Legal Studies in International, European and Comparative Criminal Law

Volume 4

The main purpose of this book series is to provide sound analyses of major developments in national, EU and international law and case law, as well as insights into court practice and legislative proposals in the areas concerned. The analyses address a broad readership, such as lawyers and practitioners, while also providing guidance for courts. In terms of scope, the series encompasses four main areas, the first of which concerns international criminal law and especially international case law in relevant criminal law subjects. The second addresses international human rights law with a particular focus on the impact of international jurisprudences on national criminal law and criminal justice systems, as well as their interrelations. In turn the third area focuses on European criminal law and case law. Here, particular weight will be attached to studies on European criminal law conducted from a comparative perspective. The fourth and final area presents surveys of comparative criminal law inside and outside Europe. By combining these various aspects, the series especially highlights research aimed at proposing new legal solutions, while focusing on the new challenges of a European area based on high standards of human rights protection.

As a rule, book proposals are subject to peer review, which is carried out by two members of the editorial board in anonymous form.

More information about this series at http://www.springer.com/series/15393

Serena Quattrocolo

Artificial Intelligence, Computational Modelling and Criminal Proceedings

A Framework for A European Legal Discussion

Springer

Serena Quattrocolo
Department of Law, Politics, Economics and Social Science
University of Eastern Piedmont
Alessandria, Italy

ISSN 2524-8049 ISSN 2524-8057 (electronic)
Legal Studies in International, European and Comparative Criminal Law
ISBN 978-3-030-52469-2 ISBN 978-3-030-52470-8 (eBook)
https://doi.org/10.1007/978-3-030-52470-8

This Springer imprint is published by the registered company Springer Nature Switzerland AG.
The registered company address is: Gewerbestrasse 11, 6330 Cham, Switzerland

To the beloved memory of Daiana, the most curious, lively and unlucky of my students: may your intellectual enthusiasm live in those who read this book.

Foreword: Let a Lawyer Write of AI

There are three different ways in which we can appreciate the role of Artificial Intelligence (AI) and of further emerging technologies in the field of criminal law. AI may entail either new forms of criminal responsibility, or new loopholes in the criminal law field, or new challenges for the rights of criminal defendants to a fair trial. The sequence of this list follows a chronological order, because scholars, first, debated since the early 1990s whether AI could ever be considered as an accountable agent in the criminal law field, due to its *mens rea*, i.e. the mental element of an offence. A decade later, in the mid-2000s, scholars increasingly focused on the material elements of a crime, in order to determine to what extent AI could ever trigger a new generation of *actus reus*. Finally, in the mid-2010s, the attention was progressively shifted to AI either as a collector of evidence in criminal investigations, or as a human substitute in the judicial decision-making process, or as a proxy of the principle of fair trial in criminal proceedings, thereby affecting the discretion of courts.

The first kind of debate on the criminal personality of AI started with the father of "robotics", Isaac Asimov in 1941. In the legal domain, this kind of debate became particularly popular fifty years later, when some brilliant scholars, such as Justice Curtis Karnow and Professor Lawrence Solum, discussed new forms of accountability and personhood for "distributed artificial intelligence", as in Karnow's 1996 paper, or for artificial intelligences, i.e. "AIs", as in Solum's seminal work from 1992. Two decades later, the advancements of technology turned this academical discussion into a hot political and ideological debate. A crucial role in this shift was played by the European Parliament's proposal from February 2017, in which the EU institution invited the European Commission "to explore, analyze and consider the implications of all possible legal solutions, (including) … creating a specific legal status for robots in the long run". Some reckon that AI can actually be considered "aware" and fulfilling the mental requirements of that which criminal lawyers discuss as intentional and negligent offences (e.g. Gabriel Hallevy's thesis). Others claim that cognition and awareness, volition and intention or reason responsiveness can be attributed to an AI system in a way that is meaningful for criminal lawyers, although no reference is necessary to human-like properties (e.g. Giovanni Sartor's stance). Most scholars note, however, that nobody would bring AI before judges today, in order to declare AI "guilty" in criminal courts. This is not to say that further forms of legal agenthood for AI make no sense, for example, in such fields as business and corporate law. Yet, it seems fair to admit, according to the phrasing of the European Parliament, that the criminal personality of AI, if ever, could only develop "in the long run".

The second kind of debate on a new generation of AI *actus reus* started with the second Gulf War in Iraq (and in Pakistan), in the mid-2000s. Years later, in the 2010 Report to the UN General Assembly, the Special Rapporteur on extrajudicial, summary or arbitrary executions, Christof Heyns, urged the then Secretary-General Ban Ki-moon to convene a group of experts in order to address "the fundamental question of whether lethal force should ever be permitted to be fully automated". A hot debate revolved around what AI can justly do in war (*ius in bello*) and when and how resort to war via AI can be justified (*ius ad bellum* or *bellum iustum*). In addition, scholars examined a wider impact of AI on a tenet of criminal law, which is traditionally summed up with the idea that "everything which is not prohibited is allowed". Similar to what occurred with a new generation of computer crimes in the early 1990s, scholars have progressively stressed that AI may soon trigger a new generation of *actus reus*, therefore affecting the principle of legality as enshrined in, for example, Article 7 of the 1950 European Convention on Human Rights. A recent literature review has proposed five areas of foreseeable threats of AI in criminal law, such as (i) new offences against the persons, e.g. harassment; (ii) sexual offences; (iii) trafficking, selling, buying and possessing harmful or dangerous banned drugs; (iv) commercial insolvency and further issues of financial markets, such as price-fixing and collusions and (v) theft and non-corporate fraud. As I like to say, these new scenarios for AI crimes are only limited by the human imagination. In the field of computer crimes, illegal systems started amending their own laws from the early 1990s, e.g. the Italian regulation 547 from December 1993; then, the international legislator intervened, so as to formalise such legal experiences through the general provisions of the Budapest convention from 2001. I think something similar will happen with a new generation of AI crimes.

The third kind of debate on how the rights of criminal defendants to a fair trial can be affected by AI has increasingly drawn the attention of experts in the 2010s to the role that AI may play as an evidence collector, as a human substitute or as a proxy of the fair trial principle in criminal proceedings. The US Supreme Court's case law is particularly instructive. In *Jones v. United States* (565 U.S. 400 (2012)) and then in *Carpenter v. United States* (585 U.S. _ (2018)), the rulings concerned the protection of the "reasonable expectation of privacy" vis-à-vis the collection of criminal evidence through the use of GPS and cell phone locations techniques, respectively. In 2017, criminal proceedings' safeguards in an age of AI ignited a popular debate in journals and newspapers because of the use of risk assessment programs by the Court of the *Loomis v. Wisconsin* case (881 N.W. 2d. 749 (Wis. 2016)). As the *New York Times* was keen to inform us on 1st March 2017, Loomis' claim was that "his right to due process was violated by a judge's consideration of a report generated by the software's secret algorithm, one that Mr. Loomis was unable to inspect or challenge". In June 2017, the Supreme Court denied Loomis' petition for a writ of certiorari. All in all, against such case law, we can suspect that this kind of debate on how AI may impinge on the rights of criminal defendants will become more and more urgent. Three reasons suggest this conjecture.

The first reason has to do with the rights of defendants to examine the algorithms of AI: some features of AI, such as the inscrutability of machine learning techniques, add a layer of complexity to traditional digital forensics. The second reason regards the role AI plays in the decision-making of judges: it is still unclear how courts should exercise their discretion when striking the balance between fair trial or due process arguments of criminal defendants and the value of AI risk assessments. The third reason hinges on the interplay between fair trial principles and the protection of personal data and individual privacy rights. In Europe, for example, the European Court of Human Rights has so far subordinated some legal safeguards of Article 6 of the Convention on fair criminal trials, to a preliminary violation of Article 8 on the right to privacy: AI will likely exacerbate the weaknesses of this stance on the interplay between criminal safeguards and privacy rights, since the right to a fair trial can be strengthened—but not replaced—by the protection of the right to privacy (and data protection). In the USA, a new generation of AI collectors of evidence will similarly stress some shortcomings of the Supreme Court's doctrine on the third-party doctrine, namely the idea that secrecy is a prerequisite for the protection of privacy rights under the Fourth Amendment to the Constitution. Further, the right to a reasonable expectation of privacy, both societal and individual, may end up with "the chicken or the egg" causality dilemma. Such reasonable privacy expectations rest on the assumption that individuals and society have developed a stable set of privacy expectations, and still, AI can dramatically change such beliefs.

Therefore, its vital scholars properly address the urgent issues of AI forensics, judiciary discretion and data protection in an age of increasingly smart AI. By comparison with the previous debates on the criminal personality of AI or on a new generation of AI crimes, it should be noted, however, that there are still few works on this subject matter. A reason may depend on recent developments of law and technology; another on the complexity of the issues that are at stake with AI. The direct and indirect impact of computational modelling on evidence gathering, much like the challenges of AI to the judicial decision-making process in criminal proceedings, do not only concern legal expertise, but scientific knowledge and technological know-how. In particular, the focus should be on criminal investigations that hinge on the use of computational techniques and AI systems, in order to understand how they may affect the principles of fair trial and the equality of arms through automatedly generated evidence. Likewise, the attention should be drawn to the distinction between deciding and predicting, between criminal justice and predictive justice. AI impacts the different steps of the criminal justice decision-making process when tackling, for example, violent behaviour and recidivism.

Few investigators, however, could have ever set the proper theoretical framework, in which to address these complex sets of issues on philosophy of law and criminal justice, legal informatics and digital forensics, machine learning and deep learning. Professor Quattrocolo's book fills this gap. Her book is timely and badly needed, because it provides an in-depth analysis on some of the most urgent legal threats brought forth by AI today. Moreover, the book is solid and yet provocative, because it will generate a multidisciplinary discussion on how the law could be used to safeguard the rights of all parties involved as AI proliferates more deeply into society. Lawyers can learn a lot about their own field, working together with computer scientists and AI developers, much as AI developers and computer scientists can reflect on the normative constraints of their work, collaborating with law professors, judges, attorneys and other legal experts. This monograph is the fruit of this essential interaction. Let the author of this book, a lawyer, write important things about AI.

Law Department
University of Torino
Torino, Italy

Ugo Pagallo

Acknowledgments

I owe gratitude to many colleagues and friends, for having inspired the thoughts I collected in this book and for having read the early versions of it. In particular, I thank Ugo Pagallo, for his intellectual generosity and for the time he devoted to helping me in this endeavour. I am grateful to my dear friend Georgia Zara, who guided me into the realm of risk assessment, Massimo Durante, Luigi Portinale, Cosimo Anglano, Margherita Benzi for their valuable suggestions. Thanks to Mina Elton, for her patience in reviewing my English, and Professors Julie O'Sullivan and Carlos Vasquez for helping with American decisions and figures. I thank Stefano Ruggeri and all the colleagues on the board of this collection, for having encouraged the publication of my work, and, of course, I thank Paolo, who always tolerates my priorities.

The research for this book has been supported by the research funding program of my home institution, the University of Eastern Piedmont, Italy, and was mostly conducted at the IALS Library, London and the Max Planck Institute for the Study of Crime, Security and Law, Freiburg i.B, which I thank.

Contents

Abbreviations

AI	Artificial Intelligence
CBR	Case-Based Reasoning
CEPEJ	Council of Europe European Commission for the Efficiency of Justice
ChFREU	Charter of Fundamental Rights of the European Union
CJEU	Court of Justice of the European Union
CoE	Council of Europe
COMPAS	Correctional Offenders Management Profiling for Alternative Sanctions
DC	District of Columbia (USA)
ECHR	European Convention on Human Rights
ECRIS	European Criminal Records Information System
ECtHR	European Court of Human Rights
FRE (US)	Fedaral Rules of Evidence
IAAIL	International Association for Artificial Intelligence and Law
ICAIL	International Conference on Artificial Intelligence and Law
ICCPR	International Covenant on Civil and Political Rights
ICT	Information and Communication Technologies
IoT	Internet of Things
IT	Information Technologies
ItCCP	Italian Code of Criminal Procedure
JHA	Justice and Home Affairs
LEAs	Law Enforcement Agencies
ML	Machine Learning
ODM	Open Data Movement
PSA	Public Safety Assessment
RBR	Rule-Based Reasoning
SAVRY	Structured Assessment of Violence Risk in Youth

Part I
Introducing the Problem

Chapter 1
Approaching the Unknown: Some Preliminary Words

1.1 Criminal Law at the Digital Turn

Traditionally, Law and Technology has been considered an oxymoron. Connecting two incompatible concepts, Criminal Law and Technology—not only Information Technology—seems to be even more inconceivable. Criminal Law is a jurisdiction's ultimate reaction to an assault upon the core values of its society and is embedded in its social culture. This topic is abundant in the European continental literature, from which we derive the idea that Criminal Law grasps national *Kulturnomen*, reproducing the general—or, at least, the most common—values of a population.[1] Thus, because cultural shifts are slow-evolving phenomena, Criminal Law throughout the world also tends to be a slow-changing factor: only established transformations can be ratified in law, not just in statutory-law legal systems.

Although law is a means to influence people's behaviour,[2] in democratic societies Criminal Law seems to be inadequate to drive normative changes in social behaviour. It instead cements accomplished processes into sets of commands, reflecting an accepted framework of social values. Indeed, this is perfectly understandable: the severity of penalties implies that the rejection of a specific conduct is shared by a vast majority of the community, just as the abolition of an offence (either statutory or judge-made) implies a general recognition of legitimacy in such conduct. If not, the legislator is imposing, non-democratically, values and rules that do not reflect common opinions and feelings. According to the European legal scholarship, this may indirectly impinge on one of the modern understandings of the rule of law. Indeed, the latter implies individuals' full understanding of the criminal

[1] See Mayer (1903), in particular p. 19, explaining the correspondence between legal norms and cultural norms; Cadoppi (2014), p. 22.

[2] See Julia Black's perspective on decentred regulation, in which law is one out of many different systems to influence social behaviour: Black (2002), p. 4.

S. Quattrocolo, *Artificial Intelligence, Computational Modelling and Criminal Proceedings*, Legal Studies in International, European and Comparative Criminal Law 4, https://doi.org/10.1007/978-3-030-52470-8_1

behaviour and command, as the basis for the duty to respect the law. One could not be expected to avoid criminal behaviours if it is not possible to fully and properly grasp what the law considers to be criminal.

However, it is undisputed that, over the past few decades, contemporary society has witnessed a computational turn, that, now we all recognise,[3] is not only a breathtaking scientific advancement, a radical change in every professional sphere, but, overall, is one of the most rapid, astonishing and wide-spread cultural changes that has ever occurred.[4] It has affected the foundations of our society[5] in such a way to permeate even the steady core of criminal law.

The first notable impact of the computational turn on the realm of criminal law has been in substantive criminal law.[6] In fact, for at least two decades, (also) the European rulers and legislators started turning their attention to new forms of offences perpetrated in the dematerialised world of IT, trying to set common minimum rules for the harmonisation of cybercrime and the consequential issues, such as competence and jurisdiction, also at the international level.[7] The Budapest Convention on Cybercrime, signed in 2001,[8] having been drafted by the Council of Europe, represented, for a huge number of jurisdictions, the first legally binding instruction to set forth specific legislation tackling such phenomenon. In fact, the first part of the document harmonised the Member States' substantive criminal law, by providing for a list of offences that the High Contracting Parties have a duty to introduce in their jurisdictions.[9] It is a common perception that harmonisation of substantive criminal law is the area in which States demonstrate major reluctance to limiting their sovereignty through international agreements: however, the Budapest Convention achieved an important score of signatures and ratifications, by almost all the members of the Council of Europe, and a long list of non-member States, including, among others, the United States of America, Australia, Israel, Japan. Incidentally, it is worth noting (more on this in Chap. 3) that the very same Convention also covers important procedural aspects, regulating the collection of evidence (e.g. such as computer search and seizure, real time collection of data traffic, etc.), jurisdiction, mutual legal assistance in cybercrime cases. However,

---

[3] Even though someone had clearly foreseen it, decades ago: Negroponte (1995); Kurzweil (2005), pp. 7, 8.

[4] Pagallo (2018), p. 1 ff.

[5] For a comprehensive overview, see Durante (2019); Garapon and Lassègue (2018), especially p. 83 ff.: "la revolution numérique bouleverse tous les compartiments de l'existence collective".

[6] Information and Communication Technologies have been seen and presented, at least initially, as a means for facilitating anti-social criminal activities: see Thomas and Loader (2000), p. 1.

[7] See the Council of Europe Budapest Convention, 23.11.2001, at https://www.coe.int/en/web/conventions/full-list/-/conventions/treaty/185/signatures.

[8] Although the Council of Europe started drawing attention on this topic in the Eighties, with the Recommendations of the Committee of Ministers R(89)9, on computer-related crimes and R(95)13 concerning problems of criminal procedural law connected with information technology. In 1996 a committee was established to draft the text of a convention about cybercrime, that than was signed in Budapest, in 2001.

[9] For an overview of the impact of the Convention see Koops and Brenner (2006).

cybercrime is not, in any way, the object of this study, and only a few references to the area of application of the Budapest Convention are covered in the book.

1.2 More Than Cybercrime

These preliminary and ancillary remarks suggest two very general observations. Firstly, if criminal law is a representation of the existing cultural context in a jurisdiction, it is not possible for it to move ahead, or keep up with scientific progress, that is reshaping social habits. Scientific progress will always precede changes and amendments in criminal law.

Secondly, the impact of the computational turn upon the realm of criminal justice turned out to be much wider than the area of 'traditional' cybercrime. Although the concept of cybercrime acknowledged at the beginning of this Century, as "computer-mediated activities which are either illegal or considered illicit by certain parties and which can be conducted through global electronic networks"[10] may not be considered wrong in itself, the phenomenon proved much more intricate and sophisticated over the decades. Today, legal research in that branch of criminal law has evolved into an attempt to theorise the application of the classic legal categories to artificial intelligence entities.[11] Moreover, the digital revolution that globally occurred especially over the last decade is having repercussions upon every aspect of the administration of criminal justice, far beyond the topics that have been addressed by the Budapest Convention on Cybercrime. Our transformation into a digital society is determining substantial changes not only in the context in which crime may occur, or in the way investigations can be carried out. Delivering justice is a human task and the sudden digital change in individuals' lifestyles is affecting the way in which such a task is performed,[12] impinging on the internal aspects of it, such as the decision-making process. These aspects will be analysed in the second part of the book.

What has been briefly observed here can be considered the cause of an undisputed trend. If regulation in the criminal area tends to follow (not to precede) social changes, the computational turn[13] occurred out of (and before) a specific legal

[10] See, among the first attempts to define the concept, Sieber (1977). Thomas and Loader (2000), p. 3. Although both research and legislation evolved significantly, it is still impossible to give one, unique and undisputed definition of cybercrime. "Cybercrime is a container term of convenience, describing a collection of acts or a field of criminal activity, rather than a single concept": Boister (2018), p. 188. Moreover, many other similar terms are often used, such as 'computer crime',' IT crime'… It has been said that the concept encompasses a whole range of terms which imply that the digital technology (not only computers) is an element of the offence. In this sense, internet connections are necessary elements, either for crimes against digital technologies and crime committed by means of digital technologies: Sieber (2008), p. 127.

[11] Pagallo and Quattrocolo (2018), p. 400.

[12] See the seminal work of Susskind (2008).

[13] de Vries (2013), all Ch. 1.

framework. On the one hand, this implies that digital advancement has been taking place in the absence of any background research on the risks it may pose to the core values of society, usually protected by criminal law. On the other hand, for a long time, and not only in Europe, the development of digital solutions overlooked the specific needs of criminal justice: existing (and pre-existing) technology leaked into (almost every) criminal justice system,[14] affording methods and solutions that were tailored for different purposes and not expressly suited for judicial use.

In particular, the computational revolution led to the availability of an enormous quantity of free data, constantly generated by digital devices; powerful computational resources, the ability to access immeasurable amounts of data in a few seconds; cheaper storage costs.[15] These conditions (access to big data and cheap, unprecedented computational power) established the grounds for offering useful solutions to criminal justice systems, even though not specifically tailored for the task. The digital turn provided not only whole ranges of data, that could be used as evidence in criminal proceedings, but also new investigation systems, based on hacking, mining and analysing huge sets of available data (private or not; personal or not). The turn not only brought the full digitalisation of collections of courts' decisions, with unrestricted access to any case-law, but also relatively sophisticated software for the analysis of it, to find patterns of predictability within judicial decisions. Moreover, the availability of an unprecedented amount of digital data shifted the attention from a code-based modelling system (code-driven regulation),[16] totally deterministic—in which the discretion is encrypted in the expert-designed code, establishing that If This, Then That—to a deep-learning modelling system, non-deterministic, in which the discretion lays in the choice of the data set (data-driven regulation) of legal texts to be used to train the system.[17] I will elaborate more extensively on this in Chap. 5.

All this happened without a proper and effective consultation between the computer scientists leading the digital revolution, and criminal law experts.[18] The literature confirms this position, indicating a growing focus, especially in the U.S., of private law on the theoretical challenges inherent in the application of automation and artificial intelligence to everyday life, since Lawrence Solum's seminal article

[14] Data mining and predictive analytics have origins in commerce: Pasquale (2015), p. 4: "At the core of information economy are Internet and the finance companies that accumulate vast amounts of digital data, and with it intimate details of their customers' – our -lives".

[15] Katz (2013), p. 916.

[16] For the distinction between code-driven and data-driven regulation, see Hildebrandt (2018), pp. 2, 3.

[17] Evans (2019), p. 260: "the modern debate between deep-learning practitioners and advocates of logic-based approaches resembles the Eighteenth century debate between empiricists and rationalists".

[18] It was 1967 when P. Souleau, a high rank French magistrate, dreamt of a joint venture between cyberneticists and judiciary to create models reproducing the most basic and repetitive parts of the judicial adjudication, in particular vehicles accidents (Souleau 1969, p. 70).

in 1992,[19] accompanied by a much slower trend in criminal law, and in criminal procedure. To some extent, this concurs with our previous assertion that the inherent characteristic of criminal law is to follow, rather than precede (or progress with) social changes…[20] For these and other reasons that will be analysed later, there are several arguments for setting the area of criminal law aside from some of the most innovative tools based on computational modelling and machine learning (Chaps. 6 and 7).[21]

1.3 A Functional Definition of AI and Other Basic Concepts

The title of this book refers, in first instance, to Artificial Intelligence. It is rather clear, though, that the term AI holds, in this context, a non-specific definition. Based on the extensive scholarship that has been published so far, the definition of AI has become a major endeavour: there is not a standard definition of what exactly AI involves.

Early 2020, the Joint Research Centre (JRC), the EU Commission's Science and Knowledge Service, delivered a comprehensive investigation on the various definitions of AI, elaborated since the 1950s, proposing "an operational definition of AI formed by a concise taxonomy and a set of keywords that characterise the core and transversal domains of AI".[22] The huge work presented by the centre not only gathered and classified the multifaceted definitions of AI available, according to the various areas of scholarship at stake, but also led to an interesting proposal of definition. According to the exhaustive report, there would be at least four common features, within the manifold range of AI definitions, including the fact that a system is based on: consideration of the real world complexity; information processing (collecting and elaborating inputs); decision making; achievement of specific goals. If these are the basic pillars of AI, the recent EU HLEG's study (High Level Experts Group on artificial intelligence) tried to elaborate a more operational concept of AI. Indeed, the latter[23] is highly specific and detailed and, according to the JRC

---

[19] Solum (1992).

[20] This attitude has been recently studied under the sociological point of view: see Christin (2017), p. 2 ff. Based on his empirical research in American local criminal courts, the author concludes that "in criminal justice innovation does not come with the glitter and appeal that it has in other sectors: it is often a source of uncertainty, as innovation arrives without the vetting of precedent".

[21] See, e.g., Breton-Darrien (2018), p. 19, suggesting that the stakeholders in the area of legal-tech accept not to mine and reuse data from criminal decisions.

[22] JRC Technical Reports, AI Watch. Defining Artificial Intelligence, Publications Office of the European Union, Luxembourg, 2020, 11.

[23] "Artificial intelligence (AI) systems are software (and possibly also hardware) systems designed by humans(2) that, given a complex goal, act in the physical or digital dimension by perceiving their environment through data acquisition, interpreting the collected structured or unstructured data, reasoning on the knowledge, or processing the information, derived from this data and deciding the best action(s) to take to achieve the given goal. AI systems can either use symbolic rules or

study, it may turn out to be too specified to apply in the non-core science realm. This assumption is also valid in our case. Although the object of the present study fits into the HLEG's definition, it is probably more suitable to introduce the topic by referring to the definition in the EC JRC Flagship report on AI,[24] establishing that "AI is a generic term that refers to any machine or algorithm that is capable of observing its environment, learning, and based on the knowledge and experience gained, taking intelligent action or proposing decisions. There are many different technologies that fall under this broad AI definition. At the moment, ML4 [*machine learning*] techniques are the most widely used".

In this sense, the term AI is the framework of this study, along with other concepts that need to be specified here.

'Computational modelling' is the second term used in the title. It refers to the simulation and study of complex systems, using mathematics and computer science. From weather forecasting models to neural network models, modelling basically means looking for laws regulating a phenomenon and translating them into a general scheme. In this broad sense, the term refers to any kind of complex system, including human behaviour and, in particular, legal reasoning. As Alan Turing argued in his seminal article of 1950, in *Mind*, 'Computing, Machinery and Intelligence', we cannot be sure, as humans, that we are not computers,[25] in the sense that human behaviour could be the consequence of a fixed and rigorous rule-set, a computation effect…[26] In his view, it is impossible to deny the existence of such rule-set, as it has not been sufficiently researched yet. Having this in mind, the term 'computational modelling' is used in this work to refer to a wide range of rule-sets, having been transformed into computational models, describing and, thus, predicting, human behaviours.

Another term often used in the book is 'algorithm'. Given the general lack of agreement, between scholars from different branches, about the definition of 'algorithm',[27] the term refers here to '*encoded procedures for transforming input data into a desired output, based on specified calculations*',[28] or, to rephrase, "*a series of steps undertaken in order to solve a particular problem or accomplish a defined outcome*".[29] In this sense, the term recalls here situations excluding individuals' intuition from the solution of a problem (or the accomplishment of a task), and replacing it with a pre-set, causational, relationship. Thus, it is possible to argue that the word 'algorithm' is used in a very general way, rather than in a

learn a numeric model, and they can also adapt their behaviour by analysing how the environment is affected by their previous actions."

[24] Craglia (2018).

[25] Turing (1950), especially § 8.

[26] Beller (2018), p. 45.

[27] For a general overview in a non-mathematics context, see the Council of Europe study about Algorithms and Human Rights, Council of Europe Publication, Strasbourg, 2018.

[28] Gillespie (2014), p. 167.

[29] Diakopoulos (2015), p. 400.

mathematical or computational sense (which do not reconcile, anyway), with the aim to point at various phenomena pushing towards non-discretional decision-making processes.

This premise is crucial in defining the sense and the boundaries of this enquiry (which will be better elaborated in Chap. 2) and in setting the basic background of the discourse: irrespective the specific definitions that the terms used in the book have in computational science, the scenario in which this study is rooted is the role of technology in the twenty-first Century society.[30]

1.4 The Structure of the Book

These preliminary and very general remarks are meant to serve as a snapshot of the current relationship between digital technologies and the realm of criminal proceedings. Such a snapshot is pivotal in outlining the framework of this book. This is neither a comprehensive exploration of the matter of AI and justice, nor an exhaustive empirical investigation into AI and criminal law. As I will clarify, this study has a precise goal and, thus, specific limits, that are outlined here. Such limits shape the structure of the book.

Against a backdrop in which legal instruments failed (and, inherently, could not but fail) to anticipate legal issues; in which for decades the technological advancement disregarded the need for scientific cooperation with criminal law scholars and practitioners, the first step is to review the existing situation, outlining all aspects directly or indirectly related to the phenomenon in question. The second step is to highlight the problems related to all aspects expressed in this framework. The third step should be, in the reader's expectations, proposing effective solutions to those problems pointed out in step 2. However, outlining solutions requires empirical research, that cannot be properly organised without having established the theoretical framework within which it should be conducted. Thus, the third step of this work is to review the fundamental principles of criminal law, both substantive and procedural, potentially jeopardised by the inevitable infiltration of computational models and artificial intelligence into the context of criminal justice. This structure will set the grounds for, in the future, a piece of empirical research testing tools and solutions that may bring together digital innovation and respect of the fundamental rights entrenched in criminal justice.

In light of these considerations, the book is divided into three parts. In **Part 1 I will introduce the problem with two chapters, the current chapter followed by an overview of the topic.**

In Chap. 2, *A Theoretical Framework for the Discussion on AI and Criminal Law*, I will present the purposes of the book and the reasons why this topic needs to be approached from a theoretical viewpoint. Firstly, I will set out the scope and the

[30] Durante (2019), p. 9 ff.

method of this study (§ 2); then I will determine the boundaries of my research by outlining its limitations: the first set of boundaries is defined by the Specificity of Criminal Law, contrary to the ability of other areas of law to react more promptly to social changes (§ 2.1.); the second set of boundaries is geographical, my work being focused on the need to frame a legal discussion about computational modelling and criminal law in Europe (§ 2.2.), given the significantly different context in non-European common-law jurisdictions; a further set of boundaries is related to the antithesis between legal traditions in common law and civil law. In fact, the application of computational models in continental jurisdictions, should not overlook the existing differences, in the structure of civilian criminal proceedings.

For the reasons explained in Chap. 2, the book proceeds into two further parts, representing the areas of criminal justice most impacted by computational modelling.

Part 2, Direct and Indirect Impact of Widespread Computational Modelling on Evidence Gathering, is devoted to the realm of evidence and to how computational modelling and the use of AI are affecting it.

Chapter 3, *Hacking by Law-Enforcement: Investigating with the Help of Computational Models and AI Methods,* deals with the methods of collecting evidence, through digital investigation instruments and hacking systems. The constant use of digital devices has encroached upon the traditional concept of privacy and the existing guarantees against LEAs' intrusion in an individuals' private sphere. In particular, the chapter focuses on the concept of privacy in Europe and, specifically, in the EU, with regard to the relationship with data protection. The effort is to assess which is the current balance between public interest (investigating crime) and private life, in the light of the digital revolution. Art. 8 ECHR, Art. 7 and 8 of the Charter of the Fundamental Rights of the EU (ChFREU) represent the legal boundaries for the intrusion into the individuals' sphere for investigative purposes, but up-dated digital forensics can easily breach those limits, with the risk of collecting unlawful pieces of evidence.

Chapter 4, *Equality of Arms and Automatedly Generated Evidence*, deals with the trial dimension of evidence. The first step is an attempt to reconstruct an eventual European minimum standard for evidence, any kind of evidence. Based on the ECtHR case law, are there conditions that cannot be derogated in evidence gathering, to be applied to every kind of evidence? What happens if an unlawful piece of evidence is admitted in the file? In particular, is such legal framework applicable to e-evidence? Although, based on the recent legal evolution, digital evidence has been specifically regulated in many jurisdictions, there is a further, wide range of digital data, that can be used as evidence in trial: 'automatedly generated evidence' is information created outside the boundaries of digital evidence, almost for commercial purposes, that can have, nevertheless, a crucial role in fact-finding. On the one hand, automatedly generated evidence can imply an intrusion into the individuals' private life. On the other hand, its opacity can create a serious knowledge-impairment between the parties of criminal proceedings. Access to source-code regulating the model that generated the evidence and *ex post* validation become the key-features of a modern theory of the equality of arms, established by the jurisprudence of the ECtHR as one of the two main features of fair trial.

Part 3, Challenges of Computational Methods to the Judicial Decision-Making Process: Deciding vs. Predicting, is then devoted to the decision-making process and the impact that computational modelling and artificial intelligence systems may have on it. It is common sense that the criminal proceeding, or at least the trial part of it, is a chain of related (not necessarily subsequent) decisions, leading to the crucial decision, about guilt. It has been argued recently that there may be activities and decisions, within that chain, that can be successfully automated, with no (or few, controlled and counter-balanced) risks for the parties.[31]

In particular, Chap. 5, *Predictability and Criminal Justice,* focuses on the meaning of 'prediction' which is a term increasingly used in the daily discussion about justice, both in the jurists' community and in the public opinion. It is important to contextualise the meaning of 'predictive justice' in the criminal law context, especially by pointing out if there is room for automated 'prediction' and foreseeability in such proceedings. In fact, the term has no normative strength and does not imply specific meaning: it can be referred to at least two main areas of judicial decision-making, that will be considered in Chaps. 6 and 7.

Chapter 6, *Predictability of Violent Behaviour and Recidivism,* deals with the use of risk assessment predictive software. Based on a reconstruction of the legal traditions, in Europe and in the US, about theories of punishment, the Chapter lingers over the scientific foundations of risk assessment in predicting violent behaviour and recidivism, in sentencing and pre-trial matters. Even in the US, where algorithmic risk assessment has been used for several decades, some interesting recent litigations show a growing concern for the compliance of such instruments with basic features of the due process. The European continental position appears to be different, for many reasons. Based on the legal tradition and on some basic principles in evidentiary law, the space for such predictive tools seems to be narrow, in Europe.

In Chap. 7, *Predictability and the Criminal Justice Decision-Making Process,* the general issue relating to the predictability of judicial decision, based on open data resources, is considered specifically under a criminal law viewpoint. Is predictability, in a digital sense, an absolute value for criminal justice? Actually, the traditional and the digital meaning of 'predictability' may not reconcile… Moreover, the analysis lingers over the relationship between the value of the precedent in continental jurisdictions, not submitted to *stare decisis* and the independence and liability of the judiciary to depart from a 'digitally predicted' precedent. In fact, the computational turn seems to have changed the inner meaning of each of these concepts.

Finally, in Chap. 8, *The Gist of the Inquiry,* the conclusions acknowledge the impossibility to dismiss computational modelling and AI from the scene of criminal justice and set the boundaries for structuring a piece of empirical research that may answer to the question: what are the best technical solutions to implement the objective advantages of computational methods within criminal proceedings, without violating the

[31] Nieva Fenoll (2018), p. 33 ff. Although many of the decisions deemed potentially automated are placed in the realm of civil procedure, the Author points out some small areas of criminal proceeding that could be automated.

guarantees of the fair trial? Hopefully, such answer will serve as the outcome of a second step of my research, that I wish to carry out in the very near future.

References

Beller J (2018) The message is murder. Pluto Press, London
Black J (2002) Critical reflections on regulation. Aust J Leg Philos 27:1–36
Boister N (2018) An introduction to transnational criminal law, 2nd edn. OUP, Oxford
Breton-Darrien S (2018) La justice predictive. Introduction à une justice 'simplement' virtuelle, in La justice predictive, Archives de Philosopie du Droit, n. 60, Dalloz, Paris
Cadoppi A (2014) Il valore del precedente nel diritto penale, 2nd edn. Giappichelli, Torino
Christin A (2017) Algorithms in practice: comparing web-journalism and criminal justice. Big Data Soc (July–December), 1–14
Craglia M (ed) (2018) Artificial intelligence: a European perspective. EU Publication Office, Luxembourg. Available at https://ec.europa.eu/jrc/en/publication/artificial-intelligence-european-perspective
De Vries K (2013) Privacy, due process and computational turn. A parable and a first analysis. In: Hildebrandt M, de Vries K (eds) Privacy, due process and computational turn. Routledge, Ch. 1
Diakopoulos N (2015) Algorithmic accountability. Digit Journal:398–415
Durante M (2019) Potere computazionale. L'impatto delle ICT su diritto, società e sapere, Meltemi, Milano
Evans R (2019) A Kantian cognitive architecture. In: Berkich D, D'Alfonso MV (eds) On the cognitive, ethical, and scientific dimensions of artificial intelligence. Themes from IACAP 2016, Springer, pp 233–262
Garapon A, Lassègue J (2018) Justice digitale. PUF, Paris
Gillespie T (2014) The relevance of algorithms. In: Gillespie T, Boczkowski P, Foot K (eds) Media technologies. MIT Press, Cambridge
Hildebrandt M (2018) Algorithmic regulation and the rule of law. Philos Trans R Soc 1–11
Katz DM (2013) Quantitative legal prediction, or- how I learned to stop worrying and start preparing for the data-driven future of the legal services industry. Emory Law J:909–966
Koops BJ, Brenner SW (eds) (2006) Cybercrime and jurisdiction. A global survey. Asser Press, The Hague
Kurzweil R (2005) The singularity is near. Viking, New York
Mayer ME (1903) Rechtsnormen und Kulturnormen. Schletter, Breslau
Negroponte N (1995) Being digital. Hodder&Stoughton, London
Nieva Fenoll J (2018) Inteligencia artificial y proceso judicial. Marcial Pons, Madrid
Pagallo U (2018) Algo-Rithms and the beat of the legal drum. Philos Technol:1–31
Pagallo U, Quattrocolo S (2018) The impact of AI on criminal law and its twofold procedures. In: Barfield W, Pagallo U (eds) Research handbook on the law of artificial intelligence. Edgar Elgar, pp 385–409
Pasquale F (2015) The Black Box Society. Harvard University Press, Cambridge
Sieber U (1977) Computerkriminalitaet und Strafrecht. Carl Haymanns Verlag, Köln
Sieber U (2008) Mastering complexity in the global cyberspace: the harmonisation of computer-related criminal law. In: Delmas Marty M, Pieth M, Sieber U (eds) Les Chemins de l'harmonisation pénale, p 127 ff
Solum L (1992) Legal personhood for artificial intelligences. N C Law Rev:1231–1288
Souleau P (1969) La logique du juge, in La logique judiciaire. PUF, Paris
Susskind R (2008) The end of lawyers? OUP, Oxford
Thomas D, Loader BD (2000) Introduction. Cybercrime: law enforcement, security and surveillance in the information age. Routledge, London-New York, pp 1–16
Turing A (1950) Computing, machinery and intelligence. Mind:433 ff

Chapter 2
A Theoretical Framework for the Discussion on AI and Criminal Law

2.1 Connecting AI, Computational Modelling and Fundamental Rights in Criminal Justice

The aim of this chapter is to demonstrate that the application of computational modelling and AI to the realm of criminal justice is a topic in need of urgent discussion. As briefly mentioned in the previous chapter, doubts and fears are growing[1] surrounding a dystopian scenario, where present, extraordinary computational power[2] is used in conjunction with the repressive powers of the State. The topic of the automatization of public functions cannot be left, at least in the traditional European approach, to the free enterprise of private stakeholders but needs to be carefully researched and tested.[3]

However, as said, any potential piece of comprehensive empirical research about the implementation of computational modelling and AI in Criminal law needs to be contained within a clear conceptual and theoretical framework. For such a purpose, it is crucial to set precise questions. Thus, it is essential to assess how much of the mistrust and fears of (European) criminal lawyers towards the most recent digital instruments is due to the fact that they (allegedly) bring non-human decision-making processes into criminal justice or, rather, that they bring algorithmic decision making-processes into it. Let's clarify this statement, that may sound slightly tautological.

[1] Pagallo (2018), p. 507 ff.; Cath et al. (2016), p. 20 ff.

[2] About computational power, Durante (2019), p. 9 ff.

[3] Catala (1998), p. 11, "*l'informatisation du droit est une chose trop sérieuse pour la laisser aux informaticiens: les jurists ont un rôle majeur à jouer dans la definition des buts, des voies et ded moyens*".

S. Quattrocolo, *Artificial Intelligence, Computational Modelling and Criminal Proceedings*, Legal Studies in International, European and Comparative Criminal Law 4, https://doi.org/10.1007/978-3-030-52470-8_2

According to a quite popular definition,[4] "*algorithms need not be software: in the broadest sense, they are encoded procedures for transforming input data into a desired output, based on specified calculations. The procedures name both a problem and the steps by which it should be solved. Instructions for navigation may be considered an algorithm, or the mathematical formulas required to predict the movement of a celestial body across the sky*". Thus, algorithms, like syllogism—the most traditional instrument of judicial reasoning—have a normative function, establishing correlations between a starting set of elements or data and a precise consequence. However, at the time being, one crucial difference between syllogism and algorithm is the basis of the normative correlation they draw: actually, the crucial difference is the set of input data. Syllogisms, indeed, may be based either on human logic and previous human experience, both limited to very few cases, while algorithms, today, are often based on statistics, driven from big data.[5] As we will see in Part III, human decisions and automated decisions rest on different patterns. The first is rooted in the recognition of a personal previous corresponding experience,[6] comparable to the one faced at present; the second, on large statistics.[7]

What is the place, then, of algorithms in a judicial proceeding? If it is true that they are not necessarily incorporated into a software and are not necessarily completely automated, they tend, however, to eradicate individual, empirical experience from the evaluation and the decision-making process, to substitute it with general or, rather, statistical evidence. As we will see in Chap. 6, when the decision-making process entails the evaluation of human behaviours—as it does, precisely, in criminal proceedings[8]—the shift from individual experience to general (or statistical) evidence, and back, implies a crucial premise. Such premise is a conceptual clarification, distinguishing between different levels of complexity in the topic addressed in this book.[9] As we will see through some enlightening examples in Chap. 6, three aspects, validity of the scientific theory; translation of the theory into algorithmic language; fully automated operation of the algorithm—are involved in some of the applications of computational modelling used in judicial proceedings at the time being, and confusing them may be detrimental to finding effective solutions to the problems tackled here.

---

[4] Gillespie (2014), p. 167. Such definition has been recently adopted by the study delivered by the Council of Europe on Algorithms and Human Rights: see https://rm.coe.int/algorithms-and-human-rights-en-rev/16807956b5.

[5] Nieva Fenoll (2018), p. 44.

[6] Tervski and Kahneman (1982), p. 4, talk about representativeness.

[7] Nieva Fenoll (2018), p. 45 ff.

[8] See the incipit of the very classical text by Tervski and Kahneman (1982), p. 3: "Many decisions are based on beliefs concerning the likelihood of uncertain events such as the outcome of an election, the guilt of a defendant, or the future value of the dollar".

[9] Chessman (2017), p. 215 ff.

2.1.1 *Algorithms and the Complexity of Judicial Decision Making*

From a conceptual point of view, a judicial proceeding and, in particular, a criminal trial, is a process to establish, beyond any reasonable doubt, whether and how a fact occurred (*actus reus*); if such fact has criminal relevance (*mens rea*); if the defendant perpetrated it and, in such a case, provided that the individual is punishable, what is the just penalty to be imposed. Although similar, this process differs from scientific investigation: while the latter begins with the observation of a phenomenon, and tries to elaborate a general pattern, valid in every case those conditions are given, the judicial decision tries to reconstruct the set of conditions that may have caused the phenomenon (criminal act) in the specific case.[10] Thus, causality is the core of both scientific and legal reasoning and, in particular, of criminal law:[11] however, the existence of a universal scientific rule or, at least, a validated scientific theory, explains why and how a category of facts may occur; the judicial decision must explain, beyond any reasonable doubt, the narrative of each specific criminal fact. How do the recent astonishing achievements in IT and AI impact on such a scenario? The answer involves, as mentioned, three steps.

The first layer of complexity surrounds the existence of a universal scientific rule or, at least, a validated scientific theory establishing correlations between a set of factors and a specific consequence. Traditionally, it is said that causality should preferably be proved on the basis of a universal rule, establishing that, given A, B will always be the result. In light of the achievements of modern science, it is doubtful that universal scientific laws exist at all...[12] In any case, when courts cannot rely on such strong correlation, they must revert to non-universal rules, allowing for a certain margin of doubt, at least at the time of ruling. It falls out of the scope of this book to linger over the burgeoning literature focusing on the relationship between science and criminal law: however, although not being the centre of our speculations, this topic is embedded in the general theme of AI and criminal proceedings, and cannot be overlooked. As highlighted in Chap. 6, the US Supreme Court delivered a decision in the 1990s that tends to be considered seminal in many jurisdictions, even outside the country, in civil-law legal orders. *Daubert v. Merrel Dow Pharmaceuticals* established a list of basic standards that the courts, throughout the world, still apply in order to admit evidence based on scientific (or technical)[13] theories. Thus, when reflecting upon the use of computational models in a judicial

[10] Psychological studies presented some evidence of the fact that inferences from causes to consequences are made with greater confidence than inferences from consequences to causes: Tervski and Kahneman (1982), p. 125.

[11] Actually, the need to reconstruct events organizing them into schemes of cause-effect relations is, first of all, a psychological commonplace: Tervski and Kahneman (1982), p. 117.

[12] There is no room here to focus on this issue. However, for an interesting overview on fallibleness and tolerance, Gilles and Giorello (2010), p. 371 ff.

[13] In fact, Kumo Tyres extended the Daubert test to technical evidence.

decision-making process (either at the pre-trial stage, in trial or at sentencing), it must be acknowledged that the first layer of complexity is characterised by the underlying scientific theory. The model must be rooted in a theory and such theory must meet minimum requirements of validation, according to the scientific community.

The second layer of complexity is consequential, because the results of such a scientific theory may be encoded into an algorithm. Acknowledging the definition given above, algorithms design a normative procedure that moves from a set of data towards a desired output, excluding subjective intuitions and arbitrariness from the process. In this way, it represents a mathematical model,[14] that can be operated by a human being, even in a criminal proceeding, provided that it is based on a sufficiently validated theory and that such theory has been correctly encoded into the algorithm. These two requirements are crucial: as we will see (Chap. 4), the possibility of reviewing, discussing, challenging[15] algorithms is a basic condition for a fair criminal proceeding, compliant with fundamental human rights.[16]

The third layer of complexity lays in the fact that the digital turn established two basic and ideal conditions to boost the use of algorithms, in every kind of decision-making process. The stunning amount of data produced (for free), daily, by digital devices and the extraordinary and unprecedented computational power now available at a very low cost, represent the ideal context in which algorithms can deliver the most effective results.[17] An algorithm operated by a human being will process a small amount of data, in a relatively long time, delivering few outputs. The same algorithm, operated through a computational model will mine limitless data in a few seconds, delivering an enormous number of outputs. In this sense, "the use of robots and AI, therefore, is just a special case of the Algorithmic Society. Big Data, too, is just a feature of the Algorithmic Society. Big Data is the fuel that runs the Algorithmic Society… To vary Kant's famous statement, algorithms without data are empty; data without algorithms are blind".[18]

Thus, it is possible to argue that, on the basis of the above-mentioned conditions, algorithms, in their essence of normative, mathematical statements/relations, are gaining momentum over subjectivity in the present day.[19] An algorithmic decision-making process is (or ought to be) opposite to an arbitrary one,

[14] For an easily-accessible definition of 'models', see O'Neil (2016), § 7.12: to create a model implies making choices about what is important to include into it or not.

[15] Chessman (2017), p. 216 talks about a twofold mechanism: (1) scientific concept; (2) its implementation.

[16] Hildebrandt (2013), p. 62; Pagallo (2018), especially § 2.3.

[17] See, in general, the remark by Zedner (2009), p. 257: "Enormous trust is placed in the capacity of technology to surmount the gravest challenges to our well-being and happiness". "Techno-credulity is widespread".

[18] Balkin (2017), 3.

[19] Plešnicar and Sugman Stubbs (2018), § 22.37. See the outstanding studies by S. Turkle about emotional interaction between humans and machines (e.g. Turkle 2006, 2008).

granting—theoretically—objectivity, accessibility and, ultimately, fairness.[20] Is it really possible to achieve such goal? There is a huge debate about transparency, which is considered to be a fundamental beacon for the fairness of algorithmic decision. However, there are doubt that transparency can grant accessibility. First and foremost, transparency is not an innate quality of algorithms. On the contrary, a substantial amount of literature has been focusing on the problem of algorithms' opacity, a situation in which the encoded procedure cannot be validated *ex post*, and thus its results cannot be (or even are not) explained and, consequently, are not justified.[21] Second, and consequently, transparency must be distinguished from accessibility, as a disclosed code may remain completely inaccessible to those who suffer the consequences of an algorithmic decision.

2.1.2 Accessibility and Transparency

Having clarified these concepts, it is possible to set the first cornerstone of the theoretical framework for this study. The need for accessibility is the quintessential feature in the discourse about the use of algorithms in decision-making processes, both in a private and public context. Such accessibility, or transparency, has specific implications when it comes to the judicial decision-making process and, in particular, to criminal trial. Thus, transparency will be the key-concept behind all the arguments that will be put under the spotlight in the following paragraphs and chapters. Reflecting on the meaning of such a concept, 'transperency' must be put in connection with 'explanability' and 'justifiability'.[22] In this sense, effective transparency depends, in the first instance, on the precision of the scientific theory underpinning it and, in the second instance, on the clarity of the language used to translate it into a mathematical formula.[23] To comply with the requirement of explanation, it seems to me that the latter quality is sufficient: a clear mathematic language allows an *ex post* reviewer to understand how the process evolved from the inputs to the outputs. However, to satisfy the need of justification, the underpinning scientific theory must be valid enough to provide a causality relationship between the set of input data and the outputs. In the context of this study, we will refer to the concept of 'validity' in the sense provided by the US Supreme Court in the mentioned case of Daubert.

In light of these arguments, it is also possible to set the second cornerstone for this enquiry. In spite of the different areas of the criminal proceeding in which computational models and AI can and could be applied (see Sect. 2.1), the general

---

[20] The validity of such argument relies on the possibility to really eradicate human biases rather than camouflage them with technology: O'Neil (2016), § 7.38.

[21] Geslevich Packin and Lev-Aretz (2018), p. 88 ff.

[22] See recently Hildebrandt (2018a), p. 2. (The topic has been deeply debated with regard to the provision of art. 22 GDPR, about automated individual decision making, including profile: see Wachter et al. (2017), p. 1 ff).

[23] Chessman (2017), p. 216. Palmiotto (forthcoming), p. 10 ff.

impression is that, allowing for the use of the most recent digital achievements in criminal proceedings may deprive courts of their discretion (and the parties of their rights). Delving into this common opinion, two main aspects must be taken into consideration, to see whether such risk is real and it is worth to be included in the framework of a theoretical study.

Firstly, irrespective of the accuracy of such an opinion, not ‘the machine’, but rather the algorithm, is what should ultimately be suspected of depriving judges of their power. As mentioned, the normative approach of mathematical modelling is supposed to objectivise a decision process, reducing non-objective criteria or indexes, based on personal culture, biases, shortcuts[24] and contingent conditions. However—secondly—the algorithmic reasoning is opposed to arbitrariness, not necessarily to discretion. In this sense, the ambition to introduce algorithms in all sorts of decision-making processes is understandable.[25] In the public sector, such ambition is driven by the need (and the duty, in some jurisdictions)[26] to grant an impartial and fair administration, in any branch of it. In the private sector, excluding arbitrariness in strategic decisions, such as hiring one applicant or another, may prove essential in gaining more profit.[27] Nevertheless, two variables must be retained. On the one hand, algorithms can help in achieving such legitimate goals at the conditions mentioned above (first cornerstone): they must underpin a valid theory (to provide effective profit) and be transparent (to provide impartiality) (see Chap. 5). On the other hand, allowing for the use of algorithms does not denote removing any discretion from the decision process:[28] there is room for the rulers to regulate the interaction between algorithms and human intuition in a way that does not deprive the process of discretion.[29] This argument is particularly valuable in those contexts in which fundamental rights—such as, e.g., the one to a fair trial—are in jeopardy and the outcomes of the decision-making process may impact significantly on the individuals’ condition (such as the nature and size of the penalty, depriving them of liberty or even life). It could be argued that discretion is not a value at all, when fundamental rights are at stake… Other forms of intelligence, such as artificial intelligence, could prove to perform better than human intuition, in all areas, even relating to fundamental rights… However, it is worth asking if and how it is possible to gauge ‘better performances’ in judging human criminal behaviour. ‘Better’ could certainly mean ‘more consistent’: as we will see in Chaps. 5 and 7, basic systems of AI can provide higher levels of consistency. However, we will also discuss if and how far such consistency is a value in criminal proceedings. As

---

[24] As to heuristics in judicial decision-making process, see, in particular, Wagner (2006), p. 281 ff.

[25] Ayres (2007), especially Ch. 5.

[26] See, e.g. Art. 97 of the Italian Constitution, providing for the duty of impartiality in every branch of the public administration.

[27] With specific regard to law firms, see Katz (2013), p. 934.

[28] See Morozov (2013), § 11.30.

[29] Gilles and Giorello (2010), p. 90 argue that there is no innate antagonism among human creativity and artificial intelligence. The statement is based on an fascinating example about the possible discovery of Kepler’s laws by machine learning systems.

said, courts ruling upon an individual's criminal liability do not perform a scientific or technical function. Judging, in general, and sentencing, in particular, are human tasks not just because they are traditionally performed by humans,[30] but because they are intended to be received, understood and accepted by the community:[31] crime is a social construct[32] and the social acceptance of a decision, rather than consistency, is the ultimate task of delivering justice.[33] In this sense, the need for discretion in all areas of the judicial decision (criminal liability, penalty, but also admission and evaluation of evidence) is inherent in the judicial function itself.

For these reasons, the legal discussion must be framed in such a way to detect (and avoid) situations in which the use of algorithms can suppress, not only arbitrariness, but also discretion. For example, such a situation may occur when algorithms are operated in a totally automated way, without any human intervention. As demonstrated in Chaps. 3 and 4, similar circumstances may prove to be detrimental to the fairness of the proceedings and, in particular, to the rights of the defence. But this is not a necessary condition. The suppression of the judge's and parties' prerogatives may be a consequence of the characteristics of the algorithm itself rather than the fact that it is performed by a machine. This distinction is not merely a formality. It is a necessary premise to addressing the topic of computational modelling, AI and criminal law from a legal point of view, because it is inherent in defining the risks that need to be considered. It is possible to find solutions only if questions are clear: to what extent does the risk to our systems of justice depend on algorithms or on computational modelling? Having clarified these two aspects, we will see that there may be different instruments to prevent different kinds of risks.

Algorithms and computational modelling are putting pressure on our systems of criminal justice, pledging high rates of efficiency. However, as mentioned, technical and scientific efficiency is a parameter not inherent to justice. Reliability, accuracy, trustworthiness of such instruments should not be measured only in terms of computer science:[34] the same concepts may have different meanings in the sphere of criminal justice, and they cannot be overlooked. For these reasons, the existing digital methods, having been applied in the criminal proceedings of many jurisdictions—with or without a proper framework of legal regulation—should be reviewed from the legal perspective.[35]

European countries, whether based on statutory law systems or not, have strong constitutional traditions. On the basis of this, the Council of Europe was able to

---

[30] See Plešnicar and Sugman Stubbs (2018), § 22.14.

[31] See the very famous Introduction in Cardozo (1921), p. 10: "What is that I do when I decide a case?" And when considering all the different elements that contribute to a decision "Some principle, however unavowed and inarticulate and subconscious, ha regulated the infusion".

[32] See Zavrsnik (2018), § 21.12.

[33] See Nieva Fenoll (2018), p. 53.

[34] Zavrsnik (2018), § 21.2 warns about the fact that "what counts as 'proper', effective and efficient police work and judicial decision-making has changed"….

[35] Zavrsnik (2018), § 21.28: These methodologies, are not developed for the study of society, in the manner that statistics in modernity was.

promote the signature and ratification of the European Convention of Human Rights and the acceptance, by the member States, of the individual application to the European Court of Human rights. Today, the common constitutional traditions are even considered a legally binding source of the EU law. Many of those constitutions, along with the ECHR and the Charter of fundamental Rights of the EU, regulate justice, often setting forth specific principles of criminal justice. In this regard, the ECHR, the EU law (within the area of the Union competences), and the national constitutions represent a legal shelter against the risk of breaching fundamental rights by using computational means in criminal proceedings. Having said this, the approach of this study is neutral: it is not based on the prejudice that the use of such means *is* inconsistent with fundamental rights. After highlighting the digital instruments that can be more easily adapted to be used in criminal justice,[36] the purpose is to assess whether their application may or may not violate some of the principles enshrined in the ECHR. To this aim, it is crucial to establish a different perspective: as mentioned, computational models and instruments, software and programs are usually assessed in terms of technical reliability, measuring their performance based on the aim to exclude errors or inaccuracy. However, for the reasons summarised above, the endeavour to hybridise (criminal) justice with such means cannot be established on the sole criterion of efficiency. Efficiency, *per se*, is not expressly mentioned in Art. 6 ECHR, as a value of the fair trial. On the contrary, such means will be confronted here by the traditional and fundamental principles regulating law enforcement, both in investigation, in trial and in sentencing. The fundamental guarantees set forth by the ECHR, such as the right to private and family life, the presumption of innocence, the equality of arms, will be used as parameters to assess the lawfulness of the application of automated instruments in criminal proceedings or, better, to assess the conditions for their lawful use.

Such a theoretical study seems crucial to establish a useful legal discussion on these terms, before rulers fall into a kind of 'digital fascination'. For the reasons that will be outlined hereafter, there is a considerable disparity between certain common-law jurisdictions and the European context, and the latter is still in the process of 'approaching the topic'. Enumerating the list of digital solutions already adopted in other jurisdictions, acknowledging their existence and, maybe, their performing rates is not enough. It is important to address the problem from the correct standpoint, which seems to be that of fundamental rights: are such instruments compatible with the presumption of innocence? Are they respectful of the equality of arms? Are they all compliant with the protection of the right to private and family life within the context of criminal proceedings? An inaccurate analysis of the problem may lead to the endorsement of computational solutions that, in the long term, may prove highly inconsistent with the principle of fair trial.[37] A situation of systematic violation of fundamental rights would be painful for individuals and, redressing it,

[36] Nieva Fenoll (2018), p. 24 ff.

[37] De Vries (2013), p. 15 ff.

extremely challenging for rulers.[38] It is better to adopt a neutral approach and reflect on it before flaws affect the fundamental rights of individuals.

For these reasons, this enquiry is meant to point-out risks, to imagine possible effects and long-term consequences of widespread use of computational modelling in criminal law. I would be sincerely satisfied if, based on the discussion that this book may foster, my arguments are defeated.

2.2 The Boundaries of the Study: A Premise

Having highlighted the purposes of this study and its approach, it is important to set the boundaries of the topic.

Even though explicitly mentioned in the title, the major limit of this work may not prove evident. In a dystopian sense (but also in a more realistic one, see Chap. 3), the union of the terms 'AI' and 'Criminal Law' suggests extremely intrusive means of surveillance, aimed to prevent crime.[39] However, surveillance and prevention fall out of the scope of Criminal Law. The latter regulates the elements of crime and the consequences of its perpetration. Thus, a criminal proceeding may exist only after a crime has (allegedly) occurred. In this sense, this study deals exclusively with the use of computational models and AI in criminal proceedings and not in policing.

It is true that, regardless certain iconic Sci-Fi scenarios, more and more LEAs have been equipped with software predicting where and when crimes are most likely to occur.[40]

On the day of writing, the main Italian newspapers reported the introduction of the so-called X-Law software, enabling a more accurate patrolling of neighbourhoods, on the basis of a set of statistical data.[41] Instruments of 'predictive policing'[42] have been used for a long time in many jurisdictions.[43] Setting aside the 'fascination' for it[44] (the Italian journals reported the immediate result of an on-site arrest,

[38] In a general sense, see Morozov (2013), § 11.27: "who would be crazy enough to oppose the march of science and suggest that perhaps some of those products need to be modified?".

[39] See Franko Aas (2009), p. 3.

[40] See Zavrsnik (2018), § 21.13.

[41] Hildebrandt (2018b), p. 12 ff.

[42] See extensively, Wilson (2018), § 19.3.

[43] See the trial results of Mohler et al. (2015), p. 1399 ff., of an algorithm based on data from American and British jurisdictions about different kind of crimes. In 21 months of testing the algorithm against specialised analysts, the results showed the first being between 1.4 and 2.2 times more accurate than the latter. The group was not totally independent, as two of the members co-founded the company that would commercialise the algorithm, while others served as external counsels for the company.

[44] Zavrsnik (2018), § 21.13, devotes a paragraph to "crime control and the fascination with numbers". 9.

see Chap. 3), such software has already demonstrated its limits, 'self-feeding' itself: actually, indicating an area as the potential site of crime, will *per se* raise the arrest rates, as more LEA units will be patrolling and monitoring that area. However, the effectiveness of such systems is not an object of this study, because this is not an area of criminal law,[45] and even less of criminal proceedings.

Inherently, the area of prevention of crime and policing—deeply intermingled with intelligence—tends to escape to rigid and precise regulation.[46] Constraining it with strict boundaries would condemn it to be less effective... Nevertheless, the absence of a clear legal framework for such a branch of law enforcement prevents this enquiry from covering this aspect. Thus, the focus is concentrated on the specificity of Criminal Law.

2.2.1 Specificity of the Criminal Law Context

Many of the reasons for justifying a criminal law approach to the topic have been anticipated in Sects. 2.1 and 2.2. Because of the values underpinning this area of law, much attention has been paid to it, in recent decades, especially in the aftermath of the second World War. The idea of recognising fair trial as a fundamental human right, within some of the most important international bills of rights—such as the Universal Declaration of Human Rights, the International Covenant on Civil and Political Rights and several regional conventions on human rights—was crucial in strengthening the culture of procedural guarantees, within any branch of the jurisdiction. However, it is with regard to criminal proceedings that rulers developed the most articulated catalogue of guarantees, establishing the presumption of innocence, but also a very detailed list of minimum standards, deeply influencing the shape of national jurisdictions: from the basic right to access to justice, to the right of having free linguistic assistance, the provisions of the ICCPR and, in particular of the ECHR, thanks to the living-instrument doctrine[47] adopted by the European Court of Human Rights (hereinafter, ECtHR), set forth a relatively strict framework for national legislators. It falls out of the scope of this study to linger over the effective level of harmonisation achieved by the ECHR and by the burgeoning case-law of the court on criminal fair trail, whose real domain reaches far beyond art. 6, covering, in the broadest sense, also art. 7 (*nulla poena sine lege*), art. 8 (right to

---

[45] Although it generally accepted that the new science of criminology helped fortifying the penal power: Foucault (1975), passim.

[46] However, some countries, like Italy, have a long tradition in providing preventive measures, not based on an alleged crime, but actually to avoid the commission of it. See, extensively, Chap. 6.

[47] Based on a precise reference inserted in the preamble of the Convention—according to which, "the object and the purpose" of the ECHR is not only the maintenance, but also the "further implementation" of human rights and fundamental freedoms, the Court started promoting (since the case of Golder v. UK,21.2.1975) an evolutionary approach, rejecting any originalistic theory in the interpretation of the document. See, Emmerson et al. (2012), p. 82.

private and family life), art. 5 (right to liberty and security) and arts. 2 and 3, in their procedural aspect (duty to set up an effective investigation on potential violations, and the right to life and the prohibition of torture respectively). On the one hand, the wording of the Convention itself regulates a range of aspects relating to the whole criminal proceeding, from the investigations and pre-trial detention, to the execution of penalties, encompassing the principle of legality. And even though the charter does not provide for a precise statute of criminal evidence, art. 6 (and 8) ECHR establish some crucial benchmarks in the collection and evaluation of it, although this is considered by the ECtHR itself,[48] to be in the realm of national legislators' discretion. On the other hand, to the extent that the States recognised the right of individuals to apply to the Commission—and, eventually, the Court—the Strasbourg case-law started building a wider structure for a convention-compliant criminal proceeding, that all national rulers had to take into account.

The reasons for such comprehensive attention to the criminal jurisdiction are many. In Chap. 1 we highlighted some of the more general features of criminal law, based on which it is possible to argue that criminal law and criminal proceedings can easily be turned into an offensive instrument, punishing and crushing the opponents, the enemies, the weakest, the non-mainstreamers.[49] Indeed, criminal law is basically about the legitimate use of violence by the State.[50] As such, a modern bill of rights cannot overlook the importance of setting strong and precise limitations to the rulers' discretion to regulate criminal affairs, in order to prevent such illiberal outcomes.

Moreover, with the entry into force of the Lisbon treaty, some ten years ago, the European Union experienced both a profound reform of its legal sources and the rationalisation of its competences, acquiring a comprehensive and penetrating power in criminal matters, substantive and procedural. Both art. 82 and 83 of the Treaty on the Functioning of the EU (hereinafter, TFEU) establish that, by means of directives, according to the ordinary legislative procedure, the Union can lay down minimum rules about: (art. 82§2), mutual admissibility of evidence in criminal proceedings; rights of individuals in criminal proceedings; rights of victims of crime; (art. 83), the definition of criminal offences and sanctions in the areas of particularly serious crime with a cross-border dimension and the approximation of criminal laws and regulations of the Member States if it proves essential to ensure the effective implementation of a Union's policy. As a result, in the past decade, a long list of directives was adopted under art. 82§2 TFEU to strengthen the procedural rights of individuals in criminal proceedings. Some of the guarantees, already provided by the ECHR, have been reiterated in the legal vest of directives—submitted to the interpretation of the CJEU—that the member States have the duty to implement in their jurisdiction, not to be subject to the consequences provided for in art. 258 and 259 TFEU.

---

[48] See, extensively, Chap. 4.

[49] See MacCorkmick and Garland (1998), p. 28.

[50] Duff and Garland (1994), p. 2 ss.

Thus, much attention is paid to the criminal proceeding within the European institutional environment, as many fundamental rights are concentrated within it, both those of the accused person and those of the victim. For this reason, the discourse around the introduction of algorithmic, computational models and AI into the area of criminal proceeding is subjected to the 'filter' of such a rich core of fundamental rights. Behind it lays the filter of national regulation, that, in some cases, is even stricter. In fact, as mentioned, at the national level, the fairness of the proceedings may acquire also another meaning. Beyond the interest of the defendant (or the victim), it may be considered to be an objective guarantee, not only to satisfy the individuals' personal interests (actually, they could consider waiving all their rights and accepting an unfair trial to be more consistent with their strategy), but also the universal interest for objective fairness in the administration of criminal justice. Despite the opinion and the strategy of the defendant, the system cannot allow unfair criminal proceedings, as this would be inconsistent with its own institutional nature.[51]

Having excluded the area of policing and prevention of crime from the scenario considered by this study, and highlighted the existence of a comprehensive framework of European guarantees surrounding the whole criminal proceeding, it is worth pointing out, now, which aspects of the latter may be most closely affected by the use of computational modelling and AI. Having regard, especially, for the northern American experience—which seems to incorporate algorithmic and digital solutions in the realm of criminal justice most extensively—such tools impact on many phases of criminal proceedings, from the investigation to the sentencing and the execution of penalties. Following the course of these interlocked stages of the proceeding, could have been a criterion for this analysis. However, in the examples that we can derive from the American experience, there seem to be patterns repeating at each different stage. During the lengthy period of a proceeding, algorithmic and computational models seem to respond to two main tasks.

The first task that can be successfully achieved by such instruments is a more effective collection of information, to be used either in the investigation and/or as evidence at the trial stage. In this way (see Chaps. 3 and 4), the digital turn offered LEAs and prosecutors many aids: a limitless amount of data to be hacked; much more intrusive hacking systems; a range of information provided by the IoT, 'ready' to be used as evidence in trial. This is the area in which the European criminal justice system has been most deeply influenced by digital solutions. In many jurisdictions, LEAs simply started using hacking systems to replace traditional interceptions, searches and seizures, almost without a specific regulation. The LIBE Committee (Civil Liberties, Justice and Home affaires) of the European Parliament commissioned a study about Legal Frameworks for Hacking by Law Enforcement: Identification, Evaluation and Comparison of Practices, delivered in March 2017 by the European Parliament's Policy Department for Citizens' Rights and Constitutional Affairs. The conclusions of this very comprehensive document focus on the same

[51] See Ferrua (2013), p. 84.

crucial aspect highlighted here above. On the one hand, the "discussions that have addressed this topic to some extent have primarily focused on the surveillance activities of the security and intelligence services", and not on the judicial aspect of hacking. Moreover, "these international-level discussions start from the point of view where surveillance activities are necessary and simply require governing laws" [...]: "however, the using of hacking techniques and the implementation of specific legislation at the national level should be subject to EU and international fundamental rights principles. [...] The right for law enforcement agencies to use hacking techniques should not be assumed but must be deemed necessary within the specific context of a Member State". Chapter 3 will delve into this aspect extensively, beginning with the first and basic fundamental principle of such a discussion, privacy. In defining the limits of this study, it is important to highlight that such a topic will be addressed exclusively from the point of view of criminal proceedings, in which it takes on a specific meaning and value. Although being extensively protected by one of the most comprehensive regulations in the world (the GDPR), privacy is not an absolute right, even in the European context.[52] When compared with other fundamental interests of society, such as (in this case) the prosecution of crime, it proves weaker, as it can be lawfully limited: privacy has its own dimension within criminal proceedings and this is regulated both by the ECHR and EU law. The first stage of our analysis will be devoted to these aspects. However, moving on from that perspective, we will see that using digitally generated (or hacked) evidence in criminal proceedings may also hinder another fundamental right: it may actually violate the right to a fair trial and the right to private life. In fact, the opacity of the algorithms regulating hacking instruments and other digital devices, generating evidence, may prevent the defence from challenging their accuracy and reliability. As explained in Chap. 4, this can hamper one of the basic aspects of a fair trial, the equality of arms, that, in its most basic meaning implies the right of the parties to challenge the opponent's evidence, not in a theoretical, but in an effective way.

The second task performed by algorithms and computational models is support in several stages of the judicial decision-making process. On the one hand, based on their stunning computational power, such instruments can rapidly mine a great deal of statistical data, helping to establish correlations between the individual's and a particular social group's behaviour and, allegedly, to predict future actions, such as violence, or violations of bail or parole conditions. On the other hand, thanks to that very same feature, open access digital instruments allow for the complete accessibility of any judicial decision delivered within a jurisdiction, including the ability to perform a search of the decision by key-words (or concepts, with the most recent technical advancements)[53] delivering, supposedly, predictability of decisions, taking into account any individual judge's variable disposition. In the US, specialised journals often refer to the 'science of quantitative legal prediction'. For example, it

[52] See Barfield and Pagallo (forthcoming), Chapter VII, Criminal Law Issues.

[53] Sobowale (2016a), referring to NexLP (private company leading the sector) most recent products, p. 20.

has been said that trying to predict the decisions of the Supreme Court seems to be a most popular hobby, at least among politicians and journalists, with very limited success… But, as the impact of the Court's decisions is crucial for society as a whole, it seems worth producing accurate models, scoring very high levels of accuracy.[54]

In this sense, it is possible to argue that the digital turn is promoting predictability to be the major feature and goal, at the same time, of criminal justice, predicting defendants' future behaviour and predicting judges' behaviour and decisions. However, the question is whether predictability has an 'autonomous concept'[55] within the realm of criminal law, that does not align with the popular meaning of the term. As said above, this issue is related to some of the most crucial and essential aspects of any legal order: the statutory nature of a jurisdiction (impinging on the relationship between judges and the law); the structure of judiciary (regulating the different levels of the jurisdiction and the relationship between lower and superior courts and the role of the latter in assuring the uniformity of the interpretation); the value of the precedent (imposing boundaries on the judges' freedom to divert from it); the very meaning of 'similarity' between two cases.

The general accessibility to the whole collection of decisions in a jurisdiction may seriously impact on two of its basic characteristics. Legal systems not being regulated by *stare decisis*—like the majority of civil-law countries—may promote a shift towards a different pattern, imposing a duty of specific reasoning on the courts in case of over-ruling. The social expectations for full consistency with the 'predicted decision' may cause judges to feel uncomfortable in departing from it, seriously impinging on the independence of the judiciary.[56] Moreover, in mining masses of data, predictive models may not distinguish between lower courts and superior courts' decisions, hampering the institutional structure of the justice system itself… These points are all crucial in determining the concept and the value of predictability, being deeply rooted in the most inherent aspects of the common-law and civil-law traditions. As such, they affect all branches of a legal system, and not only criminal justice. However, the concept of predictability has a specific meaning within the modern conception of the principle of legality. As we will

[54] See Katz et al. (2017), p. 1 ff.

[55] The term 'autonomous concept' is familiar to the European readers, having been extensively used by both the European Court of Human Rights and the Court of Justice of the European Union. The term indicates that, in the context of these two domains, a notion, applying also in the national jurisdictions, encompasses (also) different aspects and elements. The most known example is the notion of 'criminal charge', having been considered by the court an autonomous concept since the case of Engel and others v. The Nederland, 23.11.1976. For an interesting approach to 'autonomous concepts' see Letsas (2004), p. 279 ff. As said, also the Court of Luxembourg often applies the interpretative tool of autonomous concepts (sometimes overlapping with those developed by the Court of Human Rights).

[56] See the European Ethical Charter for the Use of AI in the systems of justice. Annex II, 47, delivered in December 2018 by the CEPEJ (Council of Europe), available at https://rm.coe.int/ethical-charter-en-for-publication-4-december-2018/16808f699c.

see more extensively in Chap. 7, the theory of foreseeability of criminal commands and predictability of penalties moves away from the liberal theory of criminal law and finds a place in Bentham's famous critique of British judges and the so-called 'dog-law'.[57] Men can understand the consequences of their behaviour and are able to self-determine: for these reasons, rulers must put them in a position to foresee, clearly and surely, the penal consequences of a behaviour before putting it into action.[58] It is worth asking whether this is the very same aim and function promised by computational models, mining and analysing all the decisions in a jurisdiction, searching for patterns of correspondence between decisions and judges' behaviour. Responding to this question will require a focus on the theoretical dimension of the principle of legality, as interpreted by the most recent jurisprudence.

The arguments enumerated here will be developed in the following chapters. They have been anticipated to justify the grounding of this study in the realm of criminal law and criminal proceedings, as a branch of regulation in which the issue of the use of computational modelling and AI needs to be addressed specifically. On the basis of the two different tasks set out above, the study is divided into two other parts, one focusing on evidence, the other on decision-making processes. The distinction between these two realms is not rigid, as evidence *is* actually the basis for every judicial decision-making process, about guilt or any other collateral question. However, the choice to divide the work into three parts is due to a differing pattern in the impact of technology. Apart from this first part, which is aimed to properly introduce the topic, the second relates to the process of extracting evidence through, or creating evidence by, computational models, also using artificial intelligence, while the third explores how, and how far such models can interfere with the judicial decision making-process, reshaping, transforming, altering it.

2.2.2 *Specificity of the European Context*

A second aspect of specificity in this study is geographical. There exists a lag between the US (and some others common-law jurisdictions, such as the Canadian and the Australian, e.g.)[59] and Europe, in terms of their massive reliance on digital solutions in justice systems.[60] Over two decades,[61] new branches of research and scholarship have been developed in the US, often bringing computer scientists and, in particular, models developers, to see a potentially rich new market for their software

---

[57] Bentham (1843), p. 235.

[58] Cadoppi (2014), p. 65 s.

[59] See the Australian Report in the study, A framework for hacking by law enforcement, cit., p. 111 ff.

[60] For a complete overview of American leading law-firms having turned to technological resources for the accomplishment of traditional tasks, Li (2016), p. 37 ff.

[61] See Sobowale (2016b), p. 47: "the future of legal professions started twenty years ago", referring to Discovery Cracker, the first software for legal researches.

in the realm of justice...[62] Europe, on the contrary, still seems to be relatively virgin soil.[63] Indeed, at the time being, "the use of predictive tools in criminal trials is very rare in Europe"[64] as many other algorithmic instruments are,[65] and there is room to set up a legal discussion, before the market rules overwhelm any effective possibility for it.

The reasons for such a lag seem to be multi-fold. The main aspect is that, the US represents, in the Western world, the country that most (and sooner) invested in computational sciences, leading the digital revolution. Social and cultural issues are at the base of such a trend and they have been studied in several branches of scholarship. From an economic point of view, a predominance of the private sector over the public seems to have been the most relevant influence. Similarly, the US scenario seems to be affected positively by the coexistence of strong private and public research sectors. These circumstances enhanced the development of a competitive environment, promoting a faster and wider application of computational modelling also in social sciences.[66]

A second aspect is legal, and it is twofold. Firstly, the areas of private and criminal justice are inherently distinct in any jurisdiction, as the latter is mostly based on oral hearings. This is true also in common law systems and, in particular, in the US.[67] However, in the US, the massive number of guilty pleas remarkably reduces the room for oral trials in front of the criminal courts, confining the oral activity to the disposition hearing, in which the judge delivers a decision on sentencing. This trend caused a 'bureaucratic effect', transforming the oral hearing—traditionally, the stage for intense human performances—into a more bureaucratic proceeding, concentrating the judicial discretion solely in the moment of sentencing. In this context, the need for more efficient management of data became relevant, inducing an increase in references to risk assessment methods (see Chap. 6). Secondly, the American penal doctrine's change from a rehabilitative paradigm to the idea of 'just

---

[62] The initiative of pinpointing instances of AI in judicial systems almost came from the private sector: see, European Ethical Charter for the use of AI in judicial systems and their environment. Appendix I, p. 14.

[63] See Sobowale (2016a), reporting Adam Nguyen, EBrevia's co-founder (supplying legal software based on machine learning), interest in covering the European market.

[64] See, European Ethical Charter, cit., p. 37: with the exception of HARM (Harm Assessment Risk Tool), being under experimentation at the moment in some UK court, there is no knowledge of other similar instruments.

[65] See, e.g. Ward (2018), p. 38, about the so called Priori system, a platform that pairs attorneys with clients based on detailed experience information. The service is free for the attorneys who agree to discount 25% hourly rates, while clients pay 10% of the reduction to Priori.

[66] See the comprehensive analysis of Susskind (2008), passim; see also Katz (2013), p. 909 ff.

[67] See Christin (2017), p. 8 reporting an interview with a clerk in an American local court: "here at the criminal side it's messy... It's not like on the civil side. Lawyers, Das, they negotiate, they decide on the plea... They do not kwon what's going to happen. They scribble down notes on paper sheets, they couldn't switch to paperless!".

desert',[68] deeply influenced the discourse about incarceration and rehabilitation, determining increasing rates of incarcerations.[69] This imposed, from the correctional point of view, more room for the development of computational models, meant to provide a more objective and effective management of the execution of penalties.

However, on this side of the Ocean, the use of negotiated justice is not predominant. Although the majority of European jurisdictions provide for some kind of negotiation between the prosecution and the defence,[70] essentially based on a reduction of the sanction against a very early definition of the proceeding,[71] the trial still represents the most common development in criminal cases, leaving room for oral hearings, with oral discussion and oral presentation of evidence… More unpredictable variables distinguish the typical European criminal court context from the American one. At the same time, European jurisdictions are strongly rooted in the rehabilitation doctrine: the blueprint of correctional policies is theoretically based on an individualised approach, contrary to the efficiency model promoted in the US.

In more general terms, it is possible to argue that the momentous framework for the protection of fundamental rights, established in Europe, in the aftermath of the Second World War, represents a unique factor. Firstly, many national legal orders amended the existing or adopted new constitutions, inspired by the recognition of the citizens' fundamental rights. Secondly, international organisations, such as the Council of Europe, boosted the culture of human rights, by adopting the European Convention of Human Rights and establishing the Court in Strasbourg, that represents the most effective example of implementation of human rights. The existing interaction between constitutional charters, ECHR, the Charter of Fundamental Rights of the EU created a multi-level system of protection of fundamental rights, covering also every basic aspect of criminal justice. For these reasons, the European context must be considered an autonomous area of investigation within the discourse on computational models, AI and systems of criminal justice: the hypothesis I will move from is that, in this multi-level legal system it is possible to find the instruments to face the challenges brought by the digital revolution[72] to the criminal justice.

---

[68] See Dubber and Hörnle (2016), p. 4 ff. The same trend, however, affected also the English system: see Padfiled et al. (2012), p. 974.

[69] Wacquant (2005), p. 5, reporting the US incarceration rate being, since the early 70s of the last century, two or three times that of the major European countries.

[70] Della Torre (2019), p. 595.

[71] For a recent overview on 12 European countries, Quattrocolo and Ruggeri (2019), passim.

[72] Pollicino (2020), p. 27.

2.2.3 Specificity of the Continental Context

In the previous sub-paragraphs, the spotlight was on the specificity of the criminal law context in the European region. Compared to the US, this whole area shows common trends and features, that justify the geographical boundaries of this study.

However, within the European scenario itself, there are other specificities that may impinge reflection on if and how computational models and AI should be used in criminal proceedings. An important distinction exists between common-law and civil-law jurisdictions, having important repercussions on some of the aspects that will be analysed in the next chapters.

As mentioned, one of the most remarkable effects of the use of computational models in justice systems is the impact of predictability—praised by the many advocates of open data instruments, but also deeply coveted by lawyers—on the value of the precedent. From this perspective, the English system traditionally relies on the principle of *stare decisis,* which is mostly unfamiliar to the civil law tradition. Goodhart considered it "the distinctive feature of the common law system", and, thus, the "fundamental distinction between the English and the Continental legal method".[73] Despite the progressive realignment of these two legal families over the years, having been theorised by some of the most prominent comparativists,[74] this aspect still places a remarkable distinction between the English and the continental jurisdictions.[75] This topic will be the object of a more detailed discussion—within the scope of the limited approach of this study—in Chap. 7, but it is worth highlighting here that the absence of *stare decisis* denotes a different structure of the higher Courts on the continent, which is inherent in the analysis that will follow. The number, the inner divisions, the functions of continental higher courts is unavoidably intermingled with the value and the role of the precedent: the civil law 'model' comprises the diffusion of authority within its organs and its decisions.[76] Moreover, the continental courts cannot rely on the *writ of certiorari*[77] and have to hear—in a general sense—all the cases brought before them, and huge numbers means less accessibility.[78] This is both a relevant and potent remark for the scope of this study. Delving into the value of predictability implies distinguishing between the courts of the common law and civil law systems. Also, the recruitment of and the conditions of independence of the judiciary are crucial for this topic.[79] The continental tradition of a

---

[73] Goodhart (1934), p. 42.

[74] Zweigert and Kötz (1971), p. 314 ff.

[75] See Cappelletti (1981), p. 383.

[76] Ibidem.

[77] A function that, according to Nieva Fenoll (2018), p. 37 f. could be easily automated.

[78] Although not recent, an enlightening work is that collected in a special number of the Revue international de droit comparé, by Bellet et al. (1978), passim. See, in particular, on this point, Tunc (1978), p. 441 ff.

[79] See Zweigert and Kötz (1971), p. 139 (this part of the book is reproduced and translated into the English edition, by Weir (1998), p. 124 ff.); For a more recent overview on some of the most influential European jurisdictions, see, Delmas-Marty and Spencer (2002), passim.

bureaucratic state has deeply influenced the structure of the judiciary in the main European countries, allowing for Montesquieu's classical theory to flourish: the judiciary is still, in many of those countries, an independent body of civil servants, recruited by public selection, who will progress in their career based on seniority, a feature that illustrates a significant difference with the Anglo-American system, especially with regard to the highest courts.[80] The background outlined justifies the fact that the continental judge "develops skills in technical rather than in policy-oriented decision-making".[81] In this context, the civil law supreme court judges tend towards anonymity and their names do not emerge in bold relief.[82]

However, in setting the limits of this analysis it is worth highlighting that, in comparing the European scenario with the US one from the angle of the use of AI in criminal law, some further distinctions are required within the European area itself. Some European jurisdictions provide for a jury trial, at least in most serious cases, based on the traditional bifurcation of adjudication (fact finding) and ruling on matters of law,[83] and, among these, sentencing, applying the just penalty to the convicted. At the present time, the distinction between verdict and sentence is very clear in the Anglo-American criminal jurisdictions (see England for the most serious cases, before the Crown Court),[84] where the judge determines the sanction after the fact finding has been dealt with by the jury. However, this cannot be considered a distinguishing feature of common-law, as some European continental countries, like France, also provide for jury verdict, for serious cases, followed by judicial sentencing (see, more extensively, Chap. 6).

For the purposes of this study, this topic has a specific relevance. Courts may rely, in sentencing, on different sets of information, from the ones used for the fact-finding.[85] On the one hand, there may not be sufficient factual evidence, even after a full trial, if the latter was focused on legal issues. On the other hand, there may not be evidence at all, as a consequence of an early guilty plea. Determining the basis for sentencing is crucial and in some jurisdictions information and materials that can be used for sentencing are excluded from the main file, because they cannot be

[80] Cappelletti (1981), pp. 387 and 393, where he affirms that the topic of confronting the two traditions needs to be approached under multifold aspects: "institutions and their organisations, bias and traditions, sociological backgrounds and attitudes of those who run the 'machinery'".

[81] Cappelletti (1981), p. 387.

[82] See David (2004), p. 121 f.

[83] See Langbein (2012), p. 67 ff. (See the interesting critical remark: "A judge who is kept away from fact-finding is so remote from the core function of adjudication that he is only peripherally responsible for the court's decision.")

[84] A full reconstruction of the English sentencing powers falls out of the scope here. Two aspects are worth highlighting, in these general remarks: on the one hand, the huge range of cases in which criminal sanctions are not applied by courts, rather by other public "agents who also have the role of keeping order, investigation, or preparing cases for prosecution". On the other hand, having regard to formal sentencing, the "relentless frequency" of the sentence legislation over the recent years, beside the growth of guidelines, delivered today by the Sentencing Council, established by the Coroner and Justice Act 2009 [Ashworth (2015), pp. 12 and 21].

[85] See Ashworth (2015), p. 424.

considered for the fact-finding decision-making process. This is the case for expert witnesses on the defendant's psychological character, that, in some jurisdictions, like Italy, for instance, is prohibited in fact-finding and allowed only at the correctional stage. Chapter 6, dealing with computational risk-assessment or, as is often said, recidivism prediction, will deal with the European context, distinguishing between those jurisdictions that provide for such a regulation from those that do not, traversing the traditional partition between common-law and civil-law.

In conclusion, this chapter briefly presented the scope and the boundaries of this study, justifying the object and the specificity of the selected topic. Based on this general overview, it is now possible to address each single aspect with more detail and insight. According to the scheme proposed, the first scenario for reflection on the use of computational models and AI in criminal proceedings is the realm of evidence.

References

Ashworth A (2015) Sentencing and criminal justice, 6th edn. Cambridge University Press, Cambridge

Ayres Y (2007) Super crunchers. How anything can be predicted. John Murray, London

Balkin JM (2017) The Three Laws of Robotics in the Age of Big Data, Ohio State Law Review, vol. 78, 1217-1241, p. 1219 f.

Barfield W, Pagallo U (forthcoming) Advanced introduction to the laws of AI. Elgar

Bellet P, Tunc A, Touffait A (1978) La cour judiciaire suprême. Economica, Paris

Bentham J (1843) In: Bowring J (ed) Works, V. Edinburgh

Cadoppi A (2014) Il valore del precedente nel diritto penale, 2nd edn. Giappichelli, Torino

Cappelletti M (1981) The doctrine of stare decisis and the civil law: a fundamental difference – or no difference at all? In: Bernstein H, Drobnig U, Kötz H (eds) Festschrift für Konrad Zweigert zum 70. Geburstag, JCB Mohr Verlag, Tübingen, pp 381–393

Cardozo BN (1921) The nature of the judicial process. Yale University Press, New Haven

Catala P (1998) Le droit à l'épreuve du numérique: jus ex machina. PUF, Paris

Cath C, Wachter S, Mittelstadt B, Taddeo M, Floridi L (2016) Artificial intelligence and the 'Good Society': the US, EU, and UK approach. https://papers.ssrn.com/sol3/papers.cfm?abstract_id=2906249, 1 ff

Chessman C (2017) A source of error: computer code, criminal defendants, and the constitution. Calif Law Rev 179–228

Christin A (2017) Algorithms in practice, comparing web journalism and criminal justice. Big Data & Society, July–December, pp 1–14

David R (2004) I grandi sistemi giuridici contemporanei. Cedam, Padova

De Vries K (2013) Privacy, due process and computational turn. A parable and a first analysis (Ch. 1). In: Hildebrandt M, de Vries K (eds) Privacy, due process and computational turn. Routledge

Della Torre J (2019) La giustizia penale negoziata in Europa. Cedam, Padova

Delmas-Marty M, Spencer J (eds) (2002) European criminal procedures. Cambridge University Press, Cambridge

Dubber M, Hörnle T (2016) Criminal law. A comparative approach. Oxford University Press, Oxford

Duff RA, Garland D (1994) Introduction: thinking about punishment. In: Duff RA, Garland D (eds) A reader on punishment. Oxford University Press, Oxford, pp 1 ff

Durante M (2019) Potere computazionale. L'impatto delle ITC su diritto, società e sapere. Meltemi, Milano

Emmerson B, Ashworth A, Macdonald A (2012) Human rights and criminal justice, 3rd edn. Sweet and Maxwell, London
Ferrua P (2013) Il giusto processo, 3rd edn. Zanichelli, Bologna
Foucault M (1975) Surveiller et Punir. Gallimard, Paris
Franko Aas K, Oppen Gundhus H, Mork Lomel H (2009) Introduction. In: Franko Aas K, Oppen Gundhus H, Mork Lomel H (eds) Technologies of insecurity. The surveillance of everyday life. Rutledge-Cavendish, Oxon, p 3 ff
Geslevich Packin N, Lev-Aretz Y (2018) Learning algorithms and discrimination. In: Barfield W, Pagallo U (eds) Research handbook on the artificial intelligence and law. Elgar, Cheltenham, pp 88–112
Gilles D, Giorello G (2010) La filosofia della scienza nel XX secolo. Laterza, Bari
Gillespie T (2014) The relevance of algorithms. In: Gillespie T, Boczkowski P, Foot K (eds) Media Technologies. MIT Press, Cambridge
Goodhart AL (1934) Precedent in English and continental law. Law Q Rev 40–65
Hildebrandt M (2013) Legal protection by design and the smart grid. https://works.bepress.com/mireille_hildebrandt/42/, pp 1–88
Hildebrandt M (2018a) Algorithmic regulation and the rule of law. Philos Trans R Soc 1–11
Hildebrandt M (2018b) Law as computation in the era of artificial legal intelligence: speaking law to the power of statistics. Toronto Univ Law Rev 12–35
Katz DM (2013) Quantitative legal prediction, or- how I learned to stop worrying and start preparing for the data-driven future of the legal services industry. Emory Law J, 909–966
Katz DM, Bommarito MJ II, Blackman J (2017) A general approach for predicting the behavior of the Supreme Court of the United States. SSSRN, 16.1.2017
Langbein JH (2012) Bifurcation and the bench. In: Brand P, Getzler J (eds) Judges and judging in the history of the common law and civil law. Cambridge University Press, pp 67 ff
Letsas G (2004) The truth in autonomous concepts: how to interpret the ECHR. Eur J Int Law, 279–305
Li V (2016) Techtrekkers. ABA Journal, April, 37–43
MacCorkmick N, Garland D (1998) Sovereign states and vengeful victims: the problem of the right to punish. In: Ashworth A, Wasik M (eds) Essays in honour of Andrew von Hirsch. Clarendon Press, Oxford, pp 11–29
Mohler GO, Short MB, Malinowski S, Johnson M, Tita GE, Bertozzi A, Brantingham PJ (2015) Randomised controlled field trials of predictive policing. J Am Stat Assoc 510:1399–1411
Morozov E (2013) To save everything, click here. Penguins, Allen Lane, London, ebook ed
Nieva Fenoll J (2018) Inteligencia artificial y proceso judicial. Marcial Pons, Madrid
O'Neil C (2016) Weapons of math destruction. Penguin, Allen Lane, London, ebook ed
Padfiled N, Morgan R, Maguire M (2012) Out of court, out of sight? Criminal sanctions and non-judicial decision-making. In: Maguire M, Morgan R, Reiner R (eds) The Oxford handbook of criminology, 5th edn. Oxford University Press, Oxford, pp 955–985
Pagallo U (2018) Algo-Rithms and the beat of the legal drum. Philos Technol, 507 ff
Palmiotto F (forthcoming) The impact of algorithmic opacity on fair trial rights in criminal proceedings. In: Ebers M, Canero Gamito M (eds) Algorithmic governance and governance of algorithms. Springer
Plešnicar M, Sugman Stubbs K (2018) Subjectivity, algorithms and the courtroom. In: Zavrsnik A (ed) Big data, crime and, social control. Rutledge, Abingdon
Pollicino O (2020) La sfida degli algoritmi va affrontata in base alla Costituzione, Il Sole 24 ore, 5.3.2020, 27
Quattrocolo S, Ruggeri S (eds) (2019) Personal participation in criminal proceedings. Springer, Cham
Sobowale J (2016a) How artificial intelligence is transforming the legal profession. ABA Journal, April 2016, 20–23
Sobowale J (2016b) Beyond imagination. ABA Journal, April 2016, 47–53
Susskind R (2008) The end of lawyers? Oxford University Press, Oxford

Tervski T, Kahneman D (1982) Judgment under uncertainty: heuristics and biases. In: Kahnemam D, Slovic P, Tverski A (eds) Judgment under uncertainty: heuristics and biases. Cambridge University Press, Cambridge

Tunc A (1978) Conclusion: la cour supreme idéale. In: Bellet P, Tunc A, Touffait A (eds) La cour judiciaire suprême. Economica, Paris, pp 441 ff

Turkle S (2006) A nascent robotics culture: new complicities for companionship. AAAI Technical Report series, July. https://web.mit.edu/~sturkle/www/nascentroboticsculture.pdf

Turkle S (2008) Always-on/always-on-you: the tethered self. In: Katz J (ed) Handbook of mobile communications and social change. MIT Press, Cambridge

Wachter S, Mittlestadt B, Floridi L (2017) Why a right to explanation of automated decision-making does not exist in the general data protection regulation. Int Data Privacy Law, 1–47

Wacquant L (2005) The great penal leap backward: incarceration in America from Nixon to Clinton. In: Pratt J, Brown D, Brown M, Hallsworth S, Morrison W (eds) The new punitiveness. Trends, theories, perspectives. Willan Publishing, Cullompton, pp 3–26

Wagner G (2006) Heuristics in procedural law. In: Gigerenzer G, Engel C (eds) Heuristics and the law. MIT Press, Cambridge, pp 281–301

Ward SF (2018) Doing it with data. ABA Journal, September, 35–40

Weir T (1998) An introduction to comparative law. Oxford University Press, Oxford

Wilson D (2018) Algorithmic patrol. In: Zavrsnik A (ed) Big data, crime and, social control. Rutledge, Abingdon, ebook ed

Zavrsnik A (ed) (2018) Big data, crime and, social control. Rutledge, Abingdon, ebook ed

Zedner L (2009) The inescapable insecurity of security technologies? In: Franko Aas K, Oppen Gundhus H, Mork Lomel H (eds) Technologies of insecurity. The surveillance of everyday life. Rutledge-Cavendish, Oxon, pp 257–270

Zweigert K, Kötz H (1971) Einfürung in die Rechtsvergleichung, auf dem Gebiete des Privatsrechts, I. JCB Mohr Verlag, Tübingen

Part II
Direct and Indirect Impact of Widespread Computational Modelling on Evidence Gathering

Chapter 3
Hacking by Law-Enforcement: Investigating with the Help of Computational Models and AI Methods

3.1 Investigating vs. Policing: A Necessary Foreword

As mentioned in Chap. 2, the focus of this analysis is on the sphere of criminal proceedings and, in particular, this Chapter is devoted to investigating by means of computational modelling and AI. Investigating and not policing, in general. Such a distinction does not sound familiar outside the context of the English-speaking legal orders, not only because of the lack of a specific term, such as 'policing', but also due to different legal conditions. Actually, the term 'policing' lacks of a precise translation in some of the continental languages, often being translated into the equivalent of 'surveillance'. Moreover, the term seems to represent a more active and independent role of the police, in the management of criminal files, being allowed to take initiatives that are not submitted to the control and permission of the judicial authority.[1] Nevertheless, 'policing' is a generic concept, encompassing not only criminal investigation, but also intelligence, surveillance,[2] and several other tasks, such as patrolling, responding to calls for service, maintaining order;[3] investigating allegations of crime and preparing cases for prosecution, being only a small part of it, are what is under the spotlight here. In this sense, the traditional

[1] E.g. police in England and Wales leads the investigation until the final moment of prosecution, while in a certain number of continental legal order, the prosecutor is the master of the criminal investigation and the police almost responds to her guidelines (e.g. Italy, France, Germany, Spain): see Perrodet (2002), p. 434 f.

[2] Ashworth and Zedner (2014), p. 49.

[3] Bowling et al. (2019), p. 150.

S. Quattrocolo, *Artificial Intelligence, Computational Modelling and Criminal Proceedings*, Legal Studies in International, European and Comparative Criminal Law 4, https://doi.org/10.1007/978-3-030-52470-8_3

distinction[4] between prevention[5] and repression of crime may prove effective, for the purpose of this study. There are several reasons for this.

Firstly, repression of crime, following the perpetration of it, implies the assessment of a criminal offence and the defendant's guilt. Thus, in such a specific context, policing means investigating, to gather evidence to be used in trial. On the contrary, prevention means avoiding the perpetration of a crime, and, in this sense, policing means interfering with the planning of it, by means of surveillance and other intrusive techniques. Only the first meaning is relevant here.

Secondly, the area of prevention is much lesser regulated by law than repression/investigation, for reasons of effectiveness. Were these kind of activities strictly regulated by law, they would be less effective and criminals would be able to avoid and escape them, in a much easier way. For this reason, the guarantees applicable in the realm of prevention are fewer, as the rich catalogue of rights and liberties provided for by the international bills of rights refers openly to criminal proceedings and not to prevention.[6] Although it is undisputed that the rule of law must be respected also in the realm of prevention,[7] this reiterates the exclusion of prevention from the boundaries of a criminal law inquiry.

Thirdly, prevention of crime is the area that most stimulated the application of predictive tools in the realm of criminal justice,[8] and not only in sci-fi books and novels. Besides a comprehensive literature and scholarship about such a topic,[9]

---

[4]The distinction between prevention and repression of crime spread in continental Europe in the second half of nineteenth century. But it was the eighteenth century when Blackstone set the spotlight on 'preventive justice' in his Commentaries on the Laws of England (although he recognised preventive value to punishment in itself): "this preventive justice consists in obliging those persons whom there is a probable ground to suspect of future misbehaviour to stipulate with and to give full assurance to the public that such as is apprehended shall not happen" Blackstone (1765), p. 251. About Blackstone's position see extensively Ashworth and Zedner (2014), p. 29 f.

[5]See Ashworth and Zedner (2014), p. 30. In particular, the Italian legal order provides for a specific system of preventive measures, which is quite unique in Europe (see, more extensively, Chap. 6). Measures (freezing assets or limiting personal liberty of movement and liberty itself), are aimed to prevent the perpetration of crimes, depriving the potential perpetrator of her assets or liberty. As the European Court of Human Rights assessed in the case of De Tommaso v. Italy, a vast majority of the European legal orders do not provide for similar measure. Only Austria, Switzerland, France, Russia, UK provide for similar tools (ECtHR, 23.2.2017, De Tommaso v. Italy, §§ 69, 70).

[6]As we shall see, this implies a relevant distinction between intelligence gathering and obtaining evidence to be used in trial: Ashworth and Zedner (2014), p. 51.

[7]At least in its basic standard of a prior, democratic mandate to the legislative authority, to pass, for the future, laws that are not overly vague, allowing for a discretional, arbitrary and inconsistent application: Ashworth and Zedner (2014), cit., 265.

[8]"Smart, effective, and proactive policing is clearly preferable to simply reacting to criminal acts": Perry et al. (2003). In 2009, the U.S. Department of Justice, National Institute of Justice, held the first predictive policing symposium, gathering researchers and practitioners in the field of policing, to discuss achievements and expectations in the field of the application of predictive algorithm to crime prevention.

[9]E.g. Weisburd and Braga (2006), *passim*; Benbouzid (2018), p. 1 ff.; Manning (2011).

there is a whole market flourishing on automated policing[10] and predictive policing, as PredPol demonstrates.[11]

3.1.1 Predictive Policing

According to Perry et al., "predictive policing is the application of analytical techniques—particularly quantitative techniques—to identify likely targets for police intervention and prevent crime or solve past crimes by making statistical predictions". Prediction can cover: crime (place and time with increased risk), offenders (individuals at risk of offending in the future), perpetrators' identity (profiles to match with past crimes), victims.[12] Predictive policing is gaining momentum in the field of crime prevention, along with the process of real-time data transmission,[13] fuelling the idea of a real-time cop.[14]

Predictive policing software can be based on two main different patterns. The first focuses on 'hotspots', while the second on 'crime linkage'. The 'hotspots software' mines data in order to establish correlations between geographical and social factors, having criminogenic relevance: lack of public lighting, presence of railway stations, bus stops, night clubs, schools, are considered indexes of potential offences. Thus, a combination of such factors can suggest where a crime is more likely to occur. Risk Terrain Model,[15] and PredPol are some famous examples of 'hotspots software', followed by countless similar solutions adopted, locally, by national LEAs, such as X-Law, in Italy.[16] 'Crime linking' software, on the contrary, is based on a pattern of near repeat crimes.[17] Robbery, e.g., has a high risk index of repetition within 48 h, slowly reducing over the following month.[18] Instead of places, such software targets individuals, both identified and unidentified. National and local LEAs have started using this kind of tools all over the world, in the US and in

[10] Bowling and Iyer (2019), p. 142 define 'automated policing' as "policework that has been converted so as to operate automatically".

[11] https://www.predpol.com/.

[12] Pease and Andromachi (2014), passim.

[13] With regard to the police body-worn video transmission systems, see Bowling and Iyer (2019), p. 140 ff.

[14] Wilson (2019), p. 69 ff.

[15] Caplan et al. (2017), p. 133 f.;

[16] Basile (2019), p. 12.

[17] Kaufmann et al. (2019), pp. 674–692, 679.

[18] Basile (2019), p. 12.

Europe, e.g. Precobs (Pre Crime Observation) in Germany,[19] HART in the UK[20] KeyCrime in Italy.[21]

It is clear that, although based, today, on computational modelling and AI solutions, predictive policing is rooted into criminology and sociology,[22] rather than criminal law and, for this reason, it falls out of the scope of this analysis. The basis of predictive policing is discovering patterns into criminal phenomena, outside their normative dimension but within their material essence. Some argued that "patterns form the epistemic core of predictive analytics in general, and of policing software or algorithms more specifically".[23] Due to this assumption (and even though policing falls out of this inquiry), it is important to anticipate a concept that I will elaborate on in the following chapters: "unless patterns are accompanied and contextualized by explanatory material, they render policing decisions opaque. Not only for most police operators, but also for those affected by pattern-based policing it is barely achievable to reveal and interrogate the parameters that inform the suggested interventions. The clean surface of the pattern makes it impossible to defend oneself against their results".[24] Criminal law can do little, in this perspective: as we will see in Chap. 6, with regard to the application of risk assessment tools in sentencing, scientific validity, accessibility and transparency are the parameters for measuring the reliability of these instruments, not the principles of criminal law.

3.1.2 The Realm of Investigation

Investigation, on the contrary, is a realm submitted to strict statutory regulation (even in common law legal orders) and to the general principles set forth by international bills of rights and, in particular, ECHR, as far as Europe is concerned. Not only investigations may seriously hinder the results of a criminal trial, impinging on the defendant's right to a fair trial (art. 6 ECHR, see Chap. 4), but they can also deeply interfere with other fundamental rights set forth by the ECHR, and in particular art. 8 (right to private and family life), and 10 (freedom of expression and information). There is also a huge amount of case-law by the ECtHR on the indirect violations of art. 2 (right to life), and 3, (prohibition of torture and inhuman and degrading treatments), that can be perpetrated by an incomplete and ineffective investigation.[25] Thus, investigative measures, techniques and protocols must be

---

19 Schweer (2018), p. 4. See also the presentation at https://land-der-ideen.de/en/project/precobs-software-for-predicting-crimes-355.

20 Oswald et al. (2018), p. 223 ff.

21 Parodi and Sellaroli (2019), p. 56.

22 Ashworth and Zedner (2014), p. 47.

23 Kaufmann et al. (2019), p. 689.

24 Ibidem.

25 For an updated overview see Guide on Art. 2—Right to life, edited by the European Court of Human Rights in 2018, p. 28 ff., at https://www.echr.coe.int/Documents/Guide_Art_2_ENG.pdf.

compliant with such fundamental rights, in order not to amount to a direct or indirect violation of the ECHR. As a consequence, evolution and other changes in investigative measures must be compliant with the wider framework of fundamental rights being related to (and affected by) criminal proceedings.

Having said this, the theoretical distinction between prevention and repression is not so strict in real terms. On the one hand, it has been noted that the boundaries are progressively blurring,[26] particularly in relation to the most intrusive aspects of ICTs. Not to forget that, even within the boundaries of criminal proceedings, pre-trial detention is usually (also, see Chap. 6) aimed at preventing the perpetration of serious offences…[27] On the other hand, there has always been an interference between elements gathered in preventive policing and evidence to be used in criminal proceedings. Especially in the presence of alleged, serious risks to security, the pre-trial phase of criminal proceedings proves ‘vulnerable’ to the access of materials and information that has been gathered with specific prevention purposes.[28] This is not a small issue at all, but it can be handled under the general considerations regulating evidence, under the spotlight in Chap. 4.

As anticipated, computational modelling and AI solutions proved very useful in the area of policing, not only for the purpose of preventing crimes, but also for investigating them. The digital turn obviously also affected the needs and the means of criminal investigations. Firstly, because the number of offences being perpetrated in the digital dimension is skyrocketing. Secondly, because the digital dimension of crime allows/obliges LEAs to shift the focus of their investigations from material documents and oral conversations to digital evidence, creating new phenomena, such as ‘hacking by law enforcement’ and ‘digital forensics’ (which are not necessarily diverse concepts). Although the dimension of cybercrime falls completely out of the scope of this work, there have been consequences on criminal investigations that need to be briefly addressed here. In this Chapter, the attention is devoted to the application of computational modelling and AI to investigations, with a specific focus on the risks to the right to private and family life. The breath-taking advance in digital technology is providing LEAs with extremely intrusive instruments, that seem not to be compliant with fundamental rights and with the existing national regulations on intrusive investigative measures. Of course, the range of digital technology allowing for such intrusive investigation is not necessarily based on AI. The malicious intrusion into the individuals’ private life is based on much less sophisticated instruments. However, the effectiveness of such investigations relies increasingly on the ability to mine massive quantities of data, almost in real time, and this skill is often based on neural networks, bringing the topic into the area of interest of this study.

---

[26] Vervaele (2014), p. 116.

[27] Ashworth and Zedner (2014), p. 65.

[28] Ashworth and Zedner (2014), p. 51.

3.1.3 The Dawn of Digital Investigations

Taking a small step back, it is possible to argue that, generally speaking, cybercrime[29] has boosted a huge evolution in investigations. The specificity of such criminality generated the need for different, special investigative measures: traditional policing was almost useless into inquiring into such a new phenomenon and LEAs and rule-makers had to face the reality: 'specific' crimes[30] called for 'specific' investigations. Actually, many European countries had experienced something similar in the Seventies and Eighties, with terrorism. Special powers and measures were adopted in legal orders, such as the UK (with regard to the Northern Ireland situation), Italy (to tackle a long and extremely violent period of political terrorism, in the decades between the beginning of the Seventies and Eighties), Spain (in the Eighties, against the Basque independent movement)... Besides a wider justification for pre-trial detention, the legal basis for search and seizures, wire-tapping, undercover actions, has been massively enlarged to tackle both terrorism[31] and, afterwards, organised crime, e.g. in Italy and Spain... Still terrorism represents, in many countries, a ground for special limitations of fundamental procedural rights. Cybercrime, also, is an area of criminal behaviour presenting a number of specificities.

Cybercrime is the subject, at the European macro-regional level, of the well-known Budapest Convention, open for signature of the member States of the Council of Europe on November 23, 2001. However, as said in Chap. 1, the convention has experienced a huge expansion, even among non-European countries and is now the leading international text with regard to cybercrime.[32] In transposing this important text, the Member States not only had to harmonise their criminal offences in accordance with the provisions of the Convention, but they also had to implement several procedural requirements, aimed at adapting traditional investigations and evidence to the specificities of the digital environment. It is almost thanks to the Budapest convention that the concept of 'digital evidence' has acquired a normative dimension in Europe, beginning to gain momentum, within the framework of national procedural codes and regulations. Actually, domestic norms were almost obsolete, and certainly not ready to host the new corpus of digital investigations: this pushed national rulers to regulate the brand-new area of digital investigation and evidence.

Even though there is no room, here, for a general reconstruction, it is possible to argue that cybercrime and digital evidence are expressions of a more general idea of cyberculture, rooted in the most recent development of the information society. Floridi reminds us of the distant roots of such an information society, based in the inventions of writing, printing, and mass media.[33] However, Information and

---

[29] For a definition see Flor and Oh Jang (2012), p. 13 ff.

[30] Cadoppi et al. (2019), passim.

[31] Bachmaier Winter (2012), passim.

[32] See the Council of Europe Budapest Convention, 23.11.2001, at https://www.coe.int/en/web/conventions/full-list/-/conventions/treaty/185/signatures.

[33] Floridi (2017), p. 12.

Communication Technologies (ICT) have recently boosted the phenomenon, pushing communication and information to the centre of the social and individual dimension. As a consequence, even criminal investigations followed this trend: systems of intrusion, such as wire-tapping and room bugging, have existed since the evolution in communications started to spread, and have been used to both prevent crime and repress it. Nevertheless, the proliferation of new technologies boosted more effective forms of intrusion,[34] especially because the traditional protections against public interference in private life, enacted by many national Constitutions and international bills of rights, are still based on a physical, spatial dimension, that has been deeply undermined by the digital environment, which is, now, the scene for both the perpetration of a crime and the investigation of it.

The topic of public interference into private life has been the object of a comprehensive, multifaceted, modern, constitutional legal scholarship, on both sides of the Atlantic Ocean. It is particularly complicated to address it with a partial approach, because of the almost encyclopaedic literature on it. Nevertheless, investigation is, along with prevention of crime, one of the most common grounds for balancing the fundamental right of individuals to privacy and the interference by public authorities. To this extent, it can be considered a traditional topic of criminal law. However, as said, the recent digital (r)evolution seriously affected the matter of privacy, both expanding and reducing, at the same time, the realm of the individual's private life. On the one hand, the digitalisation of communication added new, immaterial, contexts in which personal data and conversations are held. Meanwhile, on the other hand, the digital nature of such information opened it-up to more deceitful instruments of control by private subjects and public authorities. Although 'home' is still the preferential site for private life,[35] a substantial part of this private life is now invested in electronic devices, following an individual's' constant movements. This creates a sort of duplication of the personal identity; the physical side, and, now the digital side, which may or may not overlap. Accessing the digital side of this identity has become the most effective way to interfere with an individual's physical identity. Protecting the home from investigative intrusion through procedural limitations[36] and exclusionary rules, seems not to be not sufficient, at the time being. Also, the requirement of judicial authorisation for public interference[37] is losing its effectiveness, as the concepts (home, correspondence, privacy), which these procedural guarantees are based on, have increasingly blurred. The concept of "digital domicile" would possibly better fit the current need for privacy protection, as seen in § 3.2.

[34] Ashworth and Zedner (2014), p. 51.

[35] About "sanctity" of the home, see De Hert and Gutwirth (2006), p. 67.

[36] E.g. conditions limiting room-bugging and phone-tapping to some listed crimes, or restricting it to specific situations (e.g., a person who is reasonably suspected of committing a crime is present in the house).

[37] Many jurisdictions provide for a double guarantee: each interference into private life must be provided by law and authorised by a judicial authority. The judicial intervention is seen as an opacity tool: De Hert and Gutwirth (2006), p. 69.

It is possible to argue that the extensive application of computational modelling and AI in any dimension of human life intensified the blurring of some existing legal concepts: privacy, domicile, lawful intrusion for investigative purposes, seem not to have precise boundaries any longer. This Chapter and the following one are dedicated to the analysis of the impact of recent technologies in the realm of criminal evidence, in its largest dimension.

3.2 Privacy v. Investigation: A Naturally Unbalanced Relationship

There is a sphere of activity where interferences into private life or personal data may engage two distinct fundamental rights. This is the case where the interference is made as part of a criminal investigation. Although repression of crime is usually a lawful ground for limitations of the right to private life, a specific intrusion into it, with investigative purposes, may trigger both the right to privacy and the right to a fair trial. Not only because of the doctrine of 'the fruits of the poisonous tree'—eventually based on the consequences of an unlawful interference into privacy (Chap. 4)—but also because the outcomes of a lawful intrusion may be in breach of the principle of the fair trial. Thus, before focusing on evidence in Chap. 4, the accent is now on the specific threats brought to investigations by the use of computational models and AI.

As to the European context, the legal framework is based both on domestic constitutions and statutory regulations, at the national level, and the ECHR and EU provisions, at the supranational level. The European Convention on Human Rights, like other international conventions, such as ICCPR, establishes fundamental rights in both the areas of interest of investigation and evidence. The individual's right to a fair trial is enshrined in Art. 6, with specific attention to criminal proceedings in §§ 2 and 3, whereas the right to family life and private life is provided for—primarily with a negative understanding of privacy,[38] that excludes interferences by public authority[39]—by Art. 8 ECHR.[40]

---

[38] ECtHR, Kroon and others v. the Netherland, § 31. Nevertheless, the States' duty to protect individuals' right to private and family life does not merely compel the State to refrain from unlawful intrusion but may imply also positive obligations. Although a long list of positive obligation has been drawn with regard to family life, also the guarantee of private life may urge the States to positively act in order to regulate, e.g., interactions between individuals (ECtHR, Evans v. the UK, § 75).

[39] See De Hert and Gutwirth (2006), p. 71. It has been noted that the Court adopted an approach which is almost similar to the one displayed by many national constitutions: see Santolaya (2012), p. 339.

[40] Art. 8: (1) Everyone has the right to respect for his private and family life, his home and his correspondence. (2) There shall be no interference by a public authority with the exercise of this right except such as is in accordance with the law and is necessary in a democratic society in the interests of national security, public safety or the economic well-being of the country, for the prevention

3.2.1 'Private Life' in Art. 8 ECHR: Home, Correspondence and… Personal Data?

Art. 8 ECHR does not, like other international bills of rights and national constitutions, provide for a definition of what private (and family) life is. Actually, a definition of it, at the time of drafting the Convention (and the ICCPR), would have been overly difficult;[41] possibly even not suitable, as the theorisation of it was just at its dawn: actually, imposing a normative framework on an evolving concept could have been detrimental.

With the insight of the (nowadays) substantial case-law of the European Court of Human Rights, we can argue that, for the purpose of the Convention, the innate sense of the guarantee is to ensure the development, without outside interference, of the personality of any individual in her relationship with other human beings, primarily in the private, but also in the public sphere,[42] encompassing the dimension of social relationships.[43] In its text, Art. 8 ECHR refers mainly to two elements that are usually considered to be quintessential for the meaning of privacy: 'home'[44] and 'correspondence', and it is stunning indeed to discover what a comprehensive protection the Court could build on these two concepts. However, even though the individual's personal expectation of privacy is not decisive in the application of art. 8 ECHR, information about facts or conversations occurring in a public context is not, *per se*, excluded from the area of application of art. 8 ECHR. In this sense, the Strasbourg Court's doctrine seems to coincide with the traditional, philosophical definition of privacy, rooted in the individuals' right to shape their personality also on the basis of 'opacity', allowing them to exclude others from some areas of their life.[45]

However, the choice, by the drafters of Art. 8 ECHR, not to define 'privacy' in a positive way, shines the spotlight straight on the exceptions, among which the interests of criminal justice play an important role. For this reason, after having addressed the concept of 'public interference', we will focus on the (evolutive) notions of 'home' and 'correspondence', in their essence, as places from which public interference is almost excluded. Afterwards, we will try to set data protection against this scenario, to assess in what degree it is protected by the Convention.

---

of disorder or crime, for the protection of health or morals, or for the protection of the rights and freedoms of others.

[41] It is common opinion that, at the time of drafting the ECHR, the blueprint of privacy was a negative concept, that only in the following decades evolved into a positive theorisation: see Pollicino and Bassini (2017), p. 135.

[42] ECtHR, Von Hannover v. Germany (n. 2), §95.

[43] ECtHR, 16.12.1992, Niemietz v. Germany, § 29.

[44] Although the French version of the Convention refers to 'domicile', which has a broader sense: ECtHR, Niemietz v. Germany, cit., § 30.

[45] Arendt (2017), p. 87.

3.2.1.1 Interference by Public Authority

From a general point of view, Art. 8 creates a complex system of balances between competing values,[46] against "arbitrary interference by the public authorities".[47] The values enshrined in the first paragraph—family life, private life[48]—can be balanced[49] with other issues of general interest, listed thereinafter, under two central conditions. The first condition is legality; that is to say that such balance must be provided by law. The second condition is that of a necessity in a democratic society. There is substantial literature addressing the question of the sense and scope of these two provisions, and, although the issue is not central to this analysis, it is clear that the criterion of "necessity in a democratic society" is highly subjective and unspecific. The Court has tried to "objectivise" it as much as possible, introducing a further test of proportionality (between the individual position and the necessity in a democratic society). This approach should always be coupled with the principle of subsidiarity,[50] demonstrating that the intrusion was the *extrema ratio* (lesser intrusive instruments being unavailable). In addition, the Court has relied extensively on the "margin of appreciation" doctrine, in a broad context of legitimate exceptions,[51] showing a reluctance to require States to demonstrate the real "necessity" of the interference[52] and using the legality criterion as justification for such a permissive approach:[53] "the citizen gets procedural guarantees as a compensation for the lack of testing of reasonableness of the intrusion"[54] (see also Chap. 4).

Moreover, within the framework of these two main conditions, the number of general issues that can be balanced with the right to private life is extremely high. It includes national security, public safety and economic well-being of the country, prevention of disorder or crime, protection of health or morals and protection of the rights and freedoms of others.[55] When interference into an individual's right to a private life is based on one of these reasons, the court is entitled to conclude that there has been no violation. This exception is particularly relevant in cases where the intrusion has been committed by a public authority, in the context of the prevention of a crime (as expressly provided by Art. 8 Par. 2 ECHR) or of a criminal investigation. In this sense, both concepts of 'home' and 'correspondence' applied by the

46 Privacy is not an absolute but relational value...: De Hert and Gutwirth (2006), p. 74.

47 ECtHR, 13.6.1969, Marckx v. Belgium, § 31.

48 For a reconstruction of privacy as a fundamental right, at least in the western society, see De Hert and Gutwirth (2006), p. 63 f.

49 Or, actually, "weakened", see Claes et al. (2006), p. 1.

50 ECtHR, Siliadin v. France, 26.7.2005; M.C. v. Bulgaria, 4.12.2003, X and Y v. The Nederland, 26.3.1985.

51 Verbruggen (2006), p. 125: as for these exceptions there are no universal accepted standards, the Court's task to assess what is "necessary in a democratic society" is not easy.

52 De Beer et al. (2010), p. 75 ff.

53 In critical terms, De Hert and Gutwirth (2006), p. 89.

54 De Hert and Gutwirth (2006), p. 90.

55 It has been noted that the State is the first source of threat to privacy: see Claes et al. (2006), p. 2.

Court (and, previously, by the Commission), have been deeply affected by the criminal investigations' context.[56]

3.2.1.2 "Home" in the ECtHR Case-Law

Based on a comprehensive overview of the ECtHR case-law, it is possible to argue that 'home' became, through the decades, an "autonomous concept"[57] within the Convention: to this extent, it does not depend on national legal definitions and regulations. The term has always been interpreted in a very comprehensive way, including a wide variety of sites: e.g. not only the place in which an individual lives (regardless of whether she is lawfully established in it),[58] but also the one in which she has the intention to live[59] and the sites neighbouring the house; it is important to stress that, to enjoy the protection of Art. 8, home does not need to be a 'traditional' residence, but can be a cabin, a bungalow or a caravan or other kind of unfixed abode. It is possible to argue that what is relevant to the application of art. 8 is a stable, even not continuous, relationship with the place.[60] Nevertheless, the court has even recognised the Art. 8 guarantee to sports and training centres, and their annexes, in case of away events.[61] Moreover, another important topic in the case law of the Court is the extension of the guarantee of art. 8 to the places of professional activity and other business premises:[62] since the case of Niemietz, the Court recognised that, "since activities which are related to a profession or business may well be conducted from a person's private residence and activities which are not so related may well be carried on in an office or commercial premises", a rigid distinction may prove arbitrary.[63]

The resulting case law on the topic is extensive, and it has been stressed that the core of the concept theorised by the Court was essentially almost based on cases dealing with the protection of 'home' against public authorities' searches and

[56] De Hert and Gutwirth (2006), p. 91: "the transformation of Art. 8 into a source of procedural Rights and procedural conditions takes it away from the job it was designed for... to prohibit unreasonable exercises of power and to create zones of opacity".

[57] For a critical approach to the theory of ECHR 'autonomous concepts', see Letsas (2004), p. 279 ff.

[58] ECtHR, MC Cann v.UK, Buckley v. UK, Winterstein and others v. France.

[59] ECtHR, 24.11.1986, Gillow v. the UK.

[60] Nevertheless, the Court always excluded that Art. 8 encompasses the right of each family to have a home for their own alone (ECtHR, 21.11.1995, Velosa Barreto v. Portugal), or the right to keep up a specific walk of life (ECtHR, 25.9.1996, Buckley v. UK), or to affirm one own's roots in a specific area (ECtHR, 18.12.1996, Loizidou v. Turkey).

[61] ECtHR, (*National Federation of Sportspersons' Associations and unions (FNASS) and Others v. France*.

[62] *Buck v. Germany*, § 3.1; *Niemietz v. Germany*, §§ 29-31; *Saint-Paul Luxembourg S.A. v. Luxembourg*, § 37, *Popovi v. Bulgaria*, §103, (*Steeg v. Germany* (dec.); *Société Colas Est and Others v. France*, § 41; *Kent Pharmaceuticals Limited and Others v. the United Kingdom.*

[63] Niemietz v. Germany, cit., § 30.

seizures,[64] although through the decades, the judges assessed a huge variety of interferences with the conventional protection of 'home'.

3.2.1.3 And "Correspondence"

As to the concept of 'correspondence', protecting confidentiality of communications is the core guarantee of art. 8 ECHR. Thus, a long list of interactions, such as letters (personal or professional, regardless of the content and the identity of the sender or recipient, who may also be a prisoner), packages, telephone calls and their metadata, are all covered by the protection of 'private life'. More recently, the Court assessed that also emails, internet traffic, computer data stored on hard disks, mobile supports or servers fall into the scope of art. 8 ECHR.

The use of digital technologies to intrude into an individual's personal sphere and to process data relating to his or her life can be *per se* lawful, if the abovementioned conditions are respected. A successful investigation can be justified on the grounds of many of the interests that are stated by Art. 8 § 2 ECHR. However, the digital turn deeply affected the means of investigation, enlarging, as said, both the realm of private information that can be investigated and the means by which one can intrude into it. The interpretation of art. 8 was confronted with an unprecedented phenomenon, affecting the sphere of an individual's privacy in different ways: personal data, unknown at the time of drafting the Convention, rapidly became the focus of a new dimension of privacy, challenging the traditional categories. Thus, as far as Art. 8, providing for the right to a private and family life, has become the beacon against unlawful intrusions of judicial authorities into the individuals' sphere, a legitimate question arises. Does Art. 8 ECHR also provide for data protection?

3.2.1.4 Privacy and Data Protection

It is possible to argue that the European legal context nurtured the concept of data protection, producing the first international binding instrument ever: the Council of Europe drafted the Convention for the protection of individuals with regard to the processing of personal data (Convention 108), open to the signature of the Member States in 1981. Although adopted at the very dawn of the IT revolution, the history of Convention 108 is a history of success. In 2001, an amending protocol was signed, to introduce national independent authorities, for the control of data protection. In 2013 the first non-CoE State (Uruguay) signed the Convention, opening up the way for a remarkable number of extra-European signatures. Today, 55 States in the world have signed the Convention, that was up-dated in 2018, modernising the text of the Convention, in light of the accomplished digital turn.

---

[64] Harris et al. (2018), p. 319; Pollicino and Bassini (2017), p. 137.

Proliferation of data—essentially created, managed and stored in the digital environment—fostered the movement for major data protection against unlawful public intrusion.[65] However, data protection and privacy are not overlapping concepts,[66] as data protection refers exclusively to one dimension of privacy, that is to say informational privacy.[67] For these reason, the EU Charter of Fundamental Rights sets forth two separate articles for privacy and data protection (art. 7 and 8, see *infra*). Both privacy and data protection are much wider and debated concepts. Privacy, we said, is a personal sphere related to a claim of 'opacity', a realm that individuals can protect from external intrusion. Data protection, on the contrary, revolves around the idea of transparency, in collection, processing, use of date.[68] Thus, data protection and privacy share only a limited area of interference, that of personal data. According to a general definition, personal data, in CoE law (modernised Convention 108) and EU law (GDPR), is "information relating to an identified or identifiable natural person".[69] In these terms, data protection partially falls into the scope of art. 8 ECHR, and this raised questions about how the guarantee should be applied to such a sphere.

From a different point of view, data processing and other kinds of digital techniques may boost public and private power to interfere in people's privacy, challenging the overall scope of art. 8 ECHR. As to the inherent limits of this inquiry, the real intrusive power of means of digital investigation is certainly relevant with respect to the Convention. The legal basis regulating the State's interference for investigative purposes must be tailored to the actual level of intrusion into the individuals' private sphere: the existence of technological and scientific means to intrude on privacy does not mean that such an intrusion, although regulated by the law, is compliant with the Convention…

Under the first viewpoint, in recent decades, the Court worked out a "common framework of principles and conditions to be respected" in the legitimate use of data processing by public criminal authorities.[70] With particular regards to data processing, the Court has elaborated on a number of indexes which may specifically satisfy either the 'necessity' or 'legality' tests.[71] In terms of necessity, the Court often refers to "a pressing social need", as a fundamental requirement to justify the interference. Such a need must be proportional to the legitimate aim pursued by with the intrusion into personal data, via data processing and, in light of this assumption, the

[65] Durante (2019), pp. 151 ff.; 282.

[66] As to the many different concepts of privacy, Pagallo (2014), p. 225 ss.

[67] Leenes and De Conca (2018), p. 282. The concept of 'informational privacy' owes to the famous decision of 1983 by the German Constitutional Court (Bundesverfassungsgericht, decision no., 15 December 1983), ruling that, in a democratic society, citizens must enjoy the right to be aware of who knows what about their personal life.

[68] Barfield and Pagallo (forthcoming), Chapter V, Issues of Data Protection.

[69] See both General Data Protection Regulation, Art. 4 (1); Modernised Convention 108, Art. 2 (a).

[70] Sicurella and Scalia (2013), p. 437.

[71] Having been drafted in more recent years, the Charter of Fundamental rights of the EU expressly provides for protection of personal data, in art. 8.

Court often considers the effectiveness of the measures deployed by the national authorities with regard to the goal pursued. This brings to the attention of the Court possible alternative ways to protect the very same public interest,[72] by introducing a sort of *adequacy principle*, which is intended to objectivise the evaluation.

As to the legality requirement, the Court has adopted a non-formal approach. On the one hand, not every kind of legal provision satisfies this condition in Art. 8 § 1. The act providing for personal data processing must be accessible[73] and foreseeable,[74] which, according to the Court's case-law, implies (1) a clear definition of the cases in which data is processed; (2) a transparent description of the scope; and, (3) an objective set of the conditions of discretion that the public authority enjoys. On the other hand, these requirements can be achieved by the states even through administrative regulations, provided that they are accessible.[75] An Act by the Parliament is not always necessary.[76] However, in its assessment of the adequacy of the provisions aimed at meeting these requirements, the Court often tends to consider the existence and availability of judicial checks and balances,[77] thereby transforming the requirement of the "provision by law" into a control on the existence of adequately *transparent* procedural guarantees against abuse.[78]

Therefore, in summarising this extensive case-law without over-simplification, we can say that the main features of the Court's reasoning about the lawfulness of data processing are the *principle of adequacy*, embedded in the test of 'necessity in a democratic society'; and the *principle of transparency*,[79] inherent to the legality test.[80]

Yet, when data processing is performed in the interest of justice, maintaining the balance with the protection of people's privacy and their personal data can be particularly challenging because the individual is confronted directly with the state's punitive power, one of the highest and strongest expressions of the sovereignty of the nation-state.

As to the use of modern digital techniques intruding on privacy in criminal investigations and trials, the Court stated that this cannot happen at any cost. On the contrary, there must be a careful balance between the general interest of effective

[72] Sicurella and Scalia (2013), p. 442.

[73] In Kokkinakis V. Greece (25.5.1993) the Court criticized, under this viewpoint, the wording of a national law.

[74] Foreseeability played an important role in pushing the due process requirements of art. 6, and the effective remedy of art. 13 ECHR, to merge into the framework of art. 8: De Hert and Gutwirth (2006), p. 85.

[75] See the case of Kruslin V. France (24.4.1990), in which even an unwritten rule of criminal procedure was deemed to satisfy art. 8 ECHR.

[76] For a critical opinion, see De Hert and Gutwirth (2006), p. 87.

[77] ECtHR Klass v. GFR, 6.9.1978.

[78] De Schutter (2001), p. 142.

[79] "Transparency seems to have replaced legitimacy as the core value of data protection": De Hert and Gutwirth (2006), p. 80.

[80] Sicurella and Scalia (2013), p. 443.

counter-crime instruments and the important interests of private life. In particular, the Court acknowledged that "any State claiming a pioneer role in the development of new technologies bears special responsibility for striking the right balance in this regard",[81] and that the margin of appreciation of each member State is narrowed down by the existence of a large consensus between the majority of the other Member States, about the suitable application and limitations of such technologies.[82] The Court made such statements in the leading case about a DNA database, S. and Marper v. the UK,[83] concluding for a violation of art. 8 ECHR, with regard to the national legislation not providing for a precise deadline for the retention[84] of finger prints, cellular sample and DNA profiles of persons suspected, but not convicted, of any offense.

Although biometrics was specifically at stake in the case of S. and Marper, v. the UK, it seems that the principle could be extended to the use, in the investigation, of digital techniques, often based on computational modelling that will be under the spotlight hereinafter. Indeed, the Strasbourg Court (like the Luxembourg one),[85] seems to consider digital technologies more disruptive than analogic ones, and detrimental to the rights enshrined in Art. 8 ECHR. In the case of Editorial Board of Pravoye Delo and Shtekel v. Ukraine, the Strasbourg Court expressly stated that: "the risk of harm posed by content and communications on the Internet to the exercise and enjoyment of human rights and freedoms, particularly the right to respect for private life, is certainly higher than that posed by the press".[86] There are several examples in which the Court paid attention to the fact that digital 'traces' of private activities (such as browsing web sites) seems to be more vulnerable to external intrusion, regardless of the use made of such information.[87]

In § 3.3 the focus will be on the huge enlargement in information that can be mined for investigative purposes and the progressive fading of the concepts that, traditionally, enclosed and protected such information, such as home and correspondence (or communication); in § 4, the focus will be on the main issues arising from an unprecedented aggressive intrusion of LEAs in the individuals' private sphere, from the perspective of fundamental rights.

[81] ECtHR, 4.12.2008, S. and Marper v. the U.K., § 112.

[82] In the case of S. and Marper v. the UK, the Court relied on the fact that many Member States had already settled precise time-limits for retention of biometrics data belonging to suspects who were never convicted of an offence: this made the UK lack of specific terms unjustified.

[83] S. and Marper v. the U.K., cit., § 112.

[84] The Court applied a similar approach in ECtHR, 13.11.2012, M.M. v. UK, establishing a violation of art. 8 ECHR with regard to the length of retention of criminal records data.

[85] Pollicino and Bassini (2017), p. 139.

[86] ECtHR, 5.5.2011, Editorial Board of Pravoye Delo and Shtekel v. Ukraine, § 63.

[87] See, e.g., ECtHR, 3.4.2007, Copland v. UK, a case of an employer monitoring an employee's communications and internet access, without using for disciplinary or labour purposes.

3.2.2 Art. 7 and 8 of the ChFREU: A Brand-New Approach?

When referring to the protection of privacy against LEAs' interference, in Europe, it is crucial to compare the ECHR protection with that one provided by the Charter of Fundamental Rights of the European Union. Having acquired, ten years ago, the same legally binding value of the Treaties, the Charter is struggling to become a further beacon of the protection of fundamental rights in the EU member states. Art. 7 ChFREU provides, as Art. 8 ECHR, for the respect of private and family life.[88] The relationship between the rights enshrined both in the ECHR and in the ChFREU is regulated by art. 52§3 ChFREU, establishing that "the meaning and scope of those rights shall be the same as those laid down by the said Convention" (unless the Charter may grant major protection).

As to the protection of the individuals' personal sphere, the Charter is inspired, indeed, by art. 8 ECHR:[89] actually, according to the Explanations to the Charter (2007 C 303(2)), the content of art. 7 "corresponds" to that of art. 8 ECHR. Nevertheless, it is stressed that, in order to take technological developments into account, the ChFREU uses the term 'communication' rather than 'correspondence'.

Moreover, what is certainly remarkable is that the Charter encompasses a specific right to the protection of personal data, enshrined in the following Art. 8 ChFREU. According to the Explanation, the provision is rooted into (the former) art. 286 of the Treaty establishing the European Union and the directive 95/46/EC, along with art. 8 ECHR and the CoE 1981 Convention on the automatic processing of personal data. The directive 95/46 on the protection of individuals with regard to the processing of personal data and on the free movement of such data, was adopted by the European Parliament and the Council in October 1995 and represented the most specific European legal framework for personal data processing at the time the Charter was drafted.[90]

Thus, from a general point of view, the same protection deployed by art. 8 ECHR is divided into two different provisions, within the Charter. For the limited purposes of this part of the study, it is important to consider how the Charter, along with other EU pieces of legislation, affected the area of public intrusion into the personal sphere for the purpose of criminal investigations.

---

[88] Art. 7 "Everyone has the right to respect for his or her private and family life, home and communications."

[89] And to art. 12 Universal Declaration of Human Rights and art. 17 ICCPR.

[90] Some other important pieces of legislation would be adopted later: Directive 2006/24, on 15.3.2006, and Council Framework Decision 2008/977/JHA, on 8.11.2008. More on this in the text and in the next paragraph.

3.2.2.1 The Scope of Art. 7 ChFREU

As to the scope of art. 7 ChFREU, one patent difference with art. 8 ECHR is that the first does not list, as the latter does, the interests that can be put in balance with the individual right to privacy. Based on this, it has been stressed that art. 7 ChFREU needs to be read in strong interaction with other provisions of the charter itself (in particular, 17—right to property, and 8—personal data protection; 24—interests of children), as much as with other general sources of the EU law, namely, the ECHR and the constitutional traditions common to the member States (art. 6.3 TrEU).[91] Moreover, the right to private life and the specific protection for personal data processing are not absolute prerogatives and can be restricted or limited for the sake of the purpose of a general interests (art. 52 ChFREU).[92] Provided with this caveat, it is possible to argue that the CJEU case law on art. 7 ChFREU strongly built upon the principles established by the Strasburg Court. Nevertheless, there has been at least one breaking point confronting the two European legal systems, with regard to the extension of the private life privilege to legal persons and to professional and commercial premises. Actually, the CJEU originally rejected the Strasbourg extensive doctrine,[93] although the disagreement appears less evident, at the time being.[94] One of the areas in which the Luxembourg Courts showed less reluctance to extend the privilege to legal persons is, indeed, the realm of personal data. In the case of Nexans France SAS,[95] the Tribunal of the EU referred to art. 7 ChFREU, to establish the need for proportionality with regard to the public intrusion into a person's—both natural and legal—private sphere. Nevertheless, the extension to legal persons has not been general and absolute: in the case of Volker,[96] the CJEU underlined that legal persons can enjoy the guarantees established by art. 7 and 8 ChFREU if the legal person can be identified with one or more specific natural persons: proportionality has always been the key for keeping the balance between the rights established by the Charter and the social relevance of the alleged violations. In particular, in the case of ASNEF,[97] the CJEU evaluated the seriousness of the violation based on the fact that individuals have the right to stronger protection against the managing of personal data that is not accessible at all to the public, while the protection decreases if data is already accessible to the public. Such a theory was then at the basis of the decision Digital Rights Ireland, by which the CJEU declared the Directive 2006/24 invalid, as "the EU legislature has exceeded the limits imposed by compliance with

---

[91] Martinico (2017), p. 117.

[92] Pollicino and Bassini (2017), p. 143.

[93] See e.g. CJEU, 21.9.1989, Hoechst v. Commission, joint C-46/87 and 227/88.

[94] See CJEU, 22.1.2002, Roquette Frères, C-94/00, expressly referring to Hoechst.

[95] Tribunal EU 14.11.2012, Nexans v. France and Nexans v. Commission, T-135/09.

[96] CJEU, 9.11.201, Volker und Markus Schecke and Eifert, joint C-92/09 and 93/09.

[97] CJEU, 24.11.2011, Asociación Nacional de Establecimientos Financieros de Credito and Federación de Comercio Electronico y Marketing Directo c. Administracion del Estado, joint C-468/10 and 469/10.

the principle of proportionality in the light of Articles 7, 8 and 52(1) of the Charter."[98] The directive regulated the retention of data generated or processed in connection with the provision of publicly available electronic communications services or of public communications networks (in amendment of Directive 2002/58/EC), also for criminal investigation purposes.

Until the latter decision (in which the CJEU acknowledged a functional distinction),[99] the EU judicial bodies had referred jointly to art. 7 and 8 ChFREU, confirming the necessary link between the two provisions: it is worth asking, thus, why the drafters of the Charter, since its original version signed in Nice, decided to set forth two separate provisions.

3.2.2.2 Different Perspectives

There has certainly been an historical reason for distinguishing, within the Charter of Fundamental Rights of the EU, the right to private and family life and the right to personal data protection. As said, there has been an evolution, through the decades, in the European doctrine of data protection, elaborated on the basis of the negative approach that inspired the drafters of the ECHR. Nevertheless, it has been noted that this was not the main reason for establishing a brand-new independent guarantee in art. 8 ChFREU.[100] In particular, art. 8 does not represent the mere summary of the theories elaborated, over the decades, in the realm of the CoE and EU regulations and case-law, along with the doctrines of data protection worked out by the national constitutional judges: encompassing the traditional theory of consensus, art. 8 ChFREU established the statute of legitimate personal data processing, regardless of the requirement of consensus.[101]

At the time being, the CJEU case law about art. 8 ChFREU is extensive and there are many different areas that the Court recognised as falling under the scope of the guarantee. A comprehensive reconstruction falls out of our scope, and the focus will be on the aspects relating to personal data protection and criminal investigations. However, from a general point of view, it is worth noting a relevant distinction between two main historical periods, before and after the Lisbon treaty, when the Charter finally entered into force.

In any case, since the very beginning, the Court was confronted with several cases dealing with digital processing of personal data. One of the first decisions delivered by the CJEU under art. 8 ChFREU was in the case of Bodil Lindqvist,[102] relating to the unauthorised publication of personal data on an internet website. The preliminary ruling was about the interpretation of dir. 95/46 and, in particular, its

[98] CJEU, 8.4.2014, Digital Rights Ireland Ltd., joint C-293/12 and 594/12, § 69.

[99] Pollicino and Bassini (2017), p. 153.

[100] Pollicino and Bassini (2017), p. 135.

[101] Kranenborg (2014), p. 229.

[102] CJEU, 6.11.2003, Bodil Lindqvist, C-101/01.

compliance with the right of free expression. Mrs. Lindqvist claimed that Directive 95/46, implying requirements of prior consent and prior notification of a supervisory authority and a principle of prohibiting processing of personal data of a sensitive nature, was contrary to the general principle of freedom of expression enshrined in Community law. The Court adjudicated in the sense that the directive did not establish limitations incompatible with this fundamental right, holding the prior consent and notification as legitimate prerequisites for processing personal data: in so far, it apparently endorsed the same ECtHR attitude to consider digital media more intrusive than traditional media. In a following case, Satamedia,[103] Adv. Gen. Kokotte took a critical position about the decision delivered by the Court in the Lindqvist case, concluding that if publication of personal data was submitted to the subjects' consent, investigative journalism would not exist... Kokotte's opinion shone the spotlight on the need for a fair balance between the public interest and the protection of personal data from external intrusion, and, in that case, the Court found it in art. 9 dir. 95/46, providing, said the Court, for predominance of the public interest for information. However, after that case, the CJEU shifted again, and decisively, towards a prevailing protection of personal data, with the leading case of Google Spain. The decision was made the object of extensive literature[104] and it is worth mentioning it here to compare the differing attitudes shown by the court in balancing data protection with freedom of expression and with criminal investigation purposes. For this limited purpose, in Google Spain the Court departed from the Advocate general's conclusions, except in the assumption that search engine indexing *is* personal data processing, delivering to search engine managers the duty to set a balance between the overarching protection of personal data and the possible, residual public interest to access information of general relevance.[105]

As to the relationship between personal data processing and criminal investigation, a main role has been played by the CJEU in the case of Digital Rights Ireland, mentioned in the previous paragraph. The Directive 2006/24 provided for retention of personal data for a period of minimum 6 months to a maximum of 2 years (Art.6) for investigation, detection and prosecution of serious crimes (Art. 1.1).[106] After having assessed the interference of the data retention duty with art. 7 and 8 ChFREU

[103] CJEU, 8.5.2008, Tietosuojavaltuutettu c. Satakunnan Markkinapörssi Oy and Satamedia Oy, C-73/07.

[104] For an updated review, Pagallo and Durante (2019), Ch. 13; Pollicino and Romeo (2016), especially Ch. 4 and 5.

[105] Pollicino and Bassini (2017), p. 150. With regard to off line pieces of information, the Italian Supreme Court had theorized the 'right to be forgotten' in the 1990s (Corte di Cassazione, sentenza n. 3679/1998): Durante (2019), p. 132.

[106] Another very important decision was delivered by the CJEU in the case of Maximilian Schrems (Maximilian Schrems v. Data Protection Commission, C-362/14, joined party: Digital Rights Ireland Ltd.), with regard, however, to personal data processing for national security reasons, rather than for criminal investigation and prosecution purposes. In that decision, the Court outruled the Data Protection Commission decision 2000/520, based on art. 25 dir. 95/46. In decision 520, the Commission had adjudicated that personal data collected in the EU could be transferred, stored and used in the US, on the basis of the alleged adequacy of personal data protection offered by the American 'safe harbour' principle. The CJEU, based on art. 7, 8, 48 ChFREU declared the Data Protection Commission decision invalid. The same position has been recently

(§§ 32-37) the Court examined the justification for such an interference (§§ 38-69), excluding the consistency with art. 7, 8 and 52 ChFREU. Actually, the Directive failed the proportionality test, for several reasons, essentially based on the lack of precise limitations, as to the data subjects (the whole European population, regardless of any suspicion of criminality?), the range of relevant serious crimes (any, regardless of penalty limitations?), the way in which national LEAs can access retained data and, last but not least, to the period of retention, to be calculated between 6 months and 2 years, without specific criteria. Moreover, the Directive did not provide for specific protections against unlawful access to the retained data, that, based on the directive, did not need to be stored in Europe… For this long list of reasons, the Court assessed that EU legislature had exceeded the limits imposed by the principle of proportionality, declaring the directive, as said, invalid.

3.2.2.3 Secondary EU Legislation on Data Protection in the Criminal Area

What precedes is a short summary of the EU legal framework, with regard to our topic, at the time when the GDPR and, in particular, directive 2016/680 came into force. On April 27th 2016, the Regulation 2016/679 replaced dir. 95/46, protecting natural persons with regard to the processing of personal data and on the free movement of such data (General Data Processing Regulation), whose application is excluded (recital 19) for the purposes of the prevention, investigation, detection or prosecution of criminal offences or the execution of criminal penalties, including the safeguarding against and the prevention of threats to public security and the free movement of such data. Indeed, such areas falls under the scope of another specific legal act of the Union, that it is to say Dir. 2016/680, expressly devoted to the protection of natural persons with regard to the processing of personal data by competent authorities for the purposes of the prevention, investigation, detection or prosecution of criminal offences or the execution of criminal penalties, and on the free movement of such data, and repealing the Council Framework Decision 2008/977/JHA.[107] According to the title, the text does not distinguish between prevention and repression of crime, leaving the member states free to provide one unique, general regulation for the two domains.

Taking expressly into account the special balance existing between personal data and the general interest for effective criminal investigations, art. 1 of the directive

confirmed by the CJEU, in the so-called Schrems II decision, 16.7.2020, followed by strong criticism: Pollicino (2020); Bignami (2020).

[107] The Framework decision was adopted under the third pillar, before the Lisbon Treaty entered into force. FD were based on unanimity and were binding for MS only in their aims. Under the peculiar third pillar regulation, the CJEU had limited jurisdiction and the rates of implementation by MS were almost very low. In particular, the FD 2008/977/JHA applied only to the exchange of data among LEAs or judicial authorities: it did not apply to personal data collected and processed inside one national legal order.

2016/680 sets forth that "the exchange of personal data by competent authorities within the Union, where such exchange is required by Union or Member State law, is neither restricted nor prohibited for reasons connected with the protection of natural persons with regard to the processing of personal data". Based on this general assumption, art. 2 clarifies that the directive applies to the whole or partial automated processing of personal data for the said purposes (excluded: activities that fall within the scope of the GDPR; activities that fall out of the scope of the EU and the EU institutions, bodies, offices and agencies).

Thus, a wholly automated processing of personal data by LEAs is lawful, under the conditions set forth by the directive. Nevertheless, art. 11 prohibits decisions based solely on automated processing of data, producing adverse legal effects for the data subject. However, this prohibition is not absolute. Firstly, there must be an adverse legal effect on the data subject, with the exception of those situations in which there is a merely neutral legal effect or there is an adverse legal effect on a third person.[108] Secondly, Member States may authorise wholly automated decisions on the basis of the EU or national law, provided that the controller can give adequate guarantees, such as obtaining the human intervention on the part of the controller.

Chapter III of the Directive deals with the rights of the data subject, that is to say the person whose data is being processed. However, it is worth stressing that Art. 6 sets forth four different categories of data subjects, distinguishing between: persons seriously suspected of having committed a crime; persons convicted of a criminal offence; victims (even potential) of a crime; other individuals intervening in the proceedings, as witnesses, experts, or with other roles. It has been suggested that such distinctions may interfere with the fundamental rights of the individuals at stake.[109]

Art. 20 of the directive imposes that the subject's privacy protection must be taken into consideration, from the stage of designing data-mining software.[110] This should only authorise that data needed for a specific purpose (set forth by the directive itself) is processed and that, in general, unrestricted access to personal data is not permitted without the subject's consent. However, even though the text provides for an apparently wide range of access rights (in articles 13, 14, 16, in combination with art. 18), it does not afford the suspect/defendant the right to impose on the law enforcement agencies a specific duty to disclose the digital codes for software used to process data. It is premature to say whether the directive's balance between data protection and public interest is the correct one, as it is up to the member states to find a satisfying balance between these competing interests.[111] On the one hand, the individuals' interests for

---

[108] It should be considered whether such situation falls out of the scope of dir. 2016/680 and under the GDPR: in this case, the data subject would have no remedy, but this should be in the possibility of the third person suffering for the negative legal consequence of the fully automated decision.

[109] Signorato (2018), p. 97.

[110] Klitou (2014), passim.

[111] In fact, it will be up to the MS to strike a proper and effective balance between the two concurrent interests: De Hert and Papakstantinou (2016), p. 12.

the respect, even in criminal proceedings, of their personal data; on the other hand, the urgency of establishing a strict control on the application of the directive, by an independent authority, without interfering with the independence of the judiciary... The balance is not easy at all: transparency and privacy safeguarded by default seems to be the best options for the purpose. In Chap. 4 the focus will be on the risks deriving from a lack of transparency in the use of digital data as evidence in criminal proceedings. But let us focus first on how the digital turn affected the basic concepts grounding the traditional protection of privacy in our legal systems, also transforming the most common means of criminal investigations.

3.3 Is AI Transforming the Traditional Sites of Our Private Life into a Panopticon for Criminal Investigations?

In this Part of the book and in this Chapter, in particular, we worked from the assumption that the digital turn has deeply influenced the concept of privacy. As mentioned, a substantial amount of literature has been produced in the research of this topic, at least in the past decade. Thus, it is impossible to discuss the issue in a comprehensive way here. Moreover, criminal investigation represents only one specific ground for interference with an individual's privacy, and, possibly, is not the most disruptive one. Indeed, criminal investigations, being led by a public authority, tend to be regulated, more or less precisely, by general principles and statutory regulation: on the contrary, much more deceitful forms of interference have been revealed and reported recently, suggesting that private, but even transnational, interests intrude daily on people's private lives for commercial or political purposes, escaping any form of control or regulation. For these reasons, the following analysis is isolated within the boundaries of a specific enquiry, about the role and the impact of computational modelling and AI in the balance between current investigative methods and suspects' procedural guarantees.

As anticipated, the sites of the traditional protection of privacy against public interference are home and correspondence, or more generally, communication. Art.8 ECHR expressly refers to "home" and "correspondence", as does art. 18 ICCPR, along with several national constitutions in Europe. Moreover, Art. 8 covers also 'any other form of communication". As seen, the more recent Art. 7 ChFREU refers to 'domicile' and 'communication'.

However, we have seen that ICT has deeply affected each of the concepts mentioned above, starting from the idea of 'communication': all in all, we are experiencing the multiplication of the plans and environments in which a private conversation may occur and, thus, of the ways in which it can be intercepted.

3.3.1 What Is 'Communication' Today?

For the purposes of this study, it is possible to move from the hypothesis that the immense computational power at our (cheap) disposal is used for 'interactions'.[112] ICT systems may provide machine-to-machine interaction or human-computer interaction and what the several different instruments of ICT do, is to handle data. Thus, interaction, communication is (also and almost), handling, exchange of data. With a vivid metaphor, Floridi calls attention on the postulate that, as much as what our eyes can see (the spectrum of the rainbow) is a minimum part of the electromagnetic spectrum, what we can perceive of the data-managing spectrum is a negligible part of the existing machine-to-machine and human-computer interactions.[113] This scenario is disruptive, if compared with the traditional idea of communication that our legal systems still take into account, for many different reasons. Because it occurs in a non-physical environment, it almost escapes, as said, to the human perception, being often a bare machine-to-machine interaction and cannot be regulated by a traditional set of parameters, based on the physical dimension, in particular, space.[114] Thus, in addition to the common forms of communication, legal regulation should consider also the further spectrum of digital interaction that, by actively exchanging data, are forms of communication. Such framework implies at least a two-tier regulation, covering both non-digital and digital communications. Moreover, for the purpose of criminal law, the spatial dimension of communication is fundamental, both for substantive and procedural aspects. Under the substantive point of view, a digital interaction can amount, *per se*, to a criminal offence (or a part of it) and it is crucial to determine where (and when) it occurred. Under the procedural point of view, not only *locus commissi delicti* is crucial for issues like jurisdiction, but also for investigations, as interceptions and other means of investigation may be restricted, if the conversation occurs in a private context (not necessarily a private place), in accordance with international charters, national constitutions and codes of criminal procedure. It is worth underlining that investigation by digital means is becoming an increasingly successful strategy, not only with regard to those offences that occur in the digital environment, but in all kind of criminal cases.[115]

However, if the nature of communication changed over the last decades, as said, a shift must have occurred also in the way interference in communication is realised for investigative purposes... As it will be discussed in paragraph 4 (and anticipated, under a different point of view, in Chap. 2), coordination in the evolution of ICT and statutory regulation of investigation proved very hard to achieve, for several

[112] Floridi (2017), p. 9.

[113] Floridi (2017), p. 10.

[114] Even though 'hyperhistory' is a new era in human evolution, it does not transcend completely the spatio-temporal constraints in which the modern society evolved: thus, it is a matter of reframing the concepts of time and space: Floridi (2017), p. 24.

[115] Signorato (2018), p. 43.

reasons. First, because the fast and ever-advancing evolution in digital technologies would outdate even the most timely and effective reform… Second, because there is still uncertainty on the very concept of communication in contemporary days: the assumption we moved from, indeed, is far from having been fully assimilated by society. Moreover, such uncertainty is coupled with another one. Not only the existing regulations protecting private life from investigative interference refer to 'communication', but also to 'home' or 'domicile', as the place from which individuals expect to exclude any unwanted external intrusion. Obviously, the digital turn deeply affected also such concept.

3.3.2 What Is 'Home' in the Infosphere?[116]

The shift in the sense of the concept of 'communication' is also deeply affecting the traditional legal concept of 'home': both ideas of 'domicile' and 'home' (not overlapping) are undergoing a huge transformation, also as a consequence of a different idea of 'communication'. As said, 'home' (and '*domicile*', in the French version of both ECHR and ChFREU), is the place traditionally protected by law from unjustified external interference, either by public authorities and other private individuals. It has been stressed that the French version of both the ECHR and the ChFREU refers to "domicile", rather than "home", the former having been recognised a wider concept than the latter. What happens inside such premises is protected by external interference, unless it meets all the requirements provided for by art. 8 ECHR or the proportionality test within the EU legal order. On the contrary, and generally speaking, what happens or is performed outside those premises tends to fall out the scope of privacy, being almost unrestrictedly accessible. Nevertheless, national regulations and case law principles establish limitations, especially for the use in criminal proceedings of pictures, conversations, videos, recorded or intercepted in secluded areas of public places.[117]

However, the digital revolution shifted significantly the borders of the environment in which individuals perform activities (almost communicative) that they may want to keep undisclosed. Such environments can be digital, and the activities can be operated via different devices, such as computers, tablets, smartphones, digital watches and others, as we will see below. For these reasons, a strong feeling of inadequacy grew up in recent years around the concept of 'home', suggesting rather to move towards the idea of a 'digital domicile'. The concept of 'digital domicile' has been extensively researched, especially after the famous decision by the German Constitutional Court of 2008,[118] out-ruling the regional law (Nortrhein-Westphalen)

[116] The term is used by Floridi (2017), p. 24.

[117] E.g. toilets of public premises: in many jurisdictions, privacy in secluded areas of public place is protected from arbitrary intrusion and the use of intercepted conversions, pictures, videos are prohibited by an exclusionary rule (for an example see Italy, Triggiani 2019, p. 153).

[118] Bundesverfassungsgericht, Decision no. 370, 27.2.2008.

about *On-line Durchsuchung* (on-line search). According to the German highest Court, digital devices have gained the status of instruments for the development of the individual's personality.[119] In this sense, they should enjoy the same protection granted to the places where private life is traditionally located. The German decision acknowledged that the existing, ordinary, guarantees cannot fit the specificities of the 'digital privacy', due to the immateriality of the space where digital data are stored: privacy becomes 'de-located'[120] and, for these reasons, the conceptualisation of 'digital domicile' is complex.

To the purposes of this work suffice it to say that, like traditional domicile, the 'digital domicile' must be based on three main requirements:[121] (1) right to lawfully access, stay and leave a specific environment; in other words, right to log in, browse and log out a digital environment (just like checking in, staying and checking out a hotel room...; (2) right to exclude other people from such environment; (3) the private or professional nature of the activities performed in the environment. Like in the physical world, also in the digital environment there may be a matter of processing personal data in 'public areas' or 'public access areas'. In this sense, even the new concept of digital domicile is unable to offer a comprehensive 'shield' in which the data subject can effectively enjoy her right to exclude others from the access to her data... Although there is a formal distinction between the digital environments freely accessible and those requiring a registration, even with a false identity, personal data shared and stored in both contexts can hardly be protected. For example, accepting to share personal data[122] on platforms in which the users' identity may or may not be verified, opens up such information to LEAs intrusion for investigative purposes.

Against this scenario, two arguments seem crucial. Firstly, the traditional, physical dimension of domicile does not cover the whole range of human activities that individuals may not want to disclose to others. The idea of 'digital domicile' can partly help, although there are uncountable immaterial environments in which personal data can be mined and hacked, without the data subject's power to exclude other people. Secondly, not only the house is still worth the traditional protection against external intrusion, but it is also worth further layers of protection. Many systems based on AI solutions intrude our homes, with our full consent: robots, home assistant, IoT, as we will see (Sect. 3.4.1), produce, store, analyse, communicate data about what happens inside the 'sanctuary' of private life. In this sense, the house walls became transparent, vulnerable to the external intrusion, due to a constant and invisible flow of data from the inside to the outside, and the other way

[119] Flor (2009), p. 697 ss.

[120] Picotti (2004), p. 80.

[121] Signorato (2018), p. 80.

[122] The phenomenon falls under the phenomenon of extimacy (English translation for the French *extimité*, first used by the French psychoanalyst Jacques Lacan, in late Fifties), a concept having been theorised in opposition to intimacy. For a general overview, see Pavón (2014), p. 661: "extimacy indicates the nondistinction and essential identity between the dual terms of the outside and the deepest inside, the exterior and the most interior of the psyche".

around. This is not irrelevant at all for the context of this study and, in particular, for criminal investigations and evidence gathering.

3.4 Is Investigative Hacking Overarching Privacy?

In 2017, the Libe Committee of the European Parliament commissioned to the Directorate-general for internal policies (Policy Dept.: Citizens' rights and constitutional affaires), a study about the Legal frameworks for Hacking by Law Enforcement: Identification, Evaluation and Comparison of Practices. The study, based on the comparison between six Member States (France, Germany, Italy, Netherlands, Poland, UK) and three non-member States (Australia, Israel, USA), was aimed at providing, based on a summary of the international debate on the topic, an analysis of the legal basis for the EU intervention to develop concrete policy proposals, actually 12 different proposals, that are anticipated in the summary of the paper.

The initiative of the Civil Liberties, Justice and Home Affaires Committee was rooted in the assumption that "law enforcement hacking has the potential for increased invasiveness when compared with traditional coercive activities".[123] Based on this, the European Parliament Committee wanted to focus on the risks that such assumption may imply for European citizens' fundamental rights and liberties, to orient its future activity. The assumption is grounded on a general, growing opinion, that has also been elaborated in some important international acts, such as the Key Recommendations on the third UN General Assembly resolution on the right to privacy in the digital age (2016). Actually, the area of international organisation paying attention to the issue, is that of human rights and, in particular, of privacy, while justice sector bodies have initially proved less active.[124] The LIBE Committee concern was to shine the spotlight on the topic, from the specific point of view of justice.

The study delivered by the experts of DG Internal policies moves from two general arguments, of crucial importance for this analysis. First, LEAs around the world are transforming their means of investigation, based on the fact that criminality extensively relies on digital instruments and, largely, on encryption. Although the topic of encryption and criminal investigation falls largely outside the limits of this study, this first assumption is particularly relevant. Actually, to contrast such sophisticated forms of criminal activity, LEAs and judicial authorities must recur to hacking techniques, exploiting vulnerabilities within IT systems. The discussion about encryption initiated some years ago, but intensified after 2015 as a result of the famous case FBI vs Apple.

[123] Libe Report, 21.

[124] Libe Report, 23.

Second. Such hacking tools are usually developed on a commercial level, on the basis of very poor consideration for human rights.[125] This represents a serious risk for the fundamental rights, first and foremost, privacy. This is the point connecting this very general overview on investigative intrusions in private life with the main topic of this work. Using hacking instruments based on computational modelling and AI may amount to a violation, not only of privacy, but also of other fundamental rights. In many legal orders—and in some cases, also in the CoE legal system—an act performed in breach of the right to private life may violate also other fundamental rights, such as the fair trial (extensively on this, Chap. 4). This assumption is not new at all: in the previous paragraphs we focused on the balance between art. 8 ECHR, art. 7 and 8 ChFREU, with the general interest to effective criminal investigations. Although briefly, we summarised the conditions at which, under the ECtHR case law, the investigation authorities' intrusion into private life is compliant with the Convention… However, the growing invasiveness of investigative hacking instruments unbalanced such equilibrium and the traditional legal checks and balances seem not effective any longer.

Traditionally, the national jurisdictions regulated investigative interference into individuals' private life on the basis of two main resources, according with the guide-lines provided by the ECtHR case law: *ex ante* and *ex post* conditions. Usually, intrusive investigations should meet two *ex ante* requirements: on the one hand, the law must clearly list the offences in relation to which interceptions and other intrusive means can be applied (usually based on seriousness of crime) and the duration of such interception; on the other hand, the law usually imposes judicial authorisation before such means are applied (or immediately after). As to the *ex post* conditions, legal orders usually provide for remedies against unlawful investigative interference with the individuals' private sphere, almost by exclusionary rules (see Chap. 4). The concern is whether, given the shift in the meaning of 'communication' and 'home', that has been presented above, and the growing intrusiveness of hacking investigative means, such traditional safeguards are still useful.

3.4.1 Some Examples of Hacking by Law Enforcement Instruments

In the previous paragraphs much attention has been spent on the conditions, set forth by art. 8§2 ECHR for a lawful interference of public authorities into the individuals' private sphere. In particular, we lingered over the meaning of the general requirement of 'in accordance with the law'. Domestic laws should list the reasons and the ways in which such interference is allowed and this requirement should be valid also for hacking investigative means. However, listing the means for investigative hacking may prove slightly inefficient, as they tend to adapt to the specific

[125] Libe Report, 9.

conditions into which they operate: a precise description seems incompatible with their very essence. Although the Strasbourg Court applies a very wide concept of 'law', the concern is about how to establish the respect of such conditions, case by case: the more the means is peculiar, the less it is possible to regulate it, specifically, by statutory law. Thus, what is worth trying to do, in this paragraph, is to point out the main critical aspects that derive from the technical, digital, characteristics of the tools mostly used for investigative hacking. This is not an exhaustive list, nor a comparative legal confrontation, rather an overview of the most relevant clashes between digital efficiency and legal requirements.

Intrusion into the private digital sphere can be operated both by off-line and on-line means of investigation. The first group covers mainly searches and seizures of hardware, while the second encompasses malwares and all other means of remote forensics. The focus here will be concentrated specifically on the second group, covering on-line hacking for investigative purpose, although several digital tools can operate both on- and off-line.

One of the most common hacking instruments are malwares. The term encompasses several types of malicious software, with different characteristics: the name is due to the fact that such software is installed with malicious purpose, it is to say, with the user's unaware cooperation, but against her will and, possibly, against her personal interest. It can be a virus, which, like a biological virus, can replicate, reproducing copies of itself, hiding into an apparently harmless application or programme, called 'trojan horse'. Spyware is another kind of malware, collecting (and transmitting) information about the user's online activity (sites visited, purchases made online) without her consent and, of course, even not her awareness.

Malware and spyware are massively used in the investigative field, introduced by a so-called trojan horse.[126] The user, by running or installing the apparently harmless program, installs also the code of the hidden malicious software, that will colonise the hosting device. Invisible to the user of the infected device, it allows various forms of intrusion into the user's digital sphere and, in particular: (a) acquisition of information exchanged through the infected medium; (b) remote activation of geolocation, recording or audio-video recording tools; (c) access and manipulation of files present in the infected hardware. The infected device is manipulated by a remote centre, the latter being able both to up-load and down-load files and programmes from the former. For these reasons, such software is used to perform on-line searches, room bugging, on-time copies: the monitor, the webcam, the microphone and the keyboard of the infected device can be remotely controlled, delivering an unprecedented amount of information. On-line searches aim to establish a permanent control over the digital environment intruded. For this reason, they are much more aggressive than traditional searches, which are delimited in time, in place and in scope. In general terms, on-line searches do not need to be targeted on a specific aspect: technically, they consent a permanent, secret, control over the digital system, waiting for eventual

[126] Torre (2017), pp. 12–17; Pittiruti (2017), p. 69 ff.; Signorato (2018), p. 237 ff.

specific and relevant data to appear on it. This is a very clearly different context from the usual legal situation generally provided for traditional searches.

Another kind of remote control is geolocation, allowing for 'digital tailing'. Geolocation can be performed through GPS or by the exploitation of mobile devices, such as telephones and tablets. GPS is based on the transmission of a radio-signal, transmitted by a car or another object, in which a transponder has been (secretly), installed. Mobile devices, instead, can be tracked thanks to the local cells for the mobile phone service: each device, when on, is connected to a local cell (providing the service), geo-localising, with acceptable approximation, the position of it.

Among the other remote forensics means, much concern is expressed by the DG study about the exploitation of zero-day vulnerabilities.[127] LEAs can take useful advantage from the unknown vulnerabilities of a system: before the developers and, in particular, the public comes to know such vulnerabilities, they can be exploited as open doors to access wide sets of data and information. Although more often used for intelligence and prevention of crime activities, they may prove particularly useful for investigation as well.

Also crime linkage software, mentioned above, usually operates on-line, detecting (not necessarily predicting) crimes in real time. By mining and analysing big data, it is possible to profile[128] specific criminal, or potentially criminal, behaviours, allowing detection and prevention of crime. Beside policing tools, like PredPol, mentioned above, numbers of crime linkage software have been developed on the basis of specific criminal patterns. G.I.A.N.O.S., e.g., is a software used by many European banks, in order to comply with their duties in preventing money laundering, which intrudes into one of the most undisclosed areas, i.e. banking privacy. The tool processes any financial transaction exceeding € 15,000, accessing data about the individual customer (all her financial operations, their reason, frequency and amount), pointing out anomalies. Based on the aggregation of available data (reconstructing quite complex financial flows), the tool assigns a risk score, in real time, to each single operation. Based on this, the bank should proceed with the mandatory reports to LEAs, about potential money-laundering operations. MENTAS and NORCOM are similar instruments, used in the US, for detection not only of money laundering but also corruption and fraud. With specific regard to fraud in insurance, Italy developed Detector, a software detecting risky contracts, based on the access to a large data set of information, regarding the individual client.[129]

Another large area of investigative tools applying also neural networks is facial recognition. Based on the traditional human recognition, i.e. on individuals' memory, the digital systems of biometric recognition match different kind of images. The main techniques used in face recognition are the PCA (*Principal Component*

[127] Bellovin et al. (2014), espec. p. 22 ff.

[128] Hildebrandt (2008), p. 28.

[129] Costanzi (2019), 1 ff.

Analysis),[130] the LFA (*Local Feature Analysis*) and neural networks,[131] as said. Basically, such tools rely on the fact that the use of video surveillance systems for safety and prevention purposes became generally widespread among public administrations, but also in private contexts.[132] As a consequence, a multitude of frames reproducing the roundabouts of a crime scene are usually available, allowing for both the reconstruction of the facts and the pinpointing of the image of people nearby. This can enhance the identification of the victim and the offender, through the crystallization of a person's face. Those images can be confronted and matched with existing data bases, national and international, at LEAs' disposal. The metric and physiognomic analysis must be based on standardized measurements: recognition is the result of the identification of certain anatomical sites called points of "*repere*".[133] Facial recognition can usually operate both off-line and on-line. For example, *S.a.r.i.* (Automatic Image Recognition System) is a software, in use by the Italian State Police since the beginning of 2017, based on "enterprise"[134] recognition techniques, able both to compare the image of a face with those present in a database[135] and to perform in "real-time",[136] with a concomitant analysis of the faces captured by the cameras, compared with a more restricted watch-list (ten thousand images).[137] As the systems are based on correlations established by neural networks between surveillance images and existing databases, these investigative tools pose two main questions. First, massive surveillance and, in particular, the recording by CCTV of people's acts (although performed in public places) can interfere with

[130] Gulotta (2017), p. 118.

[131] See Oravec (2010), p. 155.

[132] Cfr. https://www.biometricupdate.com/201907/banco-bolivariano-selects-facephi-biometric-digital-onboarding-technology; "*The widespread use of CCTV cameras for surveillance and security applications have stirred extensive research interests in video-based face recognition. (...) Automatic face recognition technology is becoming an indispensable tool for modern forensic investigations*";Wei and Li (2017), p. 190.

[133] The most important points are: the *nasion* (root of the nose); *glabella* (point located above the root of the nose, where the skin is generally free of hair); *pronasal* (protruding point of the tip of nose); *spinal nose* (point corresponding to the nasal subset); *wingspan* (most protruding point of the nose wing); *prosthion* (upper point of the labial-nose furrow); *gonion* (lower margin of the jaw branch); *gnathion* (lower protrusion of the chin); *trichion* (hairline); *vertex* (highest point of the head); *zygion* (most protruding point of the cheekbone). For a general and in-depth analysis see Balossino and Siracusa (2004), passim.

[134] See Ministero dell'Interno – Dipartimento di pubblica sicurezza, *Capitolato tecnico, Procedura volta alla fornitura della soluzione integrata per il sistema automatico di riconoscimento immagini s.a.r.i. lotto n° 1*, available at https://www.poliziadistato.it/statics/06/20160627-ct-sari%2D%2D4-.pdf (20.12.2019).

[135] See http://www.interno.gov.it/it/notizie/sistema-automatico-riconoscimento-immagini-futuro-diventa-realta (17/6/2019).

[136] Still not in use by the Italian State Police.

[137] More specifically, the research can follow three ways: (1) on the basis of the facial image (face-based research) (2) on the basis of anagraphic or descriptive information associated with the images in the recorded people database (anagraphic/descriptive search); (3) on the combined basis of methods 1 and 2 (combined search).

privacy. Second, there may be a specific shortcoming in the matching technique, the polarization of results, due to the correlations established by neural networks. There are three phases that can give rise to the phenomenon of polarization of results: the data collection phase, the algorithm training and the preparation of information. In all these passages, the risk is to inoculate biases into the recognition system, e.g. by choosing data taken from environments that are already "polarized" *per se* (because they are not representative of the reality), the system will perpetuate this polarization in a cycle that "feeds itself".[138] Or by feeding the system, e.g., with more images of light-skinned faces than dark-skinned ones… The system would be less "trained" in the recognition of subjects with dark skin. Or, last but not least, by choosing which parameters to consider or ignore, a choice that can significantly influence the model's accuracy.

The importance of introducing this topic here is related in two ways to the assumptions we moved from. First. Some of the instruments mentioned here exploit AI and machine learning tools. For this reason, the way they operate and the results they deliver may prove unpredictable even to the LEAs applying them. As explained more extensively in Chap. 5, software designed in specific ways may escape any satisfactory *ex post* explanation of the learning process they performed… Thus, regulating their application in criminal investigation for the purpose of satisfying the condition of 'according to the law' may prove utterly difficult, and even totally useless.

Second. The wide expansion of AI home assistants, as said in § 3, is going to provide more and more precise data about any individual's private and family life to be hacked, for the widest range of purposes, including the criminal investigations one.

This scenario seems to confirm that, at the time being, privacy cannot but be recessive, when confronted with the modern investigative intrusiveness. Thus, we must ask two questions. First. Is such assumption hopelessly true, or are there legal patterns that can still reconcile privacy and digital search for evidence? Second. Should we focus all our attention on the respect for private life, or should we also consider other fundamental rights that can be affected by such means? Or better: is it possible to contrast such almighty LEAs' intrusiveness by invoking other fundamental rights? The answer to the first question in the following paragraph. The answer to the second in the following Chapter.

---

[138] For example, see "Amazon scraps secret AI recruiting tool that showed bias against women", *Reuters*, October 2018.

3.4.2 *Is Hacking Inherently Incompatible with Privacy?*

Due to the features of the tools that have been briefly presented here, it is clear that their compliance with the right to private life is submitted to a strong and in-depth test of proportionality. As said, the effectiveness of such instruments is related to their ability to adapt to the specific environment and conditions in which they operate, case by case. For these reasons, the chance (and the suitability) of providing for precise statutory regulation is highly debatable. In such framework, the respect of private life can be more effectively evaluated on the basis of a proportionality test, balancing the features of the intrusion with the specific situation, based on the seriousness of the crime under investigation, the conditions and the duration of the interference, the general interest pursued. Although rooted into the specific provision of art. 8 § 2 ECHR, the ECtHR case law often applied a similar pattern, which has been expressly adopted by the CJEU and by some national courts (and scholars), in particular the German ones.[139] Based on this, a hacking means is lawful, although not specifically regulated, whether: it is able to realise the purpose established in the general law provision; it is necessary to realise such purpose; there is an adequate balance between the limitation of the individuals' right and the prosecution of a serious criminal offence. Also, the House of Lords and the UK Supreme Court sometimes applied the proportionality test (instead of the reasonableness one).[140]

Thus, to answer to the abovementioned question, the proportionality test can assess whether a means of investigation is compatible with the right to private life, enshrined at the highest normative level by the ECHR, ChFREU, ICCPR and many national constitutions. But what happens in a criminal proceeding, if a violation of the right to privacy is assessed? Does the violation of privacy determine a direct effect on the outcome of the criminal proceeding, in which it occurred? Often, national codes of procedure and evidence acts neutralise the effects of information and data gathered in breach of individuals' privacy by exclusionary rules: given the unlawful acquisition, the evidence cannot be used by the adjudicator in the decision of the case. As said, such is the doctrine of the 'fruits of the poisonous tree'. However, it is worth stressing that not only many European legal orders depart from the doctrine 'of the poisonous tree', but also the ECtHR case law never recognised automatic, secondary consequences of violation of art. 8 ECHR, on the fair trial plan, as we will see extensively in Chap. 4.

---

[139] For a general overview, related to LEAs hacking, see Signorato (2018), p. 263 ff.

[140] House of Lords, 23.5.2001, HM the Queen v. Secretary of State for the Home Dept.; UK Supreme Court, 19.6.2013, Bank Mellat v. HM's Treasury.

References

Arendt H (2017) Vita activa. La condizione umana. Bompiani, Milano

Ashworth A, Zedner L (2014) Preventive justice. Oxford University Press, Oxford

Bachmaier Winter L (ed) (2012) Terrorismo, proceso penal y derechos fundamentales. Marcial Pons, Madrid

Balossino N, Siracusa S (2004) L'identificazione basata sul volto: metodi fisionomici e metrici, Security Forum. Edizioni ItasForum, Bergamo

Barfield W, Pagallo U (forthcoming) Advanced introduction to the laws of AI, Chapter V, Issues of Data Protection. Elgar, Cheltenham

Basile F (2019) Intelligenza artificiale e diritto penale: quattro possibili percorsi di indagine, Available at https://dirittopenaleuomo.org/contributi_dpu/intelligenza-artificiale-e-diritto-penale-quattro-possibili-percorsi-di-indagine/

Bellovin SM, Blaze M, Clark C, Landau S (2014) Lawful Hacking: using existing vulnerabilities for wiretapping on the internet. Northwest J Technol Intellect Property 12:1–64

Benbouzid B (2018) Values and consequences in predictive machine evaluation. A sociology of predictive policing. Sci Technol Stud 31:1–18

Bignami F (2020) Schrems II: the right to privacy and the new Illiberalism. Verfassungsblog, 29.7.2020

Blackstone W (1765) Commentaries on the laws of England in four books. 4th book, ch. 18

Bowling B, Iyer S (2019) Automated policing: the case of body-worn video. Int J Law Context (2):140–161

Bowling B, Reiner R, Sheptycki J (2019) The politics of the police (5e). Oxford University Press, Oxford

Cadoppi A, Canestrari S, Manna A, Papa M (eds) (2019) Cybercrime. Utet, Torino

Caplan JM, Kennedy LW, Barnum JD, Piza EL (2017) Crime in context: utilizing risk terrain modeling and conjunctive analysis to explore the dynamics of criminogenic behavior setting. J Contemp Crim Justice 33(2):417–431

Claes E, Duff A, Gutwirth S (2006) Privacy and the criminal law. Intersentia, Antwerp

Costanzi C (2019) *Big data* e garantismo digitale. Le nuove frontiere della giustizia penale nel XXI secolo, Available at www.lalegislazionepenale.eu, 21.12.2019

De Beer D, De Hert P, Gonzalez FG, Gutwirth S (2010) Nouveaux eclairages de la Notion de donné personnelle et application audacieuse du critère de proportionalité. Revue Trimestrielle des Droits de l'Homme:75–107

De Hert P, Gutwirth S (2006) Privacy, data protection and law enforcement. Opacity of the individual and transparency of power. In: Cleas E, Duff A, Gutwirth S (eds) Privacy and the criminal law. Intersentia, Antwerp, pp 61–104

De Hert P, Papakstantinou V (2016) The new police and criminal justice data protection directive. New J Eur Crim Law 7(1):7–19

De Schutter E (2001) La Convention européenne des droits de l'homme à l'épreuve de la lutte contre le terrorisme. Revue Universelle des Droits de l'Homme

Durante M (2019) Potere computazionale. L'impatto delle ICT su diritto, società e sapere. Meltemi, Milano

Flor R (2009) Brevi riflessioni a margine della sentenza del Bundesverfassungsgericht. Rivista Trimestrale Di Diritto Penale Delleconomia 22:695–716

Flor R, Oh Jang J (2012) Introduction. In: Manacorda S, Flor R, Oh Jang J (eds) Cyber-criminality: finding a balance between freedom and security. Ispac, Milano

Floridi L (2017) The fourth revolution. Oxford University Press, Oxford

Gulotta G (2017) Il volto nell'investigazione e nel processo. Nuova fisiognomica Forense. Giuffrè, Milano

Harris D, O'Boyle M, Bates E, Buckley C (2018) Harris, O'Boyle and Warbrick: law of the European convention of human rights, 4th edn. Oxford University Press, Oxford

Hildebrandt M (2008) Defining profiling: new type of knowledge? In: Hildebrandt M, Gutwirth S (eds) Profiling the European citizens. Cross-disciplinary perspectives. Springer, Cham

Kaufmann M, Egbert S, Leese M (2019) Predictive policing and the politics of patterns. Br J Criminol 59:674–692

Klitou D (2014) Privacy-invading technologies and privacy by design. Safeguarding privacy, liberty and security in the 21st century. Springer, Cham

Kranenborg HR (2014) Article 8. In: Peers S et al (eds) The EU charter of fundamental rights. A commentary. Hart Publishing, London

Leenes R, De Conca S (2018) Artificial intelligence and privacy. AI enters the house though the Cloud. In: Barfield W, Pagallo U (eds) Research handbook on the law of artificial intelligence. Elgar, Cheltenham

Letsas G (2004) The truth in autonomous concepts: how to interpret the ECHR. Eur J Int Law 15:279–305

Manning PK (2011) The technology of policing: crime mapping, information technology, and the rationality of crime control. NYU Press, New York

Martinico G (2017) Art. 7 ChFREU. In: Mastroianni R, Pollicino O, Allegrezza S, Pappalardo F, Razzolini O (eds) Carta dei diritti fondamentali dell'Unione europea. Gifffré, Milano

Oravec M (ed) (2010) Face recognition. IntechOpen, Rijeka

Oswald M, Grace J, Urwin S, Barnes G (2018) Algorithmic risk assessment policing models: lessons from the Durham HART model and "Experimental" proportionality. Inf Commun Technol Law 27:223–250

Pagallo U (2014) Il diritto nell'età dell'informazione. Il riposizionamento tecnologico degli ordinamenti giuridici tra complessità sociale, lotta per il potere e tutela dei diritti. Giappichelli, Torino

Pagallo U, Durante M (2019) Human rights and the right to be forgotten. In: Susi M (ed) Human rights, digital society and the law. Routledge, Abingdon

Parodi C, Sellaroli V (2019) Sistema penale e intelligenza artificiale: molte speranze e qualche equivoco. Diritto penale contemporaneo (6). Available at www.penalecontemporaneo.it

Pavón CP (2014) Estimacy. In: Teo T (ed) Encyclopedia of critical psychology. Springer, New York

Pease E, Andromachi T (2014) Using modelling to predict and prevent victimization. Springer, Cham

Perrodet A (2002) The public prosecutor. In: Marty MD, Spencer J (eds) European criminal procedures. Cambridge University Press, Cambridge

Perry WL, McInnis B, Price CC, Smith SC, Hollywood JS (2003) Predictive policing. The role of crime forecasting in law enforcement operations, Available at www.rand.org

Picotti L (2004) Sistematica dei reati informatici, tecniche di formulazione legislativa e beni giuridici tutelati. In: Picotti L (ed) Il diritto penale dell'informatica nell'epoca di Internet. Cedam, Padova

Pittiruti M (2017) Digital Evidence e processo penale. Giappichelli, Torino

Pollicino O (2020) Diabolical persistence. Verfassungsblog, 25.7.2020

Pollicino O, Bassini M (2017) Art. 8 ChFREU. In: Mastroianni R, Pollicino O, Allegrezza S, Pappalardo F, Razzolini O (eds) Carta dei diritti fondamentali dell'Unione europea. Giuffré, Milano, p 132 ff

Pollicino O, Romeo G (eds) (2016) The internet and constitutional law. Routledge, Abingdon

Santolaya P (2012) The right to a private and family life. In: Loca XG, Santolaya P (eds) Europe of rights: a compendium on the European convention of human rights. Martinus Nijhoff Publishers, Leiden

Schweer T (2018) Predictive Policing mit Precobs. In: Institut für Versicherungswirtschaft der Universität St. Gallen (ed) St. Galler Trendmonitor für Risiko- und Finanzmärkte. Produktund Serviceinformationen, vol 40. Universität St. Gallen, St. Gallen, pp 12–14

Sicurella R, Scalia V (2013) Data mining and profiling in the area of freedom, security and justice. New J Eur Crim Law 14(4):409–460

Signorato S (2018) Le indagini digitali. Profili strutturali di una metamorfosi investigativa. Giappichelli, Torino

Torre M (2017) Il captatore informatico. Giuffrè, Milano

Triggiani N (2019) Le videoriprese investigative e l'uso dei droni. In: Scalfati A (ed) Le indagini atipiche, 2nd edn. Giappichelli, Torino, pp 161–190

Verbruggen G (2006) The glass may be half-full or half-empty, but it is definitely fragile. In: Claes E, Duff A, Gutwirth S (eds) Privacy and the criminal law. Intersentia, Antwerp, pp 121–134

Vervaele JEA (2014) Surveillance and criminal investigation: blurring of thresholds and boundaries in the criminal justice system? In: Gutwirth S, Leenes R, De Hert P (eds) Reloading data protection. Springer, Cham

Wei X, Li C (2017) Face recognition technologies for evidential evaluation of video traces. In: Tistarelli M, Champod C (eds) Handbook of biometrics for forensic science. Springer, Cham

Weisburd D, Braga A (eds) (2006) Police innovation: contrasting perspectives. Cambridge University Press, Cambridge

Wilson D (2019) Platform policing and the real-time cop. Surveill Soc 17(1/2):69–75

Chapter 4
Equality of Arms and Automatedly Generated Evidence

4.1 Digital Evidence and Automatedly Generated Evidence

In Chap. 3 we addressed the topic of digital investigation and the intrusion into individuals' private lives for investigative purposes. Based on the Budapest Convention on Cybercrime, many jurisdictions in the world started regulating digital investigations and digital evidence, establishing criteria to guarantee minimum standards of reliability. Due to this new, immaterial dimension in which reality takes place, gathering elements for investigations and evidence for trial is shifting, more and more, from a traditional process, regulated by the law, into a digital protocol.

On the one hand, as seen in Chap. 3, traditional forms of investigation (e.g. wire-tapping, search and seizures) evolved into digital protocol-compliant standards. Therefore, many jurisdictions have (more or less extensively) faced the issue, providing a specific statute for digital evidence in criminal proceedings. Thanks to the CoE Budapest Convention on Cybercrime (Chap. 3), at least expedited preservation of stored computer data; expedited preservations and partial disclosures of traffic data; production orders; searches and seizures of stored computer data; real-time collections of traffic data; interceptions of content data, have been regulated by statutory provisions, in compliance with the basic requirements set forth by the Convention.

On the other hand, the extensive use of digital devices (often incorporating AI systems) in the everyday life of the whole world's population, has created a completely new range of data that can have decisive impact on criminal investigations and trials. In addition to 'digital evidence' (i.e. sources of information being specifically regulated for trial purposes), non-specifically regulated sources can convey crucial knowledge for criminal proceedings. Such knowledge is not based on secure protocols, because it is not conceived, unlike digital criminal evidence, with the specific purpose of being used in trial. Such knowledge usually derives from data processed for generic or commercial use, such as home assistants, IoT, or other AI

S. Quattrocolo, *Artificial Intelligence, Computational Modelling and Criminal Proceedings*, Legal Studies in International, European and Comparative Criminal Law 4, https://doi.org/10.1007/978-3-030-52470-8_4

devices, used for a variety of human activities. This second kind of information poses major challenges. Firstly, it often pertains to the most private dimension of life, such as individuals' habits, tastes, preferences inside their homes, constantly scrutinised, recorded and stored by digital devices: accessing such information amounts to the most intrusive form of surveillance, outside the formal legal boundaries provided for it. Secondly, such information is generated by a computational process that is not conceived for transparency, has commercial purposes and whose functioning is often protected by commercial licences.

Given these characteristics, should we allow this automatedly generated information to be used as evidence in criminal proceedings? Are digital evidence and 'automatedly generated' evidence different, from the viewpoint of their reliability in trial? Can we still talk about trial, fair trail, when we let such information in? The following paragraphs will try to answer all of these questions, framing them into the architecture of European fundamental rights.

4.2 Some General Reflections About Evidence in the European Context

Before addressing the specificities of digital evidence and automatedly generated evidence, some preliminary statements about evidence, in general, may be useful. The idea of presenting 'general, preliminary, statements on evidence' may appear highly ambitious. Evidence is a realm in which domestic jurisdictions hold jealously their discretion, as it represents the core of the functioning of a criminal justice system. For this reason, the level of harmonisation is low and the existence of a general statute of evidence is dubious.

Although presentation, admissibility, and evaluation of evidence are crucial aspects for the judicial outcome (marking the difference between a fair and an unfair trial), the external control on domestic laws of evidence is very limited. As a matter of fact, the international bills of rights establishing the fair trial clause, tend to display quite a timid position on evidence, especially with regard to admissibility and evaluation. The European Court of human rights,[1] e.g., often underlines that admissibility of evidence falls out of the scope of Art. 6 ECHR and of its jurisdiction, being a matter of domestic regulation:[2] as anticipated in Chap. 3, what is relevant to

[1] Firstly, the Court often reiterates that it is not the role of the Court to assess whether an applicant is or is not guilty, being the core of the Court's evaluation the overall fairness of the proceedings: see, e.g., ECtHR 12.11.2015, Sakit Zahidov, § 47. Errors of fact and of law committed by the domestic jurisdictions fall within the court evaluation in as much as they affect rights and liberties enshrined in the Convention (e.g. ECtHR, 4.3.2014, Grande Sevens v. Italy, § 158). Nor has the Convention (and the Court) a purpose to harmonise the different legal systems of the CoE member States (ECtHR, GC, 15.12.2015, Schatschaschwili v. Germany, § 109).

[2] See, e.g., ECtHR, 6.12.1988, Barberà, Messegué and Jabardo v. Spain, § 68; 14.12.1999, A.M. v. Italy,§ 24 and, more recently, ECtHR, GC, 1.6.2010, Gäfgen v. Germany, § 162: "while Article 6 guarantees the right to a fair hearing, it does not lay down any rules on the admissibility of evidence as such, which is primarily a matter for regulation under national law". Before, see also

the Court is that evidence is collected and evaluated within the framework of the overall fairness[3] of the proceedings.[4]

That the law of evidence is a matter of national law is certified and confirmed by centuries of mutual legal assistance between sovereign States. It is a sound and basic acknowledgment that traditional mutual legal assistance has been tailored upon a statement of domestic sovereignty on evidence: the basic and constant rule of *lex loci* influenced and often undermined effectiveness in mutual legal assistance proceedings. The *lex loci* rule implies that even when evidence is collected on behalf of a foreign judicial authority, based on a mutual legal assistance request, the applicable rules are the ones of the requested State, regardless of the requirements for admissibility of evidence in the requesting State. This traditional approach demonstrates that sovereign States are not prone to renounce to their law of evidence, in any case, even if the application of the domestic rules may hinder the mutual legal assistance process, by delivering to the requesting State a piece of evidence, collected abroad, that is actually inadmissible in the requesting legal order…

Nevertheless, such an attitude has been evolving within the European Union, for the last twenty years. In the last ten years of the 'three pillars system' and the first ten years after the entry into force of the Lisbon Treaty, the EU institutions promoted a more flexible approach in the circulation of (criminal) evidence.[5] Firstly, the Treaty on mutual legal assistance, signed in 2000 by a high number of EU MS, in Brussels, was meant to neutralise the negative effects of the *lex loci*, promoting more flexibility in the collection of evidence. Secondly, the so-called 'Stockholm directives', based on Art. 82§2 lett. b TFEU, enhanced approximation between national legislations on procedural rights, also allowing for an easier circulation of evidence. Moreover, Dir. 2014/41 (based on Art. 82§2 lett. a) established the European Investigation Order, with the goal to almost substitute traditional mutual legal assistance procedures between MS,[6] like the European Arrest Warrant had substituted traditional extradition. More recently, Reg. 2017/1939, introducing the European Public Prosecution Office for the protection of the financial interests of the EU, established common rules on evidence, to be applied by all MS. Although interesting and ambitious, the process going on within the EU is not substantially changing the situation in general terms. The experience of both the Stockholm directives and the other legal assistance instruments recently adopted by the EU,

---

ECtHR 26.3.1996, Doorson v. the Netherlands § 67; 23.4.1997,Van Mechelen and Others § 50; Schenk v. Switzerland, 12.7.1988, §§ 45–46; Teixeira de Castro v. Portugal, 9.6.1998, § 34.

[3] It falls out of the scope if this study to linger on this aspect. However, it is important to stress that the Court applies the 'overall fairness clause', based on which it often rejects allegations because, notwithstanding the existence of a specific violation of the Convention, it was counterbalanced by other guarantees: see ECtHR, 15.12.2011, Al-Khawaja and Tahery v. UK, § 144. For an in-depth analysis, see Cabiale (2019), p. 89 ff.

[4] In fact, "the Court's only concern is to examine whether the proceedings have been conducted fairly": ECtHR 4.6.2013, Kostecki v. Poland, § 59.

[5] Although traditional difficulties still exist: see Allegrezza (2019), p. 572.

[6] For a general overview, Mangiaracina (2014), p. 114.

highlighted a huge and decisive difference between the Member States' legal orders. Within (and also outside) the EU there is deep divergence in the treatment of unlawful, tainted, evidence. Different legal orders display different attitudes towards the effects that tainted evidence can have in criminal proceedings.

Some, mostly civil law, jurisdictions are traditionally inspired by a system of legal invalidity, based on precise categorisations. First and foremost, there is a statutory definition of the conditions for admissibility: the parties must respect such conditions if they want their evidence to be used by the Court. In addition, there is also a statutory definition of exclusionary rules and evaluation rules. If the admission does not respect the abovementioned conditions, evidence is invalid and 'procedural sanctions' are applied. Based on such sanctions, a piece of evidence is partly or completely excluded from the court's file: if partly excluded, the court can consider it only with specific purposes (e.g. it cannot be used against the defendant herself, but against co-defendants); if completely excluded, the court cannot consider it under any circumstances. Often, such jurisdictions also provide for evidence-evaluation rules: a piece of evidence with specific features (e.g. a statement from the co-defendant) cannot be taken into account by the court, unless it is supported by additional elements.

Other, like many common law jurisdictions, are not based on a legal statute of invalidity of evidence and rely on the application of exclusionary rules by the courts, based on an overall evaluation of fairness of the evidentiary procedure, like the ECtHR tends to do. This has two corollaries. The opposition between civil law and common law still plays a decisive role in the law of evidence. As a consequence, even within the EU area, it is difficult to establish acceptable and effective common rules on evidence, when domestic traditions are so profoundly divergent on the point. It is not surprising that many continental scholars have criticised the directives based on Art. 82§2 for not providing effective reactions and sanctions against the infringement of the evidentiary rules.[7] Moreover, the shift within the EU towards approximation of evidence law is isolated and has not had general effects on other jurisdictions, leaving it substantially, on the larger scale, to the discretion of national rulers.

Having said this, should we acknowledge the impossibility of any general discourse about evidence, or should we still try to determine a common pattern? Based on the previous remarks, it is crucial, for the purposes of this study, to assess what is the basic, minimum standard to open the doors of the courtroom to evidence, being it traditional, digital or automatedly generated.

[7] Bachmaier Winter (2015), p. 114; Cabiale, (2019), p. 311 ff., Caianiello (2014), p. 317 ff.; Quattrocolo (2016), p. 292.

4.2.1 The Statute of Evidence in Art. 6 ECHR

Based on the assumptions of the previous paragraph, it is possible to dismiss that a comparative approach may help in understanding whether digital and automatedly generated evidence can be assimilated into the general law of evidence of our legal systems. Trying to theorise a general statute of admissibility of that kind of evidence would be illusory. However, at least at the European level, the Convention on Human Rights and, in particular, the Strasbourg Court case law offers a general framework for the compliance of evidentiary proceedings with basic and fundamental rights.

Both in Chap. 3 and in § 2 we reiterated that the ECtHR has a specific attitude towards evidence. The text of Art. 6 ECHR addresses the topic of evidence in a somewhat fragmented way. In the absence of general provisions, specific attention has been drawn to testimony in § 3, lett. d, while lett. b provides for a set of guarantees representing the core of a fair system of evidence. Each of these provisions is part of the overall recognition of fairness and equality of arms in Art. 6§1. The Court, thus, is not in charge of assessing whether the national law of evidence is compliant with the Convention, or of checking whether the domestic regulation has been respected by the national court. The core of the Court's judgment is the review of the overall fairness of the proceeding in which the tainted piece of evidence has been used. So, the question here is: are there situations in which the Court concludes, on a regular basis, that evidence has been gathered in breach of Art. 6 ECHR? If yes, are the same situations also applicable to digital and automatedly generated evidence?

4.2.2 The Fruits of the Poisonous Tree

The admissibility of a piece of evidence depends on the respect for some basic principles and procedural rules. If the latter are disregarded, evidence may not fit the prescribed standard of reliability. In this sense, a piece of evidence is 'tainted' because it is based on a violation of the law: thus, it is traditionally said to be, 'the fruit of the poisonous tree'. For the purposes of this study, the reference is to pieces of evidence that have been collected on the basis of a violation of the defence's rights. This topic is possibly the most debated in the law of evidence. As mentioned above, every jurisdiction provides for its own rules on this, and while Art. 6 ECHR does not provide for any specific direction on it, it frames the problem generally within the clause of Art. 6§1. So, what is the attitude of the European Court of Human rights towards cases in which the applicant was allegedly judged on the basis of a piece of evidence collected through the infringement of another right or liberty, enshrined in the Convention?

As anticipated, the attitude of the Court has always been inspired by a comprehensive and pragmatic evaluation. A 'poisoned fruit' may derive from a violation of Art. 6 itself, as a consequence, e.g., of the infraction of the defendant's right to access to a lawyer; or to receive translation or interpretation, free of charge; or of her right to remain silent (*infra*, § 4.2.2.3): evidence is collected disregarding specific procedural rights and, if used, may impact on the domestic court's decision about conviction. But the violation of several other rights and liberties in the Convention may also affect the outcome of a criminal proceeding. In particular, Art. 8, protecting home and family life from external intrusions, is the clearest example (Chap. 3); but also violations of Art. 3 (prohibiting torture and inhuman or degrading treatments), Art. 2 (right to life, in its procedural aspect), Art. 10 (freedom of speech and thought) may have procedural relevance, when a piece of evidence presented in trial has been collected in breach of such provisions. The Court never adopted an 'automatic approach', establishing that the use of any 'poisoned' piece of evidence amounts, *per se*, to a violation of the fair trial. The reaction is based on the nature of the original violation. Let us focus, first, on violations of other articles of the Convention.

4.2.2.1 Violations of Art. 3 ECHR

The Strasbourg judges displayed the strongest rejection of the use of statements obtained in breach of Art. 3 ECHR in court. On the one hand, allowing for the admission[8] of such evidence "would only serve to legitimate indirectly the sort of morally reprehensible conduct which the authors of Article 3 of the Convention sought to proscribe or, in other words, to 'afford brutality the cloak of law'".[9] On the other hand, "statements obtained in violation of Article 3 are intrinsically unreliable".[10] But what about other pieces of evidence, real evidence, collected on the basis of a 'poisoned statement'? Must there be a 'causational chain' in order to exclude them? In the leading case of Gäfgen v. Germany,[11] the Court stipulated what has been defined as "a rebuttable presumption that the use of fruits resulting from confessions induced by inhuman and degrading confessions will violate the right to a fair trial".[12] Without lingering on a 'causational chain' linking different pieces of evidence, the Court simply found a violation of Art. 6 due to the fact that every piece of evidence derived from the original breach of Art. 3 ECHR, "even though that evidence is more remote from the breach of Article 3 than the evidence extracted

[8] Cabiale (2019), p. 138, noted that, with regard to evidence collected in breach of Art. 3 ECHR, the Court is inconsistent in referring to the terms 'use' and 'admission'. Excluding admission is a far stronger reaction, preventing the 'poisoned fruit' to enter the courtroom; excluding the use, instead, allows evidence in the file, although preventing the judge to consider it. However, it seems that the most recent caselaw on the point (since the case of Gäfgen v. Germany, ECtHR, GC, 1.6.2010) is becoming consistent in requiring the prohibition of the admission and not only of the use.

[9] ECtHR, 28.6.2008, Harutyunyan v. Armenia, § 63.

[10] ECtHR, 17.1.2012, Othman (Abu Qatada) v. UK, § 264.

[11] ECtHR, GC, 1.6.2010.

[12] Thaman (2010), p. 358.

immediately as a consequence of a violation of that Article".[13] Thus, what is relevant, in the Court's view, is the common genesis of evidence, all tainted by the 'initial' infringement of Art. 3 ECHR.

4.2.2.2 Violations of Art. 8 ECHR

A very different attitude was displayed by the Court with regard to violations of Art. 8 ECHR. In one of the leading cases on the matter of evidence collected in breach of the individuals' right to private life, the Court stated that it "cannot exclude as a matter of principle and in the abstract that unlawfully obtained evidence of the present kind may be admissible".[14] Compared to Harutyunyan v. Armenia (ftn. 3), the difference is patent. When violations of Art. 8 are at stake, illegality of evidence and fairness of the proceedings may co-exist, as anticipated in Chap. 3, § 4.2. Although hacking appears to be inherently incompatible with privacy, it seems that, at trial, evidence obtained in breach of Art. 8 ECHR can be admitted and used, under the condition of the overall fairness of the proceedings. In particular, the proceedings can be considered fair if "the rights of the defence were not disregarded" and the 'poisoned fruits' were not "the only evidence in which the conviction was based".[15]

The seriousness of the violation of Art. 8 does not seem to impact on the overall fairness evaluation. In the other leading case of Khan vs. UK, 12.5.2000[16] the Court found an infringement of Art. 8 ECHR, because of an unlawful bugging of private conversations. Indeed, the violation was gross, as at the time, the national jurisdiction did not provide for legal regulation of such hidden listening devices: one of the basic conditions set by Art. 8 for the legitimate intrusion into privacy, "in accordance with the law", was totally disregarded. Moreover, the Strasbourg Court acknowledged that the unlawful records were the sole and decisive evidence for the defendant's conviction. Nevertheless, the Court rejected the alleged violation of Art. 6 § 1, as the applicant was afforded the chance to challenge the authenticity of the recording.

Scholars[17] have noted that the judgement of the Court is slightly more severe when, on top of a violation of Art. 8 ECHR, evidence also displays doubtful reliability. Thus, the possible violation of Art. 6 is likely to occur not as a consequence of the previous breach of privacy, but as a result of the insufficient reliability of the evidence obtained in an illegal way.[18] In this sense, evidence collected in

[13] Gäfgen v. Germany, § 178.

[14] ECtHR, 12.7.1988, Schenk v. Switzerland, § 46.

[15] Schenk v. Switzerland, §§ 47–48.

[16] See Nash (2000), p. 268.

[17] Cabiale (2019), p. 156.

[18] Ashworth (2012), p. 157, noted that "the Court's prevailing view seems to be that violations of Article 8 and the requirements of Article 6 are two entirely separate matters. The appropriate way to deal with Article 8 breaches is to provide a remedy to the person whose right was infringed, a remedy that might be found in an award of damages".

breach of Art. 8 ECHR is considered by the Court as any other piece of evidence:[19] being tainted by a violation of privacy does not diminish its potential reliability in the courtroom, to be tested by the adversarial confrontation, at trial. Although the position of the Court in Khan v. UK has been strongly criticized,[20] the Strasbourg judges have been consistent in reiterating that "the opportunity to have knowledge of and to comment on the observations filed and the evidence adduced by the other party"[21] is the basic condition to satisfy the fair trial requirement, even when Art. 8 was infringed.

At the time being, there is no sign of any *revirement* by the Court on the matter. Nevertheless, a recent decision, in the case of Svetina v. Slovenia,[22] suggests an implicit shift in the human rights judges' position. In a case of an unlawful search and seizure[23] of the applicant's mobile phone, the Court, rejecting the alleged violation of Art. 6§1, held that the proceedings should be considered fair, because the data obtained unlawfully "were not used as evidence in the trial" and that the applicant's conviction "was based on a number of other items of incriminating evidence",[24] not related to the illegal collection of data. This decision values the fact that the unlawfully obtained data was not used at all in trial, and, incidentally, it seems to acknowledge that the judgment on the overall fairness of the proceedings might have been different, had such data been used, maybe with a decisive weight on the defendant's conviction… Such a statement[25] seems to be in disagreement with Khan v. UK, in which the Court, despite the decisive weight of the unlawful recordings on the defendant's conviction, refused to consider the proceedings unfair. Nevertheless, this cannot be considered an overruling: the Strasbourg Court adjudicates on a case-by-case basis, and we cannot derive a new position from the merely hypothetical statement reported above. The case of Svetina v. Slovenia was adjudicated rejecting the applicant's claim of a violation of Art. 6 ECHR: it is not certain at all that, had in that case the unlawful data been used at trial, the Strasbourg Court would have concluded there was a violation of the fair trial clause…

So far, we must stick to the general conclusion that a violation of a guarantee enshrined in the Convention does not provoke, as a general consequence, a violation of Art.6 if its results are used as evidence in criminal proceedings. However, in the case-by-case approach of the Court, violations of Art. 3 almost always end up in a breach of Art. 6, due to the need to deny a legal shield to evidence obtained from

---

[19] Cabiale (2019), p. 159.

[20] See e.g., Fitzpatrick and Taylor (2001), p. 349; Omerod (2003), p. 65 f.

[21] ECtHR, 23.9.2014, Cevat Soysal c. Turchia, § 64.

[22] ECtHR, 22.5.2018, Svetina v. Slovenia.

[23] In that case, there had been both a violation of the national regulation and an infringement of Art. 8 ECHR, as the applicant was not yet a suspect at the moment when his phone had been seized and searched.

[24] Svetina v. Slovenia, § 50.

[25] Somehow anticipated by ECtHR, 12.1.2012, Alony Kate v. Spain, §§ 67–81, in which the Court held the proceeding fair, because the exclusion of tainted wire-tapping from trial had broken any relationship between illegally obtained evidence and the defendant's conviction.

torture, inhuman or degrading treatment. On the contrary, infringements of Art. 8 ECHR, occurring in the collection of evidence for criminal proceedings, do not interfere, *per se*, with the overall fairness of the proceedings themselves, unless the unlawful evidence displays limited reliability. This conclusion is also confirmed by the Strasbourg case law referring to other kinds of procedural violations based on Art. 6 ECHR.

4.2.2.3 Violations of Art. 6 ECHR

As anticipated (§ 2.1), Art. 6 ECHR provides for a long list of direct and indirect procedural guarantees, the violation of which may impact on the lawfulness of evidence. A complete review of the Strasbourg Court's case law on the matter would fall out of the scope of this study, as it would focus on a burgeoning number of cases, only indirectly related to the ongoing analysis. Rather, we can try to summarise the mainstream trends of that case law, trying to find patterns that can also be applied to digital and automatedly generated evidence.

As seen in the previous paragraph, the Convention does not call for specific 'filters' excluding, systematically, the admission of unlawful evidence. The presence of a tainted item of evidence in the file is not, *per se*, an element of unfairness of the proceedings. What might be questionable, in the view of the Court, is the use of it, in the domestic adjudication of the case. Having said this, the focus must turn to 'the use of evidence'. May any possible use of it hinder the whole of the proceedings? Is a 'balanced' use of illegitimate evidence (along with lawful evidence) compatible with the Convention? The position of the Court on this point seems to be evolving.

Although based on very different cases of violation, it is possible to argue that, with regard to the use of evidence collected in breach of Art. 6 ECHR, the Strasbourg Court developed, over the decades, a common pattern, i.e. the 'overall fairness of the trial test', in which all the other specific tests, tailored for specific groups of violations, merge. A necessary caveat: the following assumptions are an attempt to generalise a trend, based on huge and complex streams of cases adjudicated by the European Court over time. Like in every national jurisdiction, the burgeoning case law of the Court may present inconsistencies,[26] and the suggested trends may not be the consequence of precise 'judicial policies'. Nevertheless, it is useful to single out patterns that could be applied to the specific kind of evidence under the spotlight here.

[26] See the statement by the Court itself in the case of Beuze v. Belgium, 9.11.2018, § 152 (with regard to a case of violation of the right to access to a lawyer): "the Court is nevertheless aware of the difficulties that the passage of time and the development of its case-law may entail for national courts".

4.2.2.4 Infringements of the Right to Confrontation

With regard to violations of Art. 6§3 lett. d, i.e. use of evidence collected in breach of the right to confrontation, the Court developed a specific test of fairness: the so called 'sole or decisive rule'. The use of statements delivered by a person whom the defendant had not the chance to examine or have examined at any stage of the proceedings, cannot represent the "sole or decisive" element for the defendant's conviction. Clearly, it does not mean that such statements cannot be admitted or used, for any purpose, at trial: they do not need to be completely irrelevant for the adjudication of any question by the court… On the contrary, not only can those pieces of evidence be admitted, but they can even be used for the adjudication of the defendant's guilt, provided that they are supported by other elements.

This approach of the Court to the matter of the 'sole and decisive evidence' has been almost consistent until 2011. It is important to remember that the Court is satisfied with almost any kind of confrontation between the defendant and the charging statements' author: there has never been a specific requirement for confrontation in trial, before the judge adjudicating on guilt.[27] In line with Art. 6§3 d, the Strasbourg Court allows for a confrontation that occurred during the investigation.[28] Over the decades, there have been several judgements[29] in which the Strasbourg judges had held that the use of such statements by national courts of such statements would not impair the fairness of the proceedings, as long as they were not the sole and decisive incriminating evidence. In 2009, in the famous case of Al Kawaja and Taheri v. UK, the Court was asked to apply the test in a very reasonable case. The result of it was the assessment of violation of Art. 6§3 d, to which the English Supreme Court[30] reacted in a very severe way, claiming that the common law procedure provides for sufficient protection of the fair trial, with no need to apply the 'Strasbourg tests'. When the case landed on the desk of the Grand Chamber of the Court, the matter of the application of the 'sole of decisive rule' had grown more political than procedural.[31] Based on this, or on other less evident reasons, the Strasbourg Court gave an arguable definition of 'decisive evidence', holding that "the stronger the corroborative evidence, the less likely that the evidence of the absent witness will be treated as decisive". Thus, 'decisive' becomes a relative concept, based on the strength of the corroborating elements. In the same way, the application of the rule also becomes, according to the Court, a matter of relativity. Paragraphs 146 and 147 of the Grand Chamber decision hold that the application of the test needs not to be "inflexible", rather it must be based on the "specificities of the particular legal system concerned and, in particular its rules of evidence".

[27] On the contrary, this is the general rule established by the Italian Constitution (Art. 111 § 4), that can be overruled only in the specific exceptions of Art. 111 § 5.

[28] Chiavario (2001), p. 238 ff.

[29] Many of which against Italy; see e.g.: ECtHR, 14.12.1999, A.M. c. Italia, § 24 (and also ECtHR 27.2.2001, Lucà c. Italia, § 40; 13.5.2005 Bracci c. Italia, § 57; 26.7.2005 Mild and Virtanen v. Finland, § 42).

[30] R. v. Horncastle, 2009, UKSC 14, in www.supremecourt.uk.

[31] Haguenau-Moizard (2012), p. 503.

Despite the reluctance of the Court to deal with the national systems of evidence, reiterated in many decisions, before and after the case of Al-Kawaja and Taheri, the 'sole and decisive rule' was transformed into a complicated (and almost discretionary?) evaluation of the guarantees provided by any national regulation on evidence. The 2011 decision also highlighted an important aspect of the right to confrontation. Indeed, the Court called attention to the need to guarantee a trial confrontation with the person who delivered the incriminating statement, if such a confrontation has not yet occurred. As a consequence, the domestic judges must inquire whether the witness' absence from trial is justified and apply all the practical solutions to allow her to participate, in a protected way.[32]

It has been noted[33] that, with Al-Khawaja and Tahery, the 'sole and decisive test' almost merged into an 'overall fairness test', based on three checks:

- first, and preliminarily: a control over the reasons for the witness' absence, and the effort made by the trial judge in granting her presence (unless a previous confrontation occurred). A negative assessment (no good reasons for the witness' absence) of this first condition entails a breach of Art. 6§3 lett. c;
- secondly (if the first check is positive): the 'decisive evidence' evaluation, based on a balance between the weight of the 'tainted' statement and the strength of the corroborating elements;
- thirdly (to be applied in any case): the 'counterbalance test', assessing whether the national system offers chances and guarantees compensating the violation of the right to confrontation.

Unlike the first condition, which is preliminary,[34] the second and the third are intertwined, because the fact that decisive evidence was used against the defendant without confrontation does not entail, *per se*, a violation of Art. 6 ECHR. The following case law of the Strasbourg Court offers several examples of guarantees that may neutralise the absence of direct confrontation with the witness, such as: the presence of a judge, during the witness statement;[35] the specific directions delivered by the judge to the jury;[36] or even a detailed reasoning by the fact-finding judge, reporting on how evidence was evaluated.[37] How far the Court moved from its position in Brandstetter v. Austria, when it held that "an indirect and purely hypothetical possibility for an accused to comment on prosecution arguments included in the text of a judgment can scarcely be regarded as a proper substitute for the right to examine and reply directly to submissions made by the prosecution"...[38]

[32] Al-Khawaja and Tahery, §§ 120–125.

[33] Cabiale (2019), p. 121.

[34] Al-Khawaja and Tahery, § 120.

[35] ECtHR, 22.11.2012, Tseber v. Tcheck Republic, §§ 61, 62.

[36] This was considered a relevant element in the case of Al Kahwaja and Tahery itself.

[37] ECtHR, 9.7.2013, Bobes v. Romania, § 46.

[38] ECtHR, 28.8.1991, Brandstetter v. Austria, § 68.

In light of these remarks, the case of Al Khawaja and Tahery set a new benchmark, holding that, provided that all efforts have been made to grant the witness' presence, 'tainted', decisive evidence can be used in trial, with no harm to the overall fairness of the proceedings, if other counterbalancing guarantees are made available to the defence.

Moreover, the Court intervened afterwards on that very same benchmark, in the case of Schatschaschwili v. Germany,[39] excluding the preliminary nature of the control over a good reason for the witness' non-attendance. Evolving from the reasoning of the 2011 case, this more recent decision comes to a different conclusion,[40] holding that "the Grand Chamber, in the light of the foregoing (see paragraphs 111–12 above), considers that the absence of good reason for the non-attendance of a witness cannot of itself be conclusive of the unfairness of a trial. This being said, the lack of a good reason for a prosecution witness's absence is a very important factor to be weighed in the balance when assessing the overall fairness of a trial, and one which may tip the balance in favour of finding a breach of Article 6 §§ 1 and 3 (d)".[41]

Concluding on this point, it is possible to highlight a trend displaying the Court's reluctance for 'automatic' tests of unfairness, as reported with regard to the 'fruits of the poisonous tree'. As a result of the 2011 and 2015 decisions, the Court openly rejected to recognise that the breach of some procedural guarantees, provided by Art. 6 ECHR, entails inevitably a violation of the fair trial clause.

4.2.2.5 Infringements of the Right of Defence

A similar trend is also to be found with regard to the fairness test relating to the violations of Art. 6§3 c,[42] providing for the individual's right to "defend himself in person or through legal assistance of his own choice". The violation of such a guarantee implies the risk that evidence—and in particular, statements by the accused—collected without the presence of a lawyer, may enter the file and be used in the proceedings, also against the defendant.

With the purpose of keeping a long story short, the leading case in such a matter is the decision delivered by the Court in the case of Salduz v. Turkey, in 2008. In that case, the Court came to the conclusion that "even where compelling reasons may exceptionally justify denial of access to a lawyer, such restriction – whatever its justification – must not unduly prejudice the rights of the accused under Article 6. The rights of the defence will in principle be irretrievably prejudiced when incriminating statements made during police interrogation without access to a lawyer are

[39] ECtHR, GC, 15.12.2015.

[40] Jackson (2019), p. 708 ff.; Casiraghi (2019), p. 1366 ff.

[41] Schatschaschwili v. Germany, § 113.

[42] Cabiale (2019), p. 127.

used for a conviction".[43] In that seminal decision, the Court established a strong exclusionary rule, that was consistently upheld by the following case law. The Salduz doctrine had a constitutive impact in several CoE countries,[44] pushing e.g. for the amendment of regulation of the *garde à vue*, in France[45] and inspiring the 2011 proposal by the EU Commission, on the measure C of the roadmap on procedural rights, that led to the approval of the Directive 2013/48.[46]

However, in 2015 the approach of the Court shifted towards a more ambiguous control, on the overall fairness of the proceedings. In this specific case,[47] the statements used against the defendant had been collected without the presence of the lawyer of his own choice. Having excluded the existence of plausible grounds for denying the accused his right to appoint a lawyer of his own choice, the Grand Chamber of the Court did not apply the specific Salduz test, rather the general 'overall fairness rule', concluding, in any case, for the violation of Art. 6 ECHR. In 2016, the Grand Chamber was asked to rule on a very reasonable case,[48] relating to the terroristic attacks that occurred in London in 2005. The applicants alleged the violation of Art. 6§3c for having been convicted on the basis of some statements collected by the police without the presence of a lawyer. Apparently, the case should fall under the Salduz doctrine, pushing towards an assessment of a violation of Art. 6. Nevertheless, the decision lingered over the very specific aspects of the case and held that "no undue prejudice had been caused by the admission of the statements at the trial having regard in particular to the counterbalancing safeguards contained in the legislative framework".[49] While shifting towards a 'softer' standard, the Court expressly went back to the Salduz doctrine, stressing that, according to that decision, the rights of the defence would only be irretrievably prejudiced "in principle" by the use of statements obtained in the absence of a lawyer. Opposing the "in principle" statement to the specific elements of the case, the court implicitly overruled the Salduz doctrine. That position was upheld by some following decisions, and, at the time being, the overall fairness test, in cases of restriction of the right to access to a lawyer, is based on a two-track control. Firstly, a check on the existence of compelling reasons to limit the individual's right to access to a lawyer, such as, "urgent need to avert serious adverse consequences for life, liberty or physical integrity". Secondly, a control over the "irretrievable prejudice" caused by the use of statements collected in the abovementioned conditions. Again, the Court sets a vague parameter, that, as in the cases of restriction of the right to confrontation, can be based on various elements, such as other

[43] ECtHR, GC, 27.11.2008, Salduz v. Turkey, 55.

[44] Jackson (2016), p. 987; Rynan (2014), p. 90 ff.

[45] Chevallier-Govers (2017), p. 67.

[46] Bachmaier Winter (2015), p. 111 ff.

[47] ECtHR, GC, 20.10.2015, Dvorski v. Croatia.

[48] ECtHR, GC, 16.12.2014, Ibrahim and others v. UK.

[49] Ibrahim and others v. UK, § 235.

counterbalancing guarantees that, in the opinion of the Court, may equalise the compression of the right to access to the lawyer.[50]

The conclusion on this point confirms the Strasbourg Court's trend to exclude the automatic assumption of violation of Art. 6 ECHR, applying to all the various cases of infringement of procedural rights (be they provided for by Art. 6 or other articles of the convention), the general test of the 'overall fairness of the proceeding'. This is, thus, the rule to take into account when reflecting upon the statute and the limits of digital and automatedly generated evidence within the framework of the Convention. The test is always the same: therefore, we need to focus, now, on what the basic features of a fair trial are. What are the elements that, given all the 'counterbalancing tests' created by the Court over recent years, can never be lacking in a fair trial?

4.2.3 The Concept of the Overall Fairness of the Proceedings

As a matter of fact, answering this question is becoming more and more difficult. As seen so far, the process enacted by the Strasbourg Court appears to be a progressive 'subtraction'. Given the conventional system of guarantees, in general; given the specific procedural guarantees of Art. 6 ECHR, the analysis of the case law demonstrates that the violation of the single protection clauses related to criminal proceedings (directly or indirectly, e.g. Art. 8), does not amount to a direct and immediate infringement of the fairness of the proceedings. In principle, the violations that have been considered so far can be compensated (with the exception of Art. 3 ECHR) by counterbalancing measures, offered to the defendant. A similar approach can also be found with regard to the provisions of Art. 6§3 lett. a and b ECHR.

These two provisions establish the right of the defendant to be informed, promptly, in detail, in a familiar language, about the accusation (lett. a) and to have time and facilities to prepare her defence (lett. b). Although lett. a is not necessarily related to evidence, as it covers the right to information all along from the start of the proceedings and throughout the proceeding, moving from the initial moment of it, lett. b is normally attributed to the disclosure of evidence. The specific problem of the disclosure of evidence is traditionally treated by the Court as an issue of joint-protection by both Art. 6§3 lett. b and § 1. The adversarial confrontation[51] of the parties on evidence is considered to be (within the conditions highlighted hereinafter) the essence of the equality of arms, a basic expression of the fair trial.[52] The

---

[50] Cabiale (2019), p. 104.

[51] The idea that the right to confrontation entails the adversarial examination at the hearing was a basic statement in the initial Court's caselaw: Barberà, Messegué and Jabardo v. Spain, § 78, highlighting that, in the context of the fair trial, § 1 and 3 of Art. 6 also mean that "the hearing of witnesses must in general be adversarial".

[52] ECtHR, 27.6.1968, Neumeister v. Austria, § 22 ('as to the law'), recognised the equality of arms as a feature of the fair trial, based on several previous decisions and pinions by the Commission.

Court reiterates, since the cases of Neumeister and Delcourt, that the equality of arms is inherent to the concept of fair trial, although not the sole and exclusive component of it.[53] In particular, in the very famous case of Brandstetter v. Austria,[54] the Strasbourg Court held that the parties must be aware of the opponent's statements and allegations and get "a real opportunity to comment" on them.[55] Thus, "an indirect and purely hypothetical possibility for an accused to comment on prosecution arguments"[56] does not fulfil the Convention requirement, being in breach of the equality of arms.

In principle, the Court proved to be compliant with such doctrine, reiterating, in several cases over the decades, the basic assumptions about the fairness of criminal proceedings established in the abovementioned decisions. Firstly, there is emphasis on the postulate that "it is a fundamental aspect of the right to a fair trial that criminal proceedings, including the elements of such proceedings which relate to procedure, should be adversarial and that there should be equality of arms between the prosecution and the defence", as recently held by the Court in the cases of Einarsson and others v. Iceland[57] and Van Wesenbeeck v. Belgium.[58] The latter stresses that "the right to an adversarial trial means, in a criminal case, that both prosecution and defence must be given the opportunity to have knowledge of and to comment on the observations filed and the evidence adduced by the other party".[59] Secondly, and more specifically, the Court has developed the 'time and facilities clause', underlining that "article 6 § 3 (b) guarantees the accused "adequate time and facilities for the preparation of his defence" and therefore implies that the substantive defence activity on his behalf may comprise everything which is "necessary" to prepare the main trial. The accused must have the opportunity to organise his defence in an appropriate way and without restriction as to the possibility to put all relevant defence arguments before the trial court and thus to influence the outcome of the proceedings".[60] Therefore, the failure to guarantee the access to the material evidence containing elements that could afford the defendant the exoneration of liability or even a reduction of the sentence is a potential violation of the equality of arms and, thus, a breach of the right to a fair trial.[61]

---

[53] ECtHR, 17.1.1970, Delcourt v. Belgium, § 28: "The principle of equality of arms does not exhaust the contents of this paragraph; it is only one feature of the wider concept of fair trial by an independent and impartial tribunal".

[54] See nt. 38.

[55] Brandstetter v. Austria, § 67.

[56] Brandstetter v. Austria, § 68.

[57] ECtHR, 4.6.2019, Sigurdur Einarsson and others v. Iceland, § 85.

[58] ECtHR, 23.5.2017, Van Wesenbeeck v. Belgium, § 67.

[59] Van Wesenbeeck v. Belgium, § 67.

[60] ECtHR, 31.3.2009, Natunen v. Finland, § 42, referring back even to the Commission's report of 12.7.1984, in the case of *Can v. Austria*, § 53, and to the more recent ECtHR, 9.10.2008, *Moiseyev v. Russia*, § 220.

[61] Natunen v. Finland, § 43.

Nevertheless, the right to disclosure of evidence is not an absolute one, as clarified by the Strasbourg judges on many occasions. In the case of Wesenbeek v. Belgium, the Court mentions compelling reasons that may justify restrictions to such a fundamental guarantee, in the light of a necessary balance with other interests, either public or private, such as the need to preserve anonymity of undercover agents and "to keep the methods used secret".[62] The framework for such balancing is two-fold. Firstly, only strictly necessary restrictions to the disclosure right are compatible with the Convention. Secondly, such limitations must be counterbalanced by other facilities and chances offered to the defence, like an independent judicial body's review of the completeness of the file.[63] According to the wording of the decision, the two conditions are both necessary, therefore a negative check on the first (excessive, unnecessary restrictions) could not be neutralised by the other compensations. For the sake of completeness, it is worth noting that issues of disclosure may be overlapping into the right to confrontation (§ 4.2.2.4): with specific regard to the abovementioned undercover agents, the refusal by a court to admit their examination in trial, to preserve anonymity, coincides with a restriction of Art. 6§3 d. Therefore, in those cases, the Strasbourg Court applies the 'Al-Khawaja three-fold test', assessing, firstly, the existence of a good reason for excluding the agents' personal appearance in court; secondly, the weight given to their statements in the light of the conviction (decisive or not); thirdly, the presence of counterbalancing factors.[64]

Thus, the paradigm of the protection afforded by the Convention to the right to discovery of evidence is very similar to the pattern outlined with regard to other specific guarantees, related to evidence in criminal proceedings. At the end of this brief exposition of the main trends in the European Court of Human Rights case law on evidence, it seems that the 'overall fairness test' is applicable to every case of alleged violation of Art. 6, based on a 'suspect' piece of evidence, with the exception of evidence collected in breach of Art. 3 ECHR. However, it is with regard to the matter of the 'time and facilities clause' that the Court seems to get to define the minimum standard of a fair trial. Realigning the right to discovery with the principle of the equality of arms, the Strasbourg judges made it clear that parties must have a real opportunity to comment and to challenge adverse evidence.[65] Regardless of all the restrictions that can be accepted under the 'overall fairness clause' (based on the doctrine of counterbalances, progressively imposed by the Court), what cannot be subtracted from a fair trial is the equality of arms, embodied by the fundamental possibility to access to adverse evidence and the effective chance to challenge it, persuasively.

As seen, the measure of such effectiveness seems to have diminished, over the years. We already noted that, although in Brandstetter v. Austria, the Court

[62] Van Wesenbeeck v. Belgium, § 70.

[63] ECtHR, 16.2.2000, Jaspers v. UK, § 56.

[64] Van Wesenbeeck v. Belgium, § 88–112.

[65] Brandstetter v. Austria, § 68.

held that an indirect and purely hypothetical possibility for an accused to challenge the prosecution's arguments would not satisfy the requirements of Art. 6 ECHR, the recent case law displayed a different approach. As a matter of fact, the 'counterbalance doctrine' ended up by valuing extremely indirect opportunities to defy adverse evidence, such as instructions given to the jury or precise reasoning, incorporated in the judicial decision… But there is another important feature of the equality of arms that helps in framing this problem and can prove particularly useful when approaching the matter of digital and automatedly generated evidence. The Court held that "the principle of equality of arms – one of the elements of the broader concept of a fair trial – requires each party to be given a reasonable opportunity to present his case under conditions that do not place him at a substantial disadvantage *vis-à-vis* his opponent".[66] This apparently vague concept is linked to another element, highlighted by the Strasbourg Court: the effective chance to comment and challenge adverse evidence, in a condition of non-substantial disadvantage against the opponent, is what allows the party to present her arguments "with a view to influencing the court's decision".[67] A real and non-hypothetical dimension of equality of arms implies that all the parties are granted the instruments to potentially influence the judicial decision of their case. It seems to me that this conclusion is also compatible also with the most recent developments in the Strasbourg case law, in terms of progressive reduction of the conventional guarantees. The very essence of a fair trial, the minimum standard that must be granted in any case, the measure of the 'overall fairness of the proceedings', is the real and effective opportunity, for all the parties, to present their arguments with the realistic expectation of influencing the adjudication of the case.

Although a process of progressive reduction of the guarantees provided by the ECtHR case law seems evident, it is doubtful whether it is due to a precise judicial policy. What is relevant for the purposes of this analysis is to point out a standard, a benchmark, to be applied in the consideration of the consequences of the use of digital and automatedly generated evidence in trial.

4.3 Automatedly Generated Evidence and Fair Trail

As seen in § 1, the process of gathering evidence through digital systems (based on computational modelling and, often, AI methods), brings kinds of proof to the trial process that depend entirely on the accuracy of the technological means being used, for their reliability.

An initial issue is related to the transformation of the investigative measures into hacking practices: under this assumption, the majority of jurisdictions passed

[66] ECHR, 7.6.2001, Kress v. France, § 72, and, before, 18.2.1997, Nideröst-Huber v. Switzerland, § 23 and Ankerl v. Switzerland, 23.10.1996, § 38.

[67] ECtHR, 12.4.2006, Martinie v. France, § 46, although referred to a non-criminal proceeding.

specific regulation for digital criminal evidence (often on the basis of the Budapest convention provisions, Chap. 3). Based on technical protocols, those recent regulations provided for standards and requirements affording a basic level of authenticity- and reliability-certification, to intervene for procedural purposes on digital supports and data.

A second issue is related to the uncontrolled production of digital data, outside the specific scope of criminal proceedings. For example, whether a person was present in one specific place, at a specific time, has always been a matter of crucial importance in criminal proceedings: today, there is plenty of digital data allegedly demonstrating this. But, if the term 'demonstrating', in criminal justice terms, means 'convincing beyond any reasonable doubt', we cannot help but wonder, as we do with any single piece of evidence, whether this data respects the standards of reliability. Or should we renounce to this control, being convinced that the digital nature of such data certifies, *per se*, its reliability? Scholars have raised a concern about the risk of the irrebuttable presumption of reliability of digital evidence, some time ago.[68] Based on the distinction I suggested in § 4.1, between digital evidence and automatedly generated evidence, the issue of reliability affects both categories, as we will see: possibly, the difference lies in the major or lower level of intensity of it. This is the core of the matter at stake here. Should we acknowledge that digital and automatedly generated evidence has a special epistemological statute, based on the intrinsic accuracy of technology, loosening the boundaries of traditional evidence law and neutralising the minimum standard of guarantees provided by ECHR? Or should we rather try to fit new evidence into the general framework that we analysed in the previous paragraphs?

4.3.1 The Essence of Fair Trial: The Equality of Arms

The goal is not an easy one. The first step is to reflect on whether and how it is possible to assess the correctness of data, which was gathered or generated by a digital system. Is there any effective chance to challenge the correctness of such data?[69] The reliability of data gathered and processed in an automated manner cannot be challenged in a 'traditional' way. Comprehensive literature, almost in every legal system, addresses the matter of evidence reliability, with specific regard to testimony. Cross-examination is considered to be the best technique, even an art, to challenge the trustworthiness of oral evidence, be it a testimony or an expert-testimony. More generally, in modern times, adversariness represents the dialogic context in which unreliability of evidence, also material evidence, is

[68] Van Buskirk and Liu (2006), p. 20 f.

[69] De Hert and Gutwirth (2006), p. 62, concerning the protection of sources by intelligence agencies.

more likely to come to light. However, these solutions do not fit the case of digital evidence.

Indeed, there is no argument for a party to challenge a piece of adverse digital evidence without having access to some technical information about the process that generated it. However, as we will see in Chap. 5, different systems of computational modelling have different levels of accessibility, allowing for a more extensive or limited *ex post* validation of a software's results. Depending on how the software was designed, there is chance or not to understand how and why it generated one specific result. In this sense, the trial party presenting that result as evidence may take advantage of their counterpart's inability to challenge the evidence's reliability.

Algorithmic modelling and AI neural networks are just the current stage of the long-enduring phenomenon of knowledge asymmetry, which is said to have begun when courts started relying on expert evidence in complicated cases.[70] The use of scientific knowledge in criminal proceedings is hardly balanced, since one of the parties—mostly usually the public one—has access to the best science and technology, having access to public financial means. Obviously, the phenomenon of knowledge impairment is not new and each cycle of the complicated relationship between science and criminal trial posed varyingly intense version of it (think of the debut of DNA profiling in courtrooms, or the use of fMRI for the assessment of the defendant's liability). The use of digital technology, as mentioned, may also denote a huge disproportion between the parties of the criminal proceedings, too. Firstly, digital data risks to being considered unflappably reliable, due to a quite common and misplaced sense of innate reliability: this will impact on the admission of it, facilitating the party presenting this piece of evidence. Secondly, the party against which the evidence is presented will hardly have the chance to challenge its accuracy, having no access to the useful information.[71] This brings the attention to the claim for transparency, that has been repeatedly mentioned in the previous chapters.[72]

4.3.1.1 Transparency as a Beacon of Equality?

Let us suppose that, as a matter of fact, transparency could be achieved by simply demanding the source code (together with inputs and outputs) of the relevant automated process.[73] This is a basic and perfectly reasonable assumption, that could enable the parties of a criminal trial to challenge the automatedly-generated evidence against them. However, there are some arguments against this hypothesis.

There is an issue related to the different kinds of protection that can support the software having generated the evidence. It can be a proprietary software. Software

[70] Brimicombe and Mungroo (2017).

[71] Vervaele (2014), p. 124.

[72] See, extensively, Hildebrandt (2013), p. 239. With specific regard to the judicial use of algorithms, Palmiotto (forthcoming).

[73] Kroll et al. (2017), p. 23.

designers/producers may decide to submit their intellectual work to licenses, protecting the secrecy of it. As we will see in Chap. 6, this has been considered a lawful limitation of the duty to disclose the sources-codes, even in criminal proceedings: a State Supreme Court in the US acknowledged that proprietary software's source-codes should not be discovered in order to let the defence access the functioning of a predictive software used for sentencing (Chap. 6, § 4). In addition, it is often necessary to keep the decision policy at the basis of the algorithmic process secret. This is of course the case for software used for investigative purposes, the effectiveness of which would be completely hampered with full disclosure. Unless investigators revert to the specifically crafted systems of accountability, such access to the digital code implies that a new algorithm should be at work for almost each subsequent investigation… Such a situation may create an impairment between prosecution and defence, in light of what the ECtHR stated with regard to analogic instruments of investigation. It is worth asking whether the decision held by the Court in the above-mentioned case of Khan v. UK could apply also to automatedly generated evidence. In that case, the Court held that the defendant had every chance to challenge the authenticity of the tapes used against him and he did not. Although the decision does not linger over these aspects, analogic audio-files had a standard system of recording, and the content of the support (used as evidence) could only having been generated in one way. Moreover, it is possible to argue that listening and observing a material tape could more easily afford the opportunity to find out whether there had been manumission of it (provided that it is the original tape) and prove its reliability. In our scenario, the reliability of the output cannot be reviewed and challenged without the disclosure of the source codes.

Although source codes are crucial in the process of *ex post* validation of a digital output, they may not be decisive. In Chap. 3 I stressed the difference between accessibility and transparency. The disclosure of the code may grant accessibility but not transparency. Firstly, experts are the only ones potentially able to validate the digital process on the basis of the source code.[74] In contrast to the assumptions related to analogic records and documents, the immateriality of digital data prevents non-experts from understanding the process that generated it and to detect possible manumissions of the process. Secondly, open-source codes may not ensure accountability in all cases.[75] Actually, *ex post* verification is often insufficient to validate properties of software that were not conceived and designed with accountability in mind.[76] Especially when machine learning systems are involved, the designers themselves may not be able to explain why and how an output was generated. This assumption demonstrates that digital evidence and automatedly generated evidence, in particular, are dramatically changing the scene in terms of the reliability and the evaluation

---

[74] Koene et al. (2017), p. 11.

[75] Kroll et al. (2017), p. 23.

[76] Kroll et al. (2017), p. 24. See in particular Art. 20 of 2016/680 EU directive, prescribing transparency as a key-features in designing algorithms and automated systems to mine data in criminal proceedings and investigations.

of evidence: for these reasons, it is possible to argue that they may ultimately change even the role of the parties and the judge in criminal proceedings.

4.3.1.2 What Does Transparency Mean in This Context?

The analysis about the relationship between automatedly generated evidence and the realm of criminal evidentiary law leads us to face what appears to be the real core of the matter. Indeed, the epistemological instruments that traditionally inspire the law of evidence seem to be useless in this new context.

The law of evidence is based on the benchmark that, pursuant to a list of legal conditions, the judge appreciates evidence through her 'intimate conviction', i.e., her human intuition. Far from alleviating the judge from any boundaries, opening her up to the realm of irrationality, the concept of 'intimate conviction' conveys the value of the judicial independence and sets the cornerstone for the modern trial. In many legal orders, the ultimate legal standard for the judicial appreciation of (criminal) evidence is 'beyond any reasonable doubt', which perfectly summarises the two main elements of the evidentiary judgment. Firstly, it is a legal judgement, because it is based on evidence lawfully admitted. Secondly, it is rational, because the judge must give reasons, demonstrating the reasonableness of her epistemological process.[77] Probability, doubt, conviction, are all processed by the human intuition,[78] the human comprehension of the facts, and the reasoning of the decision grants accessibility to that process. Even when the causation chain is based on complex scientific rules and axioms, the judicial decision must be grounded into comprehensible reasoning.[79]

Having said this, automatedly generated evidence seems hardly to fit into such a paradigm. As we will see more extensively in Chap. 5, there is little space for human intuition in the appreciation of the reliability of this kind of evidence. Having rejected the postulate 'digital=reliable',[80] the evaluation of accuracy and reliability cannot be based, in these cases, solely on logic: being a black box, the automated process that generated the piece of evidence often cannot be fully reconstructed *ex post*. The explanation, the justification of a verdict of un/reliability is traditionally based on ordinary human prudence, that seldom can be applied to a computational verification. This is what transparency should mean in the context of evidence law: either establishing standards that can always grant, *ex ante*, that reverse engineering will be possible; or setting review models, that can offer *ex post* validation of the reliability of automatedly generated data, admitted as evidence in trial.

This assumption implies two relevant consequences.

The first consequence is that the solution for this conundrum cannot be found in traditional legal culture, but in technology. Irrespective of what has always been

---

[77] Ferrua (2015), p. 157.

[78] Eggleston (2004), p. 14.

[79] Ferrua (2015), p. 88.

[80] Chessman (2017), p. 179; Van Buskirk and Liu (2006), p. 21.

done, the 'reasonableness of doubt'—about the reliability of automatedly generated evidence—cannot only be grounded in traditional judicial reasoning, rather in a sound and validated technical process. Thus, the judge is asked to perform her traditional, exclusive power to appreciate evidence, in an unprecedented way. It has been reiterated that the application of science and technique in judicial matters and, in particular, in criminal matters, affects the roles of the subjects in the proceedings, creating, first and foremost, an impairment among the parties. It is a common opinion that referring to scientific rules and postulates in the assessment of the causation chain is a trend that shifts the responsibility for adjudication from the courts to the experts. An extensive amount of literature has focused on this topic in recent decades, also highlighting the risk of opening the doors of the courtroom to junk science. Nevertheless, even in the context of a complicated confrontation of opposing scientific theories (see more extensively, Chap. 6), the judicial role has never been deprived of its own authority, in appreciating evidence and adjudicating the case. The more the assessment is complicated, the more the judge must rely on the experts' opinions. All the same, even in this scenario, the ruling rests on the judge's ability to logically analyse the elements and justify her decision. Because of its 'black box' nature, it is doubtful that the reliability of automatedly generated evidence can be reviewed; in any case, it cannot be done on the basis of traditional human prudence, but by a computational process. In this sense, there is a risk that the judicial role will undergo, in the coming decades, a loss of autonomy (and independence? See Chap. 7) in the realm of the appreciation of evidence.

The second consequence is that such a computational process must be specifically tailored to the peculiarities of the system that generated the data, admitted at trial as evidence. As the specialised literature demonstrated,[81] assessing the trustworthiness of e.g. the content and the metadata of an instant messaging conversation, implies a specific review process, that must take into account the variables of every messaging platform. While it is true that most prominent mobile forensic platforms[82] are able to decode the data stored by a large number of applications, they do not provide any explanation of how this decoding is performed, nor do they provide any guidance on how to correlate different pieces of evidence to completely reconstruct users' activities. "Therefore, unfortunately, in most cases the evidence exhibited in the trial is the mere output generated by these tools, with little or no explanation on how the evidence has been obtained from the data stored on the device".[83] This is a clear example of misplaced trust in digital data: e.g. instant messaging conversations are used daily in courts, considered fully reliable pieces of evidence, with a minimal chance for the defence to challenge their accuracy... Despite decades of research in computer forensics on the topic, highlighting the need for

[81] Anglano et al. (2017), p. 31 ff.

[82] Cellebrite LTD, 2015, http://www.cellebrite.com/Mobile-Forensics/Products/ufed-4pc; Micro Systemation, 2016, http://www.msab.com/xry/xry-currentversion; Oxygen Forensics, Inc. 2013, http://www.oxygenforensic.com/en/features/analyst; Compelson Labs, 2017, http://www.mobiledit.com/forensic-solutions/.

[83] Anglano et al. (2020), p. 11.

accurate validation of data and metadata, it is still up to the defendant to demonstrate the possible flaws of such pieces of evidence,[84] provided that she can afford to hire experts supporting the counsel…

Based on this example, it is crucial that the court must be (willing and) able to recur to reliable independent validation of the automatedly generated data. However, this can only happen under some specific conditions.

The first condition is that the software having generated the data at stake is not protected by a proprietary licence. As said, secrecy may hamper the chance to develop a valuable system of reverse engineering or, in general, ex post validation of the outputs. In fact, the balance between the rights of the parties to challenge a piece of evidence under the equality of arms clause and the protection of proprietary software depends on the domestic jurisdictions. It may be the case that, under the conditions established by the legal system, a court orders the owner to disclose the source code regulating the software at stake. However, there have been famous cases in which the local court decided not to impose disclosure (see Chap. 6§3). Nonetheless, it seems that such a balance can be obtained, in some cases, not only by means of judicial orders, but also by digital means. To some extent, one possible solution is referring back to the so called "zero-knowledge proof", that is to say cryptographic tools, allowing for proof that the decision policy that was actually used has certain properties, without disclosing what the decision policy is.[85] Such an instrument seems to allow the defence to challenge the accuracy of inculpatory evidence without implying, necessarily, the disclosure of the codes and, therefore, the rewriting of them.

The second condition is that the software is not based on machine learning solutions, that would significantly reduce the chance to usefully revert the process, in order to assess its rationale and reliability.

The third condition is that, with the software being 'accessible' under the previous two conditions, suitable and specific validation processes have already been elaborated by researchers, allowing for a reliable *ex post* review. Such a review implies that empirical research on the specific topic has been made and repeated in different circumstances, in order to be validated by independent peers. Often, the sole available literature is based on the software developers' own work, with no independent process of validation.[86]

In this sense, the assessment of reliability of automatedly generated evidence almost implies (see, however, zero-knowledge proof solutions), the recurse to independent experts (provided that they are available and have sufficient background

---

[84] See, e.g., the Italian Supreme Court decision in the case Cass., Sez. VI, 27.11.2018, n. 14395.

[85] Kroll et al. (2017), p. 30: the Authors provide a useful example. Imagine that two millionaires are out to lunch and they agree that the richer of them should pay the bill. However, neither is willing to disclose the amount of her wealth to the other. A zero-knowledge proof allows them both to learn who is wealthier (and thus who should pay the restaurant bill) without revealing how much either is worth.

[86] It is worth reminding the importance, for data accuracy, of the developing researches in the so-called *trusted computing*: see Mitchell (2005), passim; and, Oppliger and Rytz (2005), p. 16 ff.

studies): this implies to establishing an acceptable balance between the experts' opinions and the judicial authority in the adjudication of the case.[87] This argument invites us to close the circle of this long reflection on evidence. The trend, endorsed by the ECtHR, to constraint the control on the legality of evidence into the 'overall fairness of the proceeding's, delivers to the judge with a central role. Traditional evidentiary law—with exclusionary rules and evaluation rules—seems to be progressively fading, in favour of a delicate balancing test, held in the judge's hands.

Is there a risk that automatedly generated evidence induce relativization of the judicial role in the assessment of evidence reliability, forcing the judge to recur to the ICTs expert's almost unquestionable opinion? Indeed, we should look at the issue with the insight of the experience gathered with regard to other kinds of scientific evidence, such as DNA profiling or neuroscience… Initially, courts were reluctant and unfamiliar with the evaluation of such evidence, but then succeeded in 'incorporating' scientific rules into human prudence norms.

Nevertheless, the remarks above offer a guidance for the most delicate cases. Given that the minimum standard of the equality of arms is the chance to "effectively influence the court's decision", what if the defendant claims that the impossibility to assess the reliability of an automatedly generated piece of evidence deprived her of the chance to "effectively influence the court's decision"? In my opinion, it seems compliant with the principle of the equality of arms that the court discharges that piece of evidence. Given that, in many cases, technology can provide sufficient validation of automatedly generated evidence, when *ex post* validation is not available, the court should exclude the 'black box evidence' from the adjudication on the defendant's guilt, in order not to violate the basic expression of the fair trial, the equality of arms.

References

Allegrezza S (2019) Critical remarks on the Green Paper on obtaining evidence in criminal matters form one member state to another and securing its admissibility. Zeitschrift für Internationale Strafrechtsdogmatik:569–579

Anglano C, Canonico M, Guazzone M (2017) Forensic analysis of Telegram Messanger on Android smartphones. Digit Investig 2017(23):31–49

Anglano C, Canonico M, Guazzone M, Quattrocolo S (2020) Technical solutions for legal challenges: equality of arms in criminal proceedings. Global Jurist 20(1):1–12

Ashworth A (2012) The exclusion of evidence obtained by violating a fundamental right: pragmatism before principle in the Strasbourg jurisprudence. In: Roberts P, Hunter J (eds) Criminal evidence and human rights: reimagining common law procedural traditions. Hart Publishing, Oxford, pp 145–161

Bachmaier Winter B (2015) The EU Directive on the right to access to a lawyer: a critical assessment. In: Ruggeri S (ed) Human rights in European criminal law. Springer, Cham, pp 111–131

[87] Cross (2017a, b).

Brimicombe AJ, Mungroo P (2017) Algorithms in the dock: should machine learning be used in British Courts? Presentation at the 4th Winchester Conference on Trust, Risk, Information and the Law, 3 May 2017
Cabiale A (2019) I limiti alla prova nella procedura penale europea. Cedam, Padova
Caianiello M (2014) To sanction (or not to sanction) procedural flaws at EU level? A step forward in the creation of an EU criminal process. Eur J Crime Crim Law Crim Justice:317–329
Casiraghi R (2019) I nuovi approdi 'europei del diritto al confronto. Cassazione penale:1363 ff
Chessman C (2017) A source of error: computer code, criminal defendants, and the constitution. Calif Law Rev 2017:179–228
Chevallier-Govers C (2017) The Europeanisation of French criminal law. Eur Crim Law Rev:67–88
Chiavario M (2001) Art. 6. In: Bartole S, Confroti B, Raimondi G (eds) Commentario alla Convenzione europea per la salvaguardie dei diritti dell'uomo e delle libertà fondamentali. Cedam, Padova, pp 154–248
Cross M (2017a) Algorithms and Schrodinger's Justice. The Law Society Gazette, 8.5.2017. Available at https://www.lawgazette.co.uk/news-focus/news-focus-algorithms-and-schröding-ers-justice/5060964.article
Cross M (2017b) Justice by Algorithms Could "Bring Courts to an Halt". The Law Society Gazette, 3.5.2017. Available at https://www.lawgazette.co.uk/law/justice-by-algorithm-could-bring-courts-to-a-halt/5060918.article
De Hert P, Gutwirth S (2006) Privacy, data protection and law enforcement. Opacity of the individual and transparency of power. In: Cleas E, Duff A, Gutwirth S (eds) Privacy and the criminal law. Intersentia, pp 61–104
Eggleston R (2004) Evidence, proof and probability, 2nd edn., it. translation, Prova, conclusion probabilistica e probabilità, Giuffrè
Ferrua P (2015) La prova nel processo penale, I. Giappichelli, Torino
Fitzpatrick B, Taylor N (2001) Human right and the discretionary exclusion of evidence. J Crim Law:349 ff
Haguenau-Moizard C (2012) La Cour suprème britannique et la Cour européenne des droits de l'homme: une nouvelle voix dans le dialogue des juges. Revue trimestrielle des droits de l'homme:491–505
Hildebrandt M (2013) Profile transparency by design? Re-enabling double contingency. In: Hildebrandt M, de Vries K (eds) Privacy, due process and the computational turn. Routledge, pp 221–246
Jackson JD (2016) Responses to Salduz: procedural tradition, change and the need for effective defence. Mod Law Rev:987–1018
Jackson JD (2019) Common law evidence and the common law of human rights. William & Mary Bill Rights J:689–715
Koene A, Webb H, Patel M (2017) First UnBias Stakeholders workshop. Available at https://unbias.wp.horizon.ac.uk/wp-content/uploads/2017/04/UnBias_Stakeholder_1stWorkshop_report.pdf
Kroll JA, Huey J, Barocas S, Felten EW, Reidenberg JR, Robinson DG, Yu H (2017) Accountable algorithms. Univ Pa Law Rev 165:633–705
Mangiaracina A (2014) A new controversial scenario in the gathering of evidence at the European level: the proposal for a Directive on the European Investigation Order. Utrecht Law Rev:113–133
Mitchell C (ed) (2005) Trusted computing. IET, London
Nash S (2000) Secretly recorded conversations and the European Convention on Human Rights: Khan v. UK. Int J Evid Proof:268–274
Omerod D (2003) ECHR and the exclusion of evidence: trial remedies for Article 8 breaches? Crim Law Rev 2003:61–80
Oppliger R, Rytz R (2005) Does trusted computing remedy computer security problems. IEEE Secur Priv 3(2):16–19

Palmiotto F (forthcoming) The impact of algorithmic opacity on fair trial rights in criminal proceedings. In: Ebers M, Cantero Gamito M (eds) Algorithmic governance and governance of algorithms. Springer

Quattrocolo S (2016) Right to access to a lawyer in Europe: anything new under the sun? In: Petrova A (ed) Festschrift für August Nacke. Plovdiv University Press, pp 270–296

Rynan A (2014) Towards a system of European Criminal Justice. The problem of admissibility of evidence. Hart Publishing, Oxford

Thaman SC (2010) 'Fruits of the Poisonous Tree' in comparative law. Southwest J Int Law:333–384

Van Buskirk E, Liu TV (2006) Digital evidence: challenging the presumption of reliability. J Forensic Pract:19–26

Vervaele JAE (2014) Surveillance and criminal investigation: blurring of thresholds and boundaries in the criminal justice system? In: Gutwirth S, Leenes R, De Hert P (eds) Reloading data protection. Springer, pp 114–128

Part III
Challenges of Computational Methods to the Judicial Decision-Making Process: Deciding v. Predicting

Chapter 5
Predictability and Criminal Justice

5.1 From Evidence to Decision

We focused, so far, on the use of algorithmic, computational applications in the area of gathering evidence. The third part of this book is dedicated to the exploration of the impact of computational modelling and AI on the judicial decision-making process. Not that evidence is unrelated to the adjudication of a case and to the many other decisions that are usually taken during criminal proceedings... On the contrary. Evidence is the element allowing the judge to rule on any point, from pre-trial detention to assessment of guilt... The reason for distinguishing between the areas of evidence and decision-making is based on the level of interaction that computational models and AI may have with human activity. As to evidence, digitalisation offers (regardless of how much acceptance the legal systems have of digital tools) elements to be presented, advocated and appreciated by the parties and the judge. In the realm of evidence, the use of computational technologies impacts on the effectiveness of the role that the parties can play in the proceedings, offering wider and allegedly more accurate knowledge. In the realm of decision-making, computational tools are purportedly able to rationalise and to substitute human performance itself. Let us inquire into this assumption.

Computational modelling and AI focused on legal matters decades ago, because reproducing judicial functions represents one of the most challenging fields for computer science scholarship. The judicial decision-making function, either on guilt or on any other aspect, challenged and inspired computational expertise. Simulating the human decision process in judicial matters implies a huge number of variables. Computer scientists were thrilled to engage in such an endeavour, that has delivered, at present, several generations of instruments that can assist or, for instance, could allegedly substitute, the legal decision-maker, at least in one part of the process.

S. Quattrocolo, *Artificial Intelligence, Computational Modelling and Criminal Proceedings*, Legal Studies in International, European and Comparative Criminal Law 4, https://doi.org/10.1007/978-3-030-52470-8_5

It is undisputed that the topic of the substitution of humans for machines in performing decisions and judgments still represents one of the trickiest challenges in the development of AI: deciding, and not barely executing external orders, is what has traditionally distinguished humans and non-human agents. However, after Minsky's seminal definition of AI as "the science of making machines do things that would require intelligence if done by man", taking decisions is not the ultimate frontier between man and machine: in many areas, such as medicine, the goal of totally automated decision-making processes has already been achieved with success, thanks to a breath-taking advancement in computational power and, first of all, the possibility to create mathematical models representing the conditions of the case and the potential evolution of clinical and pathological situations. In almost any branch of medicine, *prediction* based on the use of biomarkers or phenotypic traits is used to select optimal effective therapy or minimize undesirable side effects.[1] In continuity with this, the term 'predictive justice' became popular in denoting software and applications developed in the area of justice, meant, as said before, to assist the parties and the judge in a judicial proceedings in taking some specific decision. It will be the aim of this study to assess the limitations and the conditions in which such assistance is viable, useful and acceptable.

For these reasons, in this part of the book, I will examine several aspects related to the phenomenon of so-called 'predictive justice'. In particular, in this chapter I will first reflect on the sense of applying the term 'prediction' to criminal proceedings, which has apparently nothing to do with forecast and *prevision*, being aimed at assessing what happened *in the past*. Then, in Chaps. 6 and 7, I will focus on the main aspects of criminal proceedings, in which the automated assistance for the decision can be applied to help human decision-makers in performing their judicial roles. In particular, at the time being, the spotlight is both on risk assessment tools—aimed to detect and quantify the risk of violent behaviour—and judgment assisting tools, establishing the potential outcome of a judicial decision on the basis of a complete collection of previous decisions.

5.2 Judicial Decision-Making and *Logique Juridique*: Two Sides of the Same Coin

Within the precise boundaries that have been set for the present analysis, it is now necessary to approach a very general and broad topic, such as that of judicial decisions. It is, of course, one of the most typical and dwelled on topics in jurisprudence, that cannot be handled comprehensively here; however, it is inherent to the current reflection to assess whether the judicial decision process can also be accurately transposed into computational models.

---

[1] Endam et al. (2018), p. 5. About individual modelling in medicine, Benzi (2019), p. 45 ff.

First and foremost, it is important to underline that within the area of cognitive science (cognitive psychology and behavioural economics are the branches that studied the decision-making process more accurately),[2] the concept of judgment is traditionally distinguished from that of decision-making. Apparently, the judicial act of adjudicating on specific questions comes under the term 'judgment', rather than 'decision-making'. Nevertheless, from a cognitive point of view, the two concepts are different. Generally speaking, 'judgment' is a cognitive performance that leads to the acquisition of a belief: based on the elements considered, it is possible to say that Ann, although very fluent in English, is actually French. On the contrary, a 'decision-making' process is a cognitive performance leading to a choice: based on the elements evaluated, we must prefer the highway n. 6 to the motorway A1. In the medical realm, for example, establishing a diagnosis is a judgment, while tailoring the most suitable therapy is a decision-making process.

What about the legal realm?[3] Judicial adjudication is an act that covers both aspects. Firstly, it entails a judgment, assessing one quality or condition; secondly, it triggers a decision-making process, ruling on the legal consequences of such quality or condition. One general feature of jurisdiction—which is common to different legal traditions—is that it is based on an action,[4] a request set by one party, wishing to obtain a (legitimate) advantage. In doing this, the judge, either in private or criminal law litigation,[5] must assess the elements of the fact alleged in the request; identify which is the most appropriate normative model to apply; verify if the first (the fact) fits effectively into the latter; to rule on the legal consequences of it.

As a cognitive process, the judicial decision-making process has been widely studied and researched, not only in jurisprudence, but also, as mentioned, in the fields of behavioural economics and social psychology.[6] With such a wide reach, this topic mostly falls out of the scope of this inquiry, with the exception of some crucial aspects that will be pivotal in the following chapters. Thus, it is worth introducing some preliminary clarifications.

Within the area of the judicial decision-making research, one essential distinction divides (popular) juries and professional judges and courts. Juries are non-professional fact-finders, usually not bound to a formal reasoning and for these reasons the decision-making process within juries is different and has been studied

[2] Cevolani and Crupi (2017), p. 182.

[3] Judicial decision-making is the object of a huge literature, in many different fields. It falls out of the scope of this work to linger over it. However, it is worth noting that there has been and there is still a large discussion over the most suitable approach to this area of research, opposing quantitative to qualitative methods [Linebach (2011), p. 4].

[4] Levin (1992), p. 96.

[5] In the European continental tradition, the prosecution is often considered an 'action', in the sense that it conveys the prosecutor's request to the judge to assess that the defendant is guilty and to sentence her to the just penalty. It is a public action, as much as it is presented by the prosecutor, who is a civil servant, and it formally encompasses the State reaction to crime. See Chiavario (1975), p. 864 ff.

[6] Wrightsman (1999), p. 17: "the field of social psychology is the most appropriate discipline for the study of judicial behavior".

separately.[7] Many factors influence it and, although not totally different from those affecting the professional legal reasoning,[8] they should be distinguished from it (infra, Chap. 6). Another important distinction, in introducing the topic of judicial decision-making, is that it seems to be deeply influenced by the legal tradition and, in particular, by the *summa divisio* between common law and civil law.[9] Actually, the deep divide between the European continental positivistic experience and the common law pragmatism still affects the approach to the study of judicial decision-making.[10]

To introduce the topic, it is possible to argue that the psychological and economical approaches were initially widely and massively applied in the common law countries and, especially, in the US. The theories of legal reasoning developed and the reviews based on them focused on various aspects, especially in the Northern American jurisdictions and courts: indeed, they analysed a cultural and institutional framework that is quite distant from the European context and the continental one, in particular.[11] However, even on this side of the Atlantic Ocean, the progressive fading of the 'positivistic rush' opened up the discussion for more articulated approaches. Although the European *logique judiciaire*[12] is strongly influenced by the predominance of statutory law, many empirical studies have been conducted in continental Europe too. To make a long story short,[13] research on both sides of the Ocean demonstrated that judicial reasoning undergoes the same kind of cognitive bias affecting common reasoning or even other areas of specialised reasoning, such as in the medical field. Based on Kahneman and Tversky's seminal studies,[14] empirical research suggests that judicial reasoning is affected by a list of heuristics[15]

[7] The first empirical research was on common law juries; however, in the last 20 years, the focus shifted towards judges: for an overview, Cevolani and Crupi (2017), p. 88.

[8] What is legal reasoning is highly debated and debatable, as much as it has also been denied, as a meaningful concept. For the purposes of this study, we can accept F. Schauer's assumption, that legal reasoning does exist, although it does not cover completely what lawyers and judges do [Schauer (2009), p. 44 it transl.].

[9] Although recently scaled down, as a result of converging trends, the distinction still matters in connection with the concept of 'legal consciousness', a range of common background of organisational schemes, concepts and meanings, reasoning schemes and advocacy techniques, characterising the role of lawyers in a certain area. [Kennedy (2006), p. 19 ff.; Marini (2012), p. 185]. Also civil lawyers argue that "thinking like a lawyer implies therefore to subscribe to a certain community and to share a certain language" [Ost (2018), p. 67]. More on the distinction between common law and civil law in Chap. 7.

[10] See Ost (2018), p. 53, suggesting that "the civil law lawyer should start to re-learn how to think about law from cases in their different dimensions".

[11] See. e.g., Edlin (2016), p. 6: "the problem with an expectation of objectivity in common law judging is that it is not the common law's expectation" and, p. 7: "the search for objectivity in common law judging is an attempt to eliminate the judge from the judgment".

[12] Hébraud (1969), p. 23 ff.

[13] For a general overview, Cevolani and Crupi (2017), p. 88.

[14] Tervsky and Kahneman (1982), p. 4.

[15] It is worth underling that the term 'heuristics', coupled with 'bias', started having a negative taint, since the Tversky and Kahneman's studies. In its original Greek meaning, the term refers to

and biases—such as representativeness, availability of scenarios, and adjustment from an anchor[16]—that tend to push the reasoning process away from rational choices, towards predictable mistakes. These are popular cognitive biases, also affecting judicial reasoning, along with others that have been theorised over the years.[17] Moreover, the literature suggests that the judicial decision is not only submitted to cognitive shortcomings, but also to other kinds of biases, depending on ideologic, cultural, personal conditions, such as those hinted, for example, by one Senator during Sonia Sotomayor's process of nomination to the U.S. Supreme Court.[18]

5.2.1 An American Overview

As to the American reality, the burgeoning literature traverses many different expertise, testifying of an issue that is not confined to the lawyers' realm, but is part of the public opinion's feelings. A leading author in the field is Richard A. Posner, a distinguished and well-known American judge. In what can be considered a seminal book of 2008, *How judges think*, he engaged in a comprehensive analysis of the trends that seem to influence judicial decision-making in the US; he could list nine different theories on judicial behaviour, all focusing primarily on the explanation of judges' decisions.[19] The theories are: attitudinal, strategic; sociological;

an exploratory behaviour, it is to say looking around and searching for information. A popular definition represents heuristics as tools needed in situations where the world does not permit optimization: Engel and Gigerenzer (2006), p. 2 f.

[16] Tervsky and Kahneman (1982), p. 3: "Many decisions are based on beliefs concerning the likelihood of uncertain events such as the outcome of an election, the guilt of a defendant, or the future value of the dollar". In such decision process, a huge part is played by the adjustment from the anchor heuristics, starting from an initial anchor value and then adjusting until an acceptable answer is found. Even when initial anchors are clearly irrational, they tend to influence deeply the final decision.

[17] See, especially, Guthrie et al. (2001), p. 778 ff.; Guthrie (2007), p. 93 ff., but also Gigerenzer (2002), passim.

[18] Years before being a nominee to U.S. Supreme Court, Sonia Sotomayor stated in an article [Sotomayor (2002), p. 87 ff.] that she would expect a wise Latina woman, with a rich personal experience, like hers, to have more chance to reach a good decision than a white, male having not lived her kind of life. During the process for her nomination to the US Supreme Court, she was criticized for letting personal background, gender, prejudices or sympathies to influence the judicial decision. In general, about the huge topic of bias in judicial decision see recently, Harrys and Sen (2018), p. 1 ff.

[19] Posner (2008), p. 19: in the complexity of the judicial decision-making process, individual rely on heuristics that are influenced, biased, by their personal background. Nevertheless, Posner's theory has been criticized for the implicit risk of justifying every irrationality and human disaster, by explaining it with the availability of heuristic: Engel and Gigerenzer (2006). p. 6. For a different classification, Baum (1997), p. 23 ff.; Levin (1992), p. 104 ff.

psychological; economic; organisational; pragmatic; phenomenological and 'legalist'.[20] Reviewing the pragmatic approach, since Holmes'[21] critique on legalism, the author underlines how deeply it is entrenched into the American legal system, still expressing one predominant (but not unique)[22] feature of the current American legal reasoning.

To over-simplify the results of Posner's study, in the Northern American society, the judicial decision-making process is influenced by different sets of factors, either objective (such as life-tenure and salary)[23] and subjective (cultural), both external (recruiting system, by vote or appointment) and internal (ethical and professional norms). In this sense, the judicial decision-making is not necessarily and purely a logic process. Some authors[24] claim that the subjective element in common law judging is a necessary and valuable part of the judicial process. Based on this remark, the consequence is that "objectivity is not the goal of the judicial function and subjectivity is not the price of judicial disfunction".[25]

Some of the theories, such as the attitudinal theory, that have been elaborated on the judicial decision-making, have been criticised or discharged, over the decades, as their models achieved low scores from the predictive standpoint.[26] This is a very important remark for this study. Especially in the American tradition, the studies and the theorisation of judicial decision-making not only try to explain how judges behave in the moment of taking a decision, but are tested on the basis of their ability to foresee, to predict, what judges will do in future cases. It seems to be common sense that "attempting to anticipate outcomes is legitimate, because these [the Supreme Court's n.d.r.] decisions have a huge impact on our everyday lives and because the justices' past writings, past decisions, and apparent values and ideologies provide much raw data for prediction".[27] Although quite tautologic, this argument reveals a crucial aspect for our further analysis. I will get back to it here after.

---

[20] With regard to Dworkin's critique to pragmatism, exposed in Dworkin (1986), spec. p. 151 f. For an overview on the 'new era of pragmatism', after Dworkin, Smith (1990), p. 409 ff.

[21] Posner (1992), p. 342.

[22] Posner (2008), p. 230: "it would be more accurate to say that most American judges are legalist in some cases and pragmatist in others; for remember that legalism is a pragmatic tactic".

[23] Posner (2008), p. 158 ff.

[24] Edlin (2016), p. 5.

[25] Edlin (2016), p. 6.

[26] Linebach (2011), p. 6; Posner (2008), p. 27.

[27] Wrightsman (1999), p. 14.

5.2.2 A European Point of View

As to the European context, it may appear very distant from the American pragmatism, especially if considered from… an American point of view![28] To the eyes of American comparative lawyers, the continental decisions process "present a coherent and carefully choreographed image of passive and mechanical judicial subservience to the codified wishes of the […] legislature".[29] Although iconic, this description is too extreme, and does not correspond to the reality.[30] In fact, also the European scholarship, researching the topic of judicial reasoning, reached conclusions that are not dissimilar to the American ones. It is undeniable, since Hume, that "any mode of evaluative argument must involve, depend on, or presuppose, some ultimate premises which are not themselves provable, demonstrable, or confirmable in terms of further or ulterior reasons. In that sense, our ultimate normative premises are not reasoned, not the product of a chain of logical reasoning".[31] Thus, even in traditional statutory systems, it must be acknowledged that the ultimate foundation of judicial reasoning is not logic but discretionary, notwithstanding the (existence of predetermined legal concepts and) formal duty to justify the decision by reasons.

Moreover, it has been noted that, despite the existence, in the civil law legal systems, of an articulated set of legal rules, the case and its features still bear a crucial relevance in the decision-making process: the application of a syllogism, without adequate consideration for the characters of the specific case, can lead to a logical but unjust outcome…[32] Shifting, precisely, from the argument that European judges "are obliged to state their reasons and any failure to do this will normally be a ground in itself for appeal", Geoffrey Samuel recently compiled a long list of questions based on the permanent contradiction between what is logic, formal, justifiable and what is not, in judging,[33] summing up the loops that have never been closed in centuries of scholarship. Are judges merely bureaucratic agents who mechanically apply the law or are they agents who have considerable freedom in resolving disputes that come before them? Can one distinguish between an 'official portrait' of judging and reasoning and an 'unofficial' one?[34]…That long, and non-exhaustive, list ends up with a crucial question for this study: "would it (or will it ever) be

[28] For a critique to the American attitude towards continental and, in particular, French legal reasoning, Lasser (2004), p. 28.

[29] Lasser (2004), p. 30, referring to the French reality: however, similar statements could be extended to other European continental legal systems, based on codifications of law.

[30] It was noted [Bell (2006), p. 70], that the French Cour de cassation "can develop the law radically, […] it can use its decisions to provoke the legislator to action. […]. It can also refuse to act and await the legislator". Of course, due to the huge amount of repetitive cases, creativity is more common at the supreme courts level, rather than the lower.

[31] MacCormick (1978), p. 5.

[32] Ost (2018), p. 59.

[33] Samuel (2016), p. 1.

[34] For the distinction among official and unofficial portrait of the judicial decision-making process, the Author refers back to Lasser (2004), p. 30 ff.

possible to produce an Artificial Intelligence programme that would permit a computer to judge and to reason like a human being?".[35]

To conclude this very general introduction to the trends in legal reasoning scholarship, in the US and in Europe, we must acknowledge the existence of elements allowing us to identify a converging view. This common view is rooted in the traditional ambiguity of the mutual relationship between science and legal reasoning,[36] between techniques and morals, that have deeply influenced both the scientific and the legal thinking, especially after the seventeenth century.[37] Such a European-rooted attitude finds a homologue in the American tension towards prediction of future judgments that, as we have seen, has been used as a parameter in assessing theories about judicial reasoning. Thus, despite the huge social and cultural divide, on both sides of the Atlantic Ocean, today, the ultimate question about judicial decision-making is "how much judges' thinking can be objectivised, in order to make it predictable, in terms to reproduce it into mathematical, computational models?" As we will see hereinafter, subjectivity and discretion—which have been acknowledged as unavoidable essences of legal reasoning—impinge on the possibility of recreating it into models.

5.3 Mathematical Modelling of Judicial Behaviours?

If curbing legal reasoning into scientific method is not a brand-new idea at all, neither is measuring and quantifying the legal phenomenon and, in particular, judicial decisions, with computational instruments, a novelty.[38]

Since 1966, the American Bar Association published the *Jurimetrics Journal*,[39] as the official publication of its Special Committee on Electronic Data Retrieval.[40] However, the term *jurimetrics* had been used for the first time by L. Loevinger, in an article released by the Minnesota Law Review in 1949,[41] as Herbert Solomon

[35] Samuel (2016), p. 2.

[36] Lasserre (2018), p. 313. From Leibnitz to Kelsen, the urgency to constraint legal reasoning into the rigorous structure of science has inspired centuries of European scholarship.

[37] It is in the Roman law that Leibnitz found inspiration for his theorization of a perfect deductive legal system. See recently Pagallo (2016), p. 23.

[38] Lebreton-Derrien (2018), p. 3.

[39] The journal first appeared in 1959, with the name Jurimetrics, directed by Layman Allen (see www.law.asu.edu). At the same time, Lucien Mehl introduced jurimetrics in France, and in Mehl (1958), p. 756 ff. he presented his work on Automatisation in the legal world from the machine processing of information to the law machine at the 1957 English National Physical Laboratory Symposium. He distinguished two kind of 'law machines': a machine to inform and a machine to decide.

[40] In the very first issue of the Journal, R.C. Lawlor, president of the ABA at the time, released the article Computers, Law and Society [Lawlor (1966), p. 53 ff.].

[41] Loevinger (1949), p. 455.

underlined in a seminal article, in 1968.[42] Loevinger considered jurimetrics as an instrument "to cut windows in the house of law, so that those inside can see out and to cut doors, so that those outside can get in". More explicitly, the term refers to any exchange of ideas and information about the relationship between law, science and technology in all areas.[43]

In that very same article, Solomon recalled the interest of some late eighteenth century probabilists[44]—Condorcet, Laplace and Buffon, in particular—in group's decision-making (and appropriate jury size), arguing that, at the time of writing (1968), the topic "does not receive the mathematical attention bestowed upon it approximately two hundred years ago".[45] Indeed, the interest in measuring and explaining the judicial decision process has not faded over the years. Interestingly, in 1837, the French mathematician Siméon Denis Poisson published his *Recherche sur la probabilitè des jugements en matière criminelle et en matière civile.* It falls out of the scope of this study to summarise the evolution of the many scientific disciplines that have engaged, over the centuries, in measuring and constraining legal reasoning into mathematical and computational models. The definition of jurimetrics remained controversial over the decades, especially because such a discipline never flourished. In a stricter sense, some intended it to be the application of the quantitative method to legal problems; a quite recent definition considerably broadens the sense of the term, encompassing "the empirical study of the form, the meaning and the pragmatics of demands and authorisations issuing from the state organisations with the aid of mathematical models and using methodological individualism as the basic paradigm for the explanation and the prediction of human behaviour".[46] Behind the different definitions provided over the years, jurimetrics testifies to a persistent need to translate and codify the judicial decision-making process into a mathematical language, which is still under discussion at the present time.

With the same attitude, AI has also started approaching legal reasoning—along with all the other realms of human activity. The new scholarship soon started to get out of the laboratories, seeking for recognition and cooperation from the legal community. In 1970, the Stanford Law Review published Buchanan's and Headrick's article *Some Speculation about Artificial Intelligence and Legal Reasoning.*[47] In 1977 the Harvard Law Review published L. Thorne McCarty's *Reflection on 'Taxman': An Experiment in Artificial Intelligence and Legal Reasoning,*[48] while in

---

42 Solomon (1968), p. 7 ff.

43 This is the definition provided by the Jurimetrics Journal itself.

44 Engel and Gigerenzer (2006), p. 2: "early probabilists were more concerned about equity than about chances".

45 Solomon (1968), p. 8.

46 De Mulder et al. (2010), p. 137.

47 Buchanan and Headrick (1970), p. 40 ff.

48 Thorne McCarty (1977), p. 837 ff.

1990 the Yale Law Journal published Edwina Rissland's, *Artificial Intelligence and Law: Stepping Stones to a model of Legal Reasoning*.[49] Meanwhile, A. von der Lieth Gardner had published her PhD thesis, *An Artificial Intellingence Approach to Legal Reasoning*.

5.3.1 A Short Overview on AI and Law

Since the beginning, it appeared clear that the realisation of the goal to bring AI programs into the field of law would bring together two different research areas, usually treated as distinct: the one on expert systems and the one on natural-language processing[50] and common-sense reasoning.[51] Although the pillars of AI have changed meanwhile, it seems particularly relevant, for the purpose of this discourse, to note that, originally, the AI approach was oriented to reflect the lawyers' own understanding of reality,[52] based on the structure of the legal task and not on the psychology of a problem-solving agent. From this point of view, a programme had to recreate a context in which legal rules were used consciously by the expert, based on the absence of behavioural regularity (unlike many other areas of human performances, like grammar, for example): "legal reasoning must thus be classified as a rule guided activity, rather than a rule-governed activity".[53] This remark relies on the same conclusion, about judicial decision-making, delivered by the burgeoning legal literature on it: rules exist, they can be transposed into a computational language, but they are not necessarily determinative of the outcome of the decision.[54] This was, and still is, a crucial aspect for any AI programme meant to reproduce legal reasoning (although major improvements were reached in this field, over the decades, based on the application of non-monotonic logic,[55] devised to capture defeasible inference,[56] that is to say the condition in which an agent reserves the right to retract a conclusion, in the light of further information). As said, the first approach was oriented towards expert systems. Expert systems, indeed, appeared to be consistent with legal culture and reasoning, as they are based on a

[49] Rissland (1990), p. 1957 ff., where the Author (trying to explain to lawyers what AI is) explicitly acknowledged that tasks involving common sense reasoning or perception, such as language understanding "are by far the most difficult for AI". It must be noted that it was not the first article about AI appearing in prestigious legal journals.

[50] Actually, computer scientists admit that law "pushes the state of the art in natural language processing to its limits": Robaldo et al. (2019), p. 113. It was 1970 when Buchanan and Headrick underlined the difficulties in giving the natural language communication enough semantics to "understand English sentences" [Buchanan and Headrick (1970), p. 44].

[51] von der Lieth Gardner (1987), p. 1.

[52] von der Lieth Gardner (1987), p. 4.

[53] von der Lieth Gardner (1987), p. 3.

[54] von der Lieth Gardner (1987), p. 119.

[55] See, recently, Strasser and Antonelli (2019), p. 1 ff. s.

[56] Prakken and Sartor (2004), p. 118 ff; Benzi and Penco (2018), p. 561 ff.

hypothetic-deductive scheme.[57] In particular, they fit the need for justification (reasoning), as rules and passages are set and stocked along the process.[58] Briefly, such a system is given an input (fact) and, on the basis of tree diagrams, it flows through the number of rules it has been provided with, until every rule has been applied and no rule is left: the last passage will deliver the output of the system. Obviously, such a model presupposes one basic condition: the translation of legal rules into mathematical, computational rules. With the insight of several decades of research, we know that satisfying this condition implies two major challenges. Firstly, translating legal rules into computational rules is a complicated, time-consuming activity, that can be performed only with regard to specific and limited areas of law. Secondly, such an endeavour implies the development of methods governing the constant dynamics of norms over time.[59]

At the time of her initial studies, Gardner worked from the question if "is there a dividing line between conclusions that can be reached deductively, without room for expert disagreement, and conclusions that depend on judicial discretion?", and she observed that "for conclusions in the second class, a program can produce at most some arguments relevant to the choice. Programs will not be in a position to make the choice until we are satisfied that we have analysed fully and encoded correctly the concepts of wisdom and justice. That time will surely never come".[60] Although Gardner's prediction may not have been defeated, the studies in non-monotonic logic have largely changed the approach to the modelling of legal reasoning, allowing for models representing the choice between conflicting arguments.[61] Let us explore how, going through the following major steps of the evolution in AI and law.

5.3.2 *The Dawn of Case-Based Reasoning*

Almost at the same time Gardner was formulating this doubt, an alternative approach came under the spotlight, drawing attention to cases rather than rules. It is possible to say that one of the most relevant changes in the AI approach to law is the progressive superseding of the expert system, rule-based reasoning (RBR), with case-based reasoning (CBR).

Case-Based Reasoning, theorized by Roger Schank in the early Eighties of the twentieth century, "is a problem solving paradigm where new problems (called target or query problems) are solved by retrieving similar problems already solved,

[57] Bourcier (2011), p. 42.

[58] Susskind (1986), p. 168 ff.

[59] See, extensively, Palmirani and Benigni (2007), p. 205 ff.

[60] von der Lieth Gardner (1987), p. 34.

[61] See, extensively, Prakken and Sartor's studies about defeasibility, since the Nineties, in particular, Prakken and Sartor (1996), p. 331 ff; Prakken and Sartor (1997), p. 25 ff.

possibly by adapting the solutions of such retrieved problems".[62] In contrast with expert systems, case-based systems are tailored to work without rules: a data-base of raw cases[63] is created, as an 'entry-level' to the system; the action of the network is to transform the value of the inputs into a signal, flowing along the connections, via several mathematical operations. The output will be a value, to be interpreted by the user. For these features, the case-based systems are particularly fit to operate in a context of vague, indeterminate, discretionary elements. Refined by Aamodt and Plaza,[64] the CBR methodology resulted in the 4R process (retrieve, reuse, revise, retain) and gained momentum in the areas of diagnosis, planning, design and, of course, legal reasoning.[65]

In fact, if it is impossible to translate all norms and acts into mathematical, computational rules, the case-based model seems to be a better option. However, it has a major weakness, residing in opacity, struggling to give account of, or to justify, its decisional process.[66] It is precisely in the domain of law that the case-based reasoning research in AI started flourishing.[67] Computer scientists admitted that "law is a particularly interesting domain for CBR researchers given that it is largely about cases".[68] But if this is certainly true for the common law, it is not necessarily correct for the civil law.[69] I will elaborate more extensively on the different approach to cases and precedents, in the two legal traditions, in Chap. 7. However, in this introductory chapter it is important to stress that the European continental legal approach[70] seems to be better represented by an expert system, rather than a case-based reasoning system, because of the different impact that the precedent has on European continental courts.[71]

---

[62] Portinale (2018), p. 41.

[63] Cases that are selected by a very general criterion, usually, utility. For the maintenance of the system, the cases inserted in the library must be constantly monitored, in order to assess whether they are still useful: the useless ones will be removed for the sake of the performance of the system.

[64] Aamodt and Plaza (1994), p. 39 ff.

[65] Portinale (2018), p. 41.

[66] Bourcier (2011), p. 45.

[67] Rissland et al. (2005), p. 1.

[68] Ibidem.

[69] See Rissland et al. (2003), p. 2, ftn. 1: in defining what law is to the eyes of computer scientists, the authors acknowledge their bias of thinking of law as the American law. Nevertheless, they claim that many of their remarks are applicable across the legal traditions. I argue (Chap. 7) that the basic difference in the value of the precedent, in common law and in civil law, has much more relevance than the authors could perceive.

[70] It has been noted that the two main AI models, rule-based and case-based, not only reflect Piaget's theory of cognitive development, but they correspond to the two main legal families, of civil law and common law: Bourcier (2011), p. 37.

[71] See Catala (1998), p. 11 ff., resuming the experience of the Montpellier laboratory for judicial documentation and the research groups of IRETIJ and Juris Data.

Although it falls out of the scope of this work to review, historically, the achievements in AI and law,[72] it is worth noting that the proceedings of ICAIL offer the most comprehensive overview on the evolution of this computational branch in the world. In 1987 the first *International Conference on AI and Law* was organised at the Northeastern University, by Hafner and Berman, followed by the publication of a rich proceedings volume. After the second international conference, in 1991, the *International Association for Artificial Intelligence and Law* was founded and went on to organise the biennial conference, to provide a forum for the presentation and the discussion of the latest research in the field.

Over the years, the CBR approach[73] was cultivated in North America, in some European countries, Australia and Japan, and brought to the realisation of many different tools. In the US, it brought, firstly, to the creation of the HYPO system, by Rissland and Ashley, which was able to solve new cases (examples) on the basis of previous court decisions,[74] of actual precedents, and that was followed afterwards by many other programmes, often combining CBR and RBR. Interaction between the two kinds of reasoning was seminal to the evolution of the field: in 1991, Rissland and Skalak presented CABARET (CAse BAsed REasoning Tool),[75] the first truly hybrid CBR-RBR reasoner, in the statutory area of US tax law. Rules and cases were not juxtaposed but intertwined in the standard functioning of the programme: once that all but one prerequisite of the rules was satisfied, the system would use cases to assess whether the predicate had actually been satisfied. This kind of interaction would be at the core of the following studies and developments towards more realistic tools; as Bench Capon and Sartor put it,[76] "the facts of the case are not givens: cases need to be interpreted, and different lawyers will interpret them in different ways. [...] Moreover, the rules that cases give rise to are inherently defeasible".[77]

In Europe, many similar projects were presented in the Nineties, such as, for example, the Dutch PROLEX, conceived for legal advice, or as the authors put it, a "first aid legal help".[78] Or the French Neurolex, trained to reproduce the decision-making process of the Conseil d'Etat with regard to matters of municipal police:[79] the algorithm efficiently performed the task of recognising which features of the litigation had a negative impact on the outcome of the case and which had a positive one.

72 For an introductory overview see Rissland et al. (2003), p. 6 ff. See also Thorne McCarty (2018), p. 55 ff.

73 First mentioned in Rissland et al. (1984), p. 288 ff.

74 Appellate precedents in the field of trade secrets law.

75 Rissland and Skalak (1991), p. 829 ff.

76 Bench-Capon and Sartor (2003), p. 97 ff.

77 Reasoning is *defeasible* when the corresponding argument is rationally compelling but not deductively valid, Koons (2017), p. 1 ff.

78 Walker et al. (1991), p. 36.

79 Bouchereau et al. (1991), p. 288 ff.

The late Eighties and Nineties represented the 'golden age', in which the field of artificial intelligence and law acquired its own independence and relevance, fuelling the trend, that then became general, of moving the attention from expert systems to CBR. In this sense, although many conditions changed over recent decades, the core of the research in the field of AI and law has long been focused on the combination of rule reasoning and case reasoning. A recent special issue of the review *Artificial Intelligence and Law*[80] was dedicated to the HYPO legacy, celebrating the first CBR system to solve examples on the basis of precedents. Concluding the article introducing that special issue, Bench-Capon[81] lists six open questions based on the scholarship following HYPO, that will need to be addressed in the near future and suggests that HYPO will continue to inspire the work of the researchers in the field for the years to come.

This over-simplified and -condensed review of more than 40 years of advancements in AI and law suggests one specific question, crucial in better clarifying the sense of this inquiry. Why did a large proportion of the European lawyers[82]—either, practitioners, judges or, in part, academics—not feel urged to approach a thrilling and burgeoning field of scholarship, such as AI and law, until recently? What did happen, in the past few years, that suddenly focused *even* our attention on the applications of AI in the many fields of law, criminal law among others?

Answering these questions will help in introducing the topics that will be considered in Chaps. 6 and 7.

5.4 What Prediction Has to Do with Criminal Proceedings?

The digital turn seems to be the most relevant fact that occurred in the last decade, having determined, along with its direct and indirect consequences, a change in lawyers' sensitivity about the interactions between their everyday practice and AI tools. Two aspects must be taken into account here.

Firstly, the global spread of digital communication and the generalised (acritical) acceptance of permanently using digital devices—producing immeasurable amounts of potentially free[83] and accessible data, every day—deeply transformed our

[80] June 2017, volume 25, issue 2.

[81] Bench-Capon (2017), p. 244 f.

[82] It must not be overlooked that some American law schools started organising seminars on AI and law since mid-Eighties. The first was given in 1984 at the Stanford Law School, followed by Harvard in 1985 and Northeastern in 1987. This created a connection between legal communities and AI [Rissland et al. (2003), p. 8] at least at the academic level. There is no evidence of when AI has begun to be considered an everyday instrument of the legal practice in the U.S. In any case, as mentioned, the ABA had shown its attention for computational science since the Sixties, with its Special Committee on Electronic Data Retrieval and the related Jurimetrics Journal.

[83] The matter of data access, usage and exploitation for free is a huge topic in literature and cannot be addressed here. For more elaboration on free access, see Chap. 7, Sect. 7.1.1.

society. As briefly seen in Chap. 2, the extent of such a revolution is still partially unknown to the majority of the global population. Although the social implications of the digital turn are not the core of this inquiry, it must be acknowledged that the over-production of digital data has boosted the research and the application of AI, also in legal tech.

Secondly, during recent past, all the branches of the European public administrations have—sooner or later, completely or partially—endorsed the shift towards a digital governance, encouraged by the European Commissions' action plans.[84] Although digital governance is the object of comprehensive scholarship, that falls out of the scope of this study, there are two aspects to be recalled here.

Firstly, the main effect of the digitalisation process has been the de-materialisation of the documents and the decisions taken by public administrations. The output of a public decision-process is now a digital document, that, theoretically speaking, can be easily accessed, retrieved and reused: among these, are also judicial decisions. This triggered, as we will see more extensively in Chap. 7, a vast movement towards free and open access to public administrations' documents, including in the area of justice, in which publicity of the decision has a specific meaning and value (Chap. 7). But there is more. As, according to popular belief,[85] security and safety are seen as a pillars of the modern political enterprise—being the tenet for enjoying any other right and guarantee—the State acts as risk-manager, anticipating and calculating risks.[86] This implies delegation from individuals to the State, but the growing lack of trust in politicians has been undermining such a traditional relationship. Hence, standardisation and automation seem to be the solution, based on considerable efficiency, consistency, reliability and predictability,[87] even though there is a serious concern for political and democratic legitimacy behind such a fascination.[88]

Secondly, the digitalisation of public administrations also conveys the claim for a more efficient, transparent and equal treatment of people involved in the process. Computational modelling and AI can offer powerful solutions for this purpose. By managing growing amounts of data in a few seconds or even in real-time, on the basis of general and apparently objective models, algorithms have become, like it or not, the banner of a more transparent and just public administration and, why not, of a more just legal action. Justice, as a branch of the public administration is undergoing the same process of expanding application of algorithm-based decision systems. Areas like criminal law, impinging on the most basic values of the society, such as life and individual liberty, have been progressively touched by algorithmic

---

[84] See, in particular, the Commission's communication about the EU e-Government Action Plan 2016–2020, available at https://eur-lex.europa.eu/legal-content/EN/TXT/PDF/?uri=CELEX:52016DC0179&from=EN.

[85] Clearly endorsing Hobbe's approach in the Leviathan, claiming for legal priority of security over civil rights: see, specifically on this point, Pagallo (2013), p. 385.

[86] Durante (2019b), p. 373.

[87] Durante (2019b), p. 377.

[88] Pagallo and Durante (2016), p. 323 ff.

decision-making processes too.[89] Some have argued that sentencing, in particular, is a governmental activity, like taxation or the application of other public policies and, therefore, it can be encoded into adequate algorithms.[90]

As a consequence, lawyers and legal scholars? all over the world have to review their attitude. On the one hand, the digitalisation of the public administration forced them to change their habits for working with material documents, files and papers, to move to a digitalised organisation of their work. On the other hand, the very same digitalisation of public decision-making processes produced new fields of litigation,[91] because, as said in Chaps. 3 and 4, algorithms, *per se*, are neither transparent nor equal.[92] As a consequence, lawyers are specialising in bringing claims against the use of algorithms to court, and judges in adjudicating such claims.

The digitalisation is hence affecting the realm of justice in several ways, with huge consequences. The most basic of such ways is the availability of, and the access to, a huge number of judicial decisions in a digital format.[93] Especially within the legal systems based on the binding value of the precedent (see Chap. 7), this produced two intertwined outcomes. Firstly, it delivered computer scientists the fuel to develop articulated and effective case-based reasoning models. The above mentioned idea of digitalising sentencing is based on extensive review of the case law of relevant jurisdictions, in order to highlight the emphasis and weight that the courts put on some key factors (e.g.: correlation between a verdict [acquittal] and a specific excuse claimed by the defendant [self-defence]): the algorithm taking into account those factors could be used for every kind of matter.[94] Secondly, digitalisation boosted the social expectation to 'predict' future judicial decisions, spreading the feeling that a computational model can—or, may be, should?—also replace human decision-making in judicial affairs, with the aim of delivering more consistent and foreseeable decisions.

This is the framework in which has developed what we are getting used to calling, even in Europe, 'predictive justice'. Thus, we must now reflect on the meaning of this term, focusing on the areas of criminal proceedings, in which this so-called predictive justice seems to have a major impact, such as the prediction of the final adjudication of the case and the assessment of the risk of violent behaviour and recidivism.

---

[89] See the document Litigating algorithms: challenging government use of algorithmic decision systems, September 2018, in ainowinstitute.org.

[90] Stoobs et al. (2017), p. 261.

[91] Ibidem.

[92] Palmiotto (forthcoming).

[93] Buchanan and Headrick (1970), p. 42, on the high costs of gathering, codifying and storing large amounts of legal information.

[94] Stoobs et al. (2017), p. 266.

5.4.1 Quantitative Legal Prediction: What Can It Do for Criminal Justice?

There is general acceptance of prediction of the Federal Supreme Court decisions in the US,[95] because of the huge impact that those rulings have on the national community. As mentioned above in Sect. 5.2.1, forecasting the decisions of the US Supreme Court has been an area of interest for scholars from different backgrounds, over recent decades. In political science research, analysing the case-law of that Court to predict the outcome of future decisions is a specific branch of study.[96] It was a matter of 'natural evolution' that the interest in prediction, the CBR modelling in AI and the digitalisation of judicial decisions, merged into a specialised area of scholarship, named *quantitative legal prediction*.[97] After a season (the so-called 'winter of AI', considering that there is no agreement on the number of winters having already occurred and likely to occur in the near future...),[98] when computer science was attempting to emulate human brain logics and functions, todays quantitative legal systems tend to reproduce the human intelligence not in the underlying logic processes but in the outcomes (provided that an AI system aims to be rational even when the human outcomes are irrational!). Quantitative legal prediction advocates claim that, on the basis of a prospering quantity of observational data, modelling is grounded in what people do[99] (and not why they do it). QLP relies specifically on this huge quantity of observational data: the human reasoners, in fact, are limited in their performance, bound solely to data they have experienced.[100] On the contrary, Big Data offers the solution for this shortcoming. Even when supported by technology in the access to a wider data-set, human actors still prove limited in their ability to processing large amounts of data, rapidly and accurately, also because of their unavoidable biases.

More specifically, the most well-known quantitative prediction tool consists of computational models based on machine learning, able to predict the US Supreme Court rulings and the Justices' behaviour in a generalised, out-of-sample context. At the core of the model, stands the recognition of a number of variables, for example, the outcome of the decision (reversed/affirmed/other).[101] Other variables have been

---

[95] Ayres (2007), p. 103 ff.

[96] Actually, Segal and Speath gave much more than a hint to such discussion, by starting the so-called Supreme Court Data Base Project, in the late Nineties of the twentieth century. See Segal and Spaeth (1989), p. 103 ff. The Authors further elaborated on the so-called 'attitudinal model', asserting that the judges base their decisions on the facts of a case juxtaposed against their personal policy preferences. See Segal et al. (2005), p. 38 f. See also, extensively, Martin et al. (2004), p. 761 ff.

[97] The literature on the point is now remarkable. See, among others Susskind (2008); Katz (2013), p. 909 ff and 911; Katz et al. (2017).

[98] See Ray (2019).

[99] Katz (2013), p. 918.

[100] Katz (2013), p. 928.

[101] Katz et al. (2017), p. 3.

introduced, based on facts that have proved significant in the determination of the outcome of previous decisions. In general, the designers engineered "features that summarise the "behaviour" of a Justice, the Court, the lower court, and differences between them".[102] According to the designers, the model largely outperformed the human prediction results, under different criteria, such as accuracy and consistency.

The French project *Open Predictive Justice*,[103] developed an algorithm predicting the outcome of administrative judicial proceedings against aliens' expulsion orders. This branch of litigation is the most accessed in the French regulatory context, with a huge number of proceedings and a big impact on human and economic costs. The model relies on supervised machine learning algorithms, mapping the function from variable inputs to variable outputs; both codes and databases are publicly available in a github repository of the project. The dataset training the algorithm is a comprehensive case-law collection of 18,000 decisions by all the French administrative courts of appeal, between 2012 and 2015. The variables covered a wide range of aspects such as: features of the fact; the presence of a certain argument; the reference to a specific piece of legislation; the nature of the parties (natural persons or public administration); the name of the presiding judge.[104] Combining the variables, it is possible to foresee the likelihood of success of the case: however, generally speaking, more variables mean more time in building-up the algorithm, and compromises between time and quality of the results may be needed.[105]

Based on similar models, many platforms and companies like, e.g. TyMetrix[106] and LegalMetric, not only offer predictive evaluations of the adequate cost of a suit, but also focus on the prediction of federal circuit courts' decisions and individual judges success rates. Thus, it is often said that such instruments, *predicting* either the length, the costs and the outcome of a potential litigation, have a great impact in pushing claimants towards mediation or other diversion instruments, avoiding litigation in court and benefitting the whole justice system.[107]

These arguments are weak.

As anticipated, Chap. 7 will elaborate more comprehensively on the problems that a case-based AI system retrieving precedents may have on many European jurisdictions. However, there are some general remarks related to the meaning of 'predictive justice' that it is worth introducing from now. In fact, before moving on in this analysis, we need to focus on the meaning of the term 'prediction' and on the sense of referring it to 'justice'.

---

[102] Katz et al. (2017), p. 6.

[103] See, extensively, Benesty (2017), p. 4 ff.

[104] Benesty (2017), p. 7.

[105] In this case, the name of the presiding judge proved to be the less relevant variable in determining the outcome of the decision and the success of the prediction: Benesty (2017), p. 8.

[106] Tymetrix Inc. was acquired by Wolter Kluwer ELM Solutions Inc.

[107] Larret-Chahine (2018), p. 293.

5.4.2 *What Does 'Predicting a Decision' Mean? The Relevance of Statistics in Criminal Matters*

Some have doubted that applying a computational model based on precedent decisions of a court means to *predict* the decision in a new case. In fact, what the programs, like the ones that have been mentioned above, can do is to provide accurate calculation[108] of how a court or a judge decided in previous cases on a similar claim. Looking at the achievement in AI from the legal point of view, it has been said that the best that the modelling of judicial decision can do, so far, is to give a model of the possible different solutions to a legal problem.[109] As a consequence, such programs can express probabilities, even high probabilities, that the court will stick to the precedent (in a common law jurisdiction), refusing to distinguish or to overrule, or that it will follow the mainstream interpretation, rejecting the more eccentric one (in a civil law jurisdiction; we will see that this distinction still has a precise meaning, although common law and civil law spheres' difference are said to be progressively blurring). Thus, it is undisputed that the first step to address the matter of 'predictive justice' is to abandon the (dystopic) idea of a machine being able to predict the outcome of a future decision, that is to say, being able to decide (we will see in a while how to translate this at the semantic level): if it is true that quantitative, predictive justice is not grounded in statistics, such a process delivers probabilities, based on what has occurred in the past and no serious scientific approach can use past events to build previsions of the future.[110] As said by Lucien Mehl, it is still the case of a law machine 'to inform', rather than a law machine 'to decide':[111] accurate statistics is what we found, e.g., in LegalMetric. But what kind of information do these probabilities, these statistics, offer and what is it valuable for?

Preliminarily, it has been noted that the core of the 'algorithmic performance' is the legal rule: if the algorithm can be positively tested in foreseeing how the judge will decide in a specific case, it is because there is a rule, that judges apply, almost invariably, in similar cases...[112] Beside the rule, other human factors and biases may play a relevant role, that QLP purports to be able to predict in terms of statistical probability.

We cannot overlook the existence of scepticism in applying probabilities and, statistics to human behaviour.[113] Given the undisputed value of statistics in hard science, it has been said that the application of probabilities to human activity is

---

[108] Lebreton-Derrien (2018), p. 5; Deumier (2018), p. 50.

[109] Garapon and Lassègue (2018), p. 229.

[110] See Dupré (2018), p. 108 (actually, for the statement reported the author refers to the text of a lecture delivered together with L. Levy Vehel at the *Entretiens Portalis*, Aix-En-Provence, June 2018, proceedings are still in press, in which they underline that quantitative justice does not rely on statistics: from the words the author reports the remarks sees a bit contradictory).

[111] See ftn 39.

[112] Benesty (2016).

[113] Durante (2019a), p. 259 ff.

non-sensical, as it is governed by uncertain rules and factors, constantly changing over the time.[114] These remarks seriously impinge on how the purported 'accurate numbers' of QLP can be used. It is arguable that this information can and should really impact both on the subjects of a judicial litigation and on the community, in the widest sense of it. But let us focus, first, on the impact on the subjects of a litigation.

The core of the matter is that some scholars stress the risk that such statistics are not reliable[115] If the instruments have to help potential parties in making their decisions, they must deliver accurate results. This depends, of course, on the characteristics of the data used as input. This can be a crucial issue in criminal law. Indeed, in many legal orders prosecutors have discretional power to drop cases they are not interested in. Within such a framework, the judicial statistics completely overlook the cases dropped by the prosecutor, either because of an 'immunity bargain', based on a deal between the suspect and the prosecutor, or other discretional evaluations. Such cases escape a complete review of precedents, as they do not even reach the trial stage. For these cases there is no judicial decision and thus they are completely overlooked by the software. This has a great impact on the reliability of the results of 'predictive justice tools'.[116]

Moreover, quantitative tools cannot be intended to function, in general, as an assessment of the risk of losing a case,[117] as the case outcome depends, in the reality, on how the parties express their arguments, on the evidence they bring, on the application of procedural rules based on incidental conditions.[118] Although modern techniques of natural language processing have reduced the gap between human and digital processing in the realm of semantics, the distinction between syntactic and semantic elaboration is still crucial. Traditionally, data is syntactically processed, while information is semantically processed: digital agents outperform human agents in syntactic analysis; humans excel in semantics, while digital technologies are not able to process data with a semantic function.[119] Given that natural language processing has been at the centre of AI and law research, since the very initial stages (above, Sect. 5.3.1) and the achievements in such a field have been great, it is still really hard to establish similarities between different cases, due to the hindrance of such a semantic gap, provided that, in law, there is no 'application', rather 'interpretation'.[120]

In any case, some argued, that even a very accurate statistic would mean little for a potential claimant. Reliable and significant statistics and probabilities do not

---

[114] Filiol (2018), p. 150.

[115] Rottier (2018), p. 191.

[116] Brigan (2018), p. 243.

[117] Dupré (2018), p. 108.

[118] Statistics are the interpretation of a certain specific reality: Lasserre (2018), p. 317.

[119] Durante (2019a), p. 162 ff.

[120] Ibidem.

produce, in the realm of justice, the same effects that they produce in economics.[121] This suggests that plaintiffs willing to have their case heard by a court may not be influenced by a reliable probability of failure.

5.4.3 *How 'Prediction' Would Impact on the Parties and the Judge?*

It is crucial to assess whether 'predictive justice' can help in promoting diversion and alternatives to judicial dispute. Being aware that a high number of variables are involved in the real adjudication of the case by a judge, the potential parties could be pushed to disregard the results of predictive justice, like they often do, today, with their lawyers' advice.[122] However, the fascination for the machine could induce some people to credit the results of predictive justice much more than they do with a human expert advice, based on the same phenomenon that induces unconscious reliance on digital and automated evidence (Chap. 4).

As to the impact on the lawyer, it has been noted that the advantages offered by the current instruments of 'predictive justice' are particularly valuable in terms of risk assessment, because they help in managing the client's risk, be it an individual or a company. In this sense, the role of the legal expert shifts towards that of an insurance company, supposed to handle and reduce its own risks[123] and the client's risk, with regard to litigation or the general compliance with the law.[124]

As to the judge, the real hazard is to paralysing the evolution of legal interpretation, by establishing a normative correlation between how rules have been interpreted in the past and how they will be in the future.[125] Such an aspect impinges on both the individuals' behaviour and on the community, as a whole. From one angle, there is a risk of distorting the judicial function (Chap. 7), compressing the judges' independence,[126] with subsequent de-responsibilisation[127] and delegitimisation of the role.[128] From another other angle, there is a general risk of giving statistical indicators, such as probabilities, a normative value, recognising to them a binding

---

[121] Lasserre (2018), p. 316.

[122] Actually, Bing and Harvold (1977), p. 229 observed: "If a legal problem is presented to a lawyer, he may predict the outcome for his client if the problem is brought before the court. If the rate of predictability is high, the client may choose to negotiate".

[123] Both TyMetrics and LegalMetric can calculate the rates of future personal success for potential junior associate lawyers.

[124] Lasserre (2018), p. 315.

[125] Marin (2018).

[126] Brigan (2018); Ferry (2018), p. 502.

[127] Abiteboul and Dowek (2017), p. 18.

[128] Lebreton-Derrien (2018), p. 11.

value and, thus, the role of source of law. In actuality there would be a binding force, which could be compared to the customary law.[129]

Also, with regard to the impact of QLP on the community, some authors have stressed the risk of endorsing a tautologic process in which what has happened in the past becomes the rule for what should happen in the future. Not only does this affect the behaviour of the subjects of a potential litigation, but also the whole dimension of human relations. The latter could undergo a process of standardisation of the human life,[130] allocating a standard value to any activity or performance and depriving the human being of a sense of justice, that would be translated into standards, quantities, measurements.[131]

Not that questions of ethics have been disregarded so far. On the contrary. It was 1972 when Joseph Weizenbaum warned computer scientists to acknowledge and accept their "enormously important responsibility to be modest in their claims".[132] Since Deborah Johnson's 1985 *Computer Ethics*, the topic has developed into an autonomous field of scholarship, sharing philosophical foundations with information ethics.[133] A comprehensive range of literature has addressed the dilemmas suggested by computer ethics and, in particular the matter of the autonomous cognitive[134] and moral agents: judging is a human act that can be, and has been, analysed, over the centuries, from an ethical point of view. Nevertheless, the aim of this inquiry is to root the discourse into the legal point of view. For this reason, the angle adopted is that of the legal professions and how they can take advantage/suffer from the application of the so called 'predictive justice' tools.

5.4.4 How Prediction Would Impact on the Quality of Justice?

Let us work from the assumption that creating computational models of legal reasoning may "improve the efficiency, comprehensibility and consistency of legal systems".[135] Actually, there are different positions on the matter and it is worth discussing them in the order suggested in the quoted passage.

---

[129] Deumier (2018), p. 61.

[130] Deumier (2018), p. 63.

[131] Lasserre (2018), p. 318.

[132] Weizenbaum (1972), pp. 176, 614.

[133] "Information ethics will not immediately be useful to solve specific computer ethics problems but it will provide grounds for the moral principles that will then guide the problem-solving procedure in computer ethics": Floridi (1999), p. 43.

[134] See, for instance, Evans (2019), p. 260, trying to reconstruct the cognitive dimension of artificial agents under the traditional Kant's vision, as "a self-legislating agent, bound by the rules he has himself constructed, reinterpreting his sensory perturbations as a coherent unified experience of an external world".

[135] Robaldo et al. (2019), p. 114.

As to *efficiency*, it is undisputed that advanced retrieving systems, based on correlations, may positively impact on some repetitive activities that do not encompass legal reasoning, in the sense of taking any judicial decision: retrieving documents or transcripts of interceptions to establish correlations could certainly contribute to a more efficient organisation of the judicial duties and schedule. Are there other efficiency issues that could be improved by 'predictive justice'? The range of applications is wide and even consistency (see below) could be considered an aspect of efficiency. Nevertheless, we should not overlook the fact that efficiency, in judicial matters, must be put in balanced with fundamental rights and principles:[136] it cannot be regarded as a value, *per se*. For this reason, much attention will be paid to this aspect in the following chapters. Thus, the ethical question "whether we need to realise 'predictive justice' tools" must be approached, bearing in mind that efficiency in justice administration is a 'balanced' concept. But that same ethical dilemma could also be rephrased, the other way around: "can we avoid to exploiting all the benefits deriving from such instruments?" Can we afford to renounce to instruments that, reproducing the conditions of judicial reasoning and decision-making, can highlight hidden human behaviours and implicit choices?[137] In this sense, the discourse about efficiency could be focused on how accurately 'predictive justice' can cast light on hidden features of the administration of justice, that cannot be appreciated by human glance. The ability to managing huge amounts of data and to establishing correlations by simulating the conditions of a judicial decision, can suggest the existence of ambiguous habits and hidden biases…[138] In this sense, the so-called quantitative or predictive tools can play a role in fostering efficiency.

As to *comprehensibility*, doubts have been expressed on the fact that predictive justice can foster the access and the *comprehension* of law by the general public, and in particular, by those who never sought access to it before. Chapter 7 elaborates on the concept of people's comprehension and acceptance of judicial decisions: accessibility to QLP tools, quickly delivering a verdict on the probability of success/failure of a potential case would not imply, in any way, a major comprehension of justice by the general public. On the contrary, I am convinced that an approach in terms of probabilities would reduce people's effort in understanding the judicial decision-making process: in such a context, people will be convinced that each ruling by a court or a judge is grounded in probability and not in legal reasoning, applying general rules to a specific case.

Finally, there is scepticism about the possibility that predictive justice tools can boost the *consistency* of legal systems. This point is crucial and needs a multi-fold approach. Both Chaps. 6 and 7 focus on the concept of consistency but it is worth anticipating that, in judicial matters, it encompasses two divergent values. Consistency is certainly a claim for equal treatment before courts and, as such, it

---

[136] Ingall-Montagnier (2011), p. 22.

[137] Bourcier (2011), p. 50.

[138] Talking about computer ethics, James H. Moore addressed the topic of the invisibility factor, claiming that if invisibility of the computational calculation is a big issue in computer ethics, the solution can be in the computer itself, being able "make the invisible visible", Moore (1985), p. 275.

strongly involves both the parties—seeking for it—and the judges, struggling to guarantee it in their decisions.[139] It has been argued that on the basis of 'predictive justice', the administration of justice could be more transparent, democratic, equal, lenient and apparently more objective.[140] However, 'equal treatment' implies that if law is the same for anybody,[141] justice is not.[142] The application of the same rule to multiple cases must bring about different rulings, respecting the principle of the individualisation of judicial decisions. The trend to homogenise decisions on the basis of what 'predictive justice' indicates to be the mainstream, can be utterly dangerous, as we will see in Chap. 7. In fact, generalisation, objectivisation can induce the suppression of the need to distinguish one case from another. And if this is true for the adjudication on guilt, it is also crucial in another area of judicial decision in criminal law, that is to say the realm of decisions on bail, sentencing and parole, in which courts are supposed to rule on the basis of the assessment of the risk of recidivism or future violent behaviour.

Before addressing these topics in Chaps. 6 and 7, it is worth clarifying another premise.

As said (above, Chap. 1), for the purpose of this study the term 'predictive justice' encompasses both predictive tools for decisions and tools for the assessment of violent behaviour and recidivism. Chapter 6 is specifically devoted to the latter but it is worth contextualising since now the problem into the general framework of the European criminal justice. Although it is very difficult to approach the topic from a general point of view, as different jurisdictions have different approaches and rules, it is possible to argue that even after the positivistic trend[143] in criminal law declined, many European jurisdictions still tolerate several 'predictive' judicial evaluations, within their criminal proceedings. Police, prosecutors and judges are often expected to decide on the suspect or defendant's liberty on the basis of a risk assessment. Notwithstanding that criminal proceedings are meant to finally assess the defendant's guilt for an act she allegedly *committed in the past*, rules of procedure often base decisions on the prevision of what the defendant *may do in the future*.

It is a common feature that judges (and prosecutors, if they can impose pre-trial measures, limiting liberty) are supposed to decide on pre-trial detention and other pre-trail coercive measures on the basis of a prevision. They are requested to foresee whether the suspect's liberty should be limited in order to preserve a specific interest of the proceedings (in particular, interest in avoiding escape, disruption or suppression of evidence; in preventing further risks for the victims and the community).

---

139 Serverin (2018), p. 45.

140 Larret-Chahine (2018), p. 293.

141 In any Italian courtroom the claim *La legge è uguale per tutti* is reported at the centre of the room. Deumier (2018), p. 62; if uniformity is a claim in the application of the law, the judicial intime conviction is a beacon for individualised justice.

142 Bouteille-Brigant (2018), p. 303.

143 Brought to its maximum extension by Cesare Lombroso, who theorized the paradigm of criminal anthropology, in the first half of the twentieth century.

In addition, the personal behavioural and psychological condition is the basis for any evaluation of the execution of the sentence and parole. The majority of the European legal orders being inspired to the rehabilitative paradigm, rather than the retributive one, the evaluation of the convicted person's future behaviour is crucial in the service of the sentence, for treatment, and for the decision about parole and similar alternative measures.

It is with regard to these two main areas of criminal proceedings that so-called 'predictive justice' is gaining momentum. However, based on the assumptions presented so far, we can argue that the use of the term 'predictive justice' is related to a real action of 'prediction'.

5.5 Brief and Crucial Matters of Semantics and Taxonomy

Let us extrapolate some key-points from the previous paragraphs to justify the assumption at the end of Sect. 5.4.

Firstly, traditionally, justice is a virtue commanding—and not foretelling, predicting—the right solution of a litigation. For instance, prediction has been largely mistrusted and rejected by law and the linkage between the name 'justice' and the adjective 'predictive' sounds unacceptable.[144] The whole range of fundamental principles of modern justice—from the presumption of innocence to the right to confrontation—are meant to objectivise the judicial decision, linking it to the facts of the case, and to value the individualisation of the decision.

Secondly, predictive tools do not deliver justice (see Chap. 6, Sect. 6.5): they can assist a human decision, providing for insights that may not appear visible to a non-computational examination. I doubt that computer scientists ever claimed to realise 'judging machines'. Nevertheless, the digital replication of what is usually a judicial act (such as delivering a verdict or ruling on bail), nurtured a certain fascination for robo-judges….

It is hard to reconstruct when and how the term 'predictive justice' started to be used in the legal field. Probably, it happened that the term 'predictive' was adopted in the legal area for incidental reasons, instead of using more accurate terms, that certainly exists, either in the English or the neo-Latin languages. Presumably, the political science scholars' habit to engaging in 'predictions' on the future decisions of the US Supreme Court influenced the spread of the term (above, Sect. 5.2.1) 'predictive justice', together with similar terms used in other fields of computational scholarship such as 'predictive medicine'. In English, 'foreseeability' would have probably fitted the concept better than predictability. However, it is in some neo-Latin languages particularly that the term 'predictable' has a specific meaning, not coinciding with the English one. In French, the term 'previsibile' is distinguished from 'prédictive' and has a different meaning. Also, in

[144] Lebreton-Derrien (2018), p. 12.

Italian, 'prevedibile', is different from 'predittivo'. We can measure and appreciate the linguistic differences on the basis of the following statement. "predictability in a legal system is the prerequisite for enabling this system to fulfil its basic functions of solving conflicts and controlling behaviour. Reduction of predictability will foster conflicts and result in appeals, and will make legislation a less-effective means of manipulation the behaviour of citizens".[145] The right term to adopt to translate this concept into French and Italian is not 'prédictivité' or 'predittibilità' but 'prévisibilté' and 'prevedibilità'.

Giving the right name to things and concepts is not an easy task. However, on the basis of what we have seen so far, it is possible to say that AI tools for the assistance of the decision, both based on precedents and on risk assessment instruments, are not decision-making agents. Even if they can foresee with a high level of accuracy how a court will decide in one case or predict cases of recidivism or an individual's future violent behaviour, they are not supposed to supersede the human decision. The act of judging is a complex cognitive task that brings into the creation of something that did not exist before: the decision. The system assisting the decision does not create anything, does not create a decision. Rather what these tools can really do[146] is to simulate the conditions in which the decision, either on guilt or on recidivism, will occur. In this sense they are 'virtual justice',[147] that can potentially exist, but only via a human act of decision.[148]

These assumptions suggest some conclusions. For the sake of a serious approach to the topic, we need to get rid of the term 'predictive justice'. It is crucial that, as lawyers, we avoid focusing the discussion on imaginary problems.[149] Although the eradication of the term 'predictive justice' from our current vocabulary is quite unlikely, using the right concepts will help in approaching the real problems from the right perspective.

In fact, we did not criticise, so far, the accuracy of the instruments of so-called 'predictive justice'. On the contrary, we envisaged the use of it as a framework for 'supportive justice', in which to recreate, to simulate the conditions of a judicial decision, taking advantage of the whole range of information that such tools can offer. But what if that information is not reliable, at least at the European level? What if the CBR-based programs, relying on complete collections of precedent decisions, misrepresent the European or, at least, the continental legal systems? What if such tools, disregarding the basic features of the institutions of civil-law legal systems, hinder the basic principles, the integrity of those very same systems?

---

145 Bing and Harvold (1977), p. 230.

146 Bourcier (2011), p. 50.

147 Lebreton-Derrien (2018), p. 9.

148 Jonas (1993), p. 50: "es muß zu Anfang Bewußtsein dasein, um dem Automaten Instruktionen, eine Aufgabe, einzuspeisen, und ebenso Bewußtsein zum Schluß, um ihm das Ergebnis, die Lösung, abzunehmen".

149 See, *mutatis mutandis*, what Chatila (2018), distinguished expert in robotics, declared to *Le Monde*: science fiction is still monopolizing the debate, while more urgent and important matters about the development and application of robotics and AI need to be discussed.

And what if, risk assessment tools do not fit the continental paradigm of rehabilitation?

These are the questions that will be addressed in the following chapters.

References

Aamodt CB, Plaza E (1994) Case-based reasoning: foundational issues, methodological variations, and system approaches. AI Communications 7(1):39–59
Abiteboul S, Dowek G (2017) Le temps des algorithmes. Le Pommier, Paris
Ayres I (2007) Super crunchers. How anything can be predicted. John Murray, London
Baum L (1997) The puzzle of judicial behavior. The University of Michigan Press, Ann Arbor
Bell J (2006) Judiciaries within Europe. CUP, Cambridge
Bench-Capon TJM (2017) HYPO's legacy: an introduction to the virtual special issue. Artif Intell Law 25(2):244 f
Bench-Capon TJM, Sartor G (2003) A model of legal reasoning with cases incorporating theories and values. Artif Intell, 97 ff (special issue)
Benesty M (2016). https://medium.com/@supralegem/supralegem-fr-open-source-la-justice-prédictive-ff351d6881c3
Benesty M (2017) L'Open Data et l'Open Source, des Soutiens Necessaire à une Justice Predictive Fiable. J Open Access Law 5(1):1–11
Benzi M (2019) Modelli individuali in medicina. Dalla classe di riferimento ai digital twins. In: Cruciani M, Gagliardi G (eds) Medicina, filosofia e cognizione. Aracne, Roma, pp 45 ff
Benzi M, Penco C (2018) Defeasible arguments and the context dependence. Paradigmi, 561–578
Bing J, Harvold T (1977) Legal decisions and information systems. Universitetsvorlagert, Oslo
Bouchereau L, Bourcier D, Bourgine P (1991) Extracting legal knowledge by means of a multilayer neural network application to municipal jurisprudence. In: Proceedings ICAIL 1991, ACM, New York, pp 288 ff
Bourcier D (2011) L'acte de juger est-il modélisable? De la logique à la justice. In: Cahièrs de Philosophie du Droit, L'E-justice. Dalloz
Bouteille-Brigant M (2018) Pour un 'transjuridisme'? In: Archives de Philosophie du Droit, La justice prédictive. Dalloz, Paris
Brigan JM (2018) Les risques accentués d'une justice pénale predictive. In: Archives de Philosophie du Droit, La justice predictive. Dalloz, Paris
Buchanan BG, Headrick TE (1970) Some speculation about artificial intelligence and legal reasoning. Harv Law Rev 23:40 ff
Catala P (1998) Le droit à l'épreuve du numérique. Jus ex Machina. PUF, Paris
Cevolani G, Crupi V (2017) Come ragionano i giudici: razionalità, euristiche e illusioni cognitive. Criminalia, pp 181 ff, 182
Chatila R (2018) *Le Monde*, special issue Dans la tête des robots, pp 11 ff
Chiavario M (1975) Appunti sulla problematica dell'"azione" nel processo penale italiano: incertezze, prospettive, limiti. Riv trim dir proc civ, 864 ff
De Mulder K, van Noortwijk K, Combrink-Kuiters K (2010) Jurimetrics please! Eur J Law Technol, pp 137 ff
Deumier P (2018) La justice prédicitive et les sources du droit: la jurisprudence du fond. In: Archives de Philosophie du Droit, La justice predictive. Dalloz, Paris
Dupré J (2018) Du droit saisi par l'IA au droit saisissant l'IA, elements de réflexion. In: Archives de Philosophie du Droit, La justice predictive, Dalloz, Paris
Durante M (2019a) Potere computazionale. L'impatto delle ICT su diritto, società e sapere. Meltemi, Milano

Durante M (2019b) Safety and security in the digital age. Trust, algorithms, standards and risks. In: Berkich D, d'Alfonso MV (eds) On the cognitive, ethical, and scientific dimensions of artificial intelligence. Themes of IACAP 2016, Springer, Cham, pp 371–383
Dworkin R (1986) Law's empire. Harvard University Press, Cambridge
Edlin DE (2016) Common law judging. University of Michigan Press, Ann Arbor
Endam LM, Sedillot E, Desorsiers M (2018) Critical entry points. Genetics and epigenetics. In: Agache I, Hellings P (eds) Implementing precision medicine in best practices of chronic airways disease. Elsevier, p 5
Engel C, Gigerenzer G (2006) Law and heuristics. An interdisciplinary venture. In: Gigerenzer G, Engel C (eds) Heuristics and the law. MIT Press, Cambridge
Evans R (2019) A Kantian cognitive architecture. In: Berkich D, D'Alfonso MV (eds) On the cognitive, ethical, and scientific dimensions of artificial intelligence. Themes from IACAP 2016. Springer, Cham, pp 233–262
Ferry SM (2018) Les algorithms à l'épreuve du droit au procès equitable. La Sem Jur, no. 11, 502
Filiol E (2018) Les risques concernent l'utilisation des algorithms dit prédictifs dans le domaine sensible de la justice. In: Archives de Philosophie du Droit, La justice predictive. Dalloz, Paris
Floridi L (1999) Information ethics; on the philosophical foundation of computer ethics. Ethics Inf Technol, 43
Garapon A, Lassègue J (2018) La justice digitale. PUF, Paris
Gigerenzer G (2002) Calculated risks: how to know when numbers deceive you. Simon and Schuster, New York
Guthrie C, Rachlinski JJ, Wistrich AJ (2001) Inside the judicial mind. Cornell Law Rev, pp 778–830
Guthrie C, Rachlinski JJ, Wistrich AJ (2007) Blinking on the bench: how judges decide cases Cornell Law Rev, 1–43
Harrys AP, Sen M (2018) Bias and judging. Harv Univ Law J, 1 ff
Hébraud P (1969) Rapport introductif. La logique judiciaire. PUF, Paris
Ingall-Montagnier P (2011) Droit pénal, procédure pénale et nouvelles technologies. In: Archives de Philosophie du Droit, L'E-Justice. Dalloz, Paris
Jonas H (1993) Dem bösen Ende näher. Suhrkamp, Frankfurt am Main, p 50
Katz DM (2013) Quantitative legal prediction, or- how I learned to stop worrying and start preparing for the data-driven future of the legal services industry. Emory Law J, pp 909 ff
Katz DM, Bommarito MJ II, Blackman J (2017) A general approach for predicting the behavior of the Supreme Court of the United States. SSRN, 1–18
Kennedy D (2006) Three globalisations of law and legal thought: 1850–2000. In: Trubeck DM, Santos A (eds) The new law and economic development. Cambridge University Press, Cambridge
Koons R (2017) Defeasible reasoning. In: The Stanford Encyclopedia of Philosophy (Winter 2017 Edition). https://plato.stanford.edu/archives/win2017/entries/reasoning-defeasible/
Larret-Chahine L (2018) Le droit isométrique: un nouveau paradigme né de la justice prédictive. In: Archives de Philosophie du droit, La justice predictive. Dalloz, Paris
Lasser M (2004) Judicial deliberations. Oxford University Press, Oxford
Lasserre V (2018) Justice predictive et transhumanisme. In: Cahièrs de Philosophie du Droit. La justice prédictive. Dalloz, Paris
Lawlor R (1966) Where do we go from here. Jurimetrics J, 53 ff
Lebreton-Derrien S (2018) La justice prédictive. In: Introduction à une justice "simplement virtuelle". In: Cahièrs de Philosophie du Droit. La justice predictive. Dallz, Paris
Levin J (1992) How judges reason. Peter Lang Publishing, New York
Linebach JA (2011) Judicial decision-making. University of Michigan, Ann Arbor
Loevinger L (1949) Jurimetrics-the next step forward. Minn Law Rev, 455 ff
MacCormick DN (1978) Legal reasoning and legal theory. Clarendon Press, Oxford
Marin JC (2018) Proceedings of the seminar 'La justice prédictive'. French Supreme Court, 12.2.2018. https://www.courdecassation.fr/IMG/Rentrée%20des%20auditeurs%20-%20Bordeaux%203.02.2017.pdf

Marini G (2012) Alessandro Giuliani: l'eredità del realismo giuridico nordamericano e l'"anxiety of influence". In: AA.VV (ed) Alessandro Giuliani: l'esperienza giuridica tra logica ed etica. Giuffré, Milano, pp 185 ff

Martin AD, Quinn KM, Ruger TW, Kim PT (2004) Competing approaches to predicting supreme court decision making. Perspect Polit, 761–767

Mehl L (1958) Automatisation in the legal world from the machine processing of information to the law machine. National Physical Laboratory Symposium No. 10, Mechanisation of Thought Processes (vol 11). In: Proceedings of a Symposium held at the National Physical Laboratory, November 26–27, pp 756–779

Moore JM (1985) What is computer ethics. Metaphilosophy, no 16, 275

Ost F (2018) (Re)Learning to think about law from cases. In: Glanert S (ed) Comparative legal reasoning. Essays in honour of Geoffrey Samuels. Wildy, Simmond&Hill Publishing, London, pp 67 ff

Pagallo U (2013) Online security and the protection of civil rights: a legal overview. Philos Technol 26(4):381–395

Pagallo U (2016) Leibnitz. Una breve biografia intellettuale. Wolters Kluwer Italia, Milano

Pagallo U, Durante M (2016) The pros and cons of legal automation and its governance. Eur J Risk Regul 323–334

Palmiotto F (forthcoming) The impact of algorithmic opacity on fair trial rights in criminal proceedings. In: Ebers M, Canero Gamito M (eds) Algorithmic governance and governance of algorithms. Springer

Palmirani M, Benigni F (2007) Norma-system: a legal information system for managing time. In: Proceedings of the V Legislative XML Workshop, Firenze, European Press Academic Publishing, 1, pp 205–224

Portinale L (2018) Case-based and multimodal reasoning: the contribution of Piero Torasso. Intelligenza Artificiale, 42–44

Posner RA (ed) (1992) The essential Holmes: selections from the letters, speeches, judicial opinions, and other writings of Oliver Wendell Holmes, Jr. The University of Chicago press, Chicago

Posner RA (2008) How judges think. Harvard University Press, Cambridge

Prakken H, Sartor G (1996) A dialectical model of assessing conflicting arguments in legal reasoning. Artif Intell Law 4(3-4):331–368

Prakken H, Sartor G (1997) Argument-based extended logic programming with defeasible priorities. J Appl Non-Classical Logics 7(1-2):25–75

Prakken H, Sartor G (2004) Three faces of defeasibility in the law. Ratio Juris 17(1):118–139

Ray T (2019) No, there will be no AI winter. Forbes, 12 September. https://www.forbes.com/sites/tiernanray/2019/09/12/no-there-will-be-no-ai-winter/#3edad93146a5

Rissland EL (1990) Artificial intelligence and law: stepping stones to a model of legal reasoning. Yale Law J 1957–1981

Rissland EL, Skalak DB (1991) CABARET: rule interpretation in a hybrid architecture. Int J Man-Machine Stud (Special Issue on AI and Legal Reasoning, Part 1), 839–887

Rissland EL, Valcarce EM, Ashley KD (1984) Explaining and arguing with examples. In: Proceedings of the fourth AAAI conference on artificial intelligence, AAAI Press, 288–294

Rissland EL, Ashley KD, Loui RP (2003) AI and law: a fruitful synergy. Artif Intell (special issue)

Rissland EL, Ashley KD, Branting LK (2005) Case-based reasoning and law. Knowl Eng Rev 20(3):293–298

Robaldo L, Villata S, Wyner A, Grabmair M (2019) Introduction to artificial intelligence and law. Editorial to the special issue on 'natural language processing for legal texts'. Artif Intell Law 27:113–115

Rottier R (2018) La justice prédictive et l'acte de juger: quelle prévisibilité pour la justice? In: Archives de Philosophie du Droit, La justice predictive. Dalloz, Paris

Samuel G (2016) A short introduction to judging and to legal reasoning. Edgar Elgar Publishing, Cheltenham

Schauer F (2009) Thinking like a lawyer. A new introduction to legal reasoning. Harvard University Press [Transl: Il ragionamento giuridico. Una nuova introduzione. Carocci, Roma, 2016]
Segal JA, Spaeth HJ (1989) Decision trends on the Warren and Burger Courts: results from the Supreme Court Data Base Project. Judicature 73:103–107
Segal JA, Spaeth HJ, Benesh SC (2005) The Supreme Court in the American Legal System. Cambridge University Press, New York
Serverin E (2018) De l'informatique juridique aux services de justice predictive, la longue route de l'accès du publique aux decisions de justice dématérialisées. In: Archives de Philosophie du Droit, La justice prédictive. Dalloz, Paris
Smith SD (1990) The pursuit of pragmatism. Yale Law J, 409–449
Solomon H (1968) Jurimetrics. Jurimetrics J, March, 7 ff
Sotomayor S (2002) A Latina Judge's voice. Berkeley La Raza Law J 13:87–93
Stoobs N, Hunter D, Begaric M (2017) Can sentencing be enhanced by the use of artificial intelligence? Crim Law J, 261 ff
Strasser C, Antonelli A (2019) Non-monotonic logic. Stanford Encyclopedia, pp 1 ff. https://plato.stanford.edu/entries/logic-nonmonotonic/#NonMonoLogiHumaReas
Susskind R (1986) Expert systems in law: a jurisprudential approach to artificial intelligence and legal reasoning. Mod Law Rev, 168–194
Susskind R (2008) The end of lawyers? Oxford University Press
Tervsky A, Kahneman D (1982) Judgment under uncertainty: heuristics and biases. In: Kahnemam D, Slovic P, Tverski A (eds) Judgment under uncertainty: heuristics and biases. Cambridge University Press, Cambridge
Thorne McCarty L (1977) Reflection on 'Taxman': an experiment in artificial intelligence and legal reasoning. Harv Law Rev 90(5):837–893
Thorne McCarty L (2018) Finding the right balance in artificial intelligence and law. In: Barfield W, Pagallo U (eds) Research handbook on the artificial intelligence and law. Elgar, Cheltenham, pp 55–86
von der Lieth Gardner A (1987) An artificial intelligence approach to legal reasoning. MIT Press, Cambridge
Walker RF, Oskamp A, Schrickx JA, van Opdorp GJ, van den Berg PH (1991) PROLEX: creating law and order in a heterogenous domain. Int J Man-Machine Stud, 35–67
Weizenbaum J (1972) On the impact of the computer on society. Science 176(4035):609–614
Wrightsman LS (1999) Judicial decision-making. Kluwer Academic, New York

Chapter 6
Predictability of Violent Behaviour and Recidivism

6.1 Is 'Foreseeing' the Future Relevant in Adjudicating a Criminal Case?

The title of this paragraph is seemingly provocative. Although a trial aims to reconstruct a fact that occurred in the past—to establish the culpability for it—criminal systems tend to attach importance also to the defendant's probable, future behaviour. As we will see, the debate about the weight the defendant's future behaviour should or should not have at sentencing is still extremely animated in criminal law and penology. It is possible to argue that the relationship between the prediction of future re-offending and the defendant's personal liberty is deeply entrenched in the design of contemporary criminal justice,[1] at least in the whole Western legal culture. For these reasons, risk assessment is one of the areas in which the digital revolution has been more intensively exploited. Risk assessment tools are based on statistical evaluation of data-sets, gathered from samples of relevant population, with the purpose of building up models scoring the individuals' personal level of potential offending or re-offending. The recent boost in computational power and the availability of large and complex sets of data, offered new fuel to this well-rooted area of research.

Although there is no room, here, for a satisfactory comparative report on the topic (it should cover a wide variety of aspects and would entail a long diversion from the main focus of this work), some common features appear at first glance, allowing for an acceptable generalisation. A preliminary warning is that we are entering a domain still deeply influenced by the distinction between common law and civil law. The whole discussion about rationales of punishment and sentencing theories is strongly affected by the legal orders' historical backgrounds, with a

[1] Ashworth and Zedner (2014), p. 27 ff.

S. Quattrocolo, *Artificial Intelligence, Computational Modelling and Criminal Proceedings*, Legal Studies in International, European and Comparative Criminal Law 4, https://doi.org/10.1007/978-3-030-52470-8_6

profound and precise distinction between the common law and the majority of the continental European countries.

Against this backdrop, the aim of this chapter is threefold, namely (1) to sum up the general terms of the eternal, philosophical discussion about the role of preventing crime in sentencing, and its repercussions on common law and civil law systems; (2) to analyse how traditional theories of risk assessment reconcile with modern computational modelling; and (3) to assess tensions with fundamental rights. Section 6.1 presents the areas of criminal proceedings in which risk assessment is more commonly used. Section 6.2 deals with rationales, theories and methods of risk assessment. Sections 6.3 and 6.4 are based on two recent North American cases, while Sect. 6.5 compares them, and Sect. 6.6 contextualise the discussion within the European human rights legal framework. Finally, Sect. 6.7 suggests some general conclusions.

6.1.1 Areas of Criminal Proceedings Requiring 'Prediction'

There are at least two areas in which the majority of the Western legal orders ground a judicial decision on a 'prediction' of the defendant's future conduct. One is bail and the second is sentencing. Usually set at the extreme points of criminal proceedings—at the very beginning, and at the very end—the decisions on both bail and sentencing reflect the basic principles underpinning criminal legal systems. In fact, they regulate limitations of personal liberty, for different aims, based on the constitutional protection offered to the latter by each jurisdiction. In any domestic legal order, arrest and pre-trial detention on the one hand, and sentencing, on the other hand, encapsulate specific theories and rationales, that developed over centuries of legal tradition. Within the limit of an acceptable generalisation, it is possible to say that pre-trial detention (here the term refers, generally, to the different domestic coercive measures imposed on the suspect before conviction) usually serves 'procedural' aims and needs: primarily, to prevent the suspect from absconding, from harming people, form dispersing evidence. Sentencing, on the contrary, is the determination of the just criminal sanction after conviction, based on specific norms or guidelines, directly reflecting which of the many theories and concepts of punishment a legal order endorsed in a certain period of time. Both decisions, on pre-trial detention and sentencing, entail a risk assessment. It may be 'procedural risk', such as, e.g., absconding, affecting the development of the proceedings, or a '*de facto* risk', such as re-offending after having served the sentence (provided that the defendant is not considered mentally disordered: these cases fall out the present analysis). The need to integrate a risk assessment into the judicial decisions on bail and sentencing is the key to understanding how important the prediction of an individual's *future* behaviour can be, in the context of an evaluation (the criminal proceeding) focused on a fact of the *past*. Accordingly, prevention of harm (for the on-going proceedings or any potential victim), is traditionally encompassed in both bail and sentencing decisions.

Although I repeatedly stressed, in the previous chapters, that the focus of this book is on repression, rather than prevention of crime, here we come to a point in which the two concepts helplessly blur. As we will see especially in Sect. 6.1.3, different legal traditions tend to allocate the need for preventing future crime under different kinds of public authorities' intervention. Actually, the risk of future dangerous behaviour may be considered either an element affecting sentencing (i.e., as an aggravating factor, like in many sentencing guidelines in common law areas), or the ground for the application of measures of correction and prevention,[2] provided by some European legal system, like Germany (*Maßregeln der Besserung und Sicherung*)[3] and Italy (*misure di sicurezza*),[4] and by, at least, other six Council of Europe member States[5] (see Sect. 6.1.3.1). Or, more precisely, such a risk can even

[2] Actually, in some legal order the criminal law system is twofold, based both on penalties and other correctional measures. Both penalties and correctional measures imply the perpetration of the offence. However, penalties are proportional to the seriousness of the criminal act that was perpetrated, while the other measures are based (or also based) on the perpetrator's social dangerousness. Such measures can be applied on top of penalties, but, in some case, even when penalties are not applicable, when the perpetrator is not punishable (e.g., for mental insanity). Being based on dangerousness, such meaasures may have an undetermined duration. See f.n 5.

[3] See ECtHR, Ilnseher v. Germany, 18.12.2018, § 48: "In accordance with a long-standing legal tradition, the German Criminal Code distinguishes between penalties (*Strafen*) and so-called measures of correction and prevention (*Maßregeln der Besserung und Sicherung*) to deal with unlawful acts. In this twin-track system of sanctions, penalties (see Articles 38 et seq. of the Criminal Code) mainly consist of prison sentences and fines, which are fixed in accordance with the defendant's guilt (Article 46 § 1 of the Criminal Code). Measures of correction and prevention (see Articles 61 et seq. of the Criminal Code) consist mainly of placement in a psychiatric hospital (Article 63 of the Criminal Code), in a detoxification facility (Article 64 of the Criminal Code) or in preventive detention (Articles 66 et seq. of the Criminal Code). The purpose of these measures is to rehabilitate dangerous offenders and to protect the public from them. They may be imposed on criminally liable offenders in addition to their punishment (cf. Articles 63 et seq.). Such measures must, however, be proportionate to the seriousness of the offences committed, or expected to be committed, by the defendants, as well as to their dangerousness (Article 62 of the Criminal Code)".

[4] As to the Italian legal order, *misure amministrative di sicurezza* are (almost) regulated by the penal code, in art. 199 ff. [see Pelissero (2008), *passim*]. They are divided into personal (incapacitating the individual's liberty) and material (incapacitating the individual's chance to dispose of her assets, such as confiscation. Some case of confiscation is regulated outside the penal code, in special statutory acts). Although based on the perpetrator's dangerousness, and on the need to protect the society from the risk posed by such danger, they must not be confused with another kind of coercive measures, regulated outside the Penal code, called preventive measures (*misure di prevenzione*). In fact, the latter are *preater delictum*, not based on the perpetration of a crime, but are meant to prevent the perpetration of it. They often consist in material incapacitation (tackling the assets of a person who is unable to justify the origin of her wealth) but also in personal limitations, like, e.g., bans to reside in a specific area. For a comprehensive overview on the history of *preater delictum* measures in Italy, see ECtHR, De Tommaso v. Italy, 23.2.2017, § III.

[5] In particular, Austria, Denmark, Switzerland, Lichtenstein, Slovakia, San Marino. For a comparative overview, see ECtHR M. v. Germany, 17.12.2009, § II B. In Denmark, Italy, San Marino, Slovakia and Switzerland, the applicable provisions do not fix a maximum duration of preventive detention. As to Germany, an initial limitation of preventive detention, up to 10 years, was abolished by a 1998 statutory act. Pursuant to the decision by the European Court of Human rights in

count under both, aggravating the sanction and establishing the basis for a preventive measure.

What is worth making clear right away, is that a consistent number of European continental jurisdictions (unlike the common law and, in particular, the American common law jurisdictions), distinguish sanctions from measures, the first being proportional to the act and, thus, almost based on retribution and the latter on the individual's dangerousness.[6] Such a distinction has a huge formal impact on domestic sentencing theories and affects the importance of prediction, as discussed in Sect. 6.1.3. Nevertheless, there is a major inconsistency in the qualification of measures based on dangerousness. As the European Court of Human Rights noted in a famous decision,[7] "the same type of measure may be qualified as an additional penalty in one State and as a preventive measure in another".[8] Although qualifications usually hold a relatively scarce importance in a comparative context, such confusion does not help with the effort for a comprehensive approach. Regardless *nomina iuris*, the focus here is on a wide range of means that courts and other public authorities (such as prison boards) may impose on people who, charged with or convicted of a crime, are considered potential re-offenders. These means, whatever their qualification, are distinguished from another range of provisions, *preater delictum* (see ftn 4). The latter do not depend on the individual having been suspected or charged with a specific offence: such 'preventive measures' (like e.g. the black-lists by several international organisations [U.N. and E.U.], against potential terrorists) are grounded in the bare suspicion that, based on specific but perfectly legal behaviours, individuals may be considered at risk of committing serious crimes, someday in the future. The focus, here, is not on *preater delictum* measures, but rather on the measures relating to the perpetration of an offence, based on a conviction or a charge.

Despite the variety of qualifications, any limitation of liberty must respect one general rule: the limitation must be provided by the law and must be proportionate to the risk that the individual's liberty would pose to the public interest. As to Europe, art. 5 ECHR provides for a binding list of grounds for the lawful limitation of personal liberty, and all measures affecting it must be supported, at any time, by "a sufficient causal connection" with at least one of such grounds.[9] According to the Court's case law, such ground, it being a lawful conviction (5.1 lett. a), the legitimate suspicion of having committed a crime (5.1 lett. b), or the need to prevent an offence (5.1. lett. c), must be sufficiently concrete and specific to justify the sacrifice of the individual's liberty. Within this basic legal framework, the assessment of the existence (and the persistence) of such risk is crucial indeed. Time elapsing may

the case of M. v. Germany (declaring that there had a violation of both art. 5§1 and 7 ECHR), a new amendment to the law entered into force in 2013.

[6] Tonry (2019), p. 293.

[7] ECtHR, M. v. Germany, 17,12,2009, § 74.

[8] The Strasbourg Court referred, in this case, to the supervision of a person's conduct after release, which is considered to be an additional penalty in France and a measure (misura di sicurezza) in Italy.

[9] M. v. Germany, § 97.

erode that justification, implying the need for constant reviews of the coercive decision.

6.1.2 Pre-trial Detention and Release

The first area of 'risk management' in criminal proceedings is that of pre-trial coercive measures: "in almost no other circumstances is the court called upon to make predictions about future conduct rather than to determine and punish events which have taken place in the past".[10] As said, art. 5 § 1 lett. c ECHR itself considers the need to prevent the suspect from fleeing or committing crimes, a legal basis for arrest. First and foremost, it is inherent to pre-trial detention (and other less coercive measures) to prevent risks for the trial to come: temporary incapacitation aims to prevent the defendant from absconding and, therefore, jeopardising the prosecution and the proceedings. Moreover, according to art. 5§1 lett. c, preventing the perpetration of offences is also considered another possible grounds for arrest and other pre-trial measures, although often criticised.[11] Let us clarify these basic statements.

It is a fundamental principle of modern law that limitations to liberty before the final assessment of the defendant's culpability should be exceptional, based on exhaustive reasoning, in order to prevent unlawful anticipation of a penalty (that… may not even be applied, at the end of the proceeding). Such a principle stems directly from Magna Charta Libertatum, and the refusal of pre-trial release, in England and Wales, is considered to be the solitary exception to the 1215 Bill of Rights.[12] Although the different legal systems are far from being harmonised under this point of view, it is possible to say that, in Europe, in compliance with that ancient and well-regarded principle, pre-trial precautionary measures have been used "to support the main criminal process (the sole justification for the derogation from Magna Charta and Art. 5 ECHR)".[13] In the legal tradition of the majority of the European countries, 'supporting the main criminal process' means preventing both the risk of absconding and tampering with evidence.[14] Yet, comparative studies demonstrate that, in recent times, many European jurisdictions departed from this tradition, to promote, instead, policing and social control goals.[15] Despite the general acknowledgement of the presumption of innocence—set forth in every European jurisdiction—the (different) purposes of punishment and pre-trial detention tend to blur. The reasons for anticipating the effect of a penalty, via remand in custody and other interim measures, are plenty and, among others, is the unreasonable length of

[10] Vogler (2013), p. 88.

[11] See Grevi (1976a), p. 44 ff., 176 ff.

[12] Cavadino and Gibson (1993), p. 69.

[13] Vogler (2013), p. 89.

[14] Ruggeri (2013), p. 227.

[15] Orlandi (2013), p. 10.

criminal proceedings,[16] certified by the European Court of Human Rights, in many member states. Whatever the causes, the effect of such a trend was to focus public opinion more on custody than on sentence, creating public expectation for an early and immediate deprivation of liberty, with less attention on sentencing. In addition, there has been a widespread widening of the legal basis for pre-trial detention to reasons of public alarm/safeguarding. The joint effect of these two trends is a major threat to the presumption of innocence,[17] as testified by comprehensive literature on the topic.[18]

The same arguments seem to be valid for the U.S. too. Protecting the community was not a traditional task of pre-trial detention[19] until the Eighties of the twentieth century. In 1984, the Crime Control Act amended the 1966 Bail Reform Act (applying to federal courts), introducing the 'danger to the community' as legitimate grounds for pre-trial detention. In recent years, only a few States regulations refer exclusively to the consideration for court appearance.[20] The US Supreme Court upheld this new task of remand in custody, stressing that "the Government's regulatory interest in community safety can, in appropriate circumstances, outweigh an individual's liberty interest".[21]

Based on these few arguments, we must acknowledge the existence of a subtle link between the presumption of innocence and the issue of predicting the defendant's future behaviour, which will be the blueprint of the whole discussion, in this chapter. This brief summary underlines the growing relevance of the defendant's future behaviour in pre-trail decisions, based i.e. on the prediction of her conduct. Moreover, we moved away from the assumption that, traditionally, pre-trail coercive measures are exceptional—last resort measures—for cases in which leaving the suspect at large would definitively hamper the results of the main process. This implies, as said, that decisions about pre-trail detention (and other coercive measures) must be justified by strong reasoning, in order to prevent abuses. Such a guarantee is enshrined in several domestic constitutions.[22] And the more custody serves social security (rather than procedural) goals, higher the need becomes for

---

[16] Orlandi (2013), p. 11.

[17] Vogler (2013), p. 89: "nothing could do more damage to the adversarial principle that to imprison one adversary so that the logistical difficulties of the case preparation are magnified and he or she will appear in court robbed of any opportunity of appearing as an innocent person".

[18] As to Spain, Moreno Catena (2013), p. 154 ff.; Grevi (1976b), p. 633 ff.

[19] For a comprehensive reconstruction of bail history in the US, see Logan Koepke and Robinson (2018), p. 1731 ff.

[20] Van Nostrand (2012), p. 2.

[21] US Supreme Court, US v. Salerno (decided on 26 May 1987), 481 U.S. 739. However, in that very same decision, Justice Rehnquist, signing the opinion of the Court, stressed that "the legislative history of the Bail Reform Act clearly indicates that Congress did not formulate the pretrial detention provisions as punishment for dangerous individuals" and that "in our society, liberty is the norm, and detention prior to trial or without trial is the carefully limited exception. We hold that the provisions for pretrial detention in the Bail Reform Act of 1984 fall within that carefully limited exception".

[22] Ruggeri (2013), p. 230.

precise justification. But how can judicial authorities deliver precise reasoning about the risks of the suspect's future behaviour? Two issues are extremely important, in this case. Firstly, codes for criminal procedure should provide precise criteria for preparing such a risk assessment,[23] and not always they do. Secondly, remand in custody and similar coercive measures are usually applied at an early stage of the proceedings, when the competent authorities have little information about both the facts that occurred and the suspect's personality, as the file is still incomplete.[24]

In this scenario, risk assessment tools appear to offer a great support, giving the judicial reasoning the 'fuel' it needs. As we will see in Sect. 6.2.1.1, the risk assessment for the pre-trial phase has specific requirements, due to the fact that the danger considered by these tools is typically related, as mentioned, to the safeguarding of the proceedings themselves.

6.1.3 Sentencing

The second area in which judges and courts are usually requested to consider the defendant's future behaviour is sentencing, considering that many continental legal orders do not provide for a clear distinction between conviction and sentencing, the former refers to the fact-finding and the burden of proof, the latter to the sanction (more on this in Sect. 6.6).[25]

This distinction has an historical root and has often been associated with the presence of a jury trial, and it is certainly a common feature in common-law legal orders.[26] At the time of the French revolution, France moved towards a system of jury trial, due to the English influence.[27] Although the philosophical debate spread around Europe, the jury courts never became the default jurisdiction for criminal

---

[23] The Italian system, based on art. 274 lett. c ItCCP, provides for specific criteria. To decide a pre-trial coercive measure, justified by the risk of offending, the judge must consider: specific circumstances of the fact (of which the individual is suspected); the suspect's personality, based on her behaviour, deeds and record of previous convictions.

[24] Pre-trial detention is usually applied at the early stage of the proceeding. However, in some jurisdiction (e.g. Italy), where the first instance decision is not final (because the parties can freely lodge an appeal), pre-trial detention can be applied until the decision becomes final (art. 279 ItCCP).

[25] Pifferi (2012), p. 342. For a general overview on the evolution of the jury trial in English criminal proceedings, see Green (1987), p. 41 ff.

[26] For an interesting description of the English jury trial at the moment when the French philosophes started studying it, see Langbein (1987), p. 16 ff; for an updated and comprehensive overview on the European approach to verdict, Thaman (2016), p. 338 ff.

[27] The English trial by jury was the archetype taken into account by the French Illuminists (not only French, however: see Beccaria in Italy e.g.). The philosophical critique to the 'ancien règime justice' was based, among others, on the need to allocate on lay judges the decision about the defendant's guilt. It is in the Montesquieu's Esprit des Lois, in 1748, that the 'judgment of the pairs' was presented to the French public as a beacon of a fair judicial system [Padoa Schioppa (1994), pp. 7, 10]. Actually, the jury trial became one of the most iconic elements of the reform of criminal justice adopted by the Assemblée Constituante.

cases on the continent. Moreover, the twentieth century raise of illiberal regimes, both fascist and bolshevik, led to the substitution of juries with professional or mixed courts in many continental countries.[28] Recently, the European Court of Human Rights surveyed the solutions adopted by the CoE countries with regard to juries in criminal matters. In the case of Taxquet v. Belgium,[29] the Court assessed that there are three different approaches to the matter. Countries that do not have (and some, never had) a jury.[30] A large group of countries providing for mixed juries, in which "the professional judges and the jurors collectively determine all questions of law and fact, the issue of guilt and the sentence".[31] Finally, a third group of countries opted for a traditional jury system.[32] Although the differences within this third group are many, "the general rule appears to be that reasons are not given for verdicts reached by a traditional jury. This is the case for all the countries concerned, except Spain and Switzerland (Canton of Geneva)".[33]

As to the neat distinction between guilt and sentence, in the adjudication, Belgium represents an interesting continental example, providing for separate deliberation. In other legal systems, belonging both to the first and second group, (e.g. Germany, Spain, Italy, Switzerland, among others), the trial court adjudicates on guilt and sentence at the same time.[34]

Interestingly enough, the bifurcation between conviction and sentencing has been theorised as a crucial instrument of modern criminology, especially by Marc

---

[28] Thaman (2016), p. 341 ff.

[29] ECtHR, Gr. C., 16.11.2010, Taxquet v. Belgium. The case was based on the fact that, until 2010, the Belgian law did not impose any kind of reasoning for the jury (Cour d'assise) guilty verdict. While the Taxquet case was pending, a reform was passed, in order to introduce a minimum standard of reasoning. The same happened, after the Taxquet decision, in France, having a similar although non-identical system. The law of 10.8.2011, amending the French code of criminal procedure, imposed a basic reasoning for convictions by the Cour d'assise [see Ambroise-Casterot and Bonfils (2011), p. 371].

[30] Taxquet v. Belgium, § 45: "fourteen Council of Europe member States have never had a jury system or any other form of lay adjudication in criminal matters or have abolished it: Albania, Andorra, Armenia, Azerbaijan, Bosnia and Herzegovina, Cyprus, Latvia, Lithuania, Luxembourg, Moldova, the Netherlands, Romania, San Marino and Turkey. In these States criminal courts are composed exclusively of professional judges".

[31] § 46: Bulgaria, Croatia, the Czech Republic, Denmark, Estonia, Finland, France, Germany, Greece, Hungary, Iceland, Italy, Liechtenstein, Monaco, Montenegro, Norway (in most cases), Poland, Portugal, Serbia, Slovakia, Slovenia, Sweden, "the former Yugoslav Republic of Macedonia" and Ukraine.

[32] § 47: Austria, Belgium, Georgia, Ireland, Malta, Norway (only in serious appeal cases), the Russian Federation, Spain, Switzerland (the Canton of Geneva until 1 January 2011), and the United Kingdom (England, Wales, Scotland and Northern Ireland).

[33] § 56.

[34] As to Portugal, the code of criminal procedure provides for a 'mitigated bifurcation', establishing a distinction between fact finding and sentencing, although as a matter of fact, there is no separation, in time, between the two decisions (see articles 368, 369, 371 of the Portuguese Code of Criminal Procedure).

Ancel[35] and the group of the so-called New Social Defence.[36] France, e.g., has recently strengthened the distinction between conviction and sentencing, with the law of 15 August 2015, on the individualisation of sentencing[37] and the following law of 23 March 2019,[38] implementing the first.

Regardless of the existence of a formal distinction (see, however, Sect. 6.1.3.2) between the decisions about guilt and sentencing, the latter represents, inevitably, the moment in which all the competing penal ideologies should reconcile: the lack of consensus about the very function(s) of punishment appears in sentencing, in the most evident way.[39] "Deterrence, retribution, rehabilitation and dangerousness represent the main competing ideologies whose implications clash with each other".[40]

Thus, although apparently too ambitious, the *fil rouge* of this analysis involves a general overview on one of the most disputed topics of criminal law, i.e. the rationales of punishment. The whole philosophical debate about the aim that criminal sanctions should achieve is influenced—although not polarised (see hereinafter)—by the opposing ideas of retribution, on the one hand (based on rigorous proportionality between criminal act and sanction), and incapacitation, on the other hand (based on the perpetrator's social dangerousness and aimed at safeguarding society from further harm). Indeed, an evaluation of criminal dangerousness cannot but be based on past facts, in order to identify possible risks of future misbehaviour. However, when such an element is taken into account at sentencing, there is a shift of the court's attention from the facts the individual has been convicted of, towards a prediction of specific crimes that she might commit in the future. The following paragraphs aim at summarising such a pressing conundrum, based on the caveat that, as said, the common law/civil law distinction still plays a relevant part in the development of the debate, that reached a climax, on both sides of the Atlantic Ocean, around the end of the nineteenth and in the first 30 years of the twentieth century. A growing reliance on psychology and sociology fostered confidence in the prediction of individuals' future behaviour and in the possibility to prevent violent and harmful conducts by those who had already been sentenced. Although rooted generally in the interest of the individualisation of punishment, the discussion led to very different results in Europe and the US, due to specific approaches to the rule of law.[41]

---

[35] In particular, Ancel (1964), p. 205.

[36] Theorised by Ancel (1954), *passim*. The doctrine criticised the traditional 'just deserts' approach to imprisonment, promoting a truly rehabilitation paradigm, in order to fulfil the goal to harmonising the social interest and the individual's one.

[37] Lasserre Capdeville (2015), p. 13.

[38] See Belloir (2019), p. 66.

[39] Lacey (1988), p. 16 ff.

[40] Norrie (2014), p. 335.

[41] Pifferi (2012), p. 326.

6.1.3.1 The European Approach

As to Europe, the paradox reached a climax with the clash between the 'classic' penological ideology, based on retribution, and the so-called positivistic ideology, and in particular the German *Moderne Schule*, inspired by the concept of criminal law as a form of social control, promoting a preventative purpose for the penalty.[42] The continental literature often defines the second theoretical trend as 'utilitarian-functionalist',[43] after Jeremy Bentham's traditional paradigm.[44] Such a theory tends to curb criminal law into an instrument to achieve a specific result, i.e., social control. In this view, culpability, the traditional foundation for penalty,[45] may not reconcile with the purpose of maintaining (or reconstructing) social order,[46] having been troubled by crime. As said, many jurisdictions, influenced by the latter, provided for a double-track system, based on both penalties and correctional measures (see ftn 2, 3 and 4), the first being proportional to the act, the second to the social risk posed by the convicted.[47] Although hypocritical,[48] such a distinction provided for the clear categorisation of desert and dangerousness, giving the latter its own specific relevance in criminological theory, resulting in one crucial consequence: many European continental jurisdictions started providing for minimum and maximum sentences, for any offence,[49] while common law systems stuck to the tradition of undetermined sentences, making sentencing a process almost breaking away from criminal law rules and principles.[50] However, as we will see hereinafter, sentencing has recently become less discretionary, even in English common-law.

In general terms, the English and Welsh system seems to represent a sort of fusion between the continental and the American traditions, or perhaps, it simply better emphasises the contradiction of those diverging legal theories. If, on the one hand, sentencing maxima now exists for many offences (and minima, for some), and sentencing guidelines, by the Court of Appeal and other bodies, flourished over

---

[42] Pelissero (2008), p. XIV.

[43] Bartoli (2005), p. 43.

[44] Although Bentham, in his theories about punishment, was very clear in rejecting unjust sanctions. As punishment is always evil, it can be accepted only if the offender's suffering can spare major suffering to others. Tonry (2019), p. 284.

[45] The principle of culpability is the premise of the state's power to punish: Kaufmann (1961), p. 15 ff.

[46] Jacobs (1993), p. 8.

[47] For an interesting overview on how the U.S. Sentencing Commission tried to reconcile these two paradigms: Dubber and Hörnle (2016), p. 9.

[48] Tonry (2019), p. 293: "extended confinement will feel like additional punishment to any affected offender".

[49] Pifferi (2012), p. 355.

[50] See Norrie (2014), p. 334: "Once we get beyond the conviction of the accused, the rules and principles of the criminal law tend to evaporate and the system becomes much more discretionary and less regulated by law".

the last decades (with some concern for judicial independence),[51] conflicting approaches were adopted in terms of preventative detention. The Criminal Justice Act 2003 introduced Imprisonment for Public Protection (IPP). Chapter 5 of the Act was entitled Dangerous Offenders and provided a list of 96 serious offences. Offenders having committed one of those crimes were presumed to be dangerous and were submitted to an indeterminate sentence, if the presumption was not rebutted.[52] Based on this, the judge would have fixed a minimum service term, after which the convicted could be released only when the parole board was convinced that she would no longer be a risk to the public. After some amendments in 2008, IPP was abandoned in 2012, due to several censures by the ECtHR and by English courts. Nevertheless, the current system still implies mandatory life imprisonment based on the risk of dangerousness for offenders who commit a second offence listed in a Schedule, attached to the Act. Also 'extended sentence' is provided, in a section of the Act, for violent and sexual offenders, who committed one of the 'listed offences'. As a result, offenders who would be submitted to IPP, before 2012, are not necessarily being treated less harshly under the new Act.[53] Moreover, the media has reported on many prisoners sentenced under the 2003 Act, who are still being submitted to the abolished regime of IPP.[54]

The recent 'back and forth' in the English and Welsh jurisdiction, echoed by the recent attention on digital predictive sentencing, demonstrates that the debate never truly polarised between retribution and incapacitation, desert and dangerousness, because these conflicting concepts are not truly completely independent, rather intertwined. Some suggest that, behind the comprehensive philosophical scholarship published over recent decades, lays the doubt that these opposing concepts (desert/dangerousness) respond to two different questions:[55] why do we punish? (desert) and how do we punish? (dangerousness).[56] Ultimately, the distinction between punishment and prevention could lay in the fact that, if the former absolutely conveys a punitive value, the latter does not necessarily do so, as incapacitation for preventive reasons does not need to be punitive.[57]

It has been correctly noted that such an unclear state of affairs depends on the factor that a criminal law system requires competing values to be balanced into equal fairness,[58] in which the weight assigned to social security must align with

---

[51] See Ashworth (2015), p. 54 ff.

[52] Redmayne (2015), p. 250.

[53] Redmayne (2015), p. 251.

[54] Grierson (2019). Although an action was announced in 2016 [Barrett (2016)], at the time of writing several prisoners were still waiting to be freed by a parole board.

[55] Ryberg (2019), p. 52.

[56] Hoskins (2019), p. 94.

[57] Redmayne (2015), p. 272; Hoskins (2019), p. 94 ff., distinguishing between intentionally burdensome treatment and non-intended burdens: the core of punishment is a deprivation of rights and liberties being burdensome; on the contrary, the deprivation would not be considered punishment.

[58] Tonry (2019), pp. 270, 291: a comprehensive jurisprudence of just punishment would incorporate proportionality, fairness, equal treatment, parsimony (offenders should never be punished more severely than can be justified by appropriate, valid, normative purposes).

human dignity, right to hope,[59] rehabilitation. Although some European Constitutions recognise the rehabilitative purpose of punishment,[60] it is undisputed that the balance between such values is not fixed, and varies over the decades, along with political and social feelings. Against this backdrop, the line between repression and prevention blurs: it actually happened in many domestic legal orders, where, despite a formal double-track system of sanctions and measures, the individual's social dangerousness (inherent to measures), ends up by overlapping into sanctions, also becoming an index in sentencing.

Cherry-picking some interesting examples among the European legal orders, art. 133 of the Italian Penal Code (*seriousness of the offence, to be considered in sentencing*), refers, specifically, in its second paragraph, to the *propensity for crime* by the convicted. For this purpose, the sentencing judge must consider: the motive that pushed the offender to commit the act; her character; her criminal record; her social behaviour, before and after the offence; her and her family's walk of life. Thus, not only may such indexes be considered by the court with regard to the defendant's dangerousness and, therefore, for the application of a measure (*misura di sicurezza*), but they must also be taken into account in sentencing, for the determination of a penalty, between the minimum and maximum provided by the law.

It is worth reminding that the Italian Penal Code dates back to 1930 and it has always been considered a synthesis between the two conflicting ideologies mentioned above, i.e. the 'classic' and the 'positive' school. In this sense, it still demonstrates how difficult it can be to draw a line between retribution and social defence, preventing the latter from also playing a role in sentencing. Although public opinion has changed a lot since 1930, with regard to these issues, art. 133 Cp has never been amended on this point. Moreover, the double-track system, based on sanctions and measures, meant to incapacitate the dangerous perpetrator, failed to deliver a good sense of major security and, more and more, penalty has become, in Italy, an instrument of repression and prevention, at the same time.[61]

As to France, the debate about the purpose of criminal law and penalty was dominated, in the nineteenth and twentieth century, by the so-called *humanisme pénal*, rooted in the *travaux préparatoirs* by the *Assemblée Constituante*, that led to the 1791 French Criminal Code.[62] It is worth noting that, in 2008, France introduced a form of post-sentence preventative detention (*rétention de sureté*), for persons with a high risk of recidivism, having been sentenced to long term imprisonment, for very serious offences committed against minor victims (homicide or manslaughter, torture, rape, kidnapping, or also for the same offences, aggravated,

59 Ashworth and Zedner (2019), p. 127ff.

60 See art. 27 Italian Constitution; the Spanish Constitution, Part 1, Chapter 2, Division 1, Section 25.2.

61 Pelissero (2008), p. XV.

62 Notwithstanding such noble tradition, a real turning-point in the execution of penalties was represented by the law of 15 June 2000 (strengthening the presumption of innocence and the victims' rights), that transformed the execution into a judicial, rather than administrative, process: see Senna (2010), p. 47.

if perpetrated on adults). Art. 706-53-13 states that, at the moment of sentencing, the Cour d'Assise can establish that, after serving the sentence, the person, on the assessment of her serious mental disorders, should be reconsidered for the application of the *rétention de sûreté*. Before release, the convicted must be examined by a board of experts, that may suggest the public prosecution office to ask the application of the *rétention*. Such a measure entails the placement of the person under medical treatment in specific public structures, for terms of one-year, and is applied by a special regional jurisdiction, and can be renewed based on art. 706-53-16.

Moreover, as said in Sect. 6.1, the scope of penalty was recently amended, in 2014, by reforming art. 130-1 of the current French Criminal Code and art. 707 of the Code of criminal procedure. Also Art. 132-1 of the Criminal Code was amended, introducing a reference to "individualisation". Actually, the provision refers to the character of the perpetrator, although this is not the sole criterion to be considered by the judge.[63] However, in continuity with the abovementioned *humanisme pénal*,[64] the reform focuses on the individual's character not to incapacitate her, but rather to tailor the best sanction for her rehabilitation,[65] provided that detention must be the last resort (art. 132-19 C.P.).

As to Germany, the determination of penalty is essentially based on Chapter two of the Criminal code, that does not involve evaluations of the defendant's future behaviour. The will and the psychological approach (*mens rea*) are evaluated only in terms of culpability for the offence the defendant is charged with. Her behaviour after the fact is taken into account as a mitigating factor, with regard to her effort to rectify the negative consequences (material and moral) of it. The German system, like the Italian one, is inspired by a rigorous two-track model, based on sanctions and measures. As said, the convicted's dangerousness can be considered for the application of a *Sicherung or Besserung Maßregel* (Sect. 6.1), which can even consist of a non-fixed term of deprivation of liberty. However, the German regulation of measures recently underwent major amendments, suggested by some of the ECtHR's and the German Constitutional Court's rulings. In fact, in its judgment of *M. v. Germany*, the Strasbourg Court held that German preventative detention (*Sicherungsverwahrung*) was a "penalty",[66] and, so far, should imply all the guarantees of Articles 5 and 7 of the European Convention. Pursuant to this judgment, the

[63] It is worth noting that the Court d'Assise, having jurisdiction for the most serious crimes, had not the duty, until very recently, to provide specific reasoning about the court's choice of the penalties, to be applied in the specific case. Such duty has been recently introduced by a decision by the Conseil constitutionnel (2 March 2018), based on the principle of individualization of penalties, enshrined by art. 8 of the Declaration des droits de l'homme et du citoyen [Dadoun (2018), p. 805 ff.].

[64] See the report by CNCDH (Commission Nationale Consultative des Droits de l'Homme) on the draft, 27.3.2014.

[65] Zentara-Logeay (2019), § 27.

[66] ECtHR, M. v. Germany, 17,12,2009, § 133: "the Court, looking behind appearances and making its own assessment, concludes that preventive detention under the German Criminal Code is to be qualified as a "penalty" for the purposes of Article 7 § 1 of the Convention".

German Federal Constitutional Court, Bundesverfassungsgericht, recommended a complete recast of the domestic system,[67] that led to the adoption of a new law on 5 December 2012 (*Gesetz zur bundesrechtlichen Umsetzung des Abstandsgebotes im Recht der Sicherungsverwahrung*).

6.1.3.2 The American Approach

As to the US, the debate about individualisation of punishment resulted in a strong shift towards undetermined sentencing, allocating the discretion over the length of the deprivation of liberty to boards of experts, rather than courts.[68] However, such a trend, theorised in the '70s of the nineteenth century, was not generally accepted. There was strong criticism about its inconstancy with the traditional principles of *nulla poena* and *punitur quia peccatum est*.[69] On the one hand, the traditional balance between powers, legislative, judicial and administrative, was at stake: not only would the undetermined sentence system remove the legislative power to establish minimum and maximum penalties from the lawmaker (as provided by the Constitution), but it would also replace the judicial discretion in sentencing, with an administrative board's arbitrariness, departing from the general principles of criminal law. On the other hand, the fundamental beacon of the whole of Western ideology, freedom of the will, seemed to be in danger. Criminal responsibility and punishment were shifted from culpability (i.e. blameworthiness of one's own free behaviour) to the realm of the perpetrator's character and criminological type. The arguments could not be more serious…

However, the advocates of 'individualised punishment' succeeded on the basis of a bitter criticism of the criminal justice system of the time. In fact, a feeling of strong dissatisfaction had grown in the US, because of the blatant differences in sentencing among the federal States. Legal historians report a huge concern for bias and the arbitrariness of courts, the latter being scarcely guided by local criminal rules in the difficult task of determining criminal sanctions. Against this backdrop, the proposal of allocating sentencing to experts' boards, operating on the basis of one common index, i.e. science, turned out to be successful. Moreover, the carrying out of the sentence and its periodical review were to be considered, more correctly, administrative duties, rather than judicial, to be performed by an administrative body.[70] Thanks to the bifurcation between verdict (on guilt) and sentence, the advocates of the undetermined sentence theory found a way to allocate the punitive power between judiciary and administrative boards that did not call for Constitutional amendments. Law still provided for a minimum and maximum sentence and courts

[67] See BVerfG, 4 May 2011, 2 BvR 2365/09, BVerfGE 128, 326.

[68] Pifferi (2012), p. 338.

[69] For a general overview, Friedman (1994), p. 159 ff., 304 ff.

[70] *Woods v. State,* 130 Tenn. 100,114 (1914).

still had the power to assess guilt, for the sake of the rule of law…[71] Apparently, this was enough to overcome the fear of 'administrativisation' of criminal justice, leading to the general spreading, between US States, of progressive treatment and experts' boards, by the 20s of the twentieth century. This was to become a benchmark, distinguishing the US and the European continental tradition, where, as said, bifurcation between verdict on fact-finding and sentencing was, and still is, rare.

In light of this situation, the twentieth century represented, in the US, the flourishing era of predictive sentencing, fuelling psycho-criminological research on the risk of violent behaviour and recidivism, that will be the subject of the following paragraphs. As a matter of fact, the results of that research pushed towards a specific paradigm: risk assessment and risk prevention have always been associated with incapacitation, that is to say with deprivation of liberty until dangerousness stops. However, as we will see hereafter, based on the evaluation of criminogenic factors, risk assessment is an instrument of measurement of anti-social behaviour, not an answer to it.[72] Notwithstanding this assumption, the debate about the most suitable balance between desert and prevention, in punishment, never ended. Recent US history in penology highlights the existence of swinging trends. In the Seventies of the twentieth century, a shift back, towards retributivism started, based on massive incarceration rates and their serious impact on minorities and poorer groups. Individualised sentencing was to be replaced by a stricter compliance to the Federal Sentencing Guides (and other guidelines developed in the different states), reducing the impact of the individual's character. However, it was in the Eighties that a new trend of 'selective incapacitation' was promoted, based on the assumption that 'career criminals' can be identified through their personal and psychological features and criminal history. Despite the serious doubts about the accuracy of prediction, the selective incapacitation doctrine was highly successful and, although perhaps not mainstream,[73] it greatly affected many North-American jurisdictions. In particular, in the Nineties, the New Penology definitively boosted the prioritisation of risk management over rehabilitation.[74]

The recent digitalisation of risk assessment tools just revived several old conundrums.[75] Firstly, is it acceptable to extend one's punishment on the basis of the risk of re-offending? Secondly, how precise and reliable are both the risk assessment's premise and results? Thirdly, is incapacitation the only possible way to address the risk of re-offending?[76]

---

[71] Warner (1899), p. 222.

[72] Zara and Farrington (2016), p. 150. In close connection, Stevenson (2018), p. 306 argues that the tool may be accurate in predicting misconducts, but the solutions taken to ameliorate the risk may even exacerbate it…

[73] Kehl et al. (2017), p. 5.

[74] See Feeley and Simons (1992), p. 449.

[75] Hannah-Moffat (2013), p. 270. See also Kehl et al. (2017), p. 6, focusing on the possibility that digital risk assessment may turn into a resurrection of selective incapacitation.

[76] See Hoskins (2019), p. 103, criticizing the intentional burden traditionally associated with incapacitation. On the contrary, measures preventing risks should be "foreseeably but non intentionally burdensome civil measures aimed at protecting members of the public".

As to the first question, the variety of the arguments is still broad. Besides those who advocate compliance of risk-based sentencing with the principle of blameworthiness,[77] others argue that predictive sentencing is not acceptable either empirically, or morally, invoking for abandoning it.[78] This brief overview of both the European and the American backgrounds highlights relevant uncertainty about the role that future risk of re-offending should play in sentencing. Even in legal orders based on a strict distinction between culpability and dangerousness (e.g. the Italian one), elements of risk assessment end up slipping into the sentencing process. The effect of this may vary according to the general criminal policy of the time: in the 1930 Italian criminal code, the outcome of risk-prediction results in a potentially aggravating factor; in the recent French amendment of the criminal procedure code, the new capacity for risk-prediction is aimed at granting a more individualised sentence, reducing the impact of imprisonment.

As to the second and third questions, the following paragraph is not ambitious enough to give decisive answers, but only to provide some basic concepts, allowing an understanding of one of the most debated issues today.

6.2 Risk Assessments, Predictive Sentencing and the 'Daubert Test': Complicated Interactions Behind the Recent Digitalisation

According to the recent history, briefly summarised above, it is clear that prediction of the defendant's future behaviour plays a crucial role in sentencing, especially in the US, but not solely. According to a recent review,[79] 39 federal States have their own risk assessment tool; In England and Wales, OASys is the offenders assessment system, routinely used in the National Offender Management Service (NOMS) within which several risk assessment instruments are employed, depending on the criminogenic needs of the offender assessed.[80] Other European jurisdictions do not seem to have institutionalised risk assessment tools.

Risk assessment is the main instrument for evaluating potential (re-)offending. The term is not specific at all, as it is used in many different technical and scientific areas. However, as noted,[81] it is in the criminal justice setting that it has received the

[77] Slobogin (2019), p. 121. The Author says that risk factors such as employment status, neighbourhood, or diagnosis are not blameworthy in themselves, but are evidence of what a person will decide to do in the future: "Risk assessment at sentencing could be said to predict future culpable choices".

[78] Tonry (2019), p. 290.

[79] Fazel (2019), p. 197.

[80] Redmayne (2015), p. 255 ff. However, the author reports a trend of the English and Welsh courts to merge the results of actuarial risk assessment with their own intuition (p. 264).

[81] Zara and Farrington (2016), p. 148.

most ambivalent reactions. Nevertheless, it has became crucial in several areas of decision-making, both at the pre-trial stage, sentencing and parole, and also in the follow-up of psychiatric situations.[82]

Based on the classical assumption that "nothing predicts behaviour like (or better than) previous behaviour",[83] "such tools include a set of risk factors, which may or may not be weighted, to provide a classification of risk (high, medium, low), a probabilistic score (i.e., a percentage probability of re-offending within a certain timeframe) or both".[84] Both in general and in specific forensic terms, the matter is the validation of methods and instruments, that must obtain acceptance by the scientific community. As demonstrated below in Sects. 6.3 and 6.4, on the basis of two real American cases, falsifiability is the core issue, the fil rouge of the whole matter of predictive sentencing. Let us summarise, then, the main features of the long-standing discussion about the scientific foundations of risk assessment.

6.2.1 Risk Assessment and the Development of Psycho-Criminological Theories

In a contemporary approach to risk assessment, it is important to start the analysis by setting the correct premise. As said in Sect. 6.1.3.2, despite a persistent trend to link risk of re-offending with incapacitation, the real purpose of risk assessment should be to inform intervention and sustain prevention by identifying rewarding alternatives to crime.[85] And the more the prediction of the risk is reliable, the more such a goal is reachable. Scholars in the field usually start by underlining the difference between probability and prediction, the first being a statement about the chance that a specific happening will occur, while the latter indicates how likely it is that such a happening will occur in a specific time-frame.[86] This theory is at the foundation of the difference between scientific research on- and practical application of risk assessment, which is crucial for our analysis: risk of recidivism or violent behaviour is not a static measure, but can vary, due to various conditions, such as a successful treatment, the intervention of positive factors (developmental and protective), the changing of the context over time, and a combination of these factors. Thus, appropriate use of risk assessment should imply awareness of these elements.

As risk always entails uncertainty,[87] identifying risk factors is the first challenge for scholars and practitioners in the field. Criminal behaviour almost always has multiple causes (although the term 'causation factor' seems more correct in the

[82] See Zara and Farrington (2016), p. 150.

[83] Kvaraceus (1966), p. 53.

[84] Fazel (2019), p. 197.

[85] Zara and Farrington (2016), p. 151.

[86] Zara and Farrington (2016), p. 151.

[87] Gigerenzer (2008), passim.

realm of social science, non-deterministic)[88] and the interaction of several factors is usually considered in an offender's risk assessment.

Thus, the first step is listing causational factors impinging on criminal behaviour. However, terminology is crucial, and risk factors should not be confused with correlates. The latter are linked to an outcome: while risk factors always precede the outcome, correlates tend to be indicators of an outcome that has already occurred.[89] Risk factors consist of two types: static and dynamic. The first do not change, like sex, or change in only one possible direction (e.g. age). The latter (dynamic) may change according to the individual's situation and they include criminogenic needs, i.e. aspects of a person, or her situation, that when changing, may imply a change in her criminal behaviour. There is no evidence that either static or dynamic factors are more reliable indicators of risk: both insufficient, *per se*, they must all be taken into account for a successful assessment. Nevertheless, it is not possible to conceive a tool considering all possible risk factors,[90] as much as it is impossible (for the most recent tools, i.e. of III and IV generation) to cover every potential protective factor (strength or protective factors reduce/neutralise the effects of risk factors and enhance resilience).[91] However, integration of different sources of information is crucial in granting reliable results.[92]

A second fundamental step in understanding risk assessment is the relationship between the group and the individual. Social sciences gather statistical data to reach general conclusions, applicable to groups of cases. The 'G2I' (Group to Individual) paradigm is at the core of the debate about forensic predictive tools. Prediction of future behaviour can only be based on the observation of a group, and is a function of group outcomes. Zara and Farrington report an iconic passage by Sir Conan Doyle, in which the author conveys this very concept, in the voice of Sherlock Holmes: "you can never foretell what any one man will do, but you can say with precision what an average number will add up to. Individuals vary, but percentages remain constant". The accuracy of a scientific prediction is based on the largest sample possible, i.e., the greatest number of cases examined. In addition, a forensic prediction is reliable if it correctly demonstrates the individual's propensity to re-offend. The scale of these two evaluations is different and, for this reason, risk assessment is often criticised for its inaccuracy in translating group phenomena into individual instances.[93] The instruments to enact practical, individual risk assessment may be different, due to the approach they use in translating psycho-criminological theories into a personal evaluation.

One main, traditional, distinction is between actuarial instruments and clinical, professional, judgment instruments. For a basic and initial distinction, it is possible

[88] Farrington (1988), p. 158 ff.

[89] Kraemer et al. (2005), passim.

[90] Zara and Farrington (2016), p. 155.

[91] Zara and Farrington (2016), p. 155.

[92] Shlonsky and Wagner (2005), p. 410 ff.

[93] Redmayne (2015), p. 258.

to say that actuarial instruments address historical and static risk factors, while professional judgment instruments take into account dynamic risk factors.

Scholarship now distinguishes between four generations of risk assessment tools.[94] The first, predominant until the fifties of the past century, was characterised by unstructured clinical judgment: correctional staff and clinical professionals (psychologists, psychiatrists, social workers) were asked to evaluate, on the basis of their professional experience, the need for extended incapacitative measures. Professional intuition was at the core of such a method and for these reasons, it was criticised for having very low inter-rater reliability (inter-rater reliability is the measure of agreement in the results achieved by independent raters, i.e. researchers measuring the same cases independently) and for crediting characteristics that are not empirically related to criminal behaviour. In summary, such instruments were not transparent and structured and could not be independently validated, allowing room for bias and arbitrary procedures.

During the Seventies, actuarial instruments developed on the basis of static factors, that could be scored and summed up to provide a low, medium or high index of risk of re-offending. Such tools are based on existing, official data sources (e.g. official records), treated in statistical terms: based on statistical rules, different items are combined, for a comprehensive risk evaluation. It is worth underling that risk factors used in actuarial tools are more likely to predict, rather than explain, recidivism.[95] And actually, the new tools proved immediately more accurate in prediction and many states in the US and Canada started assigning different supervision practices to the different scores recorded prisoners. Actuarial methods clearly outperformed clinical judgment, even when they have access to the same official data sources.

It is possible to say that, in the US, the shift towards a 'more actuarial', or evidence-based approach to sentencing was due to four main claims: judicial discretion and bias lead to unequal sentencing; risk assessment can alleviate high incarceration levels, these being both racially discriminatory and expensive; low-risk defendants should be diverted towards non-incarcerating solutions; high discretion is at odds with accountability, transparency and consistency.[96] However, it is of crucial importance to reinforce that static risk evaluations tend to portray an individual as unchangeable, without taking into account the effect of a possible evolution in her condition, influencing the risk of re-offending. Some authors claim that actuarial instruments tend to be informed by race and therefore have individual and structural racialised effects.[97] Purportedly neutral risk assessment techniques are also said to enact systemic inequality, as stressed in Sect. 6.3. In view of this, actuarial

[94] Zara (2016), passim; Kehl et al. (2017), p. 8.

[95] Spitzer and Maccarone (2007), p. 1 ff.

[96] Hannah-Moffat and Struthers Montford (2019), p. 177.

[97] Hannah-Moffat and Struthers Montford (2019), p. 179.

risk de-individualises the assessment of risk by categorising offenders based on unalterable group characteristics.[98]

A third generation of tools is based on the consideration of both risk factors and criminogenic needs, whose difference was explained above. The idea of integrating risks and needs allows for better understanding of "how the past influenced the future".[99] Structured professional judgment tries to bridge the gap between the purely clinical practice and the more scientific approach of actuarial instruments. Rooted in sound scientific knowledge, these methods leave room also for professional discretion and have practical relevance.[100] In particular, their structure allows for the validation of results. Grounded in such achievements, the fourth generation of instruments is based on the evaluation of a larger range of factors, that include risk, protective factors and responsivity factors, that affect treatment and compliance.[101] This expansion of factors allows for a more accurate analysis, in which non-criminogenic needs are also considered in the functioning of an offender. Although lacking in a significant correlation with criminal behaviour, elements such as e.g. self-esteem, anxiety, victimization issues may facilitate the positive outcome of a treatment, because criminal behaviour is the result of the complex interaction between cognitive, emotional personality, biological factors and environmental cost-rewards contingencies.[102]

In this regard, the evolution of risk assessment tools shows a progression from an intense effort to predict future offending behaviour to a stronger need to understand the reasons for offending behaviour. Along the way, hundreds of risk assessment tools have been created around the world, with general or specific purposes, some of them have been in use for decades, others are more recent. Some of them proved more accurate in prediction, some less so. Some displayed positive outcomes in the offenders' treatment, others revealed blatant discriminatory effect. Thus, the best scholarship in the field engaged in rating the validity of risk assessment tools.

For the sake of clarity, the foregoing review is based on sentencing risk assessment tools, focused on the prediction of reoffending, with a view to an individualised treatment. However, as said in Sect. 6.1, specific risk assessment tools can be tailored for the pre-trial phase, in particular for decisions on bail release. As seen in Sect. 6.1.2, pre-trial detention, usually, is applied to prevent 'procedural risk', primarily flight risk, and should not, in any way, be considered an anticipation of the subsequent punishment, such as rehabilitation or incapacitation. In fact, before a final conviction, freedom is the rule, and the decision about release after arrest (or about a pre-trial detention order) is crucial, detention being extraordinary, at this stage. For these reasons, judicial systems usually impose strongly supported pre-trial decisions, although judges have a very difficult task, in predicting the threats

[98] Hannah-Moffat and Struthers Montford (2019), p. 182.

[99] Taxman and Thanner (2006), p. 31.

[100] Hart (1998), p. 121 ff.

[101] Zara (2016), p. 10 ff.

[102] Zara and Farrington (2016), p. 165.

that leaving the accused at large could pose... In this situation, the most traditional solution is the judicial duty of extended reasoning. It is quite common, at least in several continental jurisdictions, to call for extended reasoning when pre-trial detention (or other coercive measures) is at stake. The ECtHR upheld and suggested such a solution, imposing on the public authority a specific duty to support the remand in custody with precise pieces of evidence. Another solution is looking for such evidence in the realm of risk assessment tools.

6.2.1.1 Pre-trail Risk Assessment

According to recent research,[103] one tool is widely used in the US, in pre-trial detention and release decisions: 28 jurisdictions (and among them three States) use the Public Safety Assessment (PSA)[104] to assist the judge in the decision about the risks of leaving the accused at large, before trial. The software was developed in 2013 and, according to the institution that promoted it (the Laura and John Arnold Foundation),[105] it is useful in reducing the number of individuals detained before trial.[106] Based on 9 factors,[107] the instrument is actuarial, relying on the individual's age, current charge and criminal history: race, ethnicity and geography are not taken into consideration as, according to the designers, they would not improve accuracy in prediction. The instrument is said to having been created on the basis of the largest data set ever collected, i.e. 750,000 cases, from about 300 jurisdictions: according to the designers, this makes it a nationally-wide validated tool.

The tool does not need an interview with the accused: the information can be taken out of her criminal record and other general information, known to the public authority. Based on algorithms tailored to purpose, the tool produces a scale of the individual's risk under three different parameters (FTA, Failure To Appear; NCA, New Criminal Activity; NVCA, New Violent Criminal Activity), that can be used by a judge or a court, along with the so-called Decision-Framework,[108] to decide whether the arrested will be released or detained. The peculiarity of this instrument,

---

[103] Kehl et al. (2017), p. 10.

[104] https://www.psapretrial.org/about/background.

[105] The foundation was established in 2010 by Laura (an attorney and former oil company executive), and John (an investor) Arnold.

[106] https://www.psapretrial.org/about/background. However, Stevenson (2018), p. 305, highlights that arguments and 'facts' usually reported in the discussion about risk assessment stem form non-academic reports by the agencies that designed the instruments.

[107] Age at current arrest; Current violent offense (current violent offense and 20 years old or younger); Pending charge at the time of the offense; Prior misdemeanor conviction; Prior felony conviction (prior conviction [misdemeanor or felony]); Prior violent conviction; Prior failure to appear in the past 2 years; Prior failure to appear older than 2 years; Prior sentence to incarceration.

[108] https://www.psapretrial.org/implementation/guides/managing-risk/guide-to-the-pretrial-decision-framework. According to the text, "the PSA is used to *measure* a person's pretrial risk, whereas the DF is used to help *manage* that risk".

if compared to the ones that have been considered so far, is the ability to deliver a 'Failure To Appear' index. The risk factors considered by PSA under this parameter are: Pending charge at the time of offense (Y/N); Prior conviction (Y/N); Prior failure to appear in the past 2 years (No/Once/2 or more times); Prior failure to appear, older than 2 years (Y/N).

I refer to PSA as paradigmatic of the North-American context.[109] In fact, the more that traditional monetary bail proved discriminatory towards the poorest social groups[110] (and, thus, potentially in breach of the Eighth Amendment to the Federal Constitution),[111] the quicker pretrial risk assessment tools spread around the US,[112] pushing also for the creation of pretrial services programs, focusing both on release and diversion.[113]

There are few studies focusing on the real impact of the use of pretrial risk assessment. Some researchers have highlighted that the effects of it are scarce and not permanent.[114] Nevertheless, the movement for bail reform is one rare area of bi-partisan agreement, pushing for abandoning monetary bail, in favour of effective management of risk.[115] But what is effective in predicting and managing pretrial threats? Are predictive tools accurate? This argument pushes pretrial risk assessment into the same area as sentencing risk assessment. How to measure if and how such risk assessment tools are more accurate than human intuition in predicting the risks of leaving the arrested at large?

[109] PSA was developed and piloted in Kentucky. Before the instrument was released, a local law (House Bill, 463, 2011) made the use of risk assessment mandatory in bail decisions. Since its launch in 2013, PSA spread to other 27 jurisdictions (among which, 2 other States) and has been pointed out as the scheme for a general bail review bill (Pretrial Integrity and Safety Act), presented in 2017 at the US Senate by Senators Kamala D. Harris (dem.) and Rand Paul (rep.) (read their opinion at https://www.nytimes.com/2017/07/20/opinion/kamala-harris-and-rand-paul-lets-reform-bail.html).

[110] See Criminal Justice Policy Program, Harvard Law School, Moving Beyond Money: A Primer on Bail Reform, 2016, Harvard Law School, 6 ff.

[111] The Eight Amendment prohibits "excessive bail", but, unfortunately, it does not define the meaning of 'excessive'.

[112] Stevenson (2018), p. 307.

[113] Van Nostrand (2012), p. 2.

[114] Stevenson (2018), p. 308 f., argues that the effect of the reform passed in Kentucky was an immediate boost in non-monetary release and, in general, an increase in release of moderate-risk accused. Nevertheless, in the following 2 years, the effect was reversed and the remand on custody rates became higher than they were before the reform. The introduction of PSA had no significant results in terms of release rates ad it seems that only 29% of arrested are released on non-monetary bond at the first bail setting.

[115] Stevenson (2018), p. 320.

6.2.2 Evaluation of Risk Assessment Tools

In this very short survey of risk assessment tools, one element has been repeatedly stressed. *Ex post* validation is crucial for the understanding of a tool's performance and, as said, the less methods are structured, the more their validation is difficult. Several leading experts in the field tried to rate validity of the major existing risk assessment tools, based on a list of basic standards. Zara and Farrington highlighted six basic indexes to be considered for this purpose:

a. The theoretical and developmental foundations
b. The process of construction of the instrument: its history and its established or upcoming pedigree in the scientific community
c. The identification and the inclusion of risk factors that demonstrate predictive validity
d. The inter-rater reliability (the degree to which the results achieved from independent raters, using the same instrument, are consistent)
e. The accuracy in predicting the risk of reoffending and error reduction
f. The significance/usefulness of the instrument in determining nature, severity, likelihood of future risk posed by individuals and the clinical utility in predisposing risk formulation and risk management planning.

However, talking about validity requires some crucial clarifications. First and foremost, validity is different from reliability. The latter is a measurement of precision; the first (validity), of accuracy. Validity confirms that an instrument will really measure what it is supposed to measure.[116] Thus, general validity is the ability of a method to distinguish the risk of offending between a recidivist and the rest of the non-recidivist population. Indeed, validity is the meaningfulness of a method: it is not a quality of the test, rather of the use of the test.[117] Moreover, it is important to distinguish validity in the sample on which the instrument is built on, from its validity in a different sample (construction sample/validation sample).

Other scholars, like Fazel and Wolf, also engaged in testing the performance of an instrument, based on the existence of two approaches: discrimination and calibration.[118] Discrimination is based on: sensitivity (proportion of people who actually offended, having been classified as 'high risk'), specificity (proportion of people who did not offend, having been classified as 'low risk'). Positive predictive value and negative predictive value are the measurements corresponding to sensitivity and specificity. The false negative rate, indicates the proportion of offenders who were not identified as 'high risk' by the tool, but who still offended, while the false positive rate, indicates the proportion of people who were assessed as high risk, but who did not offend. The other key to measuring the performance is calibration,

[116] Zara and Farrington (2016), p. 221.
[117] Anastasi (1982), passim.
[118] Fazel (2019), p. 198.

comparing the predicted risk with the observed risk. However, calibration is scarcely reported in literature.[119]

According to Fazel, the most recent reviews of existing risk assessment tools highlighted, in general, an insufficient availability of information about the instruments' performance and this brought her and her co-author to propose a ten-points guide for the evaluation of risk assessment tools, similar, in some aspects, to Zara and Farrington's one:

a. Did the study (deriving the tool) follow a protocol?
b. How were variables selected for the tool?
c. How were variables weighted?
d. How were other parameters selected?
e. Has internal validation been done?
f. Has the tool been externally validated?
g. Has this validation been done in the population of interest?
h. Has the validation been conducted using robust methods?
i. Has the validation study reported essential information?
j. Is the risk assessment tool useful, feasible and acceptable?

Applying this decalogue, Fazel reached the conclusion that a major number of existing tools, should probably not be used for prediction.[120] Actually, for many of them there is no sufficient evidence-base supporting their use in courts, not only because of a systematic lack of information (often due to their commercial nature), but also because the random tests always give extremely high rates of false positives and negatives.[121]

Many, although not all, of the reviewed risk assessment tools are digital, in the sense that they are incorporated into a software and take advantage of machine learning algorithms. Thus, in such cases, the calculation of 'traditional', high, medium, low rate of offending risk is automated, based on vast sets of constantly updating data, 'feeding' the predictive model.[122] Does this factor impact on the risk assessment tools' transparency? Is the digital turn further affecting the reliability of such instruments? Without anticipating the conclusions, it may be argued that the digital turn in risk assessment shifted the general public's opinion and attention towards an issue that tended to be confined, previously, into a specific professional area.

[119] Fazel (2019), p. 201.
[120] Fazel (2019), p. 208.
[121] Fazel (2019), p. 208.
[122] Kehl et al. (2017), p. 9.

6.2.3 Rating Pre-trial Risk Assessment

The evaluation of pretrial risk assessment tools is based on different contexts. First and foremost, we acknowledged (Sect. 6.2.1.1) that pretrial risk assessment is a relatively new trend, based on the recent mistrust and critique of traditional monetary bail bonds. Based on serious arguments for the unconstitutionality of monetary bail, a strong movement for reforming bail spread throughout the US, prioritising effective risk management over monetary bonds. In actual fact, the burdensome, awful, monetary bond may prove useless in bail decisions, if "in principle an algorithm could also make these predictions. Just as pixel patterns can be used to predict presence of a face, information about the defendant and their case could be used to predict flight or public safety risk".[123]

Against this backdrop, several aspects must be highlighted. Firstly, referring back to the most popular pretrial risk assessment tool in the US, at the moment, i.e. PSA, it is worth highlighting that its main difference to other actuarial instruments is the FTA index. I reported above the factors that PSA considers to be relevant for the evaluation of the individual's propensity to abscond. However, it seems that there is no comprehensive literature about the meaningfulness of those factors in terms of effective risk of flight. While criminogenic factors at the basis of sentencing risk assessment have been widely discussed by scholars, over the last century, at least, it seems to me that there is no sufficiently convincing academic literature demonstrating the relevance of the FTA factors. It seems that there is a lack of literature demonstrating that the incorporation of those factors into an actuarial instrument will outperform the judge's individual evaluation. Secondly, scholars, trying to confront algorithmic pretrial risk assessment tools to judicial decisions, cannot directly observe the judges' predictions. In fact, a defendant can be remanded in custody both because the judge estimated a high risk of absconding (or offending), or simply because the judge overestimated her ability to pay, establishing a bond that she cannot afford. Moreover, the judge's individual evaluation can be influenced by factors other than risk, such as proportion with the current charge, notwithstanding a high score in risk of absconding or offending.[124] Thus, only a rough proxy can be used as a measure of human performance in estimating pretrial risk...[125] Taking into account all these arguments, scholars have argued that it is unclear whether digital pretrial risk assessment tools really outperform humans at predicting pretrial risks.[126] On top of this, due to the fact that instruments like PSA

---

[123] Kleinberg et al. (2018), p. 240.

[124] It is worth remembering that some jurisdiction (e.g. the Italian one), provide for a specific principle of proportionality, in pretrial coercive measures, between the offence the arrested is charged with and the measure to be applied. The first index to be considered by the judge is proportionality to the current charge and the second is adequacy to the effective risk of the case (of absconding, or tampering with evidence, or offending), detention being the last resort.

[125] Stevenson (2018), p. 324.

[126] Stevenson (2018), p. 325.

are based solely on information taken out of files and records, with no need for an interview with the defendant, some have criticised their structure. It sounds contradictory to claim for reform of the bail system by suggesting instruments that are completely based on data pulled from the system under reform itself…[127] As a consequence, it was remarked, with regard to the bail reform movement in the US: "this is the stark, unfortunate irony at the heart of today's bail reform: today's pretrial risk assessment tools reflect and reinforce the very patterns of failure to appear that new, innovative policies work to change".[128]

6.3 A Famous Case of 'Predictive Sentencing' from Wisconsin…

As anticipated, in the revived international debate that developed around the theme of risk assessment and predictive sentencing, due to the use of computational models to calculate the risk of re-offending, one case has become globally known and it is Loomis v. Wisconsin. This case was definitively decided by the Supreme Court of Wisconsin on 31 July 2016[129] and was the object of the attention of key media in 2017.[130] In public opinion, this decision has become, precisely, the guide for the delegation of decision-making choices from man to machine, but, in spite of the relevant critical arguments that will be underlined, this decision entails different scenarios. The Loomis case will be confronted with another recent North-American decision, with the aim of pointing out a whole range of problems relating to the idea of using psycho-criminological risk assessment tools in criminal proceedings. As anticipated in Chap. 2, different complexity profiles overlap in this scenario. The discomfort of delegating a purely human activity to a machine is preceded by another phenomenon: the preference for algorithmic decision-makers instead of the judge's discretion. These, indeed, are not necessarily operated by a machine: we have seen that, in their essence, they are normative statements, in mathematical form that subtract an evaluation from individual intuition, to circumscribe it into a predetermined relationship.

127 Logan Koepke and Robinson (2018), p. 1751.

128 Logan Koepke and Robinson (2018), p. 1764.

129 State v. Loomis, 881 NW 2d 749 (Wis 2016). About the decision see *Criminal Law – Sentencing Guidelines – Wisconsin Supreme Court Requires Warnings before Use of Algorithmic Risk Assessment in Sentencing – State v. Loomis*, in *Harvard Law Review*, 2017, p. 1530 ss.

130 Liptak (2017).

6.3.1 The Facts of the Case

In the case decided by the Wisconsin Supreme Court, the accused, approached with five counts, had pleaded guilty in relation to the least serious two (driving a vehicle without the owner's consent and attempted violation of a checkpoint). Generally speaking, in the context of a guilty plea, the sentencing judge receives the pre-sentencing report, which offers information about the convicted person and which presents the main documentation held by the judge.[131]

In the State of Wisconsin, as in many other jurisdictions, an actuarial risk assessment tool called COMPAS[132] has been adopted, which is based both on information obtained directly from the accused, in an interview, and on the certificate of the criminal record and pending charges. Such information is processed through a computational model in relation to statistical control data, referring to a population sample not necessarily corresponding to that of the State. On the predictive level, therefore, the instrument foresees the risk of violent relapse, without however offering an explanation of this risk, based on the statistical data. As seen above, this adheres to the specific pattern of actuarial risk assessment tools.

In the case of Loomis, on the basis of the risk assessment, the local court had imposed the punishment of imprisonment for 6 years (without parole), and 5 years of extended supervision, a very high penalty, in comparison to the facts, not very serious, for which he had declared himself guilty: this attracted the attention of all national and international media.

As part of a post-conviction release request, decided by the local circuit court, the defendant disputed various forms of violation of the principle of due process. The expert witness presented by the defence pointed out some critical aspects linked to the use of the risk assessment instrument during the deliberative phase. In the first place, since COMPAS was created and designed for execution, there is a risk that, in sentencing, it may cause an overestimation of factors that, although decisive in the treatment, are not so meaningful in the measure of the penalty. Furthermore, the expert reported that the judge was not aware of the ways in which the instrument correlates the condition of the individual with the data-set of the population sample considered (a sample which, as anticipated, is not based in the State where the risk

[131] Cf. *Criminal Law – Sentencing Guidelines*, cit, p. 1537.

[132] Correctional Offender Management Profile for Alternative Sanctions. This is an actuarial tool that assesses static, non-dynamic risk: as said, the actuarial tools do not focus on the reasons of recidivism, they merely report it, evaluating risk factors through official statistics and comprehensive theoretical perspectives. On the market, the tool is marketed in the form of software, from Northpointe Inc. which holds the rights and commercial licenses. However, risk assessment tools are not necessarily software. In the Italian setting the application of risk assessment has not yet found an official recognition within the criminal justice system; however, it is widespread in other systems and has been the subject of studies by Italian authors for a long time: Zara and Freilone (2018), p. 830 ss; Zara (2013), p. 311. The psychological theories at the basis of COMPAS are explained in Brennan et al. (2009a), p. 21 ff. (Brennan lead the research team that designed COMPAS).

assessment is used). As the judge rejected the request, stating that the same sentence would have been imposed even without taking into consideration the COMPAS findings, the defence proposed an appeal (with the leave of the Court of Appeal) and renewed the complaints before the State Supreme Court.

6.3.2 The Defence's Arguments

The defendant's claims were structured into three points. The first denounced the violation of the defendant's right to be evaluated on the basis of accurate information. The second complained about the violation of the right to an individualised sentence, while the third concerned the controversial use, by the instrument, of sex among the parameters taken into consideration for the risk assessment. Indeed, the psycho-criminological theory inspiring COMPAS is also based on correlations between the information coming from the accused (with the questionnaire and the 'precedents') and the statistical data relating to social and ethnic groups, used as data sets to assess the risk of violent behaviour.

However, since the instrument is protected by trade secrets, the defence believed that the parties and the judge did not have sufficient explanations on the criteria with which the risk scores are determined, nor how the individual factors are weighed: allegedly, a blatant violation of the duty to discover. Moreover, in the defence's view, the actuarial nature of the instrument involves the use of statistical data, which would have violated, however, the right to an individualised sentence: using undetermined statistical data-sets allegedly exposes the accused to the risk of suffering the discriminatory effects of being related (inaccurately) to a social group, rather than to another. Finally, among the parameters taken into consideration by the software there is the gender, with a serious element of unconstitutionality, denounced by the defence: the defence argued that sex is used by the assessment tool as a risk factor, although, for the reasons given above, there would be no clear evidence of the parameters of its evaluation.

6.3.3 The Ruling by the State Supreme Court

Before considering the Court's conclusions, it must be emphasised that, based on the reconstruction of the defensive arguments (made by the decision), it is not clear whether the argument relating to the incontrovertible risk assessment's results was based entirely on the matter of digital evaluation or, instead, on the scientific reliability of the psycho-criminological theory, applied to the evaluation tool. As said, these two elements are overlapping but cannot be confused. Given that the object of the trade secret is the COMPAS evaluation tool as a whole, whose computational model integrates a precise scientific theory, it is impossible to understand whether the irrefutability claimed by the defence derives from the insufficient clarity of the applied scientific theory (i.e., the structure of the COMPAS) or from the digital coding with which it has been translated into the software (i.e., the translation into the digital language of the COMPAS). These are obviously two different factors: not knowing the justification of a procedural datum, because the scientific theory that produced it is not known, falls within the "traditional" problem of the application of science to criminal proceedings; on the contrary, not being able to validate a datum because it is automatedly generated by a computational process, whose rules are not known, is a different matter.

The state Supreme Court, in confirming the first instance decision, did not seem to grasp this point clearly, limiting itself to excluding the violation of due process, given the possibility, for the accused to compare the individual starting data (inputs) and the final risk assessments (output), based on the user's manual of the instrument: according to the wording of the decision, it is enough to refute the risk assessment's reliability.

The drafter of the decision, however, wanted to draw up a 'precautionary checklist', that judges must apply when using such 'predictive' tools, indicating five warnings that must always be included in the pre-sentencing report: (1) the possible existence of a trade secret that covers the software; (2) the inability of the software to carry out a highly individualized evaluation, being based on a set of data referring to social groups, not normalized with respect to the population of each State; (3) the creation of the tool for the purposes of the correctional phase, following the sentencing; (4) the existence of doubts, in the scientific community about the reliability of the computational model—albeit a secret one—which, in this case, regulates COMPAS.

In this respect, it is important to highlight that the tool at stake, developed at the beginning of the last decade, has been subjected to some practical experiments (not all of them independent), whose results have been highly contradictory. Against some partly positive conclusions,[133] some studies have highlighted the risks of discrimination[134] and of scarce significance, in terms of recurrence risk, of the parameters used.[135] A more recent study, published by the American NGO ProPublica[136] has taken up this last point, with specific regard to the criminogenic irrelevance of some factors used by the model, causing a certain stir in the public opinion. However,

[133] Brennan et al. (2009a), p. 31, pointing out the critical points, from the ethnic point of view, of the sample chosen by Fass et al (nt. 6), concluded for a positive evaluation of the results of the empirical study carried out on the COMPAS, while underlining how the software could be tested also under numerous other different parameters, not considered in that sample. An independent study carried out in 2010 on behalf of the California Department of Corrections and Rehabilitation (Farabee et al. 2010) concluded for a general reliability of COMPAS with respect to similar other control software (LSI-R) in terms of recurrence risk, reporting a lower level of reliability with respect to the profile of violent behaviour.

[134] The first was published by Fass et al. (2008), p. 1095 ff.

[135] In this sense, Skeem and Eno Louden (2007). This study was then refuted by an apparently non-independent experiment: Brennan et al. (2009b).

[136] Angwin et al. (2016), *Machine bias*, in https://www.propublica.org/article/machine-bias-risk-assessments-in-criminal-sentencing 23.5.2016.

the conclusions of the study released by ProPublica have also been strongly criticised.[137] The media's attention on this case put COMPAS under the spotlight and very recent reviews of the tool have been released, highlight its low accuracy in prediction,[138] with no better scores than untrained humans.

As mentioned, in public opinion, even in Europe, the decision by the Supreme Court of Wisconsin gained momentum not with regard to its reasons but to its ruling, confirming the first instance sentence. Media amplified the message that the ruling was mainly delivered on the basis of a digitalised risk assessment, and that the defendant had been 'sentenced to imprisonment by an algorithm'. Actually, the decision is inspired by a different approach, that relativised the impact of COMPAS on the adjudication of the case. In particular, there is one important part of the reasoning that tries to induce, in the judges, a scepticism towards these algorithmic (not necessarily digital) methods of assessing the social dangerousness of individuals. This part of the reasoning[139] did not gain as much attention as the ruling did, and did not induce, in the judges, a significant, doubtful reaction about the risk assessment tools' reliability. In fact, the decision itself reminds readers of the reason why many jurisdictions commissioned and adopted such predictive software: although designed for the correctional (and not for the decision-making) stage, is that they may assist the judges in finding allegedly objective parameters for the evaluation of social dangerousness, in order to reduce the risks of discrimination inherent in discretionary criteria. In these terms, it is possible to argue that the message in the Loomis decision is quite contradictory, inviting courts to doubt the objectivity of an instrument created… to compensate for the risk of scarce objectivity.[140] Some scholars have underlined that the mandatory written advisement in Loomis, "demonstrates that using the COMPAS does not contribute to transparency".[141]

However, the US Supreme Court rejected Loomis' petition for a writ of certiorari, confirming that the Wisconsin Supreme Court's decision clarified the matter of the application of risk assessment tools at the stage of sentencing.

[137] Flores et al. (2016), passim.

[138] Dressel and Farid (2018), p. 1342. Note that the authors are an undergraduate computer-studies major and her advisor: they set up an experimental method, tailored as a horse race between survey respondents and algorithmic risk assessment models.

[139] It should be noted, moreover, a concurrent opinion by Judge Abrahamson, which underlines, in disagreement with the majority, the need for the software development company to guarantee the judge at least a complete explanation of the functioning of the same, if not a reasoned justification of the result. There is no possibility here to focus on the essential distinction between explanation and justification of the output of an algorithm: see for all, Hildebrandt (2018), p. 3.

[140] *Criminal law – Sentencing guidelines*, cit., p. 1535.

[141] Hannah-Moffat and Struthers Montford (2019), p. 187.

6.4 A Similar Case from D.C.

The Loomis case turned the spotlight on criminal justice as a sector of the public administration in which the use of mathematical and computational models can have a very sensitive and negative impact on citizens' fundamental rights. As seen in Chap. 5, the movement claiming for transparency in the use of algorithms in public administration decisions is worldwide and also covers the area of criminal law.

A recent seminar, entitled Taking Algorithms to Court,[142] organized by the AI Now Institute of the New York University (NWY), together with the NYU Centre on Race, Inequality and the Law and the Electronic Frontier Foundation shed light on the growing number of cases of litigation between American citizens and public administrations. In many branches of the latter, there is a growing number of alleged violations of the individuals' fundamental rights, following the use of automated selection and assessment procedures. In the sessions dedicated to criminal justice, an interesting, unpublished decision by the Supreme Court of the District of Columbia[143] was reported, delivered in a case apparently very similar to State v. Loomis. Hereinafter, I will analyse the D.C. Supreme Court case, also in comparison with the Loomis case, in order to resume and underline some fundamental aspects of the topic under the spotlight.

6.4.1 *The Background*

In the context of juvenile criminal proceedings for various counts of indictment, assigned to the specialized section of the Family court, the accused had established an agreement with the public prosecutor. He pleaded guilty for felony assault and possession of a knife, in exchange for the dropping of the other charges and the non-opposition of the prosecution to parole.

Waiting for the hearing, set 2 months later, the minor was assigned to a support community and the Child Guidance Clinic's[144] social services had been asked to prepare a psychological and social risk assessment.

This evaluation, received by the judge the day before the hearing, contained a wide range of information, including the socio-family and clinical report, the observation of the minor's behaviour following the arrest, the outcome of some psychological tests, the assessment of the risk of violent behaviour—made on the basis of

[142] May 2018, available at https://ainowinstitute.org/litigatingalgorithms.pdf.

[143] 25.3.2018, Judge Okun.

[144] A specialised branch of the social service: see www.dccourts.gov.

a fairly well-known risk assessment tool, called SAVRY[145]—as well as the recommendations of the social services based on such results.

This structured tool (SAVRY) takes into consideration twenty-four risk factors[146] that are considered to be associated with the danger of violent juvenile recidivism,[147] which can be grouped into three broad categories: historical factors; factors related to the social context; risks of a personal/pathological nature. In relation to each of these areas, the tool estimates a reduced, moderate or high risk of violence in the future conduct of the accused. The final evaluation is then compared to six protection factors, or risk reduction profiles, to draw up an indication for the judge. The tool—which is not digital (it does not, in fact, have the appearance of a software, but is made up of a user's manual and cards for the evaluation of the subject), like many of these risk assessment instruments—is used by social services: the latter delivers the complete documentation to the judge before the sentencing hearing.

In this specific case, the minor had high scores in each of these three categories, balanced out by three mitigating factors. The conclusion drawn up by the social services expert on the basis of this evaluation, suggested that the defendant was at a high risk of future violent behaviour, and recommended a period of 9 months in a rehabilitation centre (residential).

The defence challenged the decision, asking the Court to exclude all the evidence based on SAVRY, including the reports prepared by the social services, also based on it, as well as any testimony or other evidence connected to it. The legal basis for excluding the evidence was Rule 702 of the Federal Rules of Evidence, as interpreted by the Federal Supreme Court in the case of Daubert v. Merrel Dow Pharmaceutics.

This is one of the most famous decisions by the US Supreme Court, that gained momentum also in many foreign and European jurisdictions, as the leading case in the field of admission of evidence based on scientific theories, in criminal trials. Against the risk of opening up the courtroom doors to junk science, the Supreme Court set the conditions for a coherent application of the Rule 702 of the US Federal Rules of Criminal Procedure, with the purpose to guide judges in the exclusion of unreliable evidence requested by the proponents. Indeed, this provision regulates

---

145 Structured Assessment of Violence Risk in Youth. It is a structured professional tool for assessing the dynamic risk in the child, which although using specific data sets, is in any case substantiated by a clinical opinion by the expert, aimed at future developments in the subject's psyche (specifically on the subject, v. Zara and Farrington [2013], p. 235 ss.). SAVRY is not a software, but a kit made of a guide and test-sheets, to administer the test.

146 *Historical risk factors*: history of violence; history of non-violent offending; early initiation of violence; past supervision/intervention failures; history of self-harm or suicide attempt; exposure to violence in the home; childhood history of maltreatment; parental/caregiver criminality; early caregiver disruption; poor school achievement. *Social/contextual risk factors*: peer delinquency; peer rejection; stress and poor coping; poor parental management; lack of personal/social support; community disorganization. *Individual/clinical risk factors*: negative attitudes; risk-taking/impulsivity; substance use difficulties; anger management problems; callous/lacking empathy; attention deficit/hyperactivity difficulties; poor compliance; low interest/commitment to school.

147 Vincent et al. (2011), p. 47 s.

expert witnesses' testimony, with a broad phrasing. Rule 702 was, then, amended[148] pursuant to *Daubert v. Merrell Dow Pharmaceuticals, Inc.*[149] Although there was no attempt to codify it, Daubert established a checklist of parameters, which are not exclusive or mandatory. *Kumho Tire Co. v. Carmichael,*[150] extended the 'Daubert test' from the scientific to the technical field. These specific parameters are: (a) whether the expert's technique or theory has been (or can be) tested (i.e. whether the expert's theory can validated in objective terms, or whether it is barely a subjective, apodictic approach, that cannot reasonably be assessed for reliability); (b) whether the technique or theory has been subject to peer review and publication; (c) the known (or potential) rate of error in the application of the technique or theory; (d) the existence and maintenance of standards and controls; and (e) whether the technique or theory has been generally accepted in the scientific community. Pursuant to these parameters (which have been complemented by the following case law), the admission of the expert witness testimony is submitted to the general application of Rule 104a FRE, placing the burden of establishing that the pertinent admissibility requirements are met on the proponent.[151] It is important for the purpose of this analysis to highlight that the amendment to Rule 702 specifically provided that the trial court must scrutinize not only the theories and methods selected by the expert, but also whether they have been properly applied to the facts of the case.

Against this background, the defence claimed the following defects in the risk assessment system used for the evaluation of risk: impossibility of falsification; absence of significant "control" literature (at least before its practical use);[152] risk of discrimination against minors belonging to poor families of colour; unavailability of data relating to the error rate and operating standards. In addition to this, with regards to the final clinical evaluation carried out in this specific case, the defence argued: the absence of adequate research on the child's personal situation by juvenile social services; the inadequate assessment of the number of "high" scores attributed to some risk factors, as well as the arbitrary measurement of the risk factors themselves.

---

[148] Rule 702: A witness who is qualified as an expert by knowledge, skill, experience, training, or education may testify in the form of an opinion or otherwise if:

(a) the expert's scientific, technical, or other specialized knowledge will help the trier of fact to understand the evidence or to determine a fact in issue;
(b) the testimony is based on sufficient facts or data;
(c) the testimony is the product of reliable principles and methods; and
(d) the expert has reliably applied the principles and methods to the facts of the case.

[149] 509 U.S. 579 (1993).

[150] 119 S.Ct. 1167 (1999).

[151] For a comprehensive overview on the application of Rule 702, see the Cornell Law School Legal Information Institute report, available at https://www.law.cornell.edu/rules/fre/rule_702.

[152] There are several studies published after the introduction of SAVRY: Vincent et al. (2011), p. 46; Vincent et al. (2012), p. 225 ss.; Zara and Farrington (2016), table 4.7, consider SAVRY a good predictor of recidivism, with good validity across settings and countries, having potential international validity.

The Government did not file the counterarguments, not even by the deadline extended by the judge, and lost, upon the defence's request, the possibility of obtaining the admission of its own expert witness at the hearing, set before the D.C. Supreme Court. At this hearing, the defence presented its expert witness, who articulated orally the reasons for the insufficient reliability, in general, of SAVRY, as well as the errors made by the experts who administered the test in that specific case.

6.4.2 *The Defence's Arguments*

The arguments by the expert witness, professor of psychology and social behaviour at the California-Irvine University, in support of the request for exclusion of the test pursuant to rule 702 of the Federal Rules of Evidence, are based on a statement of insufficiency of the reference literature previous to the application of the software in the context of the juvenile procedure. Some subsequent empirical studies were published, and the expert founded his allegations on these.

First of all, the defence argued that there is no evidence of the SAVRY's inter-rater reliability and predictive validity.[153] Furthermore, the expert reported that the user manual available for the experts (in this case, the social service preparing the pre-sentencing report), did not define exactly what was meant by low/medium/high risk level, nor did it establish the number of risk factors determining a low/medium/high social danger, in an individual. According to the circumstances of the accused, the expert denounced a reiteration of the evaluation of the same behaviour (for example, the abuse of drugs) under different parameters of risk, such as: stress, poor social relationship; impulsivity; addiction problems. However, in the expert's opinion, even in repeating the overall assessment starting from the very same rates obtained by the social service in relation to each area of risk, the accused should have reported a score ranking him in the highest level of the low level of risk or, at least, in the lower rank of the average level of risk. In no way, however, on the basis of those assessments, should the accused have been placed—as had happened—in the high level of risk, that influenced the judicial decision.

Alongside these arguments, very similar to those set out in the case of Loomis, the Court's attention was drawn to the applicability of the 'Daubert test'. Regardless of the digital format, not available for SAVRY, the question of actual refutability of a risk assessment here seems to take on a clearer and more familiar theoretical dimension. Based on the interpretation of Rule 702 promoted by Daubert, the defendant's expert witness asks the local Supreme Court to scrutinise how the first instance judge performed her role of 'gatekeeper'. Provided that the case law following Daubert shows discretion by courts in the application of the 'test', the defendant asks for the application of it to SAVRY, in order to double check its reliability.

[153] A study verified the SAVRY predictive validity with regard to Dutch juvenile: Lodewijks et al. (2008), p. 696 ff.

Against this backdrop, the D.C. decision reiterates that the Daubert checklist is the cornerstone of the control that the judge must carry out on proposed scientific or technical evidence. However, the DC Supreme Court decision faces a dilemma. In the absence of specific local precedents, the judge recalls that the courts of many other states have expressly excluded the applicability of the 'Daubert doctrine' to the sentencing phase, which is the subject of the dispute. In addition, the judge refers to the case of the State of Wisconsin v. Loomis, stressing the high risk of overestimation of the results of predictive assessment at the sentencing stage, the conclusions of which, the drafter observes, can only be taken into consideration together with other factors. Asked to rule expressly on the scientific validity of SAVRY, the local Supreme Court is confronted with a series of elements, difficult to reconcile. The drafter recalls that there is little jurisprudence on this specific point in the nine U.S.A. jurisdictions using the same software; certainly, no decision has ever ruled out the applicability of it, based on the Daubert test. The defendant's expert, though, formulated structured criticisms,[154] based precisely on the Daubert doctrine, on which the Government did not reply, failing to take part in the proceedings. Faced with such apparently insuperable impasse, the Court chooses, with pragmatism, to give value to the criticisms formulated by the expert. In particular, the decision focuses not on the general characteristics of the predictive tool, but on the practical application made of it in this specific case. Given the numerous cases of duplication of the same factor and the evident overestimation of the risk expressed in the overall judgment on the accused, the Court rules that, in the proceedings against him, the judge must not take into consideration the evaluation based on SAVRY. Neither the Government (through the prosecution), nor the social services can make any reference to the overall assessment, or to the individual risk parameters or, again, to the recommendations drawn up on the basis of the SAVRY report, at any stage of the proceedings, even after the determination of the penalty. Instead, the report about the minor, prepared by social services remains mostly usable, containing mostly references of a psychological nature.

The D.C. Supreme Court decision established some crucial benchmarks. Risk assessment tools are algorithmic in the sense that they are based on a codified procedure, connecting a certain input to precise outputs on the basis of a psycho-criminological theory. If such a codified procedure is not transparent, like in the case at stake, results may be unreliable. These kind of shortcomings should be distinguished from those deriving from the eventual automated nature of the risk assessment tool. The first issue is related to the scientific validity of the theory encoded into the model; the second, depends on the method used to encode the model.

[154] See recently (also by the defendant's expert): Skeem et al. (2019).

6.5 Is Automated Risk Assessment Different?

The argument formulated by the defence in the case of State v. Loomis, in which the risk assessment procedure is not applied by a human but by a software, is of particular importance for this book and deserves further analysis. As seen in Chap. 4, it is part of the more general topic, of the potential impossibility of challenging the accuracy of an automatically generated test, in the absence of sufficient analysis of the computational model used (Chap. 4).[155]

6.5.1 The Loomis Case as a Cornerstone?

In a general sense, this question arises as much in reference to the means of searching for evidence, as to the means of proof from which a cognitive datum generated by a fully automated process is obtained.[156] Especially in the code-driven design hypotheses (see Chap. 5), the lack of knowledge of the codes that govern the algorithms (whose application gives rise to the cognitive process data) makes it impossible to criticize the reliability of the automatedly generated test. As mentioned, this type of programming is based on articulated tree diagrams: the algorithm encodes the norm, the rule guiding, standardising the computational process in the bifurcations of the diagram and the norm explains, therefore, the output of the same process.[157] If it is not possible to discover this encoded 'standard', it is therefore impossible to demonstrate that the outcome of the computational process is unreliable.

Here lays the great importance of the argument presented by the defence in the State v. Loomis and rejected by the local Supreme Court, that, moreover, felt obliged to respect commercial secrecy. The Wisconsin supreme judges considered the discovery sufficient, given the availability, on the part of the defence, of both the COMPAS user's manual and the defendant's personal data: that was enough, in the opinion of the Court, to allow the falsification of the results obtained by COMPAS. The statement by the Court is not convincing, under several viewpoints. In fact, in the case of Loomis there has been a general lack of information on both the parameters for determining the risk within the applied psycho-criminology theory and the source code regulating the software, with a consequent, serious limitation to the chance of falsification, although the Wisconsin Supreme Court always rejected this conclusion. By reiterating that the upheld decision was not

[155] About the alleged (and irrational) presumption of reliability of digitally generated evidence, see Van Buskirk and Liu (2006), p. 20: "Courts have seemingly unflappable faith in the ability of software to render reliable evidence".

[156] In the two cases considered, the evidence having algorithmic origin, i.e. the risk assessment, is used outside the context of fact-finding, but still as a decision-making basis, in sentencing.

[157] Kehl et al. (2017), p. 28.

predominantly based on the COMPAS outputs, that Court firstly excluded any serious violation of the defendant's fundamental rights. Secondly, the Court also excluded the need for the defendant to access to the whole range of information about the functioning of the software's black box, given that the minimum condition is the possibility to challenge the data that go into the algorithm.[158]

First and foremost, the Court adopted a narrow approach in the interpretation of the issue of the trade secret, allegedly protecting the COMAPS software. It has been noted that the defence should be allowed to challenge the proprietary nature of a software, as this is often made up of a sum of general algorithms, not worth the trade secret protection.[159] Moreover, even if confirmed, trade secret protects a private, pecuniary interest, over the defendant's right to a fair trial. From a European viewpoint, this raises a serious issue of balance between competing, lawful, interests. Although it has been noted that never, in its history, the U.S. Supreme Court, "has held that an interest that is both purely private and purely pecuniary is "legitimate" enough to justify curtailing a defendant's fundamental right to present a complete defense",[160] some argued that the exclusion of a machine learning generated evidence on the basis of a free-standing due process claim would imply the (cumbersome) demonstration that such a piece of evidence offends some principle of justice deeply rooted in the people's conscience…[161]

Second, the Wisconsin Supreme Court fell into the error of the *a priori* presumption of reliability of computer programs. As extensively said in Chap. 4, the access to the source code or other solutions allowing to understand the functioning of the black box are the main way to challenge the reliability of the software output. In particular, the computational models based on self-learning mechanisms, can be hardly 'explainable', even by the designers themselves, in terms of justification of the outputs: in such cases, the software operates on the basis of normative rules that are not defined in a tree diagram codified by the designer, but are the result of mining stunning amounts of data.[162] In such cases, even the access to the source code would be insufficient to solve the lack of transparency, given the impossibility of so-called reverse engineering, or *ex post* validation of the process that generated the data, to be used as evidence.[163] "Big data-risk assessment technologies rely on machine learning. In other words, new data is constantly being inputted and processed by the existing algorithms, with the result that the parameters around risk remain in flux".[164] As seen in Chap. 4, such a situation, in judicial proceedings, may turn into a violation of the equality of arms, which according to the jurisprudence of the European Court of Human Rights, finds its very essence precisely in the possibility of

158 Barfield and Pagallo (forthcoming).

159 Chessman (2017), p. 210.

160 Chessman (2017), p. 211.

161 Barfield and Pagallo (forthcoming).

162 Burrell (2016), p. 1 ff.

163 Danaher (2016), p. 29.

164 Hannah-Moffat and Struthers Montford (2019), p. 183.

challenging and criticizing the contrary evidence.[165] As concluded in Chap. 4, if no technical solutions can assure such a minimum level of guarantee, the judge, as gatekeeper, should consider to exclude the evidence.

In the case adjudicated by the D.C. Supreme Court, the scenario was less complex. Free from its digital appearance, the predictive tool determines a violation of the rights of the defence only if it does not respect the most accredited parameters and standards in the scientific community, in the psychological field. And this is precisely the dilemma that the supreme court of the District of Columbia has faced. Although other local courts have ruled out the applicability of the Daubert doctrine to the sentencing phase, the drafter does not exclude the application of it in the present case. Indeed, the defence's request, pursuant to the current interpretation of Rule 702 FRE, is partially accepted, for the part concerning the overall individualized risk assessment, based on the SAVRY findings. Not only. Although avoiding declaring the intrinsic unreliability of the SAVRY, based on the Daubert test, the Court emphasizes the lack of confrontation with the Government. Given the importance of the decision expected—i.e., the ascertainment of scientific inadequacy, once and for all, of SAVRY—the Court expected to hear the opposing arguments (if any)... However, it being impossible, the Court focused on the specific application of SAVRY, rather than on its general, scientific reliability. In short, in the view of the Court, the defence achieved its own strategic goal—the exclusion of the risk assessment results—demonstrating, through the Daubert test, not the fallacy of SAVRY, *per se*, but of the single evaluation it made of the defendant.

On the contrary, in the Loomis case, the outcomes of the risk assessment tool—although not decisive, as the Wisconsin Supreme Court reiterated, were not excluded, like they were in the DC case, without any reference to rule 702 FRE, which instead turned out to be crucial in the second case, for demonstrating the unreliability of the psycho-criminological method, with regard to the application made on it in the specific case.

The comparison between the two decisions highlights an initial, important aspect. While the Wisconsin Court decision, although expressing articulated and appreciable reservations on the scientific validity of risk-assessment software, ended up by 'validating' these instruments, the District of Columbia Court, instead, marked an important precedent. Having submitted the use of risk assessment tools in the phase of sentencing to Rule 702 FRE, it clearly indicated that the 'Dauber test' is the only possible gatekeeper, excluding unreliable predictive software from trial.

[165] Since ECtHR 28.8.1991, Brandstetter v. Austria.

6.5.2 *Comparing Different Perspectives*

Although the conclusions of the two cases analysed are different (upholding the challenged decision, in one case, and overturning it, in the other case), there are some similarities to be highlighted.

First and foremost, in both cases, the Courts underlined the importance that the results of the risk assessment (although based on reliable instruments) are not evaluated uncritically by the judges, but always in relation to other available elements. This should, in the opinion of the Courts, neutralise the negative effects of modelled risk assessment, discriminating factors, at the first instance. Nevertheless, it is worth recalling that, under the US system, challenges of violation of the 'equal protection clause', due to alleged discriminatory effects of risk assessment, should meet the requirement of intent, based on the 1976 case of Washington v. Davis. The Davis doctrine implies that the defendant claiming the effects of discriminatory sentencing, based on risk assessment, should prove the intent to (racially e.g.) discriminate, which is an unduly burdensome proof.[166] A more fruitful approach suggests to acknowledge that (in both psychologically informed risk assessment and the digital approach), race is constitutive of the inputs that supposedly race-neutral risk assessment employ.[167]

Secondly, in both cases reported here, the assessment of "dangerousness" was applied in the sentencing phase, following the defendant's plea of guilt. Therefore, neither COMPAS, nor SAVRY, were used to determine the defendant's responsibility, it being established on the basis of the guilty plea, following bargaining with the prosecutor. Actually, in compliance with the traditional American approach to risk assessment, some have recently argued that sentencing is a governmental decision, similar to taxation or calculation of social benefits: thus, the process for coding a sentencing algorithm is no different to other decision-making processes, based on multiple variables.[168] At the time being, there are no known cases in which similar software was used, instead, in the verdict on guilt (see Sect. 6.6) and a series of indexes make this option unlikely. In the North American context, the number of declarations of guilt remains overwhelming in the mass of the proceedings[169] (realistically, both state and federal). In such cases, the judge holds the mere task of quantifying the penalty, based on a file devoid of evidence or other useful elements. To provide the judge with a minimum base for her decision, it is often necessary to

[166] Hannah-Moffat and Struthers Montford (2019), p. 185; Kehl et al. (2017), p. 24.

[167] Hannah-Moffat and Struthers Montford (2019), p. 190.

[168] Stoobs et al. (2017), p. 26.

[169] The most recent statistics, relating to the first half of 2018, show that in the American federal courts, against 77,762 defendants, there were 69,865 bargaining agreements. Incidentally it should be noted that, out of the total of the defendants, only 6004 were acquitted. Of the 71,456 convicts, 145 were judged by a court and 1447 by a jury court. All the others, as already mentioned, have pleaded guilty.

use risk assessment reports.[170] That is to say, to extend to the sentencing phase predictive software that had been created, like the COMPAS, for the executive phase and for taking decisions about parole.

In addition, many of the cases that do not go through a guilty plea, are ruled by a popular jury, expressing a guilty/innocent verdict.[171] In such cases, there is a full reconstruction of the facts, which can also help the judge in sentencing, reducing the need for risk-assessment reports. Bearing in mind these remarks, the decision by the Supreme Court of Wisconsin looks less discomforting, at least in substance. Far from allowing the use of predictive tools for fact-finding, it confirmed the use of COMPAS for assessing the 'criminal risk' with the purpose of determining punishment. What is actually impressive, in that decision, is the way in which the court ruled out the argument raised by the defence, about the potential violation of the right to fair trial. As highlighted in Chap. 4, evidence generated through software, or a computational model, rarely allows the defence to validate its genesis and, therefore, to challenge its reliability. This seems to be a case in which the 'unflappable faith' (Chap. 4) in digital evidence, seriously influenced the final decision.

Concluding on this point, it is worth highlighting that the relevance of the matter is catalysing new attention and, fortunately, is raising a discussion on it. However, some concerns had already reached the highest levels of the political bodies. It was 2014 when the U.S. Attorney General, Eric Holder, addressed the topic of risk assessment software during a rally of the (American) National Association of Criminal Defence Lawyers,[172] mainly highlighting the risk that such tools may "exacerbate unwarranted and unjust disparities" already existing in the American criminal system. In the same year, the Department of Justice's Criminal Division formalised similar concerns, related to the constitutional equal protection clause, in a letter to the Chair of the U.S. Sentencing Commission, entitled *The Promise and Danger of Data Analytics in Sentencing and Corrections Policy*.[173] If, on the one hand, the attention on this issue is absolutely important, on the other hand, the terms of such a discussion are not completely coherent: as repeatedly argued, some of the arguments against digitalised risk assessment are based on 'traditional' shortcomings of risk assessment tools and do not (or not exclusively) depend on their digital nature. However, highly regarded scholars in the field of risk-assessment have highlighted two main issues relating to digital tools. "Promises of accountability, objectivity and fairness are in conflict with the fact that algorithms are proprietary and are

---

[170] However, an interesting study assessed if and how the defence and the prosecution refer to the pre-sentencing risk assessment report in bargaining a plea of guilty: Monahan et al. (2019), p. 1 ff.

[171] See Thaman (2016), p. 379, comparing the multifaceted European context and the U.S. one, suggesting that U.S. courts should give specific reasoning on the strength of evidence in each felony case, regardless an acquittal motion by the defense. Before, see Jackson (2002), p. 517.

[172] https://www.justice.gov/opa/speech/attorney-general-eric-holder-speaks-national-association-criminal-defense-lawyers-57th.

[173] https://www.justice.gov/sites/default/files/criminal/legacy/2014/08/01/2014annual-letter-final-072814.pdf.

constantly adjusting to the data being processed".[174] Not only do these two factors affect consistency (risk scores can vary between similar individuals, based on what is considered relevant by the algorithm, in a certain place and moment); there is also a constant risk of slippage between causation and correlation factors (see above), so that anything and everything can be linked to offending.[175] In light of these assumptions, it is important to bear in mind the 'multiple layer structure' of the problem discussed here.[176] One layer is defined by the scientific dimension of the socio-criminological theory inspiring the risk assessment tool: the key to handling it has been clearly (although not expressly) confirmed by the D.C. Supreme Court decision on SAVRY, in the Daubert test. The second layer is defined by the opacity deriving from translating such theory into a model and, in particular, a computational model.[177] To address this second kind of shortcoming, the key is the equality of arms clause, presented in Chap. 4, and recalled here above (Sect. 6.5.1), as I will explain in the next paragraph.

6.6 From the European Point of View...

So far, we can assume that it is a quite common feature of jurisdictions, both in common and civil law, to take into account the defendant's character in sentencing, after the assessment of guilt. The defendant's character (bad character, in particular), is considered for the purpose of predicting her future behaviour. Therefore, the more a national order focuses such prognosis on a predictive estimation of the offender's future behaviour, the more judges tend to trust predictive risk-assessment. As seen in the previous paragraphs, this assumption needs to be framed into the present reality, in which the potentialities of computational models, now offer new frontiers for risk assessment, allowing for fast collection and mining of relevant digital data. Against this backdrop, are digital risk assessment tools ready to replace the more traditional psycho-criminological expertise on dangerousness?

In Sect. 6.2 we presented both the actuarial systems and the structured professional tools as models rooted in the principles, the axioms, the theories, of psychology: based on the degree of validation reported, such theories may be more or less regarded by the scientific community. In Chap. 5, instead, we briefly considered how computational modelling achieved astonishing results in transforming traditionally human tasks into automated processes, collecting, connecting and mining huge quantities of data in minimal periods of time. In light of this, it is possible to argue that the core of any risk assessment software is the psycho-criminological

---

[174] Hannah-Moffat and Struthers Montford (2019), p. 189.

[175] Hannah-Moffat and Struthers Montford (2019), p. 190.

[176] Chessman (2017), p. 216.

[177] Palmiotto (forthcoming), p. 10 ff., distinguishes between: technical miscodes, scientific miscodes, legal miscodes.

theory inspiring it. Having said this, it is up to the software designers to conceive the best model to deliver a fast and reliable response about the defendant (or convicted)'s dangerousness. In its essence, digital risk assessment can be compared to expert testimony: the software, though, allows for a higher number of interrogations, in a much faster time, with no need to rely on the personal presence of an expert.

The fundamental question, therefore, is whether risk assessment software should be treated as psycho-criminological expertise. Preliminarily, it is important to check what the role of the latter is in criminal proceedings. Here again, the caveat is that a comprehensive comparison would fall out of the general scope of this work, and we need to rely on broad generalisations. We must bear in mind that psycho-criminological expertise has long been considered controversial, in the European criminal debate. The background is a non-enthusiastic reaction, in the Old Continent, for the new role of psychology in criminal proceedings. More precisely, though, the discussion relating to this kind of expertise is based on the complex, general relationship between character and free will. What is the role of character in a theory of criminal culpability? Is there a correlation between the individual's character and her decision to act, criminally? So far, we focused on various instruments based on the analysis of the defendant's individual relational, familiar and social characteristics, in order to evaluate her dangerousness for future re-offending or violent behaviour in its different forms.[178] There are serious doubts that character should also play a role in the assessment of criminal responsibility for the facts under prosecution. Actually, this is a completely different procedure, in which considerations about the defendant's character would be used not for a future projection, but rather as the basis for a guilty verdict for a fact that she allegedly committed in the past. These are deeply different contexts: character in law of evidence and in sentencing has different premises and consequences, regardless of the specific penological theory (among the many mentioned above), inspiring a criminal sanctions system.

However, in many continental jurisdictions there is no clear distinction between verdict and sentence—between fact-finding and penalty—delivered in one comprehensive reasoned decision, by the judge or the court. As said in Sect. 6.1.2, in the trial, the parties must prove the facts relating to both the criminal responsibility and the determination of penalty (e.g. aspects reducing or aggravating it). The judge will consider all evidence and adjudicate, at the same time, on guilt and, if this is the case, on sentence. The absence of such a distinction may impact on the space that every jurisdiction allows for the evidence of character. In fact (as seen with regard to the D.C. Supreme Court case, Sect. 6.4), sentencing in the US escapes traditional evidentiary rules. In their task, judges have discretion to consider several aspects of the defendant's personal history, regardless of the evidence presented by the parties for the guilt phase.[179] In the decision of the case of Williams v. New York, the US Supreme Court stated that it is not an infringement of the fairness clause to use, in

---

[178] Zara and Gino (2018), p. 1 ff.

[179] Kehl et al. (2017), p. 22.

sentencing, information that is not admitted at the guilt stage.[180] Although the same US Supreme Court ruled in the case of Gardner v. Florida[181] that the sentencing phase must comply with the due process clause and the fourteenth Amendment protection, it is doubtful that the convicted has effective chance to challenge, explain or supplement the information at the basis of her sentence.[182]

6.6.1 The Overall Impact of Bad Character on Trial

Bad character evidence is a huge topic in criminal procedure. Character "is relevant in various forms and in various ways to decision-making in criminal process [...] Subjects of the criminal process are judged as actors in time, and not just as inhabitants of the present".[183] Despite the validity of this Redmayne's iconic assumption, it is difficult to address the topic of bad character evidence in a comprehensive way, not only because jurisdictions have very different approaches to it,[184] but because the concept in itself is fuzzy. The topic is part of the law of evidence that, as explained in Sect. 4.1, is utterly domestic, jealously regulated by national laws. However, the concept of 'bad character evidence' refers to a quite a large range of elements. For example, it can be a statement, by a witness or an expert, about the defendant's attitude and behaviour: a risk assessment report, acknowledging the defendant's propensity to violence or other criminal behaviour, is a bad character evidence. Or, it can be a certificate from the defendant's criminal record, demonstrating that she already violated the law. In general, the term refers to elements that can prove an interference of the defendant's character in the facts of which she is charged of, or her propensity to offend. The use that the judge can make of these elements depends on the national regulations. Some jurisdictions (see hereafter) may prefer not to rely on bad character evidence in the adjudication of guilt: having a bad character does not demonstrate, not even indirectly, that the defendant committed the crime. Some others, may value the indirect evidentiary support offered by the bad character evidence: although not related to the facts of the case, a propension to hostile reactions can cast light on the defendant's personality, which can be considered important in the reconstruction of the whole case. The bad character evidence, *per se*, conveys (or is supposed to convey) the proof of the defendant's anti-social attitude: according to domestic regulations, the judge can use such conviction to adjudicate on both guilt and sentence, or only for sentencing. However, the absence of a strong distinction between adjudication on guilt and on sentencing

[180] Williams v. New York, 337 US 241–251 (1949).

[181] Gardner v. Florida, 430 U.S., 349–359 (1977).

[182] Kehl et al. (2017), p. 22.

[183] Redmayne (2015), p. 5.

[184] In England and Wales, the bad character evidence was excluded until 2003, when the UK Criminal Justice Act allowed it: see, extensively, Redmayne (2015), p. 145 ff.

may blur the argument and the role of bad character evidence may result in being ambiguous.

In Italy, for example, according to art. 220 § 2 of the Code of Criminal Procedure, the psycho-criminological expertise on the defendant's character is allowed only after sentencing, in the correctional phase: it cannot be used either for adjudicating on guilt, or for sentencing.[185] The reasons for such a rule have been briefly mentioned above. Traditionally, a persisting mistrust in psychology is said to be the main rationale of the norm.[186] However, it seems to me that the strongest reason for it is, rather, the reluctance to value character in the decision of the case, as the defendant's personal attitudes have no evidentiary value as to the facts of the file. Based on the assumption reported above, an Italian court could not make use of any risk-assessment tool, such as COMPAS or SAVRY, in the guilt and sentencing phase,[187] given the prohibition of art. 220 § 2 ItCCP, as risk assessment reports should be considered and treated as psycho-criminological expert testimonies. Only the judge presiding over the correctional phase could rely on a risk-assessment tool, in order to decide, e.g. on parole or other prison benefits. Incorporated into a file, a digital risk assessment tool delivers reports that are the result of the application of a specific scientific theory, elaborated by scholars or clinicians, tested, verified and criticised by a community of peers. Although a digital tool does not imply the expert's personal presence in court, it delivers a result that is based on a scientific theory, according to the traditional paradigm of expert testimony: the adjudication on a matter of the case entails the application of technical or scientific knowledge, of which the judge is deprived.

In light of this, and of the complex, differing treatment that evidence of bad character may encounter under the different domestic legal systems, there is one possible, uniform, solution that can be proposed at the European level. Firstly, risk assessment reports should be submitted to the general domestic law of evidence. Secondly, regardless of the moment (and the aim) when the risk assessment

---

[185] This may sound at odds (and, actually is at odds) with the assumption (see Sect. 6.1.3.1) of art. 133.2 criminal code, providing that the judge must consider, at sentencing: the motive that pushed the offender to act; her character; her criminal record; her social behaviour, before and after the offence; her and her family's walk of life.

[186] Gialuz (2019), p. 20. The author argues that the use of digital risk assessment tools for pre-trial detention decision would not be prohibited by the exclusionary rule of art. 220.2 It.c.c.p. I believe that the only coherent way to approach and regulate the problem is to treat the risk assessment, any kind of risk assessment, as an expert evaluation, according to the existing evidentiary rules. For the Italian reader it may be interesting to wonder whether the abovementioned prohibition of psycho-criminological expertise should be applied in cases of temporary application of preventive measures (*applicazione provvisoria di misure di sicurezza*): art. 312 It.c.c.p. allows for the interim application of measures that are meant to be applied after conviction, on the basis of the defendant's dangerousness. Art. 220.2 being a general exclusionary rule, applying to the whole guilt and sentencing phase, the prohibition is applicable also in these cases.

[187] For the sake of eventual Italian readers: while psycho-criminological expertise is banned from the guilt and sentencing phase, criminal records (art. 133.2 ItCCP) and other documents relating the defendant's personality (Art. 236 ItCCP) can be considered by the judge in sentencing, as confirmed by the Italian Supreme Court decision (Sez. 6), n. 42823, 24.9.2013 Rv. 257149—01.

software is used, it should be treated as a psycho-criminological report, pursuant to the specific rules, if any, provided for it by national regulations. Moreover, whereas the national rulers decide to introduce, expressly, digital risk assessment, art. 11 of the Directive 2016/680[188] must be taken into account. In fact, it prohibits decisions, in criminal proceedings, based solely on the automated processing of data, producing adverse effects on the data subject.

6.6.2 Use of Risk Assessment in Remand in Custody Decisions

Specific attention is owed to pre-trial risk assessment tools. In fact, on the one hand, they may coincide with traditional risk assessment, insofar as they aim to predict violent behaviour. To a certain extent, I suggest to extend the conclusions presented with regard to violent behaviour risk assessment tools.

The 'bail risk assessment tools' purport to predict the failure to appear in court, which is based on different indexes, having no psycho-criminological relevance. As said in Sect. 6.2.1.1, such an area of prediction falls outside of the extensive scientific literature that has been studying criminogenic factors over the last century. There is no evidence that the FTA index is more accurate than flipping a coin, in the evaluation of the non-attendance risk. Thus, from this angle, it does not seems plausible to submit pre-trial detention risk assessment tools to the same regulation eventually provided for psycho-criminological evidence: in the part relating to the failure to appear, they are not based on a scientific approach.[189] As such, they represent an alternative to the judge's individual intuition, based on the same parameters that a human decision-maker would consider: pending charges at the time of offense; prior convictions; prior failure to appear, in the recent and less recent past...

This makes it altogether difficult to suggest a plausible normative approach. Should the pre-trial detention judge use a predictive tool to assess the risk of fleeing or absconding, or not? And if yes, under what conditions? Digital risk assessment instruments rely on general statistics, that may be of some relevance in fixing a general framework for the case: given these premises, the tool can point out how probable it is that the accused will not appear in court. Nevertheless, there are several other circumstances that the judge must take into account in each specific case. For example, the health conditions of the accused are of the utmost relevance in predicting the risk of absconding. The family situation can also heavily impinge on it... In this sense, the digital and human evaluation do not seem to exclude each other. A statistical background (easily provided by instruments like PSA), might be

[188] Art. 11: Member States shall provide for a decision based solely on automated processing, including profiling, which produces an adverse legal effect concerning the data subject or significantly affects him or her, to be prohibited unless authorised by Union or Member State law to which the controller is subject and which provides appropriate safeguards for the rights and freedoms of the data subject, at least the right to obtain human intervention on the part of the controller.

[189] Gialuz (2019), p. 20.

considered a useful overview. Moreover, an individualised decision about remand in custody implies a human-based decision, respecting the national and supranational parameters established for this matter.[190] Thus, a serious discussion about reliability and usefulness of FTA indexes is desirable. If the parameters usually taken into consideration prove to be relevant (more than flipping a coin), it could be plausible that the judicial authorities deciding about remand in custody may use it as a basis for their individualised decision. As to the European context, art. 5 ECHR establishes a set of requirements meant to assure individualised and specifically reasoned decisions on pre-trial detention (and other pre-trial coercive measures), excluding that an FTA index can be the sole or decisive parameter to decide upon remand in custody.[191]

6.7 Tentative Conclusions

The general comparison between the North-American experience and the European context has provided important components to establish a legal reflection on the impact of the digital revolution on criminal justice.

The recent release of the CEPEJ Ethical charter for the use of AI in judicial systems (Chap. 2) confirms that it is unrealistic to reject the use of digital instruments *in toto*. Although European lawyers have long displayed a lack of interest or, rather, a full rejection of automated solutions that have been adopted in other systems, there are huge advantages in computational models, such as efficiency and speed, that must not be overlooked. The excessive bureaucracy and length of the proceedings is an overarching issue, and digital technology can certainly offer viable solutions. Moreover, as explained in Sect. 6.1, national criminal jurisdictions tend to rely, often implicitly, on predictive evaluations, giving the floor to (more or less validated) risk-assessment tools, some of them completely digital: if the judge has to foresee a future behaviour by the defendant, she may feel more comfortable relying on standardised, algorithmic, statistical evaluations, able to take into account a larger number of factors, combining them together. Therefore, the existence of a need for digital applications in this area is undeniable. However, what is utterly important is to prevent the spread of these instruments on the mere basis of market rules. What is offered may not fit the standards of scientific validation that must be applied in this field, according to the Daubert doctrine. Accessibility to- and falsification of the "algorithmic test" are particular, specific problems, which do not replace, but overlap with that of the reliability of the predictive scientific method, adopted as the basis of the computational model. Against this scenario, drawing also

[190] See art. 5§1 ECHR. Suffice it to say that there is huge case-law by the ECtHR about the duty to give specific reasoning, by the judicial authority, about the necessity and proportionality test. Remand on custody must be proportioned to the aim pursued (e.g. ECtHR, 18.3.2008, Ladent v. Poland, § 55, 56) and the last resort, when less severe measures appear insufficient.

[191] Having in mind the prohibition of art. 11 dir. 2016/680... (See Chap. 3, Sect. 3.2.2.3).

on the conclusions of Chap. 4, the issue of trade secrets protecting proprietary software should be receding.[192] Irrespectively the different national regulations, it seems to me that, also in the European context, the domestic constitutions and the international bills of rights represent the ground to let the defendant's (and public) interest for a fair trial prevail on a barely economic private interest.

In this chapter, I suggested some solutions to properly face the specific matter of digital risk assessment. All the assumptions, allegations, suggestions that have been presented here, must be framed by the crucial guideline pointed out in the CEPEJ Charter, pushing towards a strictly multidisciplinary approach to the problem of the links between computational models, artificial intelligence and criminal justice. The greatest risks inherent in this relationship, in fact, derives from the incommunicability between different areas of expertise, which has long kept computer scientists and lawyers almost divided. If it is true that "it is not allowed to use as evidence elements escaping the cognitive control of the judge and the parties",[193] the multidisciplinary paradigm is the main means to reduce such a cognitive gap.[194]

References

Ambroise-Casterot C, Bonfils P (2011) Procédure pénale. Press Universitaire Française, Paris

Anastasi A (1982) Psychological testing, 5th edn. Macmillan, New York

Ancel M (1954) La defense sociale nouvelle. Cujas, Paris

Ancel M (1964) La césure du procès pénal, Problèmes contamporaines de procèdure pénale: recueil d'études en hommage à M.L. Hugueney. Siray, Paris, 205–224

Angwin J et al (2016) Machine bias. https://www.propublica.org/article/machine-bias-risk-assessments-in-criminal-sentencing. Accessed 23 May 2016

Ashworth A (2015) Sentencing and criminal justice. CUP, Cambridge

Ashworth A, Zedner L (2014) Preventive justice. OUP, Oxford

Ashworth A, Zedner L (2019) Some dilemmas of indeterminate sentences: risk and uncertainty, dignity and hope. In: De Keijser JW, Roberts JV, Ryberg J (eds) Predictive sentencing, normative and empirical perspective. Hart Publishing, Oxford, pp 127-148.

Barfield W, Pagallo U (forthcoming) Advanced introduction to the law of artificial intelligence (Ch. I). In: Constitutional law and artificial intelligence. Elgar

Barrett D (2016) Michael Gove boosts prison early release scheme despite 'Skull Cracker' scandal. The Telegraph [on-line ed.], 13 May 2016

Bartoli R (2005) Colpevolezza tra personalismo e prevenzione. Giappichelli, Torino

Belloir P (2019) Les nouveaux moyens d'individualisation de la peine dans la loi du 23 mars 2019. Gaz. Pal. 19 novembre 2019, nr. 40, 66–67

Brennan T, Dietrich W, Ehret B (2009a) Evaluating the predictive validity of the COMPAS risks and needs assessment system. Crim Justice Behav, 21 ff

Brennan T, Dietrich B, Breitenbach M, Mattison B (2009b) A response to J. Skeem, J. Eno Louden, assessment of evidence on the quality of COMPAS. www.northpointeinc.com

[192] Chessman (2017), p. 209 ff.

[193] Dominioni (2005), p. 69.

[194] Zara and Gino (2018), p. 10.

Burrell J (2016) How machines think: understanding opacity in machine-learning algorithms. Big Data Soc 1:1 ff
Cavadino P, Gibson B (1993) Bail, the law, best practice and the debate. Waterside Press, Hook
Chessman C (2017) A source of error: computer code, criminal defendants, and the constitution. Calif Law Rev, 179–228
Dadoun A (2018) L'obligation constitutionnelle de motivation des peines. Revue de Sciences Criminelles, 805 ff
Danaher J (2016) Algorithmic decision-making and the problem of opacity. Comput Law, fasc. 8, 29 ff
Dominioni O (2005) La prova penale scientifica. Giuffré, Milano
Dressel J, Farid H (2018) The accuracy, fairness, and limits of predicting recidivism. Open Dartmouth: Faculty Open Access Articles, 1342
Dubber MD, Hörnle T (2016) Criminal law. A comparative approach. OUP, Oxford
Farabee D, Zhang S, Roberts R, Yang J (2010) COMPAS validation study. Final report, currently available only on the company site holding the business license. www.northpointe.inc.com
Farrington DP (1988) Studying changes within individuals: the causes of offending. In: Rutter M (ed) Studies of psychosocial risk: the power of longitudinal data. CUP, Cambridge, pp 158–183
Fass TL, Heilbrun K, Dematteo D, Fretz R (2008) The LSI-R and the COMPAS: validation data on two risk-needs tools. Crim Justice Behav 35:1095 ff
Fazel S (2019) The scientific validity of current approaches to violence and criminal risk assessment. In: De Keijser JW, Roberts JV, Ryberg J (eds) Predictive sentencing, normative and empirical perspective. Hart Publishing, Oxford
Feeley MM, Simons J (1992) The new penology: notes on the emerging strategy of corrections and its implications. Criminology, 449–474
Flores AW, Bechtel K, Lowenkamp CT (2016) False positives, false negatives and false analysis: a rejoinder to "Machine Bias: There is Software used across the Country to Predict Future Criminals. And it is biased against the Blacks." Federal Probation, 1–23
Friedman LM (1994) Crime and punishment in American history. Basic Books, New York
Gialuz M (2019) Quando la giustizia penale incontra l'intelligenza artificiale: luci e ombre dei risk assessment tools tra Stati Uniti ed Europa, 29 May 2019. https://www.penalecontemporaneo.it/upload/6903-gialuz2019b.pdf, 1–20
Gigerenzer G (2008) Rationality for morals. OUP, Oxford
Green TA (1987) The English criminal trial jury and the law-finding traditions on the eve of the French Revolution. In: Padoa Schioppa A (ed) The trial jury in England, France and Germany, 1700–1900. Dunker & Humblot, Berlin, 41 ff
Grevi V (1976a) Libertà personale dell'imputato e Costituzione. Giuffré, Milano
Grevi V (1976b) Libertà provvisoria ed esigenze di tutela ella collettività: una questione di legittimità costituzionale. Giurit II:633 ff
Grierson J (2019) IPP sentencing in England and Wales called 'deeply harmful'. The Guardian (on-line edition), 10 November 2019
Hannah-Moffat K (2013) Actuarial sentencing: an "Unsettled" proposition. Justice Q, 270–296
Hannah-Moffat K, Struthers Montford K (2019) Unpacking sentencing algorithms. In: De Keijser JW, Roberts JV, Ryberg J (eds) Predictive sentencing, normative and empirical perspective. Hart Publishing, Oxford, 175–195
Hart SD (1998) The role of psychopathy in assessing risk of violence: conceptual and methodological issues. Leg Crim Psychol 3:121–137
Hildebrandt M (2018) Algorithmic regulation and the rule of law. Philos Trans R Soc, 1–11
Hoskins Z (2019) Against incapacitative punishment. In: De Keijser JW, Roberts JV, Ryberg J (eds) Predictive sentencing, normative and empirical perspective. Hart Publishing, Oxford
Jackson JD (2002) Making juries accountable. Am J Comp Law, 477–530
Jacobs G (1993) Das Schuldprinzip, in Rheinische-Westfälische Akademie der Wissenschaften. Vorträge G 319:7–68
Kaufmann A (1961) Das Schuldprinzip. Winter, Heidelberg

Kehl D, Guo P, Kessler S (2017) Algorithms in the criminal justice system: assessing the use of risk assessments in sentencing, responsive communities initiative. Berkman Klein Center for Internet & Society, Harvard Law School. http://nrs.harvard.edu/urn-3:HUL.InstRepos:33746041
Kleinberg J et al (2018) Human decisions and machine predictions. Q J Econ, 237–293
Kraemer HC, Lowe KK, Kupfer DJ (2005) To your health: how to understand what research tells us about risk. OUP, New York
Kvaraceus WC (1966) Anxious youth: dynamics of delinquency. Charles E. Merrill Publishing, Columbus
Lacey N (1988) State punishment. Rutledge, London
Langbein JH (1987) The English criminal trial jury on the eve of the French Revolution. In: Padoa Schioppa A (ed) The trial jury in England, France and Germany, 1700–1900. Dunker & Humblot, Berlin, 16 ff
Lasserre Capdeville J (2015) Les modifications concernant la personalization de la peine. Gaz. Pal. 23 mai 2015, nr 143, 13–17
Liptak A (2017) Sent to prison by a software program's secret algorithms. The New York Times, 1 May 2017. https://www.nytimes.com/2017/05/01/us/politics/sent-to-prison-by-a-software-programs-secret-algorithms.html?hp&action=click&pgtype=Homepage&clickSource=story-heading&module=first-column-region&region=top-news&WT.nav=top-news&_r=0
Lodewijks HPB, Doreleijers TAH, De Ruiter C (2008) SAVRY risk assessment in Dutch violent adolescents. Crim Justice Behav, 696–709
Logan Koepke J, Robinson DG (2018) Danger ahead: risk assessment and the future of bail reform. Wash Law Rev, 1731 ff
Monahan J, Metz A, Garrett BL, Jakubow A (2019) Risk assessment in sentencing and plea bargaining: the roles of prosecutors and defense attorneys. Behav Sci Law, 1–11
Moreno Catena V (2013) Spain. In: Ruggeri S (ed) Liberty and security in Europe. Universitätsverlag Osnabrück, Göttingen, 141–181
Norrie A (2014) Crime, reason and history. A critical introduction to criminal law. CUP, Cambridge
Orlandi R (2013) Introduction. In: Ruggeri S (ed) Liberty and security in Europe. Universitätsverlag Osnabrück, Göttingen, 9–14
Padoa Schioppa A (1994) La giuria penale in Francia, Edizioni Universitarie di Lettere Economia. Diritto, Milano
Palmiotto F (forthcoming) The impact of algorithmic opacity on fair trial rights in criminal proceedings. In: Ebers M, Canero Gamito M (eds) Algorithmic governance and governance of algorithms. Springer
Pelissero M (2008) Pericolosità sociale e doppio binario. Vecchi e nuovi modelli di incapacitazione. Giappichelli, Torino
Pifferi M (2012) Individualisation of punishment and the rule of law: reshaping legality in the United States and in Europe between the 19th and 20th century. Am J Leg Hist, 325–376
Redmayne M (2015) Character in criminal trial. OUP, Oxford
Ruggeri S (2013) Comparative analysis of pre-trial precautionary measures in criminal proceedings. In: Ruggeri S (ed) Liberty and security in Europe. Universitätsverlag Osnabrück, Göttingen, pp 185–243
Ryberg J (2019) Risk and retribution. On the possibility of reconciling considerations of dangerousness and desert. In: De Keijser JW, Roberts JV, Ryberg J (eds) Predictive sentencing, normative and empirical perspective. Hart Publishing, Oxford
Senna E (2010) Les ambiguïtés de l'individualisation des peines. Les Chaiers de la Justice 4:47–60
Shlonsky A, Wagner D (2005) The next step: integrating actuarial risk assessment and clinical judgment into an evidence-based proactive framework in CPS case management. Child Youth Services Rev, 409–427
Skeem J, Eno Louden J (2007) Assessment of evidence on the quality of COMPAS. http://ucicorrections.seweb.uci.edu/files/2013/06/CDCR-Skeem-EnoLouden-COMPASeval

Skeem J, Scurich N, Mohanan J (2019) Impact of the risk assessment on judges' fairness in sentencing relatively poor defendants. University of Virginia School of Law SSRN Papers series, 15 January 2019

Slobogin C (2019) A defence of modern risk-based sentencing. In: De Keijser W, Roberts JV, Ryberg J (eds) Predictive sentencing. Normative and empirical perspective. Hart Publishing, Oxford

Spitzer E, Maccarone R (2007) Research bulletin: clinical and structured assessment of sex offenders. New York State Division of Probation and Correctional Alternatives. www.dpca.state.ny.us/pdfs/somgmtbullettinmay2007.pdf

Stevenson MT (2018) Assessing risk assessment in action. Minn Law Rev, 303–384

Stoobs N, Hunter D, Begaric M (2017) Can sentencing be enhanced by the use of artificial intelligence? Crim Law J, 26

Taxman FS, Thanner M (2006) Risk, need and responsivity (RNR): it all depends. Crim Delinquency 53:28–51

Thaman S (2016) Should criminal juries give reasoning for their verdicts? The Spanish experience and the implications of the European Court of Human Rights decision in Taxquet v. Belgium. In: Petrova A (ed) Festschrtift für August Nacke. Plovdiv University Press, 338–385

Tonry M (2019) Sentencing and prediction. Old wine in old bottles. In: De Keijser JW, Roberts JV, Ryberg J (eds) Predictive sentencing. Normative and empirical perspective. Hart Publishing, Oxford, 269–293

Van Buskirk E, Liu VT (2006) Digital evidence: challenging the presumption of reliability. J Digital Forensic Pract (1):20

Van Nostrand M (2012) Legal and evidence based practices: application of legal principles, laws, and research to the field of pretrial services, 2007, Crime and Justice Institute – National Institute of Corrections. US Department of Justice, Bibliogov, Washington

Vincent GM, Chapman J, Cook NE (2011) Risk-needs assessment in juvenile justice: predictive validity of the SAVRY, racial differences, and the contribution of needs factors. Crim Justice Behav, 47 ff.

Vincent GM, Guy LS, Fusco SL, Gershenson BG (2012) Field reliability of the SAVRY with juvenile probation officers: implications for training. Law Hum Behav 36:225 ss

Vogler R (2013) England and Wales. In: Ruggeri S (ed) Liberty and security in Europe. Universitätsverlag Osnabrück, Göttingen, 87–103

Warner CD (1899) Some aspects of the indeterminate sentence. Yale Law J, 222

Zara G (2013) La validità incrementale della psico-criminologia e delle neuroscienze in ambito giuridico. Sistemi intelligenti, fasc. 2, p 311

Zara G (2016) Valutare il rischio in ambito criminologico. Procedure e strumenti per l'assessment psicologico. Il Mulino, Bologna

Zara G, Farrington DP (2013) Assessment of risk for juvenile compared with adult criminal onset: implications for policy, prevention and intervention. Psychol Public Policy Law 19(2):235 ss

Zara G, Farrington DP (2016) Criminal recidivism: explanation, prediction and prevention. Rutledge, Oxon

Zara G, Freilone F (2018) Psychological assessment. In: Arrigo BA (a cura di). The SAGE encyclopedia of surveillance, security, and privacy. Sage, Thousand Oaks, 830 ff.

Zara G, Gino S (2018) Intimate partner violence and its escalation into femicide. Frailty thy name is 'violence against women'. Front Psychol, 1–11

Zentara-Logeay S (2019) La réforme pénale issue de la loi du 15 août 2014: dans le sillage de l'humanisme pénal, Criminocorpus. Revue d'Histoire de la Justice, des crimes et des peines 9(12):2019

Chapter 7
Predictability and the Criminal Justice Decision-Making Process

7.1 Case-Based Reasoning Systems, Open-Data and the Value of the Precedent: Legal Traditions Clashing?

In Chap. 5 we summarised the progressive achievements in AI and law over recent decades, underling the important role played by the case-based reasoning approach in the endeavour of modelling the judicial decision process. In contrast with expert systems, the CBR is more likely to overcome the 'logic flaws' of legal reasoning, based on a complete collection of previous decisions. Regardless of the performance of these programmes in the task of foreseeing future decisions, two questions arise from the legal point of view. One is related to the general opacity of neural networks establishing correlations, that we abundantly commented on in Chap. 5; the other, is related to the role that precedents play in these systems.

It is a general concern for computer scientists to find complete and accurate (digital) data bases to 'instruct' CBR systems. Depending on the different fields of human activities they want to approach, program developers have to face the issue of selecting inputs: availability is, of course, the first issue and it is a quite common claim, in AI forums and conferences; quality is the second aspect, being related to the characteristics that data needs to present to be usefully inserted into the programme.

As to the legal field, an initial problem arose in the need to transform decisions into digital data. Such a technical obstacle started to be addressed, decades ago, by researchers in many legal-tech research centres and could be, then, overcome with the progressive digitalisation of public administrations, justice among all others.

At the present time, in the whole western world, judicial decisions are (created and made) available in digital format, easily transformable into the appropriate extension for the operability. A whole range of data is potentially available, in every

S. Quattrocolo, *Artificial Intelligence, Computational Modelling and Criminal Proceedings*, Legal Studies in International, European and Comparative Criminal Law 4, https://doi.org/10.1007/978-3-030-52470-8_7

jurisdiction, to be retrieved for the purpose of quantitative studies. However, availability does not mean, necessarily, accessibility. Traditionally, not every decision delivered by any judge or court in a jurisdiction is publicly accessible. Although publicity is a fundamental guarantee in modern justice, the publication of judgments and decisions is traditionally limited. As we will see hereinafter, this is a common feature in both common law and civil law, even if based on different reasons.

As mentioned in Chap. 5, the digitalisation of the public administrations (which, in Europe, has been regulated by means of directives, *infra*) is strictly related to the *open data*, an approach recently adopted by many legal orders in the world.[1] The NGO Open Government Partnership, launched in 2011, played a big role in promoting the concept of more accessible, transparent and accountable public administrations.[2] As a part of it, access to judicial decisions in the form of a data-base has become a widely accepted feature in the majority of the European jurisdictions. Open data should not be confused with the means for processing it, warned the CEPEJ at the time of the delivering the European Ethical Charter on the use of AI in judicial systems.[3] Let us try to understand what it means.

7.1.1 The Open Data Movement and the EU Approach

The Open Data Movement is a civil society movement[4] promoting more openness, of the information, documents and data-sets held by governments and public agencies, in order to allow people to access them and to take advantage of them.[5] In fact, they say, there is a huge social value in it: "putting such information into the public domain benefits society and can stimulate the economy".[6] The term "Open Government Data" became popular from 2008, after a group of advocates, in the US, released a document (late 2007)[7] providing for eight principles to be respected

[1] Charalabidis (2018), p. 1: "Data about policy-making, software code (open sources), documents, minutes, financial data and so on has been opened resulting in a large repository of government data that can be on open data portals and government websites".

[2] See www.opengovpartnership.org.

[3] See European Ethical Charter on the Use of Artificial Intelligence in Judicial Systems and their Environment, Appendix 1, p. 17.

[4] For a general overview, Novek (2017), p. 10 ss. See also Charalabidis (2018), p. 1: "the movement of opening data resembles a move from a closed to an open system".

[5] Charalabidis (2018), p. 2.

[6] See Gray and Darbishire (2011), p. 7.

[7] The so-called Sebastopol Principles, released in California on Dec. 8th 2007 by 30 open government advocates (available at http://www.opengovdata.org/home/8prinicples), setting forth that government data shall be considered open if the data are made public in a way that complies with the principles below: 1. Data Must Be Complete; 2. Data Must Be Primary; 3. Data Must Be Timely; 4. Data Must Be Accessible; 5. Data Must Be Machine Processable; 6. Data Must Be Non-Discriminatory; 7. Data Formats Must Be Non-Proprietary; 8. Data Must Be License-free.

in the enhancement of public data policies.[8] In 2013, the G8 endorsed the endeavour by adopting the Open Data Charter, although not binding.

The European scenario needs to be addressed separately. The European Union has engaged in the regulation of the reuse of public sector information since the beginning of the 2000, in relation to two of the pillars of the EU internal market: transparency and fair competition. In 2003 the first Public Sector Information directive was adopted (2003/98/EC), which was then amended in 2013, by directive 2013/37/EU. This directive provided for periodic reviews, based on which a public on-line consultation was launched in 2017. Together with an extensive evaluation of the directive and an impact assessment, the on-line consultation was the basis for a proposal to revise the 2013 directive. The new directive 2019/1024/EU entered into force on July 16th 2019, also known as the Open Data Directive, and will be implemented in the Member States by July 2021. Actually, the Open Data Directive does not focus on the citizens' access to information, rather on the economic value and impact of the re-use of public information.[9]

Reflecting on the term 'open data', it must be acknowledged that there have been several attempts to define the concept of 'openness', depending on the different areas of interests addressed. For example, as to the scientific side, the Open Knowledge Foundation provided a definition, establishing that "Knowledge is open if anyone is free to access, use, modify, and share it - subject, at most, to measures that preserve provenance and openness",[10] even though a highly regarded scholar observed that "Openness is a treasured attribute of science, but like most good things, even scientific openness has to be purposefully cultivated and judiciously deployed in order to serve its intended functions well."[11] This does not seem completely compliant with the ODM view, as it is possible to argue that in the ODM advocates' opinion, openness implies that public data should "be freely copied, shared, combined with other material, or republished as part of websites which allow users to explore, analyse, visually represent, or comment on the material, as well as transform it into other formats".[12] In fact, it has been remarked that the scope of the Open Data Movement is not only enhancing democratic participation and transparency of public administrations but it is also to generating social and economic innovation.[13]

[8] See De Filippi and Maurel (2015), p. 2.

[9] In particular, the Open Data Directive provides for: (1) publishing of dynamic data and the uptake of APIs (routine protocols and other tools for building software applications, regulating the interaction between software components); (2) limitation of the cases in which public bodies can charge more than the marginal costs of dissemination for the re-use of their data; (3) transparency requirements for agreements between private and public sector, about the re-use of the latter's data. In particular, the directive should apply also to data from public-funded research, via open access. For a complete overview, see https://ec.europa.eu/digital-single-market/en/european-legislation-reuse-public-sector-information.

[10] http://www.opendefinition.org.

[11] Jasanoff (2006), p. 42.

[12] See Gray and Darbishire (2011), p. 8.

[13] Dove (2015), p. 157. It must not be overlooked that such theory has raised a relevant criticism, as to the risk of creating a 'data divide' (along with the digital divide), as large numbers of people

Thus, according to this view, mere 'obtainability' does not grant 'openness'.[14] This makes the phenomenon particularly delicate.[15]

Moreover, a further aspect relevant to framing the meaning of 'open data' is the range of the documents affected by it, even though, it has been said, the ODM advocates did not devote much attention to this, at least in early days.[16] According to a popular understanding, the range of open data could (or should) cover "from national statistics to budgetary information, from parliamentary records to data about the locations of schools, hospitals, crimes, or post boxes".[17]

7.1.2 *Open Data and Criminal Justice*

When the discourse about open access comes to justice, there are several delicate aspects to be considered. Not only has public access to judicial decisions always played a crucial role in the organisation of judicial systems but the uncontrolled re-use of non-selected, raw, case-law for quantitative legal analysis may produce some serious flaws, as I will suggest hereinafter.

Moreover, when criminal justice is concerned, further aspects must be taken into account. Open access to criminal justice data may encompass crime rates, statistics and figures: free access to such information does not raise specific concerns, provided that the data circulated is reliable. Actually, data referring to the public administration of criminal justice may be related to a vast range of branches, such as LEAs and prosecution offices, with policing and investigation data, or Courts, and data generated within judicial proceedings… All these sets of data have traditionally been submitted to the authorities' control and even, in many cases, been kept secret. On this point, the open government advocates' argument seems crude. They admit—although acknowledging that the right to private life is a protected human right[18]—that access to data related to an investigation should only be limited in order on the unique purpose not to jeopardise it: "after the inquiry is finished and the

---

would not be able to take advantage of 'openness', rather would suffer the flaws of being the victims of such divide (e.g. being unable to protect the interests related to their personal data, accessed and used by others): see Gurstein (2011).

[14] Dove (2015), p. 158.

[15] At the European level, France is one of the countries that recently passed a law to enhance open access of State data, called 'law for a digital Republic' (2016). For a general overview on the evolution see Kambrun-Favennec (2018), p. 83 ff.

[16] Dove (2015), p. 162.

[17] Gray and Darbishire (2011), p. 8.

[18] And, to be fair, "it is not always obvious how the twin goals of opening data and protecting privacy can be mutually reconciled": Dove (2015), p. 163. It is worth noting that the topic has been addressed in such terms since the very beginning of the debate on 'open government': Michael (1981), p. 265 ff.

criminal arrested, the information could be released".[19] Such a remark expressly overlooks the presumption of innocence and the whole range of fundamental rights, recognised by international charters and treaties and national constitutions for the suspected and accused person. In general, such an approach refuses to acknowledge the distinctive privacy issues entrenched in the realm of justice and, in particular, criminal justice. For this reason, it is worth looking more closely at what *judicial* open data specifically means.

First of all, as said in Chap. 5, within the domain of justice, efficiency must be considered in a different way (we may wonder if—to use a tenet presented in Chap. 2—it can be considered an 'autonomous concept'…). If, generally speaking, efficiency is a criterion to measure the relationship between two parameters—the *best performance* in relation to a *reduced amount of means*—'judicial efficiency' implies that a third parameter is taken into account: judicial guarantees must be part of such a relationship, and be respected.[20]

Secondly, the topic of open data in judicial systems is multi-fold, covering access to courts and other judicial services, to courts' records and, of course, courts' decisions. And while the issue of open access to courts' records seems to mostly affect the aspect of privacy,[21] the Open access to judgment implies even more additional concerns.

A caveat, before deepening this topic. Law enforcement and the prisons sectors seem to be highly administrative, in the majority of the US,[22] while they tend to be more submitted to the judicial control in a certain number of European continental legal orders (e.g., Italy and France). This may affect the way data is treated and accessed.

[19] Gray and Darbishire (2011), p. 40.

[20] Jimenez Gomez (2014), p. 229: "nosotros aquí hablaríamos de un concepto de eficiencia entendida como propia del contexto judicial y, por tanto, consideraríamos la eficiencia judicial como el grado óptimo en el uso y aprovechamiento de los recursos disponibles en la oficina judicial al servicio de la administración de justicia, guardando todas las garantías legales, es decir, teniendo en cuenta dentro de este concepto no solo los recursos disponibles sino también las garantias".

[21] Sudbeck (2006), p. 268 ff. The topic touches on a large range of aspects that almost fall behind the scope of this study, delving on the concept of privacy acknowledged by the different jurisdictions. An American approach seems to consider that open access to records would imply disclosure of personal data, such as security numbers etc. A European approach would highlight that even though judicial decisions are public, the access to record is limited, not only for the reasons reported here, but also with regard to conviction and sentence. The attitude, on the two side of the ocean is very different.

[22] Hannah-Moffat and Struhers Montford (2019), p. 175.

7.1.3 Public Access to Court Record

Focusing, first, on open access to courts' records, some basic distinctions are due. The term 'record' is misleading as it refers to several different objects. These can be hearings' records and documents annexed to the case file, or criminal records, reporting final convictions and sentences.[23] The first are seldom made available, especially because they often consist of video or audio-tapes, that are not even available in a digital format.[24] However, the right to access to such materials seems to be deeply rooted in the common-law: in 1978, the US Supreme Court in the case of Nixon v. Warner Communications Inc. established that the federal and state courts of that country recognise a general common-law right to "inspect and copy public records and documents, including judicial records and documents". Nevertheless, in that very same judgment, the Supreme Court also stated that the decision to allow for access to the court's records, remains ultimately at the Court's discretion, on the basis of the specificity of each case.[25] What the Supreme Court has long considered to be, for sure, a violation of privacy, is the unrestricted access to judicial record, deprived of public interest, or, as some local Courts ruled, based on a merely economic interest.[26]

The topic of balancing public access to court records with privacy has been addressed by American courts for at least 40 years. Specific studies and pilot experimentations have been conducted in many state courts, in order to assess the peculiar impact of open access on this branch of court records. At the beginning of the last decade, The National Centre for State Courts and the Justice Management Institute, with the support of the State Justice Institute, started a national project for developing guidelines for access to records.[27] A remarkable number of proposals and solutions have been suggested, some relying on purely legal tools, others based on technical devices, such as the XML (Extensible Markup Language), allowing for some information in a document to be accessible to a particular group of users (such as judges, clerks, and other civil servants) and prohibited to others (public).[28]

As to the European area, many countries have adopted various forms of judicial open data. With specific regard to criminal records, the normative framework is

---

[23] Blankley (2004), p. 414: The specific categories of documents published online include civil court filings, bankruptcy filings, criminal documents, opinions (both "published" and "unpublished"), and even attorneys' briefs and motions.

[24] See Benesty (2017), p. 1 ff.

[25] Sudbeck (2006), p. 270. It must be acknowledged that the US Freedom of Information Act (FOIA) does not apply to court records.

[26] Sudbeck (2006), p. 271.

[27] Sudbeck (2006), p. 276. In the discourse about the matter, it has been repeatedly said that a burden to avoid or point out information that should not be disclosed should be on the attorneys' shoulders: see. Blankley (2004), p. 450. I personally do not agree with such conclusion.

[28] Sudbeck (2006), p. 282 f., providing a list of recommendations to reduce the negative impacts of public access to criminal records, i.e. Excluding publication of non court-generated documents.

multi-fold: the States have their own legislation regulating what is reported in the records and who, how and when one can access to it. Decisions, files, documents are subject to a different regulation, which is often covered by criminal procedure codes. Actually, harmonisation in this field has been modest and it essentially covers the issue of mutual exchange of record information between judicial authorities. On a regional scale, the Council of Europe 1959 Convention about mutual legal assistance provides for a general scheme of exchange of records information between foreign authorities (arts. 13 and 22). However, between the EU countries some advanced instruments have been recently adopted and implemented. The EU decisions 2009/315 and 2009/316 JHA respectively addressed the exchange of information from national criminal records and the creation of ECRIS, the European Criminal Records Information System, allowing for a complete overview of the convictions passed on one individual, in every European jurisdiction.[29] In this sense, ECRIS is not a unified European record, rather it provides a peer-to-peer access to the information related to one specific person.[30] Such legal instruments do not cover, in any way, the issue of public access to criminal records, which is still regulated under national laws.[31]

From this point of view, there is an evident fragmentation that jeopardises any attempt for a general reconstruction, not only on the two sides of the Atlantic Ocean, but also within the European context and even in the smaller area of the EU itself. However, the topic of open data criminal records seems to be almost entrenched into the Gordian knot of finding an acceptable balance between general accessibility (if not 'openness', in the sense presented above)[32] and privacy. The question here is to establish whether there is a violation of privacy, considering that judgements and sentences are public (see infra). Access, in itself, and not the means for it, seems to be the core of the legal question. Once that the database is fed with information (provided that rulers have decided if there is an issue of protection of privacy at all), a basic search-engine will accomplish the task of browsing into it, delivering a comprehensive picture of the individuals' criminal story. Apparently, the use of more sophisticated computational modelling or AI in this area of criminal law information should not induce a particularly intrusive effect: the task of the software will be to accomplish a wider, deeper and faster review of all the convictions reported by one person, delivering a better result in a much shorter time.

[29] Xanthaki (2008), p. 27 ff.

[30] Di Paolo (2011), p. 4045.

[31] While researching for this paragraph, I came across the website of a private society, named ECRIS, after the European database, that in this case stands for European Criminal Records *Services*. Against a sum of money, the platform offers access to the information in each national record, compliant with the domestic regulation, taking advantage of the fact that, thanks to the real ECRIS, the request set through one country's central record office allows discovering all the convictions ever reported by an individual in the EU countries.

[32] And, in my opinion, it should not be openness in such sense; reusability of criminal record data appears to be non-compliant with the minimum core of privacy. In this sense, it is important to raise awareness, especially in the open data movement advocates, of the specificity of this area of data.

Open access of judicial decisions, instead, is likely to create a huge side-effect that may impact on the foundations of our judicial systems. In fact, accessibility is the first, implicit step for predictability, that is the core of the analysis in this chapter.

As legal practitioners, we have all been used to, for at least two decades, relying on a comprehensive judicial data-base and mining it using search engines based on key-words. This has enormously improved the results of our researches, at least in terms of time and an increase in the quantity of the decisions mined (but also impacted on the legal profession).[33] Thanks to the open access public policies and, before it, to the tenacious effort of private legal-tech companies collecting possibly every decision delivered by any judge or court in a jurisdiction, our researches is now much faster, easier and more complete than it used to be decades ago. In addition, as we have seen, there is much more that a sophisticated AI computational model can do with this countless number of decisions, thanks to the evolutions in CBR.

Nevertheless, we cannot overlook the real impact of such systems on the European legal context and the long-term repercussions that they may have on the institutional dimension of European justice, with special regard to the criminal field.

7.2 Accessibility of Criminal Justice: The Values of the Publicity of Hearings and Publication of Decisions

It has been noted that access to legal information is inherent to the core concept of citizenship, as intended in the modern culture. Since the nineteenth century, publication became essential for the binding force of law and *ignorantia legis non excusat* became its pendant, especially in criminal matters.[34] This point is crucial in the light of this study and needs to be framed into the foundations of the European legal systems.

Let us assume, for the moment, that accessibility, publicity and publication are all intermingled terms, hendiadys expressing one crucial feature of each judicial system: its rationality. Rationality and accessibility of a legal order are intertwined: the very essence of the latter is based on the fact that people know it and (almost) adhere to it.[35] However, there are different parameters to measure rationality.

One conception ties it to statute law. In the continental version of the Enlightenment—nurturing the ideal of legal positivism—the legal certainty is embodied by the myth of codification,[36] an organised and rational system of statutory law, based on chapters, sections, subsections. Citizens and regulators all have

[33] The literature on the point is now remarkable. See, among others Susskind (2008), passim; Katz (2013), p. 911.

[34] Zeno Zenchovich (2009), p. 36 f.

[35] Bing and Havrold (1977), p. 230.

[36] Cadoppi (2014), p. 180.

the same access to the basic rules of the system.[37] Another conception ties it to the value of the precedent: someone said that there is no better way to get at the heart of a legal system than to observe the value given to prior decisions.[38] Although the idea of 'precedent' plays a crucial role in the whole western legal tradition,[39] in common law countries, *stare decisis,* has been recognised, by or large, since ancient times,[40] through the habit of law reporting. Collection and publication of the most important decisions has always been a feature of the English tradition,[41] enhancing acknowledgement and awareness of law both in judges and citizens. In more recent times—as a consequence, once again, of the Enlightenment—a more institutional and regulated system of reporting was introduced in the second half of the nineteenth century, with the establishment of the Council of Law Reporting (1865), followed shortly after by the new settlement of the courts by the Judicature Acts (1873 and 1875). The principle *stare decisis* is grounded into a hierarchical structure of courts[42] (which will prove to be a crucial feature in the contemporary approach to the topic, inspired by open data) and it is possible to say that the English *stare decisis* was strongly boosted by the reforms of the second part of the nineteenth century.[43]

Thus, it is possible to argue that on the two sides of the Channel, the rationality of the legal system stands on its own accessibility, based, on the continent, on a comprehensive codification of statutory law (framed into the Montesquieu's theory of rigid division of the powers) and, in England, on the structure of the courts and the precise reporting of the precedents.[44]

Making a decision public not only has an objective impact on the structure of the system itself; it also has subjective value. Publicity is an inherent feature of any fair trial and decision, enshrined in art. 6§1 ECHR. Actually, within the context of the ECHR, the terms 'publication' and 'publicity' do not perfectly overlap. Indeed, the jurisprudence of the Court sets a distinction, within the text of Art. 6 §1 itself. Based on the wording, the court established the right to a

---

[37] MacCormick and Summers (1997), p. 4.

[38] MacCormick and Summers (1997), p. 1. Goodhart (1934), p. 41 specifies that, the English value of the precedent differs from the continental one in the sense that, if directly on the point, it must, and not may, be followed as a pattern.

[39] Postema (1987), p. 9.

[40] Mattei (1996), p. 170 ff.

[41] Antoniolli Deflorian (1998), p. 171. Interestingly enough, the reports used to be compiled on a private basis, by lawyers for the sake of their own use: Bankowski et al. (1997), p. 321.

[42] Cadoppi (2014), p. 181; the analysis about *stare decisis* in the UK by Bankowski et al. (1997), p. 315 begins with the examination of Courts hierarchy.

[43] After the strong attacks by Hobbes and Bentham, respectively in the seventeenth and eighteenth centuries [see Postema (1987), p. 9], the nineteenth century saw a restoration of *stare decisis* [see. Extensively, Evans (1987), p. 35 ff.] and, about the half of twentieth century, Goodhart could argue that the principle of *stare decisis* had never been so rigid in England [Goodhart (1934), p. 41].

[44] Cross and Harris (1991), p. 6.

public hearing: although not absolute,[45] the guarantee of a courtroom being open to the public is crucial and the case-law of the ECtHR on it is remarkable. Then, the wording of Art. 6 expressly provides for the public pronouncement of the judgment. The meaning of such a guarantee has been rephrased by the Court, in the sense that the decision does not need to be read, in all its parts, in a public hearing: what satisfies the guarantee is the chance for anyone to consult or obtain a copy of it.[46] It is possible to argue that the Convention establishes an unrestricted right to access to the judgment, be it accompanied by reading in a public hearing or not. Thus, accessibility of the judgment is a fundamental human right, whose consequence is not necessarily the publication of any judicial decision delivered in one legal system.

It is worth anticipating that the civil law tradition systems usually provide for a generalised access to the means of appeal, based on the idea that, all the way up in the hierarchy, every superior court can amend and correct the lower court's ruling. Thus, there is a proliferation of decisions, and a huge part of them are not of general interest, as they are likely to be amended by a superior court. In this scheme, which is typical of the French, the Italian, the Spanish, but also, the German jurisdictions, the uniformity of the interpretation is also granted by a control over the publication of the decisions: if justice is public, in respect of a fundamental principle, the publication of the decisions must stay under the authority's control, in order to convey a unique interpretative message.[47]

As mentioned, at the present day, open data policies for judgments are crucial in framing accessibility of legal decisions. They push towards an unrestricted access to all the decisions delivered in one jurisdiction. On the one hand, raw data fuels CBR (case-based reasoning) programs. On the other hand, those instruments should offer an objective and representative view of the decisions delivered in any branch of the justice system, but it is not necessarily true that a generalised access to all decisions grants this. If, for the purposes of AI applications, selecting one part of the whole body can be challenging and dangerous—as this could convey, implicitly, a misrepresentation of the jurisdiction[48]—abandoning any selective criterion, allowing for free digital access to the whole case-law of a jurisdiction, does not come without the risk of serious flaws.

[45] On the one hand, a list of grounds for limiting such right is provided by Art. 6§1 itself: public policy, national security, privacy, the interests of justice are expressly listed as grounds for limitation. On the other hand, the Court jurisprudence also clarified that the presence of the public is not necessarily considered fundamental at all stages of the proceeding, especially in the appeals, when legal issues are (often) discussed. See Rainey et al. (2017), p. 301.

[46] This jurisprudence dates back to the famous case of Pretto and others v. Italy, 8.12.1983, in which the Court discharged the applicants' arguments, finding that no violation of the Convention had occurred, since the decision was accessible to anyone. See Rainey et al. (2017), p. 302.

[47] Serverin (2018), p. 24.

[48] Van Bossuyt and De Groote (2009), p. 371.

7.2.1 *The Principle of* Stare decisis *and the Publication of Criminal Decisions*

In modern times, publication is the means for both fulfilling fundamental rights of the defendant and transforming the decision into a model for later decisions.[49] In simple terms, publication means to make the decision accessible for the future, with the purpose of granting uniformity of jurisprudence.[50] As anticipated in the previous paragraph, this function is inherent in every rational legal system, although the ways to achieve it rely extensively on the institutional structure of the jurisdiction, with some relevant distinctive features between common law and civil law. The first and main feature is the principle of *stare decisis*,[51] that still represents a deep divide between these two leading legal cultures. In the terms that we will summarise hereinafter, it is said to represent the most emblematic characteristic of the common law. In this sense, it is contrasted with the civil law tradition, in which the peculiar system of means of appeal and thus, the proliferating number of decisions, brought to an authoritative control over the publication of the decisions.

Although it falls out of the scope of this study to delve into a comparative reconstruction of the value of the precedent, it is worth developing some distinctions that have been anticipated: although rooted in the ancient tradition, such distinctions are still decisive in approaching the influence of open data on the value of the precedent.[52] A main distinction must be drawn between common law and civil law countries: throughout this work there have been constant references to the fact that the precedent holds a very different relevance in the two realms, with specific reference to *stare decisis*. For sure, another distinction exists between the English and American common law and the American one: however, such a divide is not crucial for this short enquiry, and only a few references will be made to it.

7.2.1.1 *Stare decisis* in the Common Law Tradition

Preliminarily, it is worth remembering that *stare decisis* plays a specific role in the context of the value of precedents decisions. The idea that similar cases must be ruled in similar ways has nothing to do with it, this being a basic principle of justice all over the western world.[53] What really stems from the rule of *stare decisis* is the

---

[49] MacCormick and Summers (1997), p. 2.

[50] Taruffo (1997), p. 451.

[51] Blackstone (1765), p. 73, concluding the section dedicated to the precedent: "and thus much for the first ground and chief corner stone of the laws of England, which is, general immemorial custom, or common law, from time to time declared in the decisions of the courts of justice".

[52] It would be interesting to assess whether if the need for access to judicial decisions could be read in connection with the Kant's principle of publicity and his claim for the 'public use of reason' stated, in particular, in Kant (1795), p. 1995.

[53] Mattei (1996), p. 178.

binding commitment for the courts to respect the precedent, even if it appears wrong or unjust. Only this principle is an authentic expression of the common law itself. For instance, this principle is based on the idea of 'authority'. Recognising authority to a norm or to a previous decision means to establish a duty to respect it notwithstanding the real opinion of the court in the pending case. It has been argued that legal reasoning based on authority is retrospective, not only because (a norm or) a previous decision has been set in the past and does not reflect the present, but also because it demand on the judge to depart from her best appreciation of the pending case, in favour of the appreciation elaborated by someone else in the past (either a judge or a rule-maker).[54] Thus, it must be acknowledged that the authority of a decision is independent from the merit, from the correctness of that decision,[55] sometimes bringing the second judge to adjudicate in a way that she deems unjust. The idea of authority independent from correctness is a constraint that burdens the common law judge.[56] As the rule of the binding precedent has a twofold nature, operating both on a vertical level and on a horizontal one, such a constraint may have different force. On the horizontal level, the binding value of the decision extends across the judges of the same court and of the same level. On the vertical side, it expands down the hierarchy of the courts system,[57] and this is what makes the idea of 'authority without correctness' acceptable.

The institutional structure of the judiciary is crucial in understanding the sense of *stare decisis*. In the common law countries, the rational structure of the courts is complemented by the power of superior courts to select the cases to be reviewed. Especially in criminal matters, appeals to the intermediate level are also submitted to some filter, while appeals to the supreme courts are usually subject to authorisation by intermediate appeal courts.[58] This means that a small number of cases are decided by the last resort courts and, thus, few decisions per year acquire the status of superior courts' precedents, to be followed by lowers courts unless there are grounds to distinguish.[59]

With specific regard to the English common law, when the House of Lords abandoned, for itself, the ties of *stare decisis*, in 1966, after Lord Gardiner's Practice Statement on Judicial precedent, the English situation became more similar to the Northern American one, in which the Courts never felt strictly bound to the horizontal dimension of the precedent.[60] The Supreme Court, having substituted the House

[54] Schauer (2009), p. 105.

[55] Schauer (2009), p. 107.

[56] Blackstone (1765), p. 70: "the doctrine of the law then is this: that precedents and rules must be followed, unless flatly absurd or unjust: for though their reason be not obvious at first view, yet we owe such a deference to former times as not to suppose they acted wholly without consideration".

[57] Schauer (2009), p. 104.

[58] Bankowski et al. (1997), p. 318; and Summers (1997), p. 358.

[59] In this sense, it must be noted that the concept of 'leading case' is a bare doctrinal evolution, as such case has no special authority: Bankowski et al. (1997), p. 341.

[60] Cross and Harris (1991), p. 19. Mattei (1996), p. 179.

of Lords in its judicial functions, follows the same doctrine. Nevertheless, as anticipated, in the United Kingdom, a statutory regulated system[61] of publication of judicial decisions covers all areas of judicial litigations, based on a long list of sources, some of them, like the Law Reports, supervised by judges themselves.[62] In such a context, "a precedent is simply any prior decision of any court that bears legally significant analogy to the case now before a court".[63] To this purpose, the structure of the Report is crucial. Actually, the contents of the Reports are a decisive aspect, also compared to the continental tradition (see *infra*). In fact, the report must cover a long list of requirements and, between them, a statement of the facts, "always quite detailed".[64] Such a feature is decisive in determining, in the first instance, whether there is (sufficient) analogy between a pending case and the previously decided one: it has been said that "reasoning by analogy is the characteristic product of *stare decisis* and our doctrine of precedent".[65]

Afterwards, in the second instance, the content of the report is essential to establishing what is binding in the precedent and what is not. Actually, a precedent is binding only in its *ratio decidendi*, or rule of decision. This implies that "the problem is that of identifying a ratio decidendi in the precedent, and of interpreting the ratio, and debating the proper qualification of the facts of the instant case on the issue whether they do or not count as facts of the type covered by the precedent's ratio".[66] Although much effort has been made in the definition of what the *ratio decidendi* is,[67] it is up to the latter court to determine which, of the whole of the arguments deployed by the precedent decision, are the statements to be retained as *ratio decidendi*.[68] Reports are also important in assessing factors that can weaken the binding value of the precedent, such as the time elapsed or *per incuriam*, that is to say the ignorance of the court about the existing precedent or statute law.

Based on the theory of the authority *per se* of the precedent, it seems that the most challenging feature of the reasoning with precedent is distinguishing and overruling. In fact, distinguishing allows the court to depart from the precedent, because

[61] And before it, by 'prothonotaries', based on a long-lasting tradition, dating back to the days of King Edward the Second: at the expenses of the Crown, the reports were published annually and thus became known under the name of *year books*. Blackstone (1765), p. 71, recalls that, "upon the influence of Lord Francis Bacon, king James the first had appointed two reporters "with a handsome stipend for this purpose"... However, the appointment was soon forgotten and since the period of Henry the Eight to the time of Blackstone's writing, the reports had been compiled by many private and cotemporary hands", some of which more experienced, some others much more fallible.

[62] And also reporting the outlines of the arguments presented by the parties: Bankowski et al. (1997), p. 320.

[63] Bankowski et al. (1997), p. 322.

[64] Bankowski et al. (1997), p. 322.

[65] Cross and Harris (1991), p. 206.

[66] Bankowski et al. (1997), p. 337.

[67] Goodhart (1934), p. 42; see extensively, Cross and Harris (1991), p. 39 ff.; Mac Cormick (1987), p. 153 ff. For a critical (American) point of view, Schauer (2009), p. 92.

[68] Cross and Harris (1991), p. 72 ff.

it should not be applied to the pending case.[69] Thus, comparison and distinction of relevant circumstances are the normal content of common law decisions.[70] However, distinguishing is not always possible and, in such cases, rejecting is the only alternative option to sticking to the precedent. Cases of departure from *stare decisis* are exceptional both in England and in the US, although the two countries have different criteria allowing a court to the depart from a precedent. A 'special justification' is asked for by the American common law, while a "flatly absurd or unjust"[71] decision is the criterion traditionally accepted by the English common law. To echo Blackstone, the second judge is free to correct the precedent when her decision provides a better demonstration of what law is.[72] In modern times and with specific regard to criminal cases, it has been noted that the "rejection of earlier precedents and conscious use of judicial law-making is easier where there is a discernible public consensus".[73] The evolution of public feelings about what really needs to be protected by criminal law seems to be considered, by the contemporary common law judges, an index for justifying the overruling of a precedent.

Thus, although it is clear that legal certainty and predictability[74] are distinctive goals of the common law, to which the rule of *stare decisis* maintains on both sides of the Atlantic Ocean, abidance by the past decisions is balanced with some consideration for the evolution in the public opinion's feelings. It is important to stress that in the Practice Statement 1966, freeing the House of Lords from the duty to abide by its own precedent, the Lord Justice recognised that the importance of granting legal certainty through the precedent is confronted by the need to avoid injustice and gaps in the evolution of the law.[75] This remark is important for the purposes of this inquiry: the evolution of law and its interpretation is a feature that must be valued in a general reflection about the long-term impact of quantitative legal analysis.

7.2.1.2 The Precedent in Civil Law

In the civil law countries, as mentioned, some deep institutional distinctions mark a different role and value for the precedent. The first factor to consider is, of course, the existence of a huge, organised, traditional body of statutory law. For the purposes of this study, it suffices to recall an interesting passage in the Blackstone's

---

[69] Interestingly enough, it has been noted that it is almost up to the parties to cite all the relevant precedents, even those adverse to their client, pleading that it they must be distinguished: Bankowski et al. (1997), p. 342.

[70] Bankowski et al. (1997), p. 348.

[71] Blackstone (1765), p. 70.

[72] Ibidem: "the rule admits of exception, where the former determination is most evidently contrary to reason: much more if it be contrary to the divine law. But even in such cases the subsequent judges do not pretend to make a new law but to vindicate the old one from misinterpretation".

[73] Bankowski et al. (1997), p. 350.

[74] Bankowski et al. (1997), p. 334.

[75] Practice Statement 1966 3 All ER 77.

Commentaries, addressing the topic of written law in the Roman tradition. Originally resting on the people's will, expressed in the laws of the State, the written law became the will of the Sovereign, loosing that element of freedom that, for instance, went on characterising the common law.[76] For these, and much more sophisticated reasons, the statutory law represents, as much as *stare decisis* does in the common law, the essence of the civil law traditions.[77]

Another element to be taken into account is a different structure of the judiciary[78] and, first of all, of the higher courts.[79] A diffused organisation of the higher courts is a distinctive feature of many continental systems,[80] such as in France, Italy and Germany.[81] In the Italian case, at least three supreme courts must be enumerated, Corte di cassazione (the supreme court for civil and criminal cases), Corte costituzionale (the constitutional court, entitled the judicial review of laws) and Consiglio di Stato (the supreme court for administrative cases). Usually deprived of the power of *certiorari*, or to select the cases to be reviewed, these courts decide cases in thousands each, per year, and deploy greater numbers of judges, organised in different sections or chambers, adjudicating independently from each other. This has been considered to be the consequence of an historically rooted bias of the continental European tradition against judicial discretion, which has prevented the development of a form of *writ of certiorari*.[82] Primarily, this entails one main, twofold, consequence. On the one hand, the general absence[83] of any 'in-put' filter for the cases

---

[76] Blackstone (1765), p. 73.

[77] It is interesting to underling a peculiar feature of the Swiss legal system. In art. 1 of the Civil code, the legislator recognised to judge the specific duty to 'act as legislator' in case there are no written rules or customary rules to apply to the pending case. This allowed, in the recent decades, the development of a more pragmatic legal reasoning by the judges of the Swiss federal tribunal, based on the unusual recognition of incompleteness of the statutory legal system: see Werro (2018), p. 136 ff.

[78] It has been theorized that there are three different approaches from which the culture of judiciary can be studied: the personal, the institutional and the external one, the latter being related to impacts that judiciaries have on the society: Bell (2006), p. 2. There is no room in this inquiry to linger over this aspect. However, it is important to recall that the framework in which judiciaries must be appreciated is complex and multifaceted.

[79] For a general overview see Tunc (1978a), p. 8 ff.

[80] Although a comprehensive comparative study between France, Germany, Spain, Sweden and England demonstrated that the distinctions common law/civil law and Romano-Germanic/Latin are not really helpful in classifying the features and characters of judiciary in these countries: Bell (2006), p. 382.

[81] Cappelletti (1981), p. 383. On the contrary, the Italian constitution provides that any judgment and decision about liberty can be appealed to the Supreme Court (art. 111.7).

[82] In this sense, Cappelletti (1981), p. 383. Such distrust in judicial discretion is particularly relevant in the history of criminal procedure. In fact, it is always mentioned in the list of the main differences between inquisitorial and adversarial legal models, being the main reason why inquisitorial models provide for a plurality of means of appeal, allowing for a general and complete review of the first instance decision by one or more higher courts.

[83] However, many Supreme Courts, like e.g. the French and the Italian one, although deprived of the writ of certiorari, introduced filters to the admission of the cases, based on the requirements established by the law.

submitted to the continental supreme courts implies that the latter cannot orient their action on those aspects of law that, more than others, need to be clarified or modernised.[84] They have to adjudicate on any possible question submitted by the parties,[85] although it may be redundant, especially if recently adjudicated in a series of repetitive cases. This hampers the possibility of such courts to focus on their original mission, granting the uniformity of the law.[86] On the other hand, the effectiveness of such a mission is also jeopardised by the fact that it is highly diluted, between the whole number of the different supreme courts, and between the several chambers of each of them.[87] This, at least in part, deprives their decisions of authority,[88] although the Grand Chamber of such courts is usually entitled to rule on conflicts of interpretation, embodying the most authoritative opinion on the legal matter, that will be referred to and cited by the single chambers of the court and the lower courts and judges. It is worth underlining that in the French legal system there is a general and persisting ban on citing national case law, based on art. 445 of the code of civil procedure: references and arguments to previous case law, legal scholarship and comparative arguments are excluded from French judicial decisions.[89]

The decisions of the continental supreme courts tend to limit as much as possible the references to the fact, focusing on the so called 'principle of law'. It has been long discussed whether the latter and the *ratio decidendi* of common law jurisdictions overlap:[90] there is certainly a difference from the angle of the relevance of the material facts. Because they have jurisdiction over matters of law, and not of fact, the decisions of many continental supreme courts have long been long published in a summarised way, reporting only the principle of law, with no reference to the facts.

This situation generated the opinion,[91] fiercely disputed by an opposite theory,[92] that the civil law judges do not feel the same need for certainty as their common law colleagues do, the priors being supported by the force of the existing codification, and, long ago, by the roots of the Roman law.

Within this scenario, is there a specific theory of the value of the precedent? Certainly, the continental systems do not implement the principle of *stare decisis*, in the rigid sense endorsed by the English common law since the nineteenth century. Nevertheless, it is unrealistic to claim that in continental law there is absolute denial of the importance of case-law: on the contrary, the continental Supreme Courts are

[84] Tunc (1978b), p. 436: modernising the law is the main function of supreme courts, according to the Author's conclusions; Cappelletti (1981), p. 385.

[85] There are, of course, admissibility requirements, but they imply just a minimum deree of diligence by the parties.

[86] Tunc (1978b), p. 440 f.

[87] Taruffo (1997), p. 448.

[88] Cappelletti (1981), p. 383.

[89] Bobek (2013), p. 99.

[90] Bankowski et al. (1997), p. 337.

[91] See Goodhart (1934), p. 61 f. The opinion is endorsed by Cross and Harris (1991), p. 11 f.

[92] Zweigert Kötz (1971), p. 316.

traditionally invested with the function of granting uniformity in the interpretation of the law, by means of a consistent case-law.[93] It has been suggested that the best way to understand the role of the precedent in civil-law is to delve more extensively into the interaction between the foundations of domestic legal theories and the institutional, cultural and social impact of the legal order in its complexity.[94]

Moving on from the previous remarks about the structures of the continental supreme courts, a further layer of investigation focuses on the composition of the judiciary itself.[95] Descending from the Westphalian tradition of the nation-state, many modern continental legal orders are based on a bureaucratic model of judiciary.[96] Judges are civil servants,[97] recruited on the basis of a public selection[98] between law schools graduates who have been (before or after the selection) specifically trained in technical juridical matters.[99] For these reasons, they tend to develop "skills in technical rather than in policy-oriented decision-making".[100] This also has an impact on a trend of anonymity of the judges in delivering decisions. Often excluding the possibility for concurrent or dissenting opinions to be attached to a judgment, the continental jurisdictions tend to limit the relief of personal opinions.[101]

Nevertheless, it must be acknowledged that some of the continental systems have proved to be the ideal ground for building up a highly independent judiciary. Although the scholarship on the independence of judiciary is burgeoning and cannot be addressed in a comprehensive way, the topic is crucial for the problems considered in this study.

---

[93] See, e.g., art. 65 of the Italian Judiciary Act (*Ordinamento giudiziario*), establishing that the Supreme Court of Cassation must provide for the exact application of law, the uniformity of the interpretation of it, and the substantive unity of the legal order.

[94] Cappelletti (1981), p. 389.

[95] For a comprehensive comparative approach to judiciary recruitment in seven democracies (England, US, Germany, France, Spain, Portugal, Italy), see Guarnieri and Pederzoli (2002), p. 46.

[96] Oberto (2003), p. 14.

[97] See, however, Switzerland: judges are elected by the Federal Assembly on a political basis. Such system has long been in the radar of GRECO, the Council of Europe's Group of States against Corruption, that released its last report earlier 2019: https://rm.coe.int/fourth-evaluation-round-corruption-prevention-in-respect-of-members-of/168094e860. Unfortunately, the report on the implementation of the measures suggested about judicial recruitment is negative: the committee of the Council of Europe found out that there is no domestic discussion about the possibility to amend the current system.

[98] For a worldwide overview, see Bellet et al. (1978), passim: each national report covers the recruiting policies for judiciary. For more recent European perspective, Delmas Marty and Spencer (2002), passim. For a comparison between France and England, see Cross and Harris (1991), p. 13. For a complete overview on the Italian system see Oberto (2013).

[99] Salas (2002), p. 491 ff.

[100] Cappelletti (1981), p. 387.

[101] Edlin (2016), p. 8. In some continental jurisdictions, judges are not supposed to sign their decision because it "should in principle be the same decision that any other judge in that tradition would reach in the same case".

Firstly, the most common continental recruiting scheme[102]—public selection and training of young law schools' graduates, who will be introduced into the civil service[103]—allowed for a certain level of diversity within the judiciary. Although this argument should be approached also from a sociological point of view, for the purpose of this study it is possible to argue that the public selection of junior legal experts has allowed for a more diverse access to the judicial functions in several continental European countries, especially since the 70s of the last century. Many of the social groups that had been previously been excluded from careers in the judiciary took advantage of the objective and standardised requirements, at the basis of a public selection. This integrated new cultural approaches, for example in the Italian,[104] French and German judiciary, although the composition of the national society is a major variable in this context.[105] While diversity is a persistent problem in the English judiciary,[106] at the time being there seems not to be such a compelling issue in the majority of the continental countries, where the public selection has allowed, at least, for some interplay, within the judiciary, between different social groups and, certainly, genders.[107] In this sense, diversity is an element assuring a higher level of independence, which is primarily granted, in some of the continental countries, by self-governing bodies, composed in part of representatives of the judiciary and of the political power (the Parliament or the head of the State).[108]

Secondly, unravelled by the ties of a strict *stare decisis* rule,[109] the civil law judge can prove ready to reverse the dominating jurisprudence, endorsing a new interpretation of the law, maybe suggested by one of the parties of the case. It is general common sense that, the continental supreme courts usually overrule their precedent

[102] Salas (2002), p. 493.

[103] See Posner (2010), p. 129.

[104] Violante (2009), passim.

[105] Bell (2006), p. 19 underlines that the research about this topic is very rare, and data are patchy. The social context of each European country is particular and any general approach will prove inappropriate. The mix of diverse components in each national society is unique and depends on geography, ethnography, history and colonialism… Thus, a comprehensive discourse about diversity in judiciary should be based on a diversified approach for each country. On the basis of high educational qualifications, the prerequisite for recruitment, the average European member of judiciary has middle-class backgrounds.

[106] Access to legal profession is the requisite for a further access to the highest level of judiciary: see Webley et al. (2016), p. 198 ff. See The Guardian editorial, 12.5.2017, The Guardian view on judicial diversity: time, gentlemen, please.

[107] In December 2015 the Italian media informed that the number of women in judiciary was higher than men, although acknowledging that women in the highest seats were less than one third. In France, in April 2018, 66% of judiciary were women, with a stunning relationship, within the youngest group of judges (30–34 years), of 29 men against 100 women (figures from by the French Ministry of Justice).

[108] Salas (2002), p. 494.

[109] Paradoxically, it has been noted that in France, the Cour de Cassation is not used to cite its own precedents. It does not mean, of course, that the Court feels totally free to disregards its own precedent, but the typical style of the decision does not encompass citations from previous case-law: Taruffo (1997), p. 454.

by endorsing lower courts' decisions, departing from the predominant case-law. In this sense, the 'vocational engagement of the Supreme Courts to modernise the law', as suggested by Tunc, is rather an ability to intercept and to endorse the new interpretative trends, deriving from the evolving society.

7.2.2 *The Value of the Precedent from the Comparative Angle*

As said, several comparative studies have argued that, if it is true that the civil law judges are not bound to the precedent with the same ties as their common law colleagues, one trend pushes towards a realignment between the two realms. Sometimes it has been stressed that the contrasts between the two legal domains have been "too often too much exaggerated".[110] In the previous paragraph I highlighted both diverging and converging factors, such as the traditional opposition between the "declaratory" theory and the 'constitutive' (positive) theory, lying at the basis of the binding value of both precedents and statutory law.[111] With the insight of the continental (and national) scholar, it is difficult to minimise the impression that, in some continental jurisdictions, the force of the Supreme Court decisions in granting uniformity of the jurisprudence is progressively weaker. The stunning number of cases and of decisions, the growing inconsistency between chambers of the same court, are seriously hampering, in some cases, the mandate of the Courts, to grant uniform trends in jurisprudence.[112]

The overview of the most relevant aspects of the attitudes presented by the major legal families towards the precedent, is meant to support a further step in this analysis, with regard to the outcomes that a generalised practice of judicial prediction based on open data could cause on this scenario.

In this chapter, we began from the co-existence of 'quantitative legal prediction' methods and the massive phenomenon of open data. As it has been highlighted, these two factors provide for the following conditions: accessibility to (potentially) every decision delivered by a national court, in civil, regulatory but also criminal matters; analysis of all the decision by CBR and/or ML algorithms. At the same

---

[110] MacCormick and Summers (1997), p. 12.

[111] Taruffo (1997), p. 458, highlighting that in every system the declaratory or constitutive nature of the courts is crucial. However, a critical approach to English common law, denies that neither the declaratory theory, nor the positivist one can justify the absolute authority of the precedent: Wesley Smith (1987), p. 87: "*stare decisis* cannot be law, precedents cannot be absolutely authoritative. Judges owe their fidelity, not to the pronouncements of predecessors, but to the law".

[112] As to Italy, see Canzio (2014), p. 231: every judge of the court writes average 400 decisions per year. And the number of the judges at the Supreme court is very high, higher than in any other Supreme Court: Lupo (2014), p. 11. A comprehensive study on the organization and functioning of the Court, based on empirical research, was published by Di Federico (1969), passim: unfortunately, the empirical research has not been updated.

time, it has been highlighted that the role of the judiciary and of judges in particular,[113] is deeply rooted in the institutional and social context of a jurisdiction, as much as it has huge influence on the public opinion as well. Although we already anticipated the topic of the general effects of AI tools in Chap. 5, it is now time to put together all the different lines of analysis that were introduced, to deepen the inquiry on the role of the judge, both in the short-term and in the long-term period. Four factors must be put together here: (1) the availability of performing computational models and algorithms to analyse comprehensive data-sets of case law; (2) potential availability of any decision delivered by the courts of a jurisdiction via open data; (3) the different value of the precedent in common law and civil law; (4) the complex role of the judiciary within the institutional, political and social context of a nation. Based on these factors, we must ask ourselves what may the impact of such AI instruments on the role and the function of the judges be? Is the judicial function gaining or loosing from the availability of performing computational models? We must not forget that, in Chap. 5, we already criticised and rejected the term 'predictive justice', discharging the most useless and 'science-fictional' meaning of it. Indeed, much of the answer that we can give to the previous question depends on a serious analysis of the expectations that lawyers have for computational modelling. Assuming that no one is interested in predicting but rather in simulating, in pre-considering all the relevant options of a case, it is now time to ask if that simulation, that pre-consideration is compliant with the fundamental rights established in Europe by the European Convention of Human rights, by the Charter of fundamental rights of the European Union and by many domestic constitutions. Two principles are at stake here: both the independence and the impartiality of the judge may be hampered by the widespread use of quantitative legal analysis systems.

7.3 Computational Modelling and Predictability of Decisions: An Enquiry in Three Steps

The aspiration of eradicating arbitrariness from the judicial decision-making process is an old one.[114] The French revolutionary "*juge bouche de la loi*" is the beacon of such an aspiration and the recent shift towards predictability of the judicial decision-making process has been sometimes compared to that ancient aspiration.[115] Actually, the comparison seems to me far too general, as the context in which the claim was brought, the late eighteenth century, was characterised by a tyrannical

[113] The term judiciary may encompass different roles: in some countries, prosecutors are member of judiciary, although they do not exercise any formal judging power, while in other countries (England and Wales Crown Prosecution Service) middle rank civil servants. On the complexity of translating the term, Bell cit., 2ff.

[114] On the legalistic theory, see Posner (2010), p. 41.

[115] Dupré (2018), p. 106.

legislation, administered by oral and arbitrary justice.[116] Nothing similar to that situation exists at the present time, although the general claim for more effectiveness of justice should not be overlooked. In fact, if it is true that attuning the concept of efficiency within the realm of justice requires a specific balance (supra Chap. 5), it is also true that justice delayed means justice denied. Thus, a legal study on the theoretical framework for the use of computational modelling and AI in criminal proceedings must investigate which outcomes—positive or negative—such modelling can have on the institutional and social dimensions of (criminal) justice. For this purpose, the inquiry should move on in three steps.

7.3.1 Step One

So far, we focused on how the human legal reasoning has been studied and reproduced in AI, first through expert systems and, more recently, by CBR and ML algorithms. In Chap. 5 we have briefly summarised the evolution of the computational approach to the crucial problem that legal reasoning is a rule-guided but not a rule-governed human activity.[117] However, it is necessary to reverse the question and to assess what impact the artificial legal reasoning may have on the traditional human judicial reasoning. The first relevant issue is related to the role of the precedent: we will first approach it from a general point of view and, afterwards, from a European perspective.

7.3.1.1 Establishing Relevant Variables

When referring to a precedent, either in common law or in civil law, the judge applies a form of analogy, comparing a certain number of variables, on the basis of which a precedent can prove relevant for the solution of the pending case. Although the intensity with which judges follow such a scheme depends on the institutional foundations of the system (these being less intensive in civil law countries), it is traditionally up to the judge to point out the relevant variables and to establish a correspondence between them. Within a computational model, the number of factors, variables, involved in the decision-making process is crucial: it can be established *ex ante*, and once for all, e.g. in expert systems; or, in machine learning, it can be left to the training set, during which the system will be fed with a sufficient number of decisions, to allow it to recognise the relevant variables: the factors selected during the training set, will be applied in the predicting set.

Thus, both in expert system and in case-based models, the relevant factors to be applied to a case are pre-established, depriving the individual of the control of the

[116] Bobek (2013), p. 98.

[117] von der Lieth Gardner (1987), p. 3.

out-lining of the judicial problem: if the legal analysis at the basis of the engineered model is correct, the variables should be correct; however, there is much subjectivity and discretion in the way variables can be fixed into a linguistic frame and this has an impact, together with human error, on the exact list of relevant variables, especially in legal matters. Based on correlations between vast amounts of information, the result of the AI process is a high possibility of correspondence between a group of words and a certain decision, having been previously adopted. In the first instance, this does not exclude the chance of wrong correlations. Moreover, we know that in a judgment, reasons do not give full account of the decision-making process, rather represent an *ex post* validation of the decision taken. For these reasons, although computational models can be trained to learn from previous mistakes, they may be not able to effectively establish the real causality of a judicial decision, due to the fact that the factor that really pushed the judge to adjudicate the case is not realistically reported and reflected in the reasoning. This reiterates the conclusion that their results belong to the realm of the likelihood that the model captures a pattern of decision in similar cases.[118] However, such patterns are even more complicated to establish in criminal law.

In fact, the number of factors/variables interfering in the decision of a criminal case is extremely high, depending both on the substantive and the procedural nature of the judgement. Many different layers of evaluation coexist within a criminal case and finding significant correlation depends on the combination of them all. A 'significant correlation' is one establishing that in previous corresponding cases, the court consistently adjudicated in one way. Before listing the most relevant variables of a criminal case, it is important to be reminded that many of the continental European jurisdictions do not provide for a clear distinction between the verdict on guilt/innocence and the determination of the penalty. Both verdict and sentence must be adequately justified in the reasoning. The relevant variables can be divided into: i) ***substantive*** and ii) ***procedural***. The substantive variables can be distinguished into: a) *material* and b) *legal*. The material variables refer to: a1) factual (*actus reus*) and a2) subjective (*mens rea*) elements.

i) ***Substantive***; a) *material*; a1) factual variables:

- the conduct
- the subsequent natural event
- causality
- the circumstances of the case, aggravating or mitigating
- in case of attempt (or other forms of inchoate offence), the stage of development in the action

i) ***Substantive***; a) *material*; a2) subjective variables:

- *Mens rea* (bearing in mind that different legal systems provide for different classifications of *mens rea*)

---

118 European Ethical Charter, Appendix I, p. 27.

- Liability
- Complicity (in some jurisdiction, like the Italian e.g., complicity refers to the material aspect and not the subjective one)
- Propensity towards crime

i) ***Substantive***, b) *legal* variables:

- *Nomen iuris*
- Any legal condition impinging on the sentence, such as recidivism and other forms of habitualness in re-offending
- Statute of limitation (usually depending on *nomen iuris*: e.g. classifying the facts under a different *nomen iuris*, the statute of limitation may not occur)
- Continued or concurrent offences.

Moreover, as the majority of the European continental countries do not distinguish between verdict and sentencing, a long list of further variables needs to be evaluated for the determination of penalty. Penal codes usually provide judges with a list of criteria, either objective or subjective, to help in calculating the quality and the amount of penalty. Moreover, as mentioned above (Chaps. 5 and 6) this is often the realm of prediction, in which the judge must foresee, on the basis of various aspects, the future behaviour of the convicted, to include it in a comprehensive evaluation of the fact and of the offender.

ii) ***Procedural*** variables are much more complicated to list. Although not the only relevant aspect, the evidence process is the factor that most affects the possibility to establish relevant variables, to build up useful correlations. All the elements listed above must be appreciated on the basis of evidence provided by the parties (although many European legal orders recognise the judges *ex officio* power of introducing decisive evidence): based on such evidence, the judge must reach conviction beyond any reasonable doubt, on each of the listed points. However, the whole evidence process relies on discretional judicial evaluations. It is highly debatable that a quantitative computational model can grasp useful correlations in the realm of sentencing, not because of an intrinsic limitation of AI techniques. In this field, establishing similarities between different cases is particularly complicated, because the factors listed above are discretionally weighted by the judge, in each case. For instance, comparing two cases from the standpoint of the judicial evaluation of mitigating and aggravating circumstances may prove pointless: given the same circumstances, judge 1 may consider the aggravating circumstances predominant, while judge 2 may reach the opposite conclusion. And, although a machine learning system is trained to learn from previous errors, there are no right or wrong decisions, but only decisions giving different, discretional interpretation of the same factor.

As to the procedural aspects, selection and admission of evidence is the first step of a crucial process that will bring the judge to 'establish the truth', in the adjudication of the case. Every legal order provides for different criteria to admit evidence, and it is difficult to generalise. However, it is possible to argue that, all over the world, the courts' activities must orient the fact-find towards the truth:[119] "courts are encouraged to pursue these basic goals through admitting and taking into consideration any evidence that appears to be factually relevant for the disposition of the case".[120] 'Relevance' is a multi-fold concept that not only undergoes the typical process of a discretional evaluation, but can vary significantly, depending on the stage of the procedure in which it is applied.

Moreover, criminal evidence evaluation is a factor that seriously impinges on the effectiveness of a computation model. In fact, at least at the time of writing and probably for many years to come, evidence in criminal proceedings is mostly oral. Documents are valuable and frequently used evidence, of course; however, witnesses and expert-witnesses are key evidence in the majority of the cases. The evaluation of the accuracy, reliability and relevance of each piece of evidence is crucial in the decision of a case and cannot be standardised into a computational model. Based on very similar factual elements and evidence, two cases can be decided in different ways, because of a different evaluation of reliability and accuracy of a witness or expert witness. As mentioned in Chap. 4, evaluating reliability of oral evidence is, at the time being, mostly based on personal intuition. Especially in Europe, theories about neuro-scientific analysis for the assessment of reliability are not generally accepted. Moreover, the justification of such a subjective evaluation is tricky. Seldom does the reasoning give account of why the judge deemed a piece of evidence unreliable: it is a matter of objectivising a feeling, an intuition and, consciously, the judge may not be able to explain what really induced her to consider a piece of evidence reliable or not.

There is more on evidence. In many European continental jurisdictions, the law of criminal evidence rests on exclusionary rules,[121] often based on the theory of 'nullities'.[122] And if the most serious violations trigger a sort of automatic non-use clause, a true "balancing of various considerations should occur only where the violation is not properly characterised as fundamental".[123] As the ECtHR case-law confirms (Chap. 4), using or excluding an unlawful piece of evidence is a mayor decision, which is usually based on balancing interests:[124] sometimes "courts tend to balance even clear constitutional violations against other important interests, and

[119] Interestingly enough, the Italian Code of Criminal Procedure never mentions the word 'truth'. Due to the large doctrinal discussion about the existence of different concepts of truth, a judicial and an historical one, the rulers decided not to use the term.

[120] Turner and Weigend (2019), p. 257.

[121] Turner and Weigend (2019), p. 256: "Every legal system recognizes exclusionary rules as a reaction to particularly serious violations".

[122] Thaman (2013), p. 410.

[123] Thaman (2013), p. 408.

[124] Rationales of exclusionary rules are multiple: first, finding the truth, but also upholding judicial integrity, deterring police misconduct and, of course, promoting respect of fundamental rights: see Turner and Weigend (2019), p. 257.

often will suppress neither the direct, nor the derivative evidence resulting from them".[125]

Not that evidence is the only procedural variable impinging on the outcome of a criminal proceeding... Competence, for instance, can be a crucial factor. Not only because of territorial reasons (one local court tends to adjudicate consistently on a specific legal issue, but in contrast with other courts, located in different areas of the country):[126] based on the connection with other misconducts, the competence for a criminal fact may change, in favour of a different or higher court. If an offense is ordinarily adjudicated by a lower court (lay judge), when it comes to a higher court (magistrate court) for reasons of connection with other offences, it may be adjudicated in a different way.

There may be many other procedural variables that can affect the outcome of the criminal proceedings, distinguishing it from any other that has occurred previously or subsequently. More specific examples would be too rooted in national procedural rules, while the approach here is general, as much as possible. The sense of reflecting on these aspects is that attaching a correlational value to these variables is arguable. What I mean is that, from the point of view of the legal practitioner in criminal law, there seems to be a doubtful advantage in quantitative legal prediction. Correlations may not be significant for the outcome of the proceedings. Computational modelling based on criminal case-law seems to be able to offer more sophisticated systems of retrieving previous decisions but can hardly simulate the outcome of a future decision, because of the high number of variables involved in the judgment and the high level of discretion entrenched in the decisions, especially in terms of evidence evaluation.

7.3.1.2 Establishing Relevant Patterns in a Single Judge's Decisions

It is possible to extend the conclusions here above to the specific aspect of quantitative legal analysis focusing on the single judge's' behaviour. As mentioned, the personal role and relief of individuals in taking a decision is much less evident in continental courts than in common law ones. However, among the metadata of a decision, easily accessible through open data,[127] the presiding judge's name is always accessible and this may bring to establish correspondence between a specific judge and rejection or upholding rates, pointing out purported personal biases or suspicion of bias.[128] Can predictive tools really highlight a personal bias? A 'prediction' is based on correlations between a list of variables and the background of the comprehensive case-law on which the model is trained. It has been noted that such a scheme is inherently unable to single out the truly causative factors of a decision, as they are entrenched into the interpretative framework governing any individual's

---

[125] Thaman (2013), p. 426.

[126] Serverin (2018), p. 45: local courts would benefit of 'predictive justice' in the sense of recognizing the public opinion expectation for equal treatment at a local level.

[127] Serverin (2018), p. 44.

[128] See European Ethical Charter, Appendix I, cit., p. 29.

decision-making process.[129] Especially when a court decision is at stake, there is a need to isolate, if possible at all, the impact of any individual in the process of adjudicating the case. Theoretically, such an endeavour could only be handled under the umbrella of different social-science disciplines, in the attempt to reconstruct the most realistic cultural framework as possible.[130] Moreover, another factor impinging on the real causative factor is the frequency with which a judge or a court adjudicates on a specific legal issue: whether they occasionally deal with a problem or are familiar with it is a relevant aspect to be considered, that, however, may escape the computational model analysis. For all these reasons, France has recently banned the re-use of the judge's' name, for purposes of quantitative legal prediction.[131] This introduces us into the second aspect of this issue.

7.3.1.3 The Role of the Courts and the Binding Value of Their Decisions

We repeatedly mentioned the fact that the performance of a computational model of legal reasoning depends (at least initially) on the data-set of decisions injected into the system. Potentially, that data-set can be comprehensive, exhaustive, if a legal system provides for open access to the whole national case-law. Of course, such case-law can be selected and organised, based for example on one specific court: e.g., the US Supreme Court or the French Appellate Administrative Courts, as in two examples mentioned above. However, training the model on the whole case-law, thanks to the availability, via open data, of all the decisions delivered within the jurisdiction, would hamper the value of the precedent, either in common law but, specifically, in civilian jurisdictions. As said, the hierarchy of courts is at the basis of any legal system. In common law countries, it allows the application of a strict *stare decisis* principle, with the rigid duty to abide by the *rationes decidendi* established by the superior courts. In continental Europe, the duty to grant uniformity in the interpretation of the law rests with the Supreme Courts, whose case-law sets forth the framework for interpreting statutory law.

It is possible to argue that, a widespread use of predictive software would enact, with regard to the common law systems, a trend narrowing down the room for distinguishing.

---

[129] Ibidem.

[130] Benesty (2017), p. 4, observes that it is not relevant for the purposes of the instrument to determine the individual role of each judge.

[131] There has been a serious debate in France on the matter of publishing the name of the judges who delivered the decision. Art. 33 loi n° 2019-222 du 23 mars 2019 de programmation 2018-2022 et de réforme pour la justice, not only provides that the publication of elements identifying the individuals involved in the proceeding is prevented whether hampering their right to security and privacy. Such guarantee is extended to their families and the professionals. It also expressly prohibits the re-use the names of judges and registrars for the purposes of predictive quantitative legal analysis.

As to the civil law countries, injecting an uncontrolled amount of first instance (and lower instances) decisions would be highly disruptive, confusing 'quantity' with 'quality'.[132] As I explained in the comparative approach, the continental lower courts' decisions are not subject to the duty to respect the precedent. If a first instance decision by a lower court disregards the interpretation of the law endorsed by higher courts and, in particular, the Supreme court, it may be reversed by the court of appeal or the supreme court itself, as the right to appeal, for both the defence and the prosecution, is generally quite wide. Infusing the training data-set with lower courts' decisions, which are not final (and seldom become final, because of the broad amending power of the superior courts),[133] would reverse the logic of the whole legal system, denying any difference in the authority of the decisions by the Supreme Courts and those of lower courts and judges. The fact that in many first instance decisions a matter of law has been solved in one specific way, does not mean that that case was actually and finally solved in that precise way: the upper court may reverse the first instance decision. For these reasons, only supreme courts' decision should be considered.

Moreover, as demonstrated above, especially in civil law jurisdictions, the final outcome of a case does not depend, necessarily, on the adjudication, on the merit, of the legal question at stake. Many side-factors can impact on it, like statute of limitation, for example.

Trying to merge all these aspects into a common framework, it is possible to argue that the civilian legal systems would be deeply transformed by the effects of widespread use of quantitative 'legal prediction' instruments. The consolidated hierarchy of legal sources would be reversed, as to the relationship between statutory laws and case-law,[134] but also in the confusion of a generalised, unrestricted consideration of all decisions.

However, there are differing points of view. Some authors appreciate the possibility to let the first instance case-law finally emerge, from the mist in which it is usually immersed.[135] The advocates of this theory argue that, based on a generalised access, by open data, the lower courts' decisions will enter a positive loop via 'predictive' algorithms, generating new knowledge, allowing for a form of 'cognitive predictive justice'.[136] Such a point of view rests on the critique developed by some American authors, against the European trend of focusing only on superior courts' decisions, shining the spotlight on only the 'difficult cases', those in which the best arguments and means are deployed... This would limit the focus to a very small and particular area of justice, leaving the simple cases—that is to

---

[132] See European Ethical Charter, Appendix I, cit., p. 19.

[133] Usually, decisions in civil law countries are considered final when no ordinary means of appeal is available any longer. However, a first instance decision, totally departing from the supreme court case law, could become final, if none of the parties appellate it. Nevertheless, its value as a precedent is irrelevant, because, if appealed, it would have been likely reversed.

[134] Brigan (2018), p. 244.

[135] Deumier (2018), p. 54.

[136] Deumier (2018), p. 55.

say, the major part of the case-law—out of the doctrinal discourse. Actually, as said, in the majority of the cases, the case-law of the European continental supreme courts is not restricted to 'difficult cases' but, due to the absence of a writ of certiorari, they are usually forced to linger over repetitive cases.

Others argued that 'predictive justice' will finally suppress the fundamental distinction between civil law and common law, based on a common aspiration to predictability.[137] Thanks to predictive justice, in fact, a new legal system would be founded: the theory of the 'isometric legal system' relies on the fact that the entire collection of judicial decisions would be equally measured by a computer programme and the results of such measurement would acquire normative value. In this sense, the informatisation of law would become an alternative source of legal normativity. The 'isometric legal system' would be more democratic, reducing the relevance of the political power and endorsing the judges' power. In fact, it would respond to the general public's opinion expectation of renovation of justice, which is generally considered dysfunctional.[138] It is needless to say, on the basis of the analysis drawn so far, that this theory is arguable. I do not subscribe to the opinion that judicial discretion is more democratic than political discretion. It is not possible to elaborate comprehensively on this point, as it touches on the foundations of institutions and societies. However, the 'isometric' theory confirms our remarks about the crucial impact that comprehensive CBR computational models may have on the institutional structure of the civil law legal systems. They can disrupt it, regardless of the positive or negative consideration that one can have of such a radical change. I would personally consider it negative, for the following reasons.

7.3.2 Step Two

Under the previous point we focused on the fact that the injection of a mass of precedent into a computational system can alter the balance between lower courts' and superior courts' case-law, that has a specific meaning and value in the civil law jurisdictions. This would be the first stage of a shift towards a system of *stare decisis*. The second stage would be based on the specific relationship that any single judge would have with the outcome of a 'predictive process'. Would the 'prediction' acquire a normative status, the authority of a source of law, as some authors argue? This would depend on the attitude shown by judges and by the general public opinion. We know that civil law judges do not have a duty to follow the precedent. French judges even have a ban on referring to and citing previous decisions... Thus, the point is to reflect on how such an alteration of the system would impact on the attitude of the civilian judge towards the decision-pattern singled-out by the programme. What would justify the departure from the result of the AI prediction, even

[137] Larret-Chahine (2018), p. 292.

[138] Larret-Chahine (2018), p. 293.

though the system does not provide for *stare decisis*? Quantitative prediction can outline trends in decision-making patterns. The issue to be discussed here is the value to be recognised in such trends. It has been acknowledged that the litigators, especially private parties, may benefit from these instruments in terms of deploying potential strategies. However, the most delicate aspect of it is the repercussions on the judicial decision-making process. It is doubtful whether the recurrence of decision patterns grants them with authority. In light of the remarks above, it is possible to argue that neither in the *stare decisis* systems, nor in the European continental tradition, does recurrence *per se* mean that a certain decision, or pattern, must be followed because it is authoritative or is uniform. However, some authors have suggested that regularity in the application of the law may legitimately expect to become a source of law.[139]

Especially reasoning from a criminal law point of view, I strongly disagree with this opinion. Firstly, recurrence is based on correlations and some correlations may be wrong. Secondly, it is necessary to have regard to the range of decisions used to train the computational model. Recurrence may be representative within the dataset covering the case-law of one specific court: mixing lower courts and higher courts' decisions dilutes the authority of the judicial interpretation, indicated as the more likely to be adopted. But even if it is reasonably possible to say that there are areas of homogeneous case-law in which recurrence is the clue for a generalised interpretation of the law, I still doubt the authority of the result. Can statistics rest on high numbers of first instance decisions that have then been quashed or amended by superior courts? Numerical preponderance does not provide such an application of the law of the authority, which derives exclusively from the validation by a superior or supreme court. There must be a selection of cases, based on the superior courts' decisions.

Traditionally, civilian judges who do not share a previous interpretative pattern do not need (and cannot be requested) to justify a departure from it.[140] Would they feel free to keep on doing the same when a sophisticated algorithm showed the preponderance of a different solution even though they do not deem it just for the case? Or would they feel constraint to depart from the 'prediction' only for compelling reasons, such as those provided in common law countries? If this was to happen, the clearest consequence would be a deceptive shift of the continental systems towards a binding value, not of the 'precedent', but of the repetitiveness of a decision pattern. Of course, it must be acknowledged that even in those systems, in which there is no formal duty to provide for stronger reasoning when departing from (or overruling) the Supreme court jurisprudence, judges prudentially deploy a more articulated reasoning, if rejecting the interpretation of a higher court. Disregarding the 'most authoritative interpretation of the law' is not deprived of any consequence, even for the continental judges (see after). However, the question here is not the judge's awareness of the law and its interpretation, but her freedom

---

[139] Deumier (2018), p. 61.

[140] Buat-Menard and Giambiasi (2017), p. 1483.

to apply it only if she deems it just for the specific case: that is to say, the question is the *intime conviction*.[141] Once that a 'prediction' exists, what are the consequences for disregarding it? There are aspects, both institutional and social, impinging on the answer to such a question.

In the continental traditions, the judiciary are high ranking civil servants, required to respect several sets of legal requirements and disciplinary standards. Although there is no room for a comparative overview on the disciplinary regulation in the European countries, it is possible to say that the judiciary is submitted to disciplinary regulation and proceedings, administered by the self-governing bodies, such as the French or Italian *Conseil supérieur de la magistrature* or by the ministry of justice (implying a certain level of political control over the judiciary). One disciplinary duty is, usually, life-long training and respect of the supreme court interpretation.[142] Moreover, gross mistakes in the interpretation of the law—endorsed by the domestic supreme court or by the Court of Justice of the EU—amounts to a tort or even a crime, if a gross negligence caused damages to the parties or the State, and *mens rea* is proved. The question is, once again, whether quantitative prediction is delivering a result[143] that is equivalent to the concept of 'authority of the precedent' that has been so far recognised in most of the legal systems of the world.

Thus, if repetitiveness in the application of the law would become a normative factor, it is worth wondering whether disregarding it would trigger disciplinary or civil liability for the judiciary. Despising the prediction would amount to neglecting one relevant source of law and, thus, to a disciplinary fault. Based on the same argument, the judge's behaviour, frustrating the expectations of the litigators may amount to a tort. There is an interesting aspect to consider, here. Normally, the litigators always have opposite expectations about the outcome of the proceedings: such expectations are at the basis of their strategy and the judge is perfectly aware of this. Curiously, quantitative judicial prediction could unify the parties' expectations into an apparently neutral prediction, based on what occurred in previous cases. Once that the expectation about the ruling is purportedly objectivised into the result of an AI predictive process, the adjudication of the case does not belong, any longer, to the dynamic of the litigation itself. Due to the general public's opinion's and the parties' common expectation, the judge could feel constrained into the 'predicted' solution of the case, unless she can give reinforced reasoning for departing from it. On the one hand, the judge may feel discouraged from engaging into the complicated activity of distinguishing or overruling the 'prediction', due to the social pre-acceptation of the 'statistical decision'. On the other hand, non-mainstream decisions would become easily detectable,[144] encouraging an external control over the single individual. This brings us, inevitably, to

141 Brigan (2018), p. 250.

142 See e.g. Italy.

143 Deumier (2018), p. 61.

144 Mouriesse (2018), p. 135.

reflect on the impact that 'predictive' instruments may have on the institutional dimension of the judicial function and, in particular, on the judicial prerogatives of independence and impartiality.[145]

7.3.3 *Step Three*

The social constraints impinging on the judicial *intime conviction* must be analysed in the light of art. 6 ECHR.[146] Excluding even the slightest possibility to wonder whether 'predictive tools' may be considered "judges", in the sense of art. 6.1 ECHR, the question is to shine the spotlight on if and which fundamental prerogatives of the judicial function could be hampered by a large-scale use of quantitative prediction systems.

A burgeoning case-law of the ECtHR established that the fundamental guarantee of judicial independence is multifaceted. It implies different layers of action, both external and internal to the judiciary, objective and subjective.[147] As to the external dimension, independence is traditionally related to the classical Montesquieu's theory of division of state's powers. In this sense, it implies an institutional organisation preventing any form of external control or interference by other public authorities over the exercising of the judicial function. The Strasbourg case-law identified many situations that can be related to such a dimension, including, e.g. the national recruiting system for the judiciary and the interference of military power. Of course, the most dangerous external incursion into judicial independence is represented by other public powers and authorities.[148] Nevertheless, also private interference in the function may also be detrimental and thus, contrary to the Convention. Social constraint is a negative factor impinging on judicial independence, regardless of the form that it holds: a large-scale access to 'prediction' can be a serious risk for constraint over the judge, who would feel 'encouraged' to follow the normative force of numbers... and this would have an impact also on the internal side of independence.

As to the internal control, the Court has stressed the importance that the organisation of judicial offices allows each individual to perform her task without being

---

[145] Brigan (2018), p. 248.

[146] Ferrié (2018), p. 498.

[147] Rainey et al. (2017), p. 297: "the subjective element involves an enquiry into whether the personal conviction of a judge in a particular case raises doubts about his or her independence or impartiality [...] The objective element involves determination of whether, in terms of structure and appearance, a party's doubts about the tribunal's independence and impartiality may be legitimate".

[148] See, e.g., ECtHR, Tourancheau et July c. France, 24.11.2005, spec. § 78: in the case about the alleged violation of art. 10, based on the applicants' conviction for opinions expressed in a press article, the court recognized that the conviction was necessary in a democratic society to guarantee impartiality of the judicial function. The decision has been recalled in many further cases about art. 10 ECHR.

influenced by other judges, from higher courts or from the same court: freedom from her peers' influence.[149] This reminds us of the provision in the French code of civil procedure, preventing the judge from referring to or to citing previous decisions of other courts or that very same court. Pushing judges to use and follow the 'prediction' would mean to constraining them into the respecting of the decisions taken by other judges, that she should comply with. The intensity of the constraint would vary: from a moral-suasion to a precise disciplinary duty to follow the prediction, clearly impinging on the independence of each single judge. All these aspects could impinge on the decision-making process, influencing the individual's freedom of the will.

Based on the source exercising it, this interference can also impact on impartiality. The European Court of human rights has repeatedly stressed the importance, not only of guaranteeing effective impartiality, but also to displaying it, so that the parties of the proceedings and the general public have the feeling that the judge has been impartial. The refrain often used by the court, "justice must not only be done, justice must seem to be done",[150] sounds peculiar, if applied to our topic. In fact, advocates[151] of 'predictive justice' claim its position to guarantee more transparency,[152] democracy, impartiality: as said, it would embody the popular demand for a more equal and consistent judicial treatment. Although not convinced of this argument (see *supra*), we must push our analysis a little bit further, wondering whether the consequence of widespread use of quantitative instruments would not have the opposite result. Due to the pre-comprehension of the case, based on a 'prediction', the judge could be, or could appear to be less inclined to listen to the parties' arguments, statements, evidence.[153] We already mentioned that large-scale reliance on quantitative legal analysis would seriously affect the dynamics of the litigation, reducing the importance of the parties' role. But the less the parties count, the less the judge is inclined to invest actively in the decision of the case, the more the system is likely to stop its evolution. The context that has been described here is characterised by standardisation, by a multi-fold action reducing the likelihood of dystonic decisions. In different ways, a generalised use of 'predictive instruments' would tend to nullify the virtuous bottom-up spin that induces changes in legal interpretation, in any legal systems. Discouraging potential litigants to avoid going to court; pushing lawyers to stick to arguments that proved successful in previous cases; inducing judge to respect the precedent, even if it is not part of the legal culture, would reduce, extremely, any advancement of the legal culture. 'Predictive justice' is incompatible with overruling[154] and evolutionary interpretation.

---

[149] In a case dealing with a military court, the European Court stated the importance of avoiding internal influences based on the rank of the judges: ECtHR, Findlay v. UK, 25.2.1997.

[150] Which was apparently used first by an English barrister…

[151] Larret-Chahine (2018), p. 293.

[152] Benesty (2017), p. 7.

[153] Brigan (2018), p. 248; Ferrié (2018), p. 502 f.

[154] Brigan (2018), p. 245.

Thus, there is a conceptual bug in the idea of quantitative judicial prediction. The sum of the factors that have been highlighted here can have the devastating effect of stopping the evolution of law. After an initial period of 'downwards standardisation' (having incorporated a massive quantity of first instance decisions). the case-law on which the model is trained would settle, reaching growing constancy. Consistency will raise the figures of correct predictions leading to a situation in which the hypothesis of overruling, and, thus, of modernisation of the jurisprudence will be minimised. Modernisation is the most fundamental function of a supreme court, it being the head of the whole judicial system. However, the evolution usually moves from the lower layer of the judicial activity; modernisation is shifted by the efforts of lawyers who, representing their client, induce a change in the court's interpretation of a legal factor. Relying on more and more accurate predictive services, lawyers will stop engaging in the effort of promoting modern, new, even revolutionary interpretations of the law, condemning such a human task (interpretation) to lose all its humanity...

Despite a critical approach, we must consider that a question could be raised, with specific regard to criminal matters. Criminal law is the realm in which the interests at stake are of the highest level: the state power to punish, the interest of the victims for the assessment of the harm they have suffered against the defendant's expectations related to life, liberty and her right to a fair trial... The variables to be taken into account are more and more complicated to assess, as only the criminal judgment implies a deep and profound investigation into the psychological (*mens rea*) and mental conditions (insanity) of the defendant. Is predictability not crucial in this sense? Is predictability not a core element of the rule of law or, in the European continental traditions, of the principle of legality? These legitimate, appropriate questions lead the discourse into the core of this enquiry.

7.4 Prediction and Predictability

Having introduced some general concepts in Sect. 7.1 and reflected upon the roots and the value of the precedent, in common law and civil law, in Sect. 7.2, it is now time to approach the fundamental question. How does quantitative legal prediction cope with the concept of predictability in criminal proceedings?

Before approaching the core of this crucial question, it is worth recalling the linguistic flaw that has been highlighted previously (Chap. 5). The term 'predictability' has several counterparts in the majority of the neo-Latin languages and in German and, probably, the most appropriate are the less assonant. As we will see, the sense in which the idea of 'predictability' comes to the attention in criminal law is that of legal certainty, which is probably more respondent to the term foreseeability. The Italian language offers a valuable example: to predict should be translated into 'predire', and foreseeability corresponds to 'pre-vedere': while 'pre-dire' literarily means fore-say, 'pre-vedere' means to fore-see. Such distinction will be useful in the conclusions of this paragraph.

Having said this, most of the domestic legal orders in continental Europe are inspired to a strict legality principle. In the widest and principal sense of it, the provision is a formal limitation to legislators with regard to their power to rule in criminal matters. Usually inserted in the national constitutions, the principle of legality is a material constraint to the future rulers (about how they will be allowed to exercise their power with regard to criminal law) and to the judges (about how they should, or rather should not, interpret criminal provisions).[155] In recent times, the constitutional framework for the principle of legality has enlarged, having been encompassed into the most important charters of fundamental rights at the regional level.[156] Both Art. 7 ECHR and, more recently, art. 49 ChFREU establish the principle of legality, although not in identical terms.

For the purpose of this study, the attention must be drawn to the central *dictat* of this principle, setting forth that the legislator must adopt clear and undisputed legal provisions, because the first and main guarantee derived by citizens from the principle of legality is the right to certainty of criminal law.[157] As to the meaning of legal certainty there has been much debate, that cannot be summarised here. Of course, each domestic constitutional court tends to have its own interpretation of it:[158] for the purposes of this study, it is suitable to refer to the interpretation of art. 7 ECHR[159] and 49 ChFREU.

Formally, art. 7 ECHR only provides for the prohibition of the retrospective application of criminal law. However, the European Court of Human Rights interprets art. 7 in the sense that "only the law can define a crime and prescribe a penalty. While it prohibits in particular extending the scope of existing offences to acts which previously were not criminal offences, it also lays down the principle of the application of a penalty by analogy. It follows that offences and the relevant penalties must be clearly defined by law. This requirement is satisfied where the individual can know from the wording of the relevant provision, if need be with the assistance of the courts' interpretation of it and after taking appropriate legal advice, what acts and omissions will make him criminally liable and what penalty he faces on that account".[160]

Preliminarily, it must be acknowledged that there is an important debate going on about the meaning of 'law', for the purposes of art. 7. It is certainly not only the

---

[155] Constitutionalism places an onus on all the powers, even the legislative branch, to subject themselves to limits and material obligations. Fossas Espalder (2018), p. 3; Ferrajoli (2007), p. 567.

[156] Fossas Espalder (2018), p. 4.

[157] See what one of the most influential twentieth century Italian scholars said about certainty of law: *"[l'uomo], per fare un passo, ha bisogno di vedere dove va. La previsione precede l'azione come la luce dei fari precede la marcia d'un veicolo nella notte. E quanto più la marcia è veloce, tanto maggiore ha da essere lo spazio illuminato dai fari. Perciò, se oltre ad essere giustizia il diritto non fosse certezza, non offrirebbe la garanzia dell'azione"*, Carnelutti (1953), p. 178.

[158] Villaverede Menéndez (2018), p. 36.

[159] It is worth remembering that art. 7 ECHR cannot be derogated based on art. 15, in any case, even not in case of war.

[160] RCtHR 21,10.2003, Del Rio Prada v. Spain, §§ 78, 79.

formal legal provision, as the Court said, but also the interpretation of it by the Courts, national and international. It is generally recognised that the huge impact of both ECtHR and CJEU is determining a new role for jurisprudential interpretation, even in the systems that are essentially based on statutory law.[161] Such a phenomenon reiterates and boosts the importance of certainty of the law: the more courts are entitled a 'creative' role, even in the realm of criminal offences, the more the principle of foreseeability plays a crucial role, as the normative provision is mostly diluted between the statutory outline and its judicial interpretation. In these conditions, accessibility and foreseeability of the normative command become more difficult.[162] People need to know how to behave in order to avoid perpetrating a crime and being punished: the more the relevant normative provision is diluted among different legal sources, the less people may rely on legal certainty, especially if there are inconsistencies in the jurisprudential interpretation of the law. In this sense, I certainly recognise the existence of a query for more certainty, that is repeatedly used by advocates of 'predictive justice' as an argument in favour of it. In the following paragraphs I want to reflect on this point: given a serious need for legal certainty with specific regard to criminal offences, is the computational modelling the right response?

7.4.1 Comprehension of the Legal Command and Culpability

Based on the German concept of *Unzumutbarkeit*, a popular theory of continental criminal law states that the comprehension of the penal precept is a basic condition for criminal liability. The theory was elaborated by the German doctrine, to extend the very narrow discipline of excuses, provided by the criminal code:[163] perpetrators, committing a crime in the compelling circumstances to save themselves or others from serious detriment, should not be punished. In fact, no other human behaviour could be expected, in such a situation, than the perpetration of the offence: abidance to the law cannot be expected, is not due, in such a situation. Seemingly, if the individual is not in the position of understanding what the criminal law imposes or bans, her compliance with the law cannot be expected.[164] Inconsistency in the judicial interpretation of a criminal command can affect the foreseeability of what is legitimate and what is not. "The foreseeability of the legal consequences of our actions is one of the dimensions of legal certainty".[165] More precisely, certainty guarantees that individuals, before acting, can foresee these three aspects: whether

[161] Zagrebelsky (2018), passim.

[162] Viganò (2016), p. 213 ff.; Donini (2002), p. 1165 ff.; Di Giovine (2006), passim.

[163] See, e.g., Mayer (1915), p. 302 ff.

[164] Fiorella (2018), p. 418. Scarano (1948), p. 163: "*possiede una sua configurazione autonoma distinta dalle altre cause codificate di esclusione della colpevolezza*".

[165] Garcia Amado (2018), p. 178.

their conduct will be considered legitimate; if illegitimate, whether it will amount to a crime; what punishment they may undergo.[166] Of course, the intimate sense of the protection deployed by the principle of legality is to prevent individuals from undergoing an harsher treatment than what they could foresee at the moment they behaved, or misbehaved: the principle of legality does not prevent more favourable consequences or even harsher non-criminal consequences.[167]

Although focused on the 'accessibility' of the criminal provision, such foreseeability is a not a purely objective concept. Rather, it may be influenced by several aspects, some of which are subjective. The case-law of the European Court of Human Rights covers a wide variety of cases in which the alleged violation of art. 7 ECHR would depend on different factors.[168] The Court did not apply a unique interpretative pattern, but adopted at least three different criteria, not always consistently.[169]

In some cases, the Court adopted an 'evolutionary' concept to interpret the principle of legal certainty. In particular, in the cases of S.W. v. United Kingdom and C.R. v. United Kingdom, the Court ruled upon applications dealing with alleged violations of art. 7 ECHR, in relation to the cases of two husbands convicted of rape of their wives. In fact, although the Sexual Offences Act 1956, in its consolidated version in force at the time of the facts, did not mention it, the 'marital immunity' had been long considered an excuse, based on a statement by Sir Matthew Hale CJ in his History of the Pleas of the Crown, published in 1736. However, at the beginning of the Nineties, when the facts of the cases had occurred,[170] the Law Commission released an opinion, discharging such a trivial interpretation and establishing that marriage is a partnership of equals. Nevertheless, the applicants argued that their right to legal certainty had been violated, as a consequence of their convictions, because, allegedly, at the time of the facts the case-law of the English courts was still considerably consistent with the 'marital immunity' doctrine. Rejecting both cases, the European Court referred to an "evident evolution" towards treating such conduct as within the scope of the offence of rape: "the evolution had reached a stage where judicial recognition of the absence of immunity had become a reasonably foreseeable development of the law". In this sense, the Court endorsed a concept of foreseeability that implies the duty of individuals to appreciate, to consider, the legal precept within the framework of the present time's culture and sensitivity.[171] What is legitimate and what is not under the law of the time also depends on the social culture and the attitude of the case law to keep the pace with it. Thus, if a

---

[166] Viganò (2016), p. 213 ff.

[167] Garcia Amado (2018), p. 179: based on the fact that in many European legal systems, the same behavior may amount to both a criminal and a civil violation, the global conditions applied to the offender may be harsher as to the penalty, but can be harsher from the private law point of view.

[168] Manes (2012), p. 278 ss.

[169] Santangelo (2019), p. 344.

[170] At the end of 1989 in C.R. v. UK and at the beginning of 1990, in S.W. v. U.K.

[171] Osborne (1996), p. 406 ff.

change in the interpretation of the law is not based on an evolutive path, but it is due to a sudden change in the orientation of the Courts, like in the case of Pessino v. France[172] or Del Rio Prada v. Spain, there is a breach of art. 7 ECHR, as "there was no indication of any perceptible line of case-law development in keeping with the [eventual] Supreme court judgement".[173] However, what the Court holds for a "perceptible line of a case-law development"[174] is not always clear, as in the cases of Soros v. France[175] and Contrada v. Italy, hereafter.

In other cases, the court applied a subjective criterion, based on the specific knowledge and expertise of the applicant. Interestingly enough, adjudicating on the alleged violation of art. 10 ECHR, in a Swiss case, the Court rejected the applicant's claim on the basis of the principle of foreseeability and accessibility of law. In fact, in this specific case, the applicant, an Italian local radio station also broadcasting programs in Switzerland, claimed that the ban of the radio emissions in Switzerland, on the basis of a multi-fold and complicated regulation in international telecommunications law, had violated the radio's right to free speech and opinion under art. 10 ECHR. In the uncertainty of the applicable law, not even foreseeable with the assistance of a lawyer, the radio was convinced of being allowed to legitimately broadcast its programmes beyond the Swiss border. Nevertheless, in this case the European Court stated that, under the Convention, it is expected that companies engaging in specific economic fields, are aware of the applicable law,[176] "if necessary with the help of advisers".[177]

In other cases, the court applied a more objective parameter. In the cases of Sunday Times v. UK, Kokkinakis v. Greece, Dallas v. UK the court focused on the material possibility of the applicants to access the legal precepts, even though not explicitly expressed in a piece of statutory law. In Sunday Times v. UK and Dallas v. UK, the applicants were arguing the uncertainty related to the offence of 'contempt of court', which is based on a common law command and not on a statutory act. In both cases, the Court excluded the violation of art. 7 ECHR, the case-law about the contempt of court being clear and accessible.[178] In the specific case of

[172] ECHR, 10.10.2006, Pessino v. France, § 36 f.

[173] Del Rio Prada. cit., § 117.

[174] Ibidem.

[175] ECHR, 6.10.2011, Soros c. France, in which the Court stated that although neither the French supreme court, nor a court of appeal had ever ruled on the new offence, with which the applicant was charged, lower courts had delivered decisions on the merit of similar cases, excluding a violation of art. 7 ECHR. Moreover, the Court applied the 'subjective test', considering that (§59) the applicant quality of international entrepreneur, urged him to be aware of the criminal risk implied in the investment he was planning.

[176] The Court completely overlooked this criterion in the case of Pessino v. France, who was an entrepreneur in the real estate field, having been convicted for urban planning offences, and in the case of Dragotoniu e Militaru-Pidhorni v. Rumania, 24.5.2007, § 35.

[177] ECHR, 28.3.1990, Groppera Radio AG and others v. Switzerland.

[178] However, with regard to Dallas, it has been noted that the Court completely failed to apply the 'subjective test'. The applicant had no specific legal competences, helping her to understand the criminal consequences of her act (while serving as juror, she browsed the internet for information

Kokkinakis v. Greece, the Court excluded the violation of the Convention in a case in which the penal code provision (proselytism) was actually vague, ("although for the specific purpose to keep pace with the changing circumstances"),[179] but supplemented by "a body of settled national case-law".

It seems, however, that in the case of Contrada v. Italy (3), all these criteria have been differently interpreted by the court. The applicant, an Italian former hi-rank police officer, was finally convicted for '*concorso esterno in associazione mafiosa*' (external interference with a mafia organisation), an offence that is not formally provided for by the Italian Penal Code, but has been created on the basis of a judicial interpretation of art. 416-bis P.C. (*associazione mafiosa*), that was finally recognised by the Supreme Court in a 1994 decision.[180] Before that moment, other decisions had applied the concept of 'external interference' in a criminal organisation, such as terrorist organisations, but not yet for mafia ones. In the case of Contrada, the European Court established that there had been a violation of art. 7 ECHR in relation to the facts that occurred before 1994, as the doctrine of 'external interference' had been applied until that moment only to other kinds of criminal organisations. Such decision seems inconsistent with all the main precedents of the Court, not only with S.W. v. U.k, C.R. v. UK, Del Rio Prada v. Spain and, in particular, in the case of Soros v. France and the decision in the case of Jobe v. UK.[181] Also the 'subjective' parameter, developed in the case of Groppera and in a number of following cases, seems overlooked, considering that Contrada was a high-rank police officer who should have known and foreseen the risk of being charged of 'external interference' with a criminal organization. In the decision that declared Jobe's application inadmissible, the court had expressly stated that, although at the time of the facts there was not yet a consolidated case-law about the meaning of 'reasonable excuse' in the crime of terrorism, "the concept of 'reasonable excuse' was not new under English law",[182] as it could have been found under other English statutes... In this sense, the 'evolutive test' has been disregarded in Contrada,[183] because irrespectively of their personal position and profession, people should have been aware of the existence of a "perceptible line of a case-law development", in recognising the criminal relevance of 'external interference' with a criminal organisation.

Although within a framework of inconsistent application of the subjective and objective tests, and with the exception of Contrada v. Italy, the Court has displayed quite a strict attitude in recognizing a violation of art. 7 ECHR. Having repeatedly

---

about the defendant). Such decision was criticized (A. Santangelo, cit., 340), especially because it was followed by a statutory reform (Criminal Justice and Court Act 2015) of the offence, due to the concern of the Law Commission about the uncertainty of the common law 'jurors content of court'. Before the European Court decision, the Law Commission had already expressed its concern about the situation (Law Commission, Report 304, 9th December 2004).

[179] ECHR 25.5.1993, Kokkinakis v. Greece, § 40.

[180] Manes (2018), p. 125 ff.

[181] ECHR, Dec. 14.6.2011, Jobe v. UK.

[182] Jobe v. UK, § A.

[183] Be Blasis (2017), p. 141.

stressed that, for purposes of legal certainty, individuals should seek competent legal advice, the Court sets a high standard of duty on the individuals and their counsels in extending and up-dating their knowledge about the relevant criminal law and case-law, both with regard to acts and omissions that will determine criminal liability and to the penalties they would face in that account: "offences and the relevant penalties must be clearly defined by law".[184] Neither the Convention, in art. 7, not the Court refer to the foreseeability of the decision of a specific case, but rather to the normative command, defining the criminal misbehaviour and the subsequent penalty.

For these reasons, this short overview on some of the most relevant decisions of the European Court of Human Rights is meant to demonstrate that the fundamental guarantee of 'predictability' implies something more (an individualised treatment) and something less (foreseeability of the decision) of what 'predictive justice' purports to offer.

7.4.2 Useful Semantic Distinctions

At this point in the reflection, it is useful to recall two Italian terms that I introduced above. In fact, the distinction between 'pre-vedere' (fore-*see*) and 'pre-dire' (fore-*say*, i.e. pre-dict, based on etymology) is based on the same difference between 'foreseeability of the criminal law' and 'predictive justice'.

The fundamental right of legal certainty, established by the main bills of human rights in the world, is a guarantee of accessibility, comprehensibility, awareness that people must have of the penal consequences of their behaviours. The interpretation by the Strasbourg Court reiterates that it is a matter of cognitive comprehension, the complexity of which implies the suitable intervention of a counsel. The court demonstrates awareness that, in a modern and complex society, statutory law cannot but be vague, in order to be of general applicability:[185] for this reason, people may not be able to appreciate on their own the real meaning of the legal precept.

It could be said that this 'counselling task' could be perfectly performed by 'predictive justice': people would not need legal counsel any longer, with the availability of a quantitative prevision system. I do not argue that this would be, per se, negative or positive. Rather, I think that this would not be the implementation of a more effective foreseeability in criminal law.

In fact, 'predictive justice' is not aimed to clarify the meaning and the comprehension of legal precepts, but to predict the outcome of a potential litigation. It is a prediction of the success rate of an action[186] and not an instrument to clarify

---

[184] See Del Rio Prada, cit., § 79.

[185] See, among others, Kokkinakis, cit., § 40; Del Rio Prada, cit., 92.

[186] In civil matters, the consequence would be that of shifting the legal system towards a model based on actions, on writs, like in the ancient common law tradition. Actually, there is trend in legal

the interpretation of the law.[187] In this sense, such instruments are not supposed to foster the principle of legality and the accessibility of the criminal precept. Rather, they are about the personal expectation[188] about the decision in each specific case, and this is much more than the core guarantee protected by the principle of legal certainty. But there may also be something less. It is arguable how much a popular access to such instruments would benefit the awareness, the comprehension of what is really legitimate or not. Reducing the recourse to professional counsels, the generalised reliance on 'predictive justice' may lead to misunderstandings of the real meaning of the norms.

Moreover, the expectation of a specific result is not encompassed in the core of the principle of legality:[189] it depends on a wide range of variables (see *supra*) in each case that, within the framework of the ban of retrospective application of criminal law, may escape to foreseeability.[190] The expectation of a result implies an action of pre-diction, of fore-saying the verdict, while the principle of legality only implies the possibility to fore-see, to figure out, the abstract consequences[191] of an action.

The difference between these two situations is the individualisation of the penal treatment. If pre-diction is much more than what the principle of legality requests, the individualisation of the judicial response is what 'predictive justice' ignores. Based on the long list of variables mentioned above, individualisation is crucial not only in sentencing but throughout the criminal proceedings. And if the popular demand for more equal treatment would be satisfied by the large-scale use of predictive systems and the consequent standardisation of judgments, then that demand would have been mistaken. The result of a judgment *must* depend on the peculiar circumstances of each case, otherwise other fundamental rights would be violated, such as art. 6 ECHR.

This critical analysis was meant to be a sort of risk assessment with regard to a certain attitude towards 'predictive justice'. Having first criticised the use of the term itself (Chap. 5), I went through a number of concerns that an a-critical approach to the topic has raised. In concluding this reflection, I cannot but reiterate that the criticism displayed is focused on two specific aspects. Although some jurisdictions,

---

doctrine suggesting to found the litigation not on the claim for the respect of a substantive right, but on the existence of a corresponding action…

[187] Serverin (2018), p. 42.

[188] Garcia Amado (2018), p. 181.

[189] ECtHR, 23.2.2017, De Tommaso v. Italy, § 107: "a norm cannot be regarded as a "law" unless it is formulated with sufficient precision to enable citizens to regulate their conduct; they must be able – if need be with appropriate advice – to foresee, to a degree that is reasonable in the circumstances, the consequences which a given action may entail. Such consequences need not be foreseeable with absolute certainty: experience shows this to be unattainable. Again, whilst certainty is highly desirable, it may bring in its train excessive rigidity, and the law must be able to keep pace with changing circumstances".

[190] Usually, procedural law is ruled by the principle *tempus regit actum*…

[191] Garcia Amado (2018), p. 181.

like France,[192] decided to exclude the use (and reuse) of judicial data for purposes of quantitative analysis from the realm of criminal justice, I do not argue that these instruments are detrimental. As far as the expectations towards their application are realistic and respectful of the fundamental principles, there can be positive consequences, from several points of view. In terms of '*machine à informer*', the advanced systems based on CBR and machine learning can reduce the time required for legal researches and provide practitioners with more accurate reports. However, this neutral, even positive scenario implies two conditions. Firstly, computers scientists must recall Weizenbaum's quest for modesty in their claims.[193] Secondly, lawyers and, in particular criminal lawyers, need to abandon their twofold attitude towards AI, sometimes totally dystopic, sometimes recklessly fascinated: the balance, as ever, stays midway, resting basically on a full comprehension of what AI really is, on the one hand, and a strong commitment to fundamental rights, on the other hand.

References

Antoniolli Deflorian L (1998) Il ruolo del precedente giudiziario nel common law inglese. In: Vincenti U (ed) Il valore dei precedenti giudiziali nella tradizione europea. CEDAM, Padova, pp 167–234

Bankowski Z, MacCormack DN, Marshall G (1997) Precedent in the United Kingdom. In: MacCormick RS (ed) Summers, interpreting precedents. Ashgate-Dartmouth, Aldershot

Be Blasis S (2017) Oggettivo, soggettivo ed evolutivo nella prevedibilità dell'esito giudiziario tra giurisprudenza sovranazionale e ricadute interne. Diritto penale contemporaneo 4:141. www.penalecontermporaneo.it

Bell J (2006) Judiciaries within Europe. CUP, Cambridge

Bellet P, Tunc A, Touffait A (1978) La cour judiciaire suprème. Une enquête comparative. Economica, Paris

Benesty M (2017) L'Open Data et l'Open Source, des Soutiens Necessaires à une Justice Predictive Fiable. J Open Access Law, 1–11

Bing J, Havrold T (1977) Legal decisions and information system. Universitetsforlaget, Oslo

Blackstone W (1765) Commentaries on the Laws of England, I. Clarendon Press, Oxford

Blankley KM (2004) Are public records too public - why personally identifying information should be removed from both online and print versions of court documents. Ohio St Law J, 413–450

Bobek M (2013) Comparative reasoning in European Supreme Courts. OUP, Oxford

Brigan JM (2018) Les risques accentués d'une justice pénale predictive, in Archives de Philosophie du Droit, La justice predictive. Dalloz, Paris

Buat-Menard E, Giambiasi P (2017) La mémoire numérique des décisions judiciaires. Dalloz Actialité p. 1483

Cadoppi A (2014) Il valore del precedente nel diritto penale, 2nd edn. Giappichelli, Torino

Canzio G (2014) La Corte assediata. Giuffré, Milano

Cappelletti M (1981) The Doctrine of Stare Decisis and the civil law: a fundamental difference – or no difference at all? In: Bernstein H, Drobnig U, Kötz H (eds) Festschrift für Konrad Zweigert zum 70. Geburstag, JCB Mohr Verlag, Tübingen, 381–393

[192] Art. 33 loi *n° 2019-222 du 23 mars 2019 de programmation 2018-2022 et de réforme pour la justice.*

[193] Weizenbaum (1972), p. 614.

Carnelutti F (1953) La morte del diritto. In: AA.VV. (ed) La crisi del diritto. CEDAM, Padova
Charalabidis Y et al (2018) The world of open data. Springer, Cham
Cross R, Harris JW (1991) Precedent in English Law. Clarendon Press, Oxford
De Filippi P, Maurel L (2015) The paradoxes of open data and how to get rid of it: analysing the interplay between open data and sui-generis rights on databases. Int J Law Info Technol 1:1–23
Delmas Marty M, Spencer J (eds) (2002) European criminal procedures. CUP, Cambridge
Deumier P (2018) Le justice predictive et les sources du droit; la jurisprudence du fond, in Archives de Philosophie du Droit, La justice predictive. Dalloz, Paris
Di Federico G (1969) La Corte di cassazione. Laterza, Bari
Di Giovine O (2006) L'interpretazione nel diritto penale. Giuffré, Milano
Di Paolo G (2011) La circolazione dei dati personali e del casellario giudiziario. Cassazione penale, 4034–4048
Donini M (2002) Le garanzie istituzionali della legalità penale e un 'nuovo' ruolo della Corte di Cassazione a fianco o al posto del vecchio? Cassazione penale, 1165–1181
Dove ES (2015) Reflections on the concept of open data. Scripted 2:154–166
Dupré J (2018) Du droit saisi par l'IA à l'IA saisissant le droit. In: Archives de Philosophie du Droit, La justice predictive. Dalloz
Edlin DE (2016) Common law judging. University of Michigan Press, Cambridge
Evans J (1987) Change in the doctrine of precedent during the nineteenth century. In: Goldstein L (ed) Precedent in law. Clarendon Press, Oxford, 35-72
Ferrajoli L (2007) Principia Juris. Teoria del diritto e della democrazia, I. Laterza, Bari
Ferrié SM (2018) Les algorithms à l'épreuve du droit au procès équitable. La Semaine Juridique 11:498
Fiorella G (2018) Le strutture del diritto penale. Giappichelli, Torino
Fossas Espalder E (2018) Material limits on the criminal legislator: their interpretation by the Spanish Constitutional Court and the European Court of Human Rights. In: Pérez Manzano M, Lascuraín Sanchez JA, Mínguez Rosique M (eds) Multilevel protection of the principle of legality in criminal law. Springer, Cham
Garcia Amado JA (2018) On the principle of criminal legality and its scope: foreseeability as a component of legality. In: Pérez Manzano M, Lascuraín Sanchez JA, Mínguez Rosique M (eds) Multilevel protection of the principle of legality in criminal law. Springer, Cham
Goodhart AL (1934) Precedent in English and continental law. Law Q Rev, 1–52
Gray J, Darbishire H (2011) Beyond access: open government data & the right to (re)use public information. SSRN, 3–89
Guarnieri C, Pederzoli P (2002) The power of judges. OUP, Oxford
Gurstein M (2011) Open data: empowering the empowered or effective data use for everyone? 7 Feb 2011. www.firstmonday.org
Hannah-Moffat K, Struhers Montford K (2019) Unpacking sentencing algorithms. In: De Keijser JW, Roberts JV, Ryberg J (eds) Predictive sentencing. Hart Publishing, Oxford, 175–195
Jasanoff S (2006) Transparency in public science: purposes, reasons, limits. Law Contemp Probl 69:21–45
Jimenez Gomez CE (2014) Desafios de la modernizacion de la Justicia en los tiempos del Gobierno Abierto. Revista Digital de Derecho Administrativo 12:225–239
Kambrun-Favennec E (2018) L'ouverture des données publiques: un préalable à la justice predictive, La justice predictive, Archives de philosphie du droit. Dalloz, Paris, 83-97
Kant I (1795) In: Hoffe O (ed) Zum ewigen Frieden. Zweite Anhang. Akademie, Berlin
Katz DM (2013) Quantitative legal prediction, or- how i learned to stop worrying and start preparing for the data-driven future of the legal services industry. Emory Law J, 909–966
Larret-Chahine L (2018) Le droit isométrique: un nouveau paradigm juridique né de la justice prédictive, in in Archives de Philosophie du Droit, La justice predictive. Dalloz, Paris
Lupo E (2014) La Corte assediata. Giuffré, Milano
Mac Cormick DN (1987) Why cases have rationes and what these are. In: Goldestein L (ed) The precedent in law. Clarendon Press, Oxford

MacCormick DN Summers RS (1997) Introduction. In: MacCormick DN, Summers RS (eds) Interpreting precedents. Ashgate-Dartmouth, Aldershot
Manes V (2012) Art. 7. In: Bartole S, De Sena P, Zagrebelsky V (eds) Commentario breve alla Convezione europea per la salvaguardia dei diritti dell'uomo e delle libertà fondamentali. Cedam, Padova, 278 ff
Manes V (2018) Retroattività, diritto e processo penale (da Scoppola a Contrada). In: Padula C (ed) Le leggi retroattive nei diversi rami dell'ordinamento. Editoriale scientifica, Napoli, 125–143
Mattei U (1996) Il modello di common law. Giappichelli, Torino
Mayer ME (1915) Der Allgmeine Teil des Strafrechts. C. Winter, Heidelberg
Michael J (1981) Open government and data protection. Br J Law Soc:265–260
Mouriesse E (2018) Quelle transparence pour les algorithmes de justice prédictive? In: Archives de Philosophie du Droit, La justice predictive. Dalloz, Paris
Novek BS (2017) Right-based and tech-driven: open data, freedom of information and the future of the government transparency. Yale Hum Rights Dev Law J, 1–47
Oberto G (2003) Recruitment et formation des magistrats en Europe. Etude comparative, Editions du Conseil de l'Europe, Strasbourg, 1–162
Oberto G (2013) Judicial independence in its various aspects: international basic principles and the Italian experience. http://giacomooberto.com/reportkiev2013.htm
Osborne C (1996) Does the end justify the means? Retrospectivity, Art. 7 and the material rape exception. Eur Hum Rights Law Rev, 406 ff
Posner RA (2010) How judges think. Harvard University Press, Cambridge
Postema GJ (1987) Some roots of our notion of precedent. In: Goldstein L (ed) Precedent in law. Clarendon Press, Oxford
Rainey B, Wicks E, Ovey C (2017) Jacobs, White and Ovey The European Convention on Human Rights, 7th edn. OUP, Oxford
Salas D (2002) The role of the judge. In: Delmas Marty M, Spencer J (eds) European criminal procedures. Cambridge University Press, Cambridge, 488–540
Santangelo A (2019) Ai confini tra common law e civil law: la prevedibilità del divieto nella giurisprudenza di Strasburgo. Rivista italiana di diritto e procedura penale, 332–357
Scarano L (1948) La non esigibilità nel diritto penale. Humus, Napoli
Schauer F (2009) Thinking like a lawyer, a new introduction to legal reasoning. Harvard University Press, Cambridge [Italian edition, Carocci, Roma, 2016]
Serverin E (2018) De l'informatique juridique aux service de justice prédicitive, la longue route de l'accès public aux decisions de justice dématérialisées, in Archives de Philosophie du droit. La justice predictive, Dalloz, 23-47
Sudbeck LE (2006) Placing court records on line: balancing the public and private interests. Justice System J 3:268–285
Summers RS (1997) Precedent in the US. In: MacCormick DN, Summers RS (eds) Interpreting precedents. Ashgate-Dartmouth, Aldershot
Susskind R (2008) The end of lawyers? OUP, Oxford
Taruffo M (1997) Institutional factors influencing precedents (1997). In: MacCormick DN, Summers RS (eds) Interpreting precedents. Ashgate-Dartmouth, Aldershot, 451 ff
Thaman S (2013) Balancing truth against human rights: a theory of modern exclusionary rules. In: Thaman S (ed) Exclusionary rules in comparative law. Springer, Dordrecht
Tunc A (1978a) Synthèse. In: Bellet P, Tunc A, Touffait A (eds) La cour judiciaire suprème. Une enquête comparative. Economica, Paris, 8 ff
Tunc A (1978b) Conclusions: la Cour supreme idéale. In: Bellet P, Tunc A, Touffait A (eds) La cour judiciaire supreme. Une enquête comparative. Economica, Paris, 436 ff
Turner JI, Weigend T (2019) The purposes and functions of exclusionary rules: a comparative overview. In: Gleß S, Richter T (eds) Do exclusionary rules ensure a fair trial? Springer, Cham
Van Bossuyt H, De Groote B (2009) Free access to law and judicial decisions: solutions and challenges from a Belgian point of view. In: Peruginelli G, Ragona M (eds) Law via the Internet. Epap, Roma, 371–384

Viganò F (2016) il principio di prevedibilità della decisione giudiziale in materia penale. In: Paliero CE, Moccia S, De Francesco G, Insolera G, Pelissero M, Rampioni R, Risicato L (a cura di) La crisi della legalità. Il "sistema vivente" delle fonti penali, Edizioni Scientifiche Italiane, Napoli, 213–265

Villaverede Menéndez I (2018) A dialogue between courts. The case law of the European court of hr and the Spanish constitutional court on the principle of legal certainty. In: Pérez Manzano M, Lascuraín Sanchez JA, Mínguez Rosique M (eds) Law multilevel protection of the principle of legality in criminal law. Springer, Cham

Violante L (2009) Magistrati. Einaudi, Torino

von der Lieth Gardner A (1987) An artificial intelligence approach to legal reasoning. MIT Press, Cambridge

Webley L, Tomlinson J, Muzio D, Sommerlad H, Duff L (2016) Access to a career in legal profession in England and Wales. In: Headworth S, Nelson RL, Dinowitzer R, Wilkins DB (eds) Diversity in practice. OUP, 198–225

Weizenbaum J (1972) On the impact of the computer on society. Science 176:609–614

Werro F (2018) The Swiss Federal Tribunal and its pragmatic pluralistic method. In: Glanert S (ed) Comparative legal reasoning. Wildy, Simmonds & Hill Publishing, London, 136 ff

Wesley Smith P (1987) Theories of adjudication and the status of *Stare Decisis*. In: Goldestein L (ed) Precedent in law. Clarendon Press, Oxford, 73–87

Xanthaki H (2008) The European criminal record: analysis. In: Stefanou C, Xanthaki H (eds) The European criminal record. CUP, Cambridge, 27–58

Zagrebelsky V (2018) La Convenzione europea dei diritti dell'uomo e il principio di legalità nella materia penale, in ius17@unibo.it, 2018 no. 2

Zeno Zenchovich V (2009) Legal information as an essential aspect of citizenship. In: Peruginelli G, Ragona M (eds) Law via the Internet: free access, quality of information, effectiveness of rights. European Press Academic Publishing, Florence, 33–40

Zweigert K, Kötz H (1971) Einfürung in die Rechtsvergleichung, auf dem Gebiete des Privatsrechts, I. JCB Mohr Verlag, Tübingen

Chapter 8
The Gist of the Inquiry

8.1 A Personal Result

When I began 'approaching the unknown', it is to say, the topic of the impact of AI and computational modelling on criminal justice, it was from the standpoint of my traditional criminal procedure scholarship, domestic, European and comparative. To be precise, I can remember exactly how the interest commenced.

It was during a lunch break, in London, discussing with a colleague and friend, professor of jurisprudence, who had started researching the field of legal-tech and AI and law, many years before. Based on his extensive study of the field, he addressed the matter of the opacity of algorithms, arguing that this could have specific, detrimental effects on evidence and, in general, on the fair trial. He asked me about my impressions, as a criminal lawyer. Although I had very confused ideas about what an algorithm is, the importance of the issue seemed to me to be crucial, from the very beginning. Despite the 'starting point' being evidence, the most 'classic' topic for criminal lawyers, I began, that day, a long journey that brought me far from my 'comfort zone'. Over these intervening years, I went through a selection of literature from very distant areas of scholarship, some of them having no, or at least very few, contact points with criminal procedure. Other areas of law, of course (substantive criminal law, jurisprudence, comparative law, data protection, administrative law), but also logic, basic rudiments of computer science, of psychology... And the selection was certainly insufficient, as there are probably many other aspects that I could have included in my inquiry.

As a result of this experience, the first acknowledgment to share is that the digital turn blurred the thresholds between different areas of scholarship, in an unprecedented way. This is not another example of the 'traditional' issues between science and criminal justice, it is actually much more than this. I repeatedly stressed the importance that courts stick to the Daubert doctrine, which is the general (almost world-wide) benchmark for the admission of expert (and technical) evidence into

S. Quattrocolo, *Artificial Intelligence, Computational Modelling and Criminal Proceedings*, Legal Studies in International, European and Comparative Criminal Law 4, https://doi.org/10.1007/978-3-030-52470-8_8

criminal trials. But, as extensively underlined in Chaps. 2 and 6, this only relates to the most basic layer of complexity inherent in the computational models that can be used in the criminal justice field. There are other layers of complexity that reach far beyond this aspect.

Actually, the impact of the digital revolution is so global and so profound that the conventional concepts and glossary are insufficient to approach it. There is no way to address the new challenges brought by the digital dimension to law, solely with the instruments of law. Thus, the starting point for a researcher is to cross into other areas of scholarship, letting concepts, methods and languages circulate, in a multidisciplinary environment.

However, this does not mean that the legal culture is unfit to face the issue and to find viable solutions for it. On the contrary, the legal culture must become the pillar, the mainstay, in the discussion about the application of AI and other digital technologies in criminal proceedings. There is a lack, so far, of a genuine legal debate about it, at least in Europe. The first demonstration of this enquiry is that, to start a process for a useful legal debate on the point, the legal culture must undergo a preliminary hybridization with other areas of scholarship.

8.2 Competing Values, Prevailing Guarantees

Moving on from the previous acknowledgment, the achievements and the future developments of AI in criminal justice must be framed into a solid, updated, multidisciplinary legal approach. This is the second recognition of this work. If AI solutions and other digital instruments are to be applied in criminal proceedings, they must be conceived and designed to serve the specific purposes of criminal justice. This implies that, based on the enlargement of the legal focus, suggested above, computer scientists willing to develop solutions for criminal justice must also work with lawyers. The validation of AI and other digital solutions to be used in the field cannot be based solely on computational parameters and standards. On the one hand, software designers may pursue e.g. consistency, rapidity, cheapness, which are not *per se* relevant values in the realm of justice. On the other hand, software developers are often actors in the private sector, looking for profit and for the protection of their product by trade secrets. As a consequence, there may be an apparent competition between these values and the procedural guarantees established both by domestic constitutions and international bills of rights, such as the protection of private and family life or the equality of arms. However, as I highlighted, such competition is barely apparent, as the only acceptable, systematic approach to the matter is that the basic principles of the fair trial must prevail.

From this viewpoint, the European context can rely on very strong and valuable legal beacons, able to balance the risks inherent to the application of AI and other digital solutions to criminal proceedings. From the angle of the protection of the individuals' privacy from intrusions for investigative purposes, both the CoE and the EU legal systems developed a sophisticated set of guarantees. As acknowledged in Chap. 3, the traditional concepts of home and correspondence evolved in the recent European case law and legislation, also in order to cover the brand-new sector of data protection. In this sense, the unprecedented intrusiveness of digital, hacking instruments, used in criminal investigations, is counterbalanced by a solid culture of respect of privacy. From the angle of evidence, i.e., the fair trial, the European context displays a multilevel system of protection. Besides the national regulations, regulating the law of evidence in their codes of criminal procedure (but in some case, also in the Constitutions), the European Convention on Human Rights and the ECtHR case law built a comprehensive set of values, with regard to the use of tainted evidence and the right to confrontation in criminal trials. It is exactly within this set of values that the issue of digital and automatedly generated evidence must be framed. For the reasons extensively reported in the book, evidence generated by digital software cannot be challenged and scrutinised in traditional ways. As a matter of fact, evidentiary law is still based, essentially, on the traditional concepts of testimony and material evidence, that do not encompass the specificities of digital evidence and, in particular, of automatedly generated evidence. Against this backdrop, it is of crucial importance to highlight and contrast the risk that digital evidence is considered to be reliable *per se*. For many reasons approached in the previous Chapters, data generated by digital software and used as evidence in trial can be incorrect, unreliable, manipulated, biased... Accordingly, the first solution is to avoid the digital fascination and to stick to evidentiary law, both at the domestic and regional level, to establish the need to demonstrate, case by case, the relevance and the reliability of each piece of digital evidence.

8.3 Digital Solutions for Legal Conundrums

Given the need to avoid any irrebuttable presumption of trustworthiness of digital evidence, there is a further important acknowledgement. As said above, this kind of evidence cannot be challenged and evaluated in a traditional way. In order to argue that a piece of digital evidence is unreliable, there must be the chance to access the 'black box' that generated it, both from the viewpoint of source codes and the inputs inserted in it. An independent reviewer, a qualified computer scientist, must be able to access it and examine how it runs the software. There is no way to apply the traditional epistemological heuristics to evaluate the genuineness and reliability of such a piece of evidence: in this scenario, the solution to the classic legal dilemma, the trustworthiness of evidence, is exclusively digital.

Based on the 'Daubert doctrine' (supra, Chap. 6), setting the conditions for the use of scientific and technical evidence in criminal trials, *ex ante* transparency is the ideal standard, generating evidence designed to be validated. If *ex ante* solutions are not applied, we must rely on reverse engineering, on digital forensic validation, to admit or reject a piece of evidence, provided that such solutions are available. When the software having generated the data used as evidence cannot be neither successfully submitted to *ex post* review (because, e.g. it is based on machine learning systems, and there is no way to explain the results on the basis of the inputs), such a piece of evidence should be rejected or excluded from the file. Only digital *ex post* review can certify the reliability of a piece of digital evidence and, given the assumption established in the previous paragraph, reliability must be demonstrated case by case.

This assessment is crucial in revitalizing the role of the judge in this scenario. Although unable to themselves evaluate such reliability, it is of crucial importance that courts are not prone to accept and recognise a false 'unflappable trust' in digital evidence, that would make it into a 'special' and 'unique' kind of evidence, escaping the basic requirements of ordinary evidentiary law. And it is the role of the judge that our further assumptions will touch upon.

8.4 Adjudicating and Predicting Are Different Activities

After having addressed the matter of automatedly generated evidence, this inquiry lingered extensively over the applications of AI and computational modelling purportedly assisting judges in their decision-making processes.

Firstly, Chap. 6 analysed the realm of predictive risk assessment tools, intended to assist the judge or the court in delivering a decision that implies a prediction. As discussed, it is possible to say, even without a deep comparative investigation, that there are several situations in which penal codes and criminal procedure codes expect the judge to base her decision on a prediction of the defendant's future behaviour. Starting from pretrial detention and bail, the judge must try to foresee whether the arrested person will try to abscond or to disperse and jeopardise evidence, in order to take a decision on her liberty. Further into the proceedings, there are many occasions in which the prediction of the defendant's future behaviour plays a crucial role, especially in sentencing. Based on a very general comparison, I highlighted that, across the dominant western legal culture, the prediction of recidivism and future violent behaviour is very often taken into account in the determination of a just penalty for the fact the defendant has been convicted of. With regard to these kinds of digital elements too, I focused on the two-tier evaluation process that courts must apply. First and foremost, they must strictly apply the *Daubert test*, in order to assess the scientific foundation of the criminological theory founding the risk assessment. Then, they must face two further layers of complexity, represented by: (1) the correct translation of the theory into a software and (2) the presence of errors significatively affecting the functioning of the software. In this sense, the conclusions established in Chap. 6 are a further elaboration of the acknowledgments attained in the previous steps.

Secondly, Chap. 7 focused on the meaning and the value that existing software of quantitative legal prediction can have in criminal justice. Working from the acknowledgment that open data and openness of the judicial decisions are different phenomena, the analysis recognises that the digitalisation of public documents and, in particular, of judicial decisions, has made the whole case law of a jurisdiction available for reuse by quantitative analysis software, purportedly able to predict courts' future decisions.

Based on the assumption foreseen in Chap. 5, the term 'prediction' (associated with this kind of software) seems incorrect. Indeed, the results delivered by such software is not a prediction, rather an accurate analysis of the variables that can affect the judicial decision. Indeed, 'predictability' (apparently offered by such software) is highly valued by the advocates of quantitative legal prediction, who stress the importance of individuals being able to rely on predictable consequences of their behaviour, against the risk of uncertainty that derives from inconsistent and obscure case-law. The analysis lingered over this aspect, as it is particularly important in criminal law. The foreseeability of the penal consequences of the individuals' behaviour (in terms of both liability and punishment), is an essential element of the modern theory of the principle of legality. Nevertheless, I highlighted that foreseeability is something different from predictability: while the first is a beacon of the rule of law, a fundamental right of every individual, the latter is not covered by the principle of legality. While individuals must be able to foresee the penal consequences of their free will, it is not essential that they are put in the position to predict the decision that will be delivered in their case. Based also on the difference existing between 'predicting' (*fore-say*) and 'foreseeing' (*fore-see*) in some neo-Latin languages, I argued that predictability is not an essential part of the principle of legality.

Concluding Chap. 7, I focused on some risks that an extensive use of quantitative legal prediction software may cause over the long-term, in civil law jurisdictions. Based on a basic comparison of the role of the precedent in the two main legal families, common law and civil law, I tried to elaborate on the impact that software based on precedent decisions may have on legal orders, that do not rely on the principle of *stare decisis*. Usually, in civil law legal orders, courts are not bound to the precedent: the supreme courts have the role of granting uniformity in the interpretation of the law. In such a scenario, first instance judges are not bound to follow the supreme court's precedent… It will be up to appellate courts or the supreme court to reverse the first instance decisions, which are inconsistent with the most authoritative interpretation. Against this background, I tried to figure out the consequences of quantitative legal prediction: the latter would induce expectations within public opinion, that the judge sticks to the results of the predictive software… Such expectations may push the judge to adhere to the solution 'suggested' by the software, giving up her qualities of independence and impartiality. In this sense, I did not prove that quantitative legal prediction violates the principles of judicial independence and impartiality. I simply suggested that CBR and quantitative legal prediction may more easily fit common law legal orders or, at least, legal orders based on *stare decisis*. Moreover, introducing spurious elements into a system may induce long term consequences, that could reach far beyond the trend recently acknowledged in comparative law, progressively reducing the most evident differences between legal families.

Conclusively, I presented my personal, inherent conviction about the essential, unavoidably human nature of judging. As criminal law—and law, in general—is a social normative construction, judging cannot be but a social, human activity, delivered by humans and devoted to humans, who must be able to understand and accept it. I cannot assume that I proved this: I am aware that new trends, in the near future, may depart from this theory… Nevertheless, this long journey across many different branches of scholarship has profoundly shaped my personal conviction in the sense that I have reported here.